To our families and especially to Mary Beth Klofas

Consulting Editor: *George Cole*

Brooks/Cole Publishing Company
A Division of Wadsworth, Inc.

Printed in the United States of America

10   9   8   7   6   5   4   3   2   1

Library of Congress Cataloging-in-Publication-Data

Klofas, John.
    Criminal justice organizations : administration and management
  John Klofas, Stan Stojkovic, David Kalinich.
     p. cm.
  Includes bibliographies and indexes.
  ISBN 0-534-11952-2
    1. Criminal justice, Administration of.   2. Criminal justice,
Administration of—United States.   I. Stojkovic, Stan.
II. Kalinich, David B.   III. Title.
HV7419.K56   1989
364'.068—dc20   89-15918
                                            CIP

Sponsoring Editor: *Cynthia C. Stormer*
Editorial Assistant: *Mary Ann Zuzow*
Production Coordinator: *Fiorella Ljunggren*
Production: *Sara Hunsaker, Ex Libris*
Manuscript Editor: *Pamela Howell Fischer*
Permissions Editor: *Carline Haga*
Interior Design: *Sharon L. Kinghan*
Cover Design: *Victoria A. Vandeventer*
Interior Illustration: *Art by Ayxa*
Typesetting: *Kachina Typesetting, Inc.*
Cover Printing: *The Lehigh Press Company*
Printing and Binding: *The Maple-Vail Book Manufacturing Group*

Criminal Justice Organizations: Administration and Management

John Klofas
Rochester Institute of Technology

Stan Stojkovic
University of Wisconsin–Milwaukee

David Kalinich
Michigan State University

Brooks/Cole Publishing Company
Pacific Grove, California

Preface

Studying criminal justice from the established perspectives of management and organizations is a relatively recent development. Perhaps, in the past, attention to the problem of crime and attention to the offenders themselves diverted attention away from the organizations of the criminal justice system. In the late 1960s and 1970s, however, increasing attention was paid to management in criminal justice. Presidential commissions strongly advocated that the management process be taken into consideration and called for improvements in planning, information systems, and the utilization of human resources.

Since then, theory and research from the areas of management and organizations have become influential in criminal justice. A variety of public and private enterprises exist to train criminal justice managers, and the study of management is a staple in criminal justice curricula.

These courses play an important role in criminal justice education, but publications have not kept pace with the subject matter, and we have found ourselves growing increasingly impatient with the selection of books in this area. We have been committed to considering management issues as they run through the entire criminal justice system but have found few books that take this broad perspective. We have been committed to integrating theory and practice but have not been comfortable with the way these issues are joined in available works.

After changing books frequently and forcing students to work from stacks or photocopied articles, we hoped to address these problems by writing this book on management and administration in criminal justice. It became clear that many decisions had to be made about how material should be approached and about what material should or should not be included. The collective answers to these questions became the perspective from which the book is written. We describe here several characteristics of the approach we have taken.

Themes of the Book

A focus on criminal justice. A focus on criminal justice is not as obvious as it first seems. Over the years, we have found it necessary to rely heavily on the general literature of management as a framework within which to study criminal justice. At times the integration of that material has not been as smooth as we would have liked. In this book, we avoid tacking criminal justice onto management theory and instead endeavor to integrate the two. In doing so we draw on the literature of management, organizations, the human services, and criminology in an effort to consider the implications of these perspectives for the management and administration of criminal justice. Our task, as we see it, is to provide an enriched discussion of criminal justice rather than a watered-down discussion of management.

A systemwide focus. Some books address management within the separate components of the criminal justice process. They either limit themselves to one type of organization or sequence discussions of managing the police, courts, and corrections. We have, instead, selected to examine issues we find to be relevant throughout the criminal justice system. Each chapter, then, discusses a management topic as it relates to the police, courts, and corrections. We acknowledge that there are significant differences in these organizations and that there is some merit in studying them separately. We have, however, chosen a systemwide focus for two reasons. First, our own teaching experience suggests the merits of a broad approach to the topic in advance of or, if necessary, instead of a specialized focus on one component of the system. This approach prepares students to study or work in a range of criminal justice settings. Second, we believe that the topics covered in these chapters are equally relevant throughout the system and that considering how those topics affect all components is informative.

A focus on theory, research, and practice. Our justification for discussing the broad range of criminal justice is buttressed by our focus within the chapters. We have sought to integrate theory, research, and practice in each of the topic areas. Although chapter 1 describes some broad perspectives on organizational theory, we do not place the management of criminal justice within any single theoretical context. In each chapter, we examine a range of theories and concepts developed in the management and organization literature, and we consider how these theories relate to criminal justice. We also focus on the research in criminal justice as it supports or fails to support current management perspectives. Finally, each chapter also considers how the theories and research bear on the practice of managing criminal justice. Whether we are discussing motivation or organizational effectiveness, then, the goal is to move from theoretical propositions to practical considerations.

Although our presentation ranges from the abstract to the concrete, our focus is not on preparing students for any particular management task; that can best be accomplished through further, narrowly targeted coursework and through experience. Our aim is to introduce students to the broad set of concepts, research, and practices that form a sound foundation for the management and administration of criminal justice.

Organization of the Book

Topics in management do not lay out as neatly as they may appear. For example, can organizations be effective if their personnel are not motivated or are improperly trained or socialized? What, then, is the justification for dealing with motivation and effectiveness as completely separate issues? In this book, we combine the chapters into four parts integrated by some frame of reference, although some overlap is necessary and some division is artificial. Part One describes the broad set of concepts that undergird later discussions of criminal justice management. Part Two focuses on how individuals are affected by and influence criminal justice organizations. Part Three addresses group behavior, and Part Four considers processes, including decision making and effectiveness.

To make the material on criminal justice management and administration as accessible as possible, we have included a number of features in each chapter.

Each chapter begins with several *introductory quotations* selected to highlight the complexity of the concepts discussed within the chapter. You may wish to begin and end your reading of the chapters by referring to these quotations.

Chapters end with *case studies* designed to highlight issues raised in that chapter. The case studies come from the real world or are fictionalized accounts that draw on real-world experiences. As you read them, you should consider how the case studies reflect the major themes in the chapters.

The *questions for discussion* carry the reader beyond the chapter material itself into applications in settings encountered in criminal justice. We also hope that interested students will further their study by examining the *suggested readings*.

Citations to important material are contained within the text. The complete *references* are found at the end of the book. Rather than rely on footnotes, we have left the references in the text so that readers can readily identify the sources of significant material. We have also attempted to be thorough in supplying references in the hope that students interested in particular topics will follow-up their study in the original works.

Goals of the Book

Our goal in writing this book was to produce an integrated text on the management and administration of criminal justice organizations. We aimed at a mid-range discussion of these issues, tackling neither the broad philosophical questions that necessarily underlie the management of a system of social control nor the narrower daily operations that necessarily take place within such a system. We hope that students of criminal justice will find our approach useful and that they will also go on to consider those large issues necessary for a fair and equitable system of justice as well as the focused issues necessary for an effective and efficient criminal justice system.

Acknowledgments

In writing this book we have had assistance from many people whose efforts deserve acknowledgment. Claire Verduin guided the project in its early stages and showed the courage to support our efforts even after she met the authors. Cindy Stormer continued the encouragement and was influential in bringing the manuscript to draft. The burden of molding the work of three authors into its final form fell on several people. The book has benefited from the fine work of Fiorella Ljunggren, Sara Hunsaker, and Pamela Fischer, and we are grateful for their efforts.

We would also like to express our gratitude to the following reviewers for their insightful and constructive comments: William G. Archambeault of Louisiana State University, George Cole of the University of Connecticut, James M. Poland of California State University at Sacramento, Philip W. Rhoades of Corpus Christi State University, Jeffery Senese of Indiana University at South Bend, and Gennaro F. Vito of the University of Louisville.

John Klofas
Stan Stojkovic
David Kalinich

Contents

PART 2

The Individual in Criminal Justice Organizations   49

CHAPTER 3

Problems of Communication   51

CHAPTER 4

Motivation of Personnel   78

CHAPTER 5

Job Design   101

CHAPTER 6

Leadership   122

CHAPTER 9

Organizational Conflict 194

PART 4

Processes in Criminal Justice Organizations 219

CHAPTER 10

Decision Making 221

CHAPTER 11

Organizational Effectiveness 251

CHAPTER 12

Change and Innovation 274

PART 1

THE NATURE OF CRIMINAL JUSTICE ORGANIZATIONS

The study of criminal justice organizations and management emerged during the 1970s as a vital part of the criminal justice curriculum. Concern with crime was part of the great social agenda of the day and was fueled both by reports of presidential commissions and by federal funding. Criminal justice organizations were considered a loosely connected system ranging from the police to courts and corrections. Scholars and managers began to examine criminal justice within the framework of traditional organizational studies. Theory and research on organizations have continued to encompass criminal justice organizations and to identify their common and their unique features. Part One of this book explores those features with two aims. First, these chapters examine where criminal justice organizations fit within the broad body of organizational theory, and, second, the chapters provide a general foundation for the discussion of specific topics in the coming chapters.

CHAPTER 1

Basic Concepts for Understanding Criminal Justice Organizations

☐ What Is an Organization?
☐ What Is Management?
☐ Open-System Theory
☐ Complex Goals
☐ Complex Environment
☐ Complex Internal Constituencies
☐ Summary
☐ Case Study
☐ For Discussion
☐ For Further Reading

R: That's a contact in terms of "We'll take a look at this" or "Judge, what can you do about this?" or "Judge, what can you do about that?"

I: Are these attorneys or political figures?

R: Oh, anybody. Anybody. Political figures, people who you might not want to call political figures, people who worked in campaigns, that kind of thing.

I: So the telephone lines are open?

R: Yeah.

I: And they pay attention to it?

R: Oh, sure. The chambers are open, and that's a very difficult thing to deal with.

> (Prosecutor being interviewed about extramural influences on judges, from Eisenstein, Flemming, and Nardulli, 1988:85.)

Dear Wardens:

Attached is a copy of our response to the officious and intrusive conduct of the mastership. We have tried to be tolerant and meet the demands of the court and its Master but reached a point where the security and safety of our units have been endangered. We have therefore felt it necessary to resort to the courts and ask for dissolution of the mastership.

> (Letter from Texas Prison Director W. J. Estelle to his wardens regarding his response to the court-appointed special master in the case of *Ruiz* v. *Estelle,* from Martin and Ekland-Olson, 1987:199.)

Organizations are a significant part of our lives. We are immersed early in schools and scouting, churches and athletic teams. We continue in colleges and universities, military service, employment, and our organized social life. This immersion in organizations continues throughout our lives, and, in the end, our obituaries will include a chronicle of our organizational attachments.

Among the many organizations that touch our lives are those of the criminal justice system. Many Americans will be only indirectly involved in these organizations. They may find themselves fighting a traffic ticket in court or touring the local jail while serving on a grand jury. Other Americans will find themselves immersed in the criminal justice system when they are processed as offenders. Still others will be employees of criminal justice organizations. This book is about the management and administration of those organizations, and the goal of this chapter is to lay a basic foundation from which to study them.

Our ties to organizations differ, as do the size, structure, and purpose of those organizations. The analysis of those differences forms a large part of organizational research and theory, from which this book draws. Our approach to this material is eclectic. We do not intend either to introduce a new organizational theory as it applies to criminal justice or to reflect any single theoretical perspective in this book. Instead, our goal is to provide an overview of organizational theory and research as it applies to criminal justice.

We cannot proceed, however, without devoting special attention to some key theoretical concepts and ideas. In this chapter we define and describe those that have come to be widely accepted and that we feel are necessary as a foundation for the study of criminal justice administration and management.

What Is an Organization?

This may seem like a straightforward question. We all know when we are in an organization, and criminal justice organizations should not be an exception. The police officer, probation officer, and prison guard are certainly aware of their organizational attachments. But identifying organizations is not the same as defining them, and an adequate definition of organization continues to be the subject of debate among scholars (see Hall, 1982:28).

Definitions of the term *organization* hinge on three important issues: structure, purpose, and activity. The issue of structure was raised by Weber (1947), who first distinguished the corporate group from other forms of social organization. For Weber, the corporate group was marked by limited admission to the group and by a structure that usually involved a leader and a staff. Weber's ideas lead one to think of organizations as bureaucracies—that is, as entities requiring a particular formal structure. In Weber's bureaucratic model, that structure included a rigid hierarchy of offices, a clear division of labor, and formal rules that govern action. Many organizations, however, do not possess a bureaucratic structure. For example, Clynch and Neubauer (1981) point out that trial courts can be viewed as organizations, but they lack the attributes of bureaucracies. Trial courts are relatively autonomous units not closely tied to a larger structure. Their formal rules are often ignored, as is evidenced by the fact that the presumed adversarial nature of the courtroom has often been revealed to be much more cooperative than the rules would suggest.

Barnard dealt with the issue of structure in a way much more consistent with Clynch and Neubauer's view of the courts. His basic definition of an organization is "a system of consciously coordinated activities or forces of two or more persons" (Barnard, 1938:73). Such a definition suggests boundaries but allows for a variety of organizational structures and makes it clear that courts, public defenders' offices, and other key components of the criminal justice system may profitably be studied as organizations.

Barnard's definition leaves the second issue, that of purpose, open. But other theorists have viewed the pursuit of goals as fundamental to organizations. Etzioni, for example, describes organizations as "social units deliberately constructed and reconstructed to seek specific goals"

(1964:3). The goal question is complicated however. Although it seems clear that the police, courts, and corrections agencies all have goals, the waters get murky quickly when we try to spell them out. The police prevent and solve crimes, but they also maintain due process, reduce community conflicts, and seek to provide a good working environment for officers. Courts may pursue justice but temper that with mercy. They may also have retribution, deterrence, humaneness, or equity as goals. Among the goals of corrections organizations are punishment, rehabilitation, maintenance of order, and, perhaps, avoiding publicity. Even profit-making corporations must balance short- and long-run profit goals, quality and quantity concerns, and pollution or environmental interests. Thus, organizations have many goals, and their goals often conflict. It is important to avoid the oversimplification of viewing organizations as pursuing a single goal or even a most important goal.

The third issue is whether organizations themselves act or whether organizations are simply collections of individuals who act. We will deal with this question in several of the following chapters in detail. At this time, however, we acknowledge that our view in this book is that organizations do act. In this view, leadership in organizations is more than the leadership of individuals. Likewise socialization in organizations involves not simply the attitudes and values held by individuals but also an organizational ethos. Decision making, too, is shaped by influences beyond those of individual decision makers.

The three issues discussed here shape the view of organizations that underlies this book. According to that view organizations require some boundary and structure but are not limited to rigidly bureaucratic forms. Organizations pursue goals, but those goals are complex, multiple, and often conflicting. And, finally, organizations act in that their influence extends beyond that of individual members. For this analysis, then, we may define an organization as a collective that has some identifiable boundary and internal structure and that engages in activities related to some complex set of goals. Our particular focus in this book is on those collectives engaged in activities related to criminal justice.

What Is Management?

This too seems to be a straightforward question. Like organizations, however, management seems easier to identify than to define. The names of managers can be found high on the organizational chart. Their offices may give them away, as may their salaries. But the function of management is not as clear in criminal justice as in many other types of organizations.

Management has been defined as "the process by which the elements of a group are integrated, coordinated, and/or utilized so as to effectively and efficiently achieve organizational objectives" (Carlisle, 1976). In this definition, management is a process in the sense that it is ongoing; it is not an end in and of itself. Instead, management is directed at the attainment of organizational goals. We have little trouble with this view as long as the complexity of those goals is appreciated.

This definition ignores the notion of office. It does not say whether management is a function of a specific office or is spread throughout an organization. Usually we associate management with a particular office or point on the organizational chart. In this book, however, we prefer to view management as a function that may not be the sole responsibility of any particular office. Although we recognize that wardens, chiefs of police, and others are managers, we also believe that even front-line police and corrections officers exercise some management responsibility. There are two reasons for this view. First, front-line staff supervise others. Whether police are directing citizens at the scene of a crime or corrections officers are controlling the routine of inmates, front-line staff manage people. In this sense they are neither fish nor fowl. Their positions are at the bottom of the organizational hierarchy, while their work requires that they manage many people in difficult situations.

Lipsky (1980) discusses a second reason for viewing the management function as not limited to particular offices. He argues that front-line staff in street-level bureaucracies, which include most of those working in criminal justice, determine organizational policy. They do so because the nature of their work requires that they exercise a great deal of discretion, and the collective use of that discretion reveals organizational policy. In these organizations, then, it may be productive at times to consider the hierarchy as inverted. Front-line staff may exercise considerable power in influencing the direction of the organization.

Management of organizations thus is not the sole province of executives. It is best thought of only as the process by which organizational members are directed toward organizational goals. This view of management suggests that many workers in criminal justice influence the direction of their organizations and that the study of management, therefore, is important to anyone interested in criminal justice.

As Hall (1987:35) warns, "Discussions of definitions can be quite deadly." Still, some appreciation of the complexity of the terms *organization* and *management* is necessary for understanding this book. Organizational theory also provides a number of other concepts that are central to understanding administration and management in criminal justice. We discuss them in the following sections.

Open-System Theory

In the past, many students of organizations have focused exclusively on what occurred within the organizations they studied. Perhaps the model of that approach is found in the work of Frederick Taylor (1919, 1947). As we will see in later chapters, one of Taylor's chief concerns was with increasing the efficiency of work through the design of jobs. Such an orientation ignored many variables outside the workplace that could influence the efficiency of labor. As we will discuss in detail, it was not until the advent of the human relations school that managers began to consider extraorganizational influences.

Taylor's orientation reflects a closed-system view, in which organizations are regarded as unresponsive to their environments, as self-contained. To the organization, the factors in the environment are unchanging constants. Such an approach to analyzing organizations has some appeal in the sense that it reassures us that relevant variables are clear, easily understood, and controllable. The model has its origins in systems theory, the view found in biology, mechanics, and other fields, which assumes that complex entities are composed of interrelated parts. Thus, as closed systems, organizations are composed of elements that are all related to one another. In this view, communication follows the lines of hierarchy; power and authority are a function of office; and change is slow and directed by management.

Although this approach to analyzing organizations may be adequate in some circumstances, it is now seen as too simplistic for most studies of organizations. In criminal justice, for example, a closed-system analysis would suggest that the causes of a prison riot could be found only in administrative practices and procedures, types of inmates, and other such internal variables. Clearly, however, the 1972 riot in New York's Attica prison cannot be explained without reference to the political climate of the times. Likewise, the prison riots of the middle and late 1980s cannot be understood without reference to conservative criminal justice policies and the resulting overcrowding in prisons.

Eisenstein, Flemming, and Nardulli (1988) revealed the limitations of closed-system views of criminal justice organizations in their study of trial courts. These authors are critical of the view that the courts can be understood as simply applying the law. They concluded that the great differences they found in nine criminal courts could not be understood by focusing on only the legal aspects of the courts. They suggest that the metaphor of the courts as communities is productive. This view recognizes differences in the extent of prosecution–police interaction, political relationships of judges, and approaches to plea bargaining, among others. These differences originate in the community context and the environment of the courts, and they influence both the process and product of the legal system.

The community analogy suggests the usefulness of an open-system view of the courts. In this framework for analysis, organizations are viewed as constantly interacting with their environments. In business, for example, profitability fluctuates with the availability of raw materials, consumer interests, and even taxes, tariffs, and the value of the dollar relative to foreign currency. In criminal justice, isolated heinous offenses have led to major changes in legislation and policing practices. Public conservativism has led to tougher sentences, which in turn have caused prison and jail crowding and increased prisoner violence. The influence of the environment need not be so dramatic however. State laws permitting unionization of public employees have had tremendous effects in criminal justice. Even changes in local economies have affected the number and qualifications of applicants for police and corrections jobs.

In their social–psychological analysis, Katz and Kahn (1978) describe organizations as open systems characterized by inputs from the environment, throughput (the process of changing those inputs), and outputs (the product or service of an organization). They point out that this simple model offers some advantages over closed-system analyses. First, it highlights the importance of studying organization–environment relations. Second, because the organization cannot be equally open to everything in the environment, it highlights the need to study the selection process. For example, how are job descriptions determined? What makes some constraints on decisions more important than others? How are criteria for measuring effectiveness determined? Finally, the open-system approach indicates we should also study how organizations affect their environments. It permits us to see that organizations are not necessarily passive. For example, high-profile crime-control efforts that reassure the public may lead to increased police budgets. In some states, corrections officials have used the threat of releasing prisoners to obtain support for prison construction. Community-treatment programs have been closed because they have negatively affected their environments through high recidivism rates or notorious offenses by their clients.

Complex Goals

We first discussed the question of organizational goals in our effort to define the term *organization.* The point is important enough, however, to risk redundancy here. The organizations of the criminal justice system have multiple and conflicting goals. We will deal here with the consequences of this complexity.

The implications of having multiple and conflicting goals were first spelled out in a classic work by Simon (1964). To be successful, organizations must endeavor to meet all their goals. For example, profit-making firms must meet production goals, quality goals, environmental-protection goals, and many others. Simon pointed out, however, that the pursuit of all these goals impinges on the degree of goal attainment. Borrowing from the field of mathematics, Simon used the notion of a Pareto Optimal Solution to show that organizations inevitably seek satisfactory levels of attainment of several goals simultaneously rather than attempting to maximize attainment of each goal.

Goals thus not only provide direction but also serve as constraints or limits. For example, a manufacturing firm has both production and sales goals. For the sales force, production goals limit the quantity of items they can sell; and, for production workers, sales goals may set limits on the quantity of items they can produce. In criminal justice, the police may strive to control crime, but due process goals constrain their effectiveness. Likewise, prosecutors may seek justice through rigorous prosecutions, but they are limited by the goal of not having crowded dockets. Plea bargaining may represent the Pareto Optimal Solution to these multiple and conflicting goals in the prosecutor's office.

Although complex and conflicting goals may thus serve as constraints, they need not be viewed in negative terms. For example, the limitations due process requirements put on police powers are fundamental to our freedoms. Wright (1981) argues that goal conflict is in fact desirable and that a unified criminal justice system with consensus about goals would be undesirable. Goal conflict, according to Wright, permits the expression of diverse viewpoints and provides for the mediation of interests so that no single perspective dominates. Goal conflict may also promote efficiency in offender processing by enhancing the adaptability of the system. Studies of effectiveness in criminal justice, of corruption and subcultures in criminal justice organizations, and of how these organizations change or fail to change all require an understanding of multiple and conflicting goals.

Complex Environment

As with the other topics in this chapter, we will return to organizational environments throughout the book. The following chapter deals with the topic in detail. In this section we briefly examine the impact of the environment on criminal justice organizations.

Some researchers have attempted to specify how environments impinge on different types of organizations. For example, Lipsky (1980) argues that the conflicting goals of human services organizations are the result of unresolved disagreements in society at large. The police too will always be subject to criticism as they pursue both crime control and due process because the public cannot agree on what goal or what balance of goals is appropriate.

Walmsley and Zald (1973) agree with Lipsky that public organizations absorb conflict from their environment. They also describe other effects of the environment on public organizations. They argue that because the productivity of public organizations such as the police or prisons is difficult to measure, the structure of those organizations is more closely tied to public beliefs about what the organizations should do than to what goes on in those organizations. For example, the public view is that prisons should attempt to rehabilitate offenders. Prisons, therefore, maintain elaborate treatment divisions despite the fact that the staff members of those divisions are engaged primarily in security functions such as classification and discipline. Likewise, Duffee (1986:65) points out that the modern police department continues to be organized along paramilitary lines, which were instituted when police were first organized to put down labor unrest and protect the wealthy. The structure of the courts, too, more closely reflects beliefs about what they should do than about what they actually do. Their rigid structure is a reflection of faith in the adversarial process, but it is widely acknowledged that the courts function in a much more collegial than adversarial way.

Walmsley and Zald (1973) also point out that not only is organizational structure affected by the environment but so is the way in which these public organizations are evaluated. First, clients are not the legitimizers of these organizations, so service delivery may not be rewarded. For example, prisoners are not viewed as legitimate evaluators of their prisons. Second, because the marketplace does not determine the value of public organizations, they are generally evaluated on the importance of their mission rather than on the results they achieve. The enforcement of laws and dispensing of justice are seen as important missions. Police and courts, therefore, are valued despite difficulties in measuring productivity. But the value placed on these organizations may diminish if public views change even though the organizations' effectiveness does not change. With the movement away from the treatment model, for example, probation agencies were devalued until they took on the more valued roles of intensive custodial supervision, pretrial release evaluation, and home detention.

As this brief discussion indicates, in public organizations like those of the criminal justice system, environmental influences are quite complex. In the next chapter we examine those influences in depth.

Complex Internal Constituencies

Our discussion of basic concepts for this book must include one additional subject. One way of viewing organizations is to consider them arenas in which struggles for power occur (Hall, 1982:300). Perhaps the most obvious examples are workers' struggles for increased wages and better working conditions. Although the external environment of organizations is complex, then, there are internal constituencies that are also relevant to organizational form and function.

In criminal justice the literature is just starting to acknowledge the potency of these internal groups. As noted, clients often are not the legitimizers of criminal justice organizations. They cannot, however, be regarded as wholly insignificant. The prisoners' rights movement clearly illustrates the point that even inmates can dramatically influence prisons. Although these changes have also involved powerful external groups, inmates clearly exercise some power not only through their individual lawsuits but also well beyond court mandates. As a result of litigation, prisons have become more bureaucratized, prison staff have become more demoralized, and a strong movement to establish prison standards has begun (Jacobs, 1983b:86).

Internal constituencies are clearly not limited to clients. They may include groups of employees who come to pursue a distinct set of interests. Departmental legal counsel and budget managers, for example, set requirements that constrain organizations. Likewise, groups such as court stenographers and secretaries have special goals. In fact, the most significant internal constituency in many criminal justice organizations today may be the work force. Through traditional grievance mechanisms and now through collective bargaining, labor is having an increasingly significant effect. The public-employee unionization movement of the 1960s paved the way for organized labor in corrections and more recently in policing. Unionization has dramatically changed the role of management and influenced everything from job and shift assignments to occupational safety. In some prisons guards and prisoners have even united to call for better and safer institutions (Jacobs, 1978).

Summary

This chapter provides a brief foundation for the discussions in the rest of the book. We have covered concepts that we regard as central to understanding criminal justice administration and management. It is important to bear in mind that these concepts are not presented here as indisputable facts but as analytical tools. For example, criminal justice organizations may be studied as open or closed systems. But it is not the organizations that are open or closed, only our analysis. For the purposes of this discussion we find important benefits in viewing criminal justice organizations as open systems interacting with and responsive to their environment.

Likewise, we prefer a rather general definition of the concept of organization. For this analysis, organizations are not limited to groups with specific structural arrangements or groups that pursue limited and clearly defined sets of goals. Similarly, we regard managing as a general process or function that, to some extent, is performed by a variety of organizational members.

Apart from these basic definitions we have identified three concepts that seem particularly germane to criminal justice organizations. First, those organizations pursue many and often conflicting goals. Second, the organizations operate in a complex environment that exercises considerable influence. And, third, internal constituencies in these organizations are becoming increasingly powerful.

This is, no doubt, a difficult chapter, full of rich theoretical concepts that we have just begun to discuss. Students with a penchant for theory will wish to investigate the suggested readings and to follow up on the citations in the chapter. Students without such a penchant can be relieved that the chapter is over. It does, however, cover topics to which we shall return time and time again, and we feel it provides a needed background. That background will first come into use in the next chapter, where we explore the organizational environment of criminal justice in detail.

--- **CASE STUDY** ---

Who's Running This Organization Anyway: Jail Structure, Goals, and Environment

The Marion County Jail serves as the detention facility for the county, the city of Indianapolis, and the cities of Beech Grove, Lawrence, Southport, and Speedway—a total population of approximately 800,000. The four-story jail, completed in 1965, had an official capacity of 776. It was built with security and control as the primary concerns and was, according to one observer, obsolete before it opened.

Just a few years after the jail opened it was the subject of a lawsuit which was not fully settled until a new . . . wing was completed. . . . Briefly, the events and charges are as follows: In September 1972, a suit was filed by the Legal Services Organization (LSO) on behalf of pretrial detainees at the Marion County Jail. Named as defendants in the suit were the sheriff of the county, the jail commander, the commissioner of the State of Indiana Department of Corrections, the mayor of Indianapolis, and specific members of the Board of County Commissioners. The complaint, brought under Section 1983 of the Civil Rights Act (42 U.S.C. 1983), alleged violations of the pretrial detainees' rights under the First, Fourth, Fifth, Sixth, Eighth, Ninth, Thirteenth, and Fourteenth Amendments to the United States Constitution. At issue were overcrowding, [poor] physical and sanitary conditions, failure to classify prisoners for housing assignments, inadequate medical and dental care, lack of recreation, of contact visits, and of access to telephone and mail services.

Because of crowding, detainees were sometimes required to sleep on the floor in the shower rooms. Although mattresses were provided, mattress covers often were not. Jail issue clothing consisted of dresses for females and trousers for males. The prisoners wore the underwear they had on when admitted. Although they could purchase more underwear, as well as towels and pillows, or receive them from a visitor, indigent prisoners often had to do without. No provision was made to launder clothing or towels. Though these could be washed in cell-block basins, it was against regulations to hang them up to dry.

All detainees could purchase postage and writing materials. They were allowed to mail only one letter per day containing no more than one piece of paper. Jail officials read all correspondence to and from family and friends. Telephone calls were not permitted except by special arrangement.

There was no recreation program or exercise area. Playing cards could be purchased, and there was a meager library. Detainees could exercise only in the open area of the cell block. No televisions or radios were available.

There was no regular dental program, no provision for medical examinations, no law library. Visits were "closed." The detainee visited from inside the cell block looking through a small plexiglass window and talking through a metal grating. Only two visitors were allowed per week. Children were never permitted.

In 1975 a consent decree and partial judgment corrected many of the physical and sanitary problems. New jail rules were formulated and submitted to the court. These covered the sanitizing of mattresses, issuance of jail clothing and provisions for laundering these, improvements in medical and dental care, counseling services, and more liberal correspondence rules. However, many of these were "paper" changes only.

A 1976 court order required attention to all areas left unresolved by the consent decree. The judge ordered that clothing be issued and laundered weekly; that a bed above floor level be provided for each detainee along with sheets, pillow, blanket, and mattress cover. He ordered that telephone calls be permitted "in reasonable number and for a reasonable length of time without censorship," and that correspondence opportunities be greatly expanded.

Contact visiting was ordered with the visitation schedule to be equal to that provided by the state for the convicted. Reasonable facilities for both indoor and outdoor recreation were also ordered. The court recognized that many deficiencies resulted from lack of funds but ordered that appropriations be made in order to correct them.

Defendants' official response was the appointment of a steering committee, with representatives of the mayor, the county commissioners, and the sheriff as members, to select consultants who would propose solutions. The contract to the consultants was let by the Department of Metropolitan Development, an arm of city government attached to the mayor's office.

The consultants' report was submitted fourteen months later in June of 1977. In January and February 1978 the mayor's office and the sheriff's office submitted memoranda based on the report to the court advocating certain of the compliance options that particularly addressed the problem of overcrowding. These memoranda were followed by the plaintiffs' memorandum in opposition to some of the proposed solutions.

In August 1978, interrogatories to the sheriff were propounded by attorneys for the plaintiffs and were answered in the required thirty days by the sheriff. There were eighty-seven questions, and it was clear from the responses that no major concerted effort had been made to implement the judgment of the court. Neither the 1977 nor the 1978 sheriff's budgets had allocated funds for compliance, nor had the sheriff requested special funds. Whatever improvements had been made had come from the jail's normal operating budget. The 1979 budget request included $12 million for an addition to the jail, but it was denied by the county commissioners.

In 1979, seven years after the suit was initiated, the jail commander sent letters to jail officials throughout the country seeking advice and assistance in achieving compliance. During this year also, the Sheriff's Department assumed command of the city lockup. All prisoners were then booked at the lockup and transient prisoners (held for up to three days) were not transferred to the jail. This had the immediate effect of reducing the population. But on December 28 lawyers for the plaintiffs filed three motions: an order to show cause why defendants should not be held in contempt of court and assessed fines and damages of over $300,000; a motion to appoint a special master to oversee compliance with the order issued three years earlier; and a motion to restrain further incarceration of detainees at the Marion County Jail.

These motions produced immediate action. By January 14, 1980, an Ad Hoc Jail Committee had been appointed which included criminal court judges, city–county councilmen, representatives of the mayor's office, the sheriff's office, the prosecutor's office, the auditor's office, and the Greater Indianapolis Progress Committee (GIPC), a privately funded citizens group advisory to the mayor.

In the court's stipulation and order of May 1980, the GIPC was appointed jail commission, and two [additional] commissioners were named. The court held in abeyance the show-cause order and the motion to restrain incarceration but ordered further progress toward compliance within six months and recreation, televisions, and radios and private attorney–client conference booths by July 1, 1980. Threatened with a contempt-of-court citation, the defendants began to engage seriously in compliance attempts. A new classification system went into effect in March 1980; in July, both contact visits and outdoor exercise were begun; by August, private attorney–client cubicles were in use; and by the end of the summer there was a television set for each cell block.

The Ad Hoc Jail Committee met regularly throughout the year and ordered an update of the 1977 consultants' study, which was submitted in December. In December the City–County Council passed a resolution to undertake a survey of jail renovations and additions. The federal court judge cooperated . . . by accepting improvements and postponing action on the 1979 motions.

In April 1981, expansion of the jail and a necessary bond issue were approved by the City–County Council. Architects' drawings were approved in June of 1982, construction bids were accepted in the fall, and contracts signed in December. Construction began in April 1983. This new addition would bring the jail into full compliance in all areas requiring additional space and structural change.

By March 1983, compromises had been made on the larger issues: outdoor recreation was available once per week rather than daily; holding cages had been converted for contact visitation by setting up folding chairs on each side of the bars; cubicles were made available for attorney–client conferences; telephones had been installed in each cell block with sixteen to twenty-four hours of access per day (collect calls only); and a law library was in operation. Compliance was lax in other areas: mattresses were not hygienically treated on a regular basis; clean clothing was not regularly issued; the promised counselors were interns from a nearby university's school of social work; and often there were not quite enough blankets, pillows, or towels for every inmate. [From "Jails and Judicial Review," by N. E. Schafer. In D. Kalinich and J. Klofas (Eds.), *Sneaking Inmates Down the Alley*, 1986. Courtesy of Charles C. Thomas, Publishers, Springfield, Illinois.]

Case Study Questions

1. From the discussion of conditions in the jail, what would you say its goals were? How did those goals change over the course of the suit?

2. How would you describe the role of internal and external constituencies in the saga of this jail case?
3. How would you describe the role of management in the course of this legal action? How effective was it at directing the organization, and what constraints was it under?

For Discussion

1. Using the concepts discussed in this chapter, describe your local probation department. What is its structure? What management functions are performed and by whom? What people and organizations outside the agency exert an influence on it? How does that influence show in organizational structure or process?

2. Discuss the goals of a victim-witness program. In what ways are they complex or conflicting? In what ways do some goals serve as constraints? Now consider those goals in the context of where the program is located. Will they differ if the program is attached to the prosecutor's office or if it is an independent unit?

3. Using both a closed-system analytical framework and an open-system framework, describe your local jail. How might these frameworks lead to different views of how effective the jail is or of the causes of jail violence? Describe how jails are affected by their environment and how they may influence that environment.

4. Sheriffs' departments usually carry out a variety of tasks including enforcing laws in rural areas, serving summonses, maintaining courthouse security, and managing the jail. In light of this variety of tasks, what internal and external constituencies are powerful? How is the importance of those constituencies affected by the fact that county sheriffs are elected officials?

For Further Reading

Duffee, D. *Correctional Management: Change and Control in Correctional Organizations.* Prospect Heights, Ill.: Waveland, 1986.

Eisenstein, J., Flemming, R., and Nardulli, P. *The Contours of Justice: Communities and Their Courts.* Boston: Little, Brown, 1988.

Katz, D., and Kahn, R. L. *The Social Psychology of Organizations.* New York: Wiley, 1978 (especially chapters 1–3).

Langworthy, R. *The Structure of Police Organizations.* New York: Praeger, 1986.

CHAPTER 2

The Criminal Justice System in Its Environment

☐ Defining the Environment of the Criminal Justice System

☐ The Political Environment

☐ Task Environment Elements Specific to the Criminal Justice System

☐ Environmental States

☐ Organizational Response to the Environment

☐ Managing Environmental Forces

☐ Implications for Administrators

☐ Summary

☐ Case Study

☐ For Discussion

☐ For Further Reading

If one believes in the "great man" theory of history, universities and community colleges are indebted to California Highway Patrol Officers Lee Minikes and Robert Lewis for the proliferation of the hodgepodge of academic criminal justice programs, criminal justice professors, and educated practitioners. They are the officers who were unfortunate enough to attempt to arrest a drunk driver in the Watts community in Los Angeles, California, during the summer of 1965, which sparked the Watts racial riot, which was likely awaiting a reason to happen. The Watts riot led to racial riots across the country, which, in turn, led to responses from the federal, state, and local levels of government. The governmental response, especially from the federal level via the creation of the Law Enforcement Assistance Administration, had a lasting impact upon most criminal justice agencies through the nation on at least two dimensions. The standard of living for police officers increased dramatically and the educational opportunities, and requirements, for criminal justice practitioners increased dramatically. Moreover, the symbol structure of the criminal justice system was altered in an attempt to make it appear democratic rather than repressive and in the hands of well-educated "professionals" rather than insensitive racists. While conditions of poverty may not have been improved over the last two decades, the environmental upheaval of the racial riots has had unexpected but lasting impacts upon the system of criminal justice [Kalinich, 1987].

Our Korean colleague turned to several of his fellows and proceeded to summarize a year of education with consumate oriental terseness. He said, "Crime affects criminal justice; criminal justice does not affect crime" [Duffee, 1980].

Our opening excerpts make the point that the environment in which the system of criminal justice is immersed has an impact on its substance and form because it, like all organizations, is an open system and ultimately governed by environmental forces (Perrow, 1986). In this chapter we discuss the interdependence of the criminal justice system and its environment. Our focus is on the constraints environmental forces place on the system. As we will see, these forces affect the mission of the system and its individual agencies as well as its objectives, policies, procedures, and day-to-day practices. In addition, we discuss how environmental forces allocate resources and personnel to the criminal justice system. Finally, we argue that environmental forces can be stable or complex and unpredictable; they often push the criminal justice system in contradictory directions. However, environmental forces will be the final determinants of the effectiveness and efficiency of that system. In short, we describe here how environmental forces send mixed messages to members of criminal justice agencies and how those agencies attempt to survive in an often conflicting environment.

Defining the Environment of the Criminal Justice System

In a loose sense, we may define an organization's environment as any external phenomenon, event, group, individual, or system. This sweeping definition can be broken down into finite dimensions to make the concept of the interdependence of an organization and its environment understandable.

The environment of an advanced society is composed of at least technological, legal, political, economic, demographic, ecological, and cultural forces (Hall, 1982). Each of these plays a role in creating, maintaining, changing, or purging organizations. As environmental conditions change, demands for goods and services, legal and resource limitations, and support for and opposition to the programs of both public and private organizations may also change. To adapt to new demands, constraints, and pressures, new bureaus or businesses may be created, and existing agencies may alter their missions or policies. Agencies, public or private, that fail to meet changing demands, expectations, or constraints may suffer severe loss of resources or public support before they catch on. Those agencies that fail to catch on may become extinct.

It is easy, for example, to understand how technological changes affect our lives as well as our organizations. Our ability to mass-produce electricity has improved our lives in general and made organizations increasingly productive. Yet the blessing has cursed us with acid rain and other pollution that may damage us severely in the not-too-distant future. To deal with the negative effects of pollution, the government, through new or existing agencies, has attempted to regulate the utility companies in response to public demands (political forces) for clean air and a safe environment. Every similar effort by government to regulate organizations or individuals will, in some manner, necessitate the use of agencies of the criminal justice system. We discuss here each of the environmental forces and, through the use of examples, examine the effect of each on the criminal justice system. Figure 2-1 displays the environmental conditions as forces that affect the criminal justice system.

Technology

Technology has had many direct and indirect effects on the criminal justice system. The introduction of the automobile into our society is an excellent example. The automobile allowed police agencies to increase the efficiency of patrols. Yet autos became a major social-control problem for the criminal justice system to deal with because they expanded the range of operations for thieves, became valuable items to steal, and created

Figure 2-1 How Environmental Conditions Affect the Criminal Justice System

Environmental conditions	Public demands and constraints	Criminal justice system	Expected product
Legal Political Demographic Ecological Technological Economic Cultural	Demands for services Legal constraints Resource allocation Support for and opposition to programs	Mission Policies Procedures Practices	Services Social control Protection of society

traffic problems. Also, the current resurrection of neighborhood polic-ing indicts the use of police cars for patrol; the use of patrol cars is, in fact, a major impediment to police efficiency and police–community relations.

Law

Legislation and court decisions provide the basic rules and authority for the criminal justice system. This system is mandated to enforce statutory criminal law, determine the guilt or innocence of offenders, and apply sanctions to criminal offenders. The procedures for arresting, adjudicat-ing, and punishing criminal offenders are defined by legislation and case law. For example, the Miranda warnings imposed by the Supreme Court on the police caused a procedural change in police agencies (although they had little substantive effect on the outcome of police work) (Walker, 1985). In the area of corrections, the courts have granted inmates a number of rights that have caused procedural changes. Perhaps the most significant result has been the increased standard of care for inmates, such as adequate medical treatment and protection from harm.

The Civil Rights Act of 1964 has also had an impact on the criminal justice system. The requirement of equal opportunity has changed the personnel composition of criminal justice agencies so that they include more minorities than they did before. Women are now police and correc-tions officers, positions that were traditionally male. Agencies have to recruit from minority groups to meet affirmative-action guidelines. Con-sideration has to be given to assimilating minorities into the pre-dominantly white, male system. Policies and procedures protecting minorities from racial and sexual harassment have to be developed within criminal justice agencies. In some prison systems, preservice training now includes courses for female corrections officers to help them cope with the unique problems they face in male prisons. Changes in the legal sector of the environment have thus created a new set of constraints to which the criminal justice system must adapt.

Economic Conditions

Clearly, the resources available to public bureaucracies limit their numbers and scope. In a highly productive society, a great many resources are available, but many organizations are required to produce and distribute goods and services as well as to regulate the production and distribution system. These organizations compete for resources, however plentiful. In our society, business cycles cause production and employment rates to fluctuate, and the resources allocated to public agencies fluctuate along with business cycles.

The criminal justice system is affected by the business cycle even though it derives its funds from government rather than the marketplace. It competes with private and public organizations and with other regulatory agencies for existing resources. For example, during times of high unemployment, criminal justice agencies have a large labor pool to pick from and have the opportunity to be highly selective in recruiting personnel. During periods of prosperity, criminal justice agencies have little difficulty in obtaining resources but cannot be highly selective in personnel recruiting because members of the labor force have so many career choices.

Economic conditions may influence the criminal justice system in other ways. To the extent that unemployment rates affect crime rates and jail and prison populations, economic conditions affect the work load of criminal justice agencies. The research on correlates between unemployment rates and crime rates is conflicting (Thompson, Svirdoff, and McElroy, 1981). However, the literature indicates that prison populations and sentencing rates increase as unemployment increases and vice versa (Yeager, 1979). In spite of the lack of certainty in this area of research, it serves as a good example of how environmental conditions beyond the control of the criminal justice system can affect it. Workhouses were built during the fifteenth century to incarcerate large numbers of unemployed and vagrant citizens of London (Barnes and Teeters, 1959). In this historical instance, a corrections system was created, in part, as a result of economic conditions.

Demographic Factors

Factors such as the age, sex, race, ethnicity, and number of people in a community all have an impact on organizations. For example, roughly 71 percent of criminal activity is carried out by individuals under the age of twenty-five (Reid, 1982). A community with a high proportion of individuals under the age of twenty-five will probably have a relatively high crime rate. Large cities tend to have higher per capita crime rates than smaller communities, and cities with more citizens of lower rather than higher economic status also have higher per capita crime rates (Sutherland and Cressey, 1978). A sudden influx or exodus of people creates a new set of demographic characteristics within the community that, in turn, can alter crime patterns. For example, an increase in the population of a state generally indicates that the state will soon be building additional prisons (Benton and Silberstein, 1983).

The flight of the working- and middle-class population to the suburbs has left inner cities with the poor and minorities and has created a new clientele for urban police departments. The flight to the suburbs has also significantly eroded the tax base for major cities (Grubb, 1982; Danziger and Weinstein, 1976; Frey, 1979) and has limited resources for their criminal justice systems at a time when they have to deal with a problematic population.

Cultural Conditions

Culture can be defined briefly as the collective norms, values, symbols, behaviors, and expectations of the members of a society. Ultimately, a society's political and economic system reflects its culture. Thus, laws are codified social norms. Moreover, the roles attributed to a society's organizations are based in its culture. In other words, the missions, constraints, images, symbols, and validity of organizations are rooted in a society's cultural makeup. Society's dictates are imposed on bureaucracies through its political–legal system, which is linked to its cultural and social fabric. This is especially true for the criminal justice system; it is expected to carry out its duty of providing safety for the public in a manner the public approves of. However, American culture is heterogeneous and dynamic, and the demands on and expectations of its institutions often conflict.

For example, during the racial riots of the 1960s and the anti-Vietnam War riots that took place during the early 1970s, many citizens were outraged by the conduct of the police. Charges of racism and brutality were common. However, other individuals approved of the conduct of the police during the riots. Demands for "law and order" and the use of coercive force to end rioting and looting dominated the rhetoric of many groups. In general, liberals viewed the social-control problems as a result of poverty, racism, and a justice system biased against the lower class. Conservatives, however, viewed the civil disobedience, rioting, and looting simply as lawless conduct and advocated the increased use of coercive force to deal with it (Rosch, 1985).

These conflicting views of crime and civil disorder are an excellent example of the lack of consistency in norms and values among the members of our society. Our cultural mix can create homogeneous or heterogeneous demands (Hall, 1982) depending on the issues at hand as well as our collective or individual perceptions of the issues. When demands are heterogeneous, government and organizations must work to appease or mitigate conflicting interests, or must ignore one set of interests in favor of others.

A striking historical example of our conflicting norms can be seen in our attempt to eliminate the consumption of alcohol through federal legislation. The Eighteenth Amendment (Volstead Act), passed in 1919 and repealed in 1933 (the Twenty-First Amendment), created our infamous period of prohibition. Basically, a coalition of politically powerful moral and religious groups created the amendment, which made the consumption of alcoholic beverages for recreational purposes illegal. The amendment was intended to make the nation righteous by preventing a large number of Americans from consuming alcohol. The law was to be implemented by the criminal justice system at the federal, state, and local levels. However, alcoholic beverages were nonetheless consumed by "good citizens" from all walks of life. Beer and gin were often homemade, but bootleggers and members of organized crime supplied most of the beverages to the consuming public. The values and preferences of large numbers of Americans seemingly were ignored by the prohibition lobby. In effect, the criminal justice system was mandated to enforce a law that a great number of people would not follow. In fact, stories from the "roaring twenties" recount the corruption of local law enforcement officials who allowed speakeasies to openly market beer and liquor. While the amendment ignored the wishes of "drinking" citizens, local criminal justice systems ignored the amendment. Hence the power the "moral" minority had over others was mitigated in favor of the "drinking" minority by the practices of local criminal justice systems.

In many respects, our present attempts to control the consumption of recreational drugs, such as marijuana, heroin, and cocaine, resemble our efforts at prohibiting the use of alcohol (Warren, 1978). Again, a large enough minority of American citizens form a lucrative market that attracts suppliers of illegal recreational drugs. Traditional organized crime has its share of the illegal market, and new criminal cartels have been formed to supply illegal drugs to consumers. However, despite increased enforcement efforts we seem unable to prevent the marketing of a product demanded by a substantial number of citizens with just the application of coercive force.

Because demands placed on the political–legal system and ultimately on the criminal justice system often conflict, criminal justice agencies have difficulty establishing priorities. Justice may, therefore, be applied inconsistently within a particular criminal justice system and differently from system to system. As a result there will always be some dissatisfaction with the performance of the criminal justice system among certain members, groups, or forces in its environment.

Ecological Conditions

Ecological factors are components of an environment such as climate, geographical location, size of a community, and economic base—industrial, service, agrarian. Ecological factors make a major contribution to the total environment of an organization and subsequently affect its mission and constraints. A small city in the midst of a farm area is profoundly different from a small city with an industrial base, and both are profoundly different from a large industrial community. Small agricultural communities tend to have homogeneous cultures and a history of relative stability. The criminal justice system typically does not receive mixed signals from community members. An immediate link between criminal justice agencies and community members exists because citizens typically have access to political leaders and criminal justice officials and probably associate with them on a rather consistent social basis. From an operational point of view, most of the community members are probably well known to the local police, and many problems are handled informally based on local preference rather than on formal procedures.

As communities change from agrarian to industrial, migration patterns bring in new citizens who may have values different from those of the old citizens, thus creating a heterogeneous environment for the criminal justice system. In addition, crime patterns may change, and an increased number of social-control problems may require formal rather than informal processing. Large urban, industrial communities offer an even more complex environment for criminal justice agencies to work within. Values of community members and their demands for services from governmental and criminal justice agencies may vary greatly. Social-control problems are handled with formality. Criminal justice bureaucracies become large, and their members may not be easily accessible to citizens. Therefore, direct input from community members into criminal justice agencies may be limited.

Geographical conditions also have an impact on both the services demanded in a community and the resources available. In northern cities, winter climates create traffic hazards. Western areas have forest fires and droughts. Coastal areas or lakes and streams present safety hazards. Areas that attract tourists have distinctive social-control problems. For example, Las Vegas attracts more than its share of drifters and criminals as well as legitimate tourists looking for excitement. Little imagination is needed to consider how the problems the Las Vegas criminal justice system faces compare with those of stable industrial or rural communities.

Political Conditions

Political conditions can affect an organization directly through pressures from constituents and clients and indirectly through governmental action. The governmental response to political conditions can be passed on to organizations and agencies in a number of ways. To focus on public agencies, governments can alter agency budgets, change mandates, alter the composition of top administrative personnel—which often happens after an election—or write legislation that changes the purpose or power base of a bureaucracy. Court decisions that affect the operations or mission of an agency are made in the existing political climate and are not exempt from political forces. As suggested previously, a body of case law has evolved as individual rights have become a deep political concern.

Political pressure can be placed directly by interest groups on criminal justice agencies rather than through the governmental structure. For example, Mothers Against Drunk Drivers (MADD) has been successful in causing police agencies to be concerned with the safety hazards created by drunk drivers. The MADD group has been able to focus national attention on the highway safety problem created by drunk drivers, which has, in turn, pressured courts to impose stiffer penalties and police to increase the frequency of arrest of those driving under the influence of drugs or alcohol. The National Association for the Advancement of Colored People is a well-organized political force that has historically placed direct pressure on police agencies for fair treatment of black citizens and for equal opportunity employment within criminal justice agencies. In addition, the American Friends Service Committee (1971) has a history of attempting to bring humane reform to our prison system. We often also hear general pleas from the public at large for tougher criminal sentencing. Judges, being elected officials, are vulnerable to such pressures.

Much of what has been discussed in this section on political conditions within the environment is based on cultural considerations. Cultural views and values become political when we try to operationalize them or make them part of the official domain of government. A society utilizes its political–legal system to perpetuate its most basic values. In addition, the political–legal system becomes a conduit between the forces of the environment and governmental agencies by rendering the conflicting demands and needs of the environment into manageable mandates for governmental agencies. Thus criminal justice agencies are linked directly to and must be most responsive to the political environment they function within.

The Political Environment

The political environment of the criminal justice system can be thought of as a complex decision-making apparatus containing both formal and informal overlapping subsystems (Fairchild and Webb, 1985). The formal political system includes legislative bodies at the federal, state, and local levels. These bodies pass legislation that determines and limits the operation of the criminal justice system. These bodies also allocate to criminal justice agencies resources that can have a substantial impact on operations. Legislative bodies in theory pass on demands from the general public to public service agencies. They are also subjected to the potential influence of pressure groups, whose goal is to influence the policies or operations of the criminal justice system (Fairchild, 1981; Stolz, 1985).

The court system, while a component of the criminal justice system, also is a part of the formal political system. The court system, especially the federal system, regulates the operations of criminal justice agencies. The regulation imposed by the courts is, in theory, based on statutory and case law and constitutional law, much of which is constantly being redefined by new court decisions or case law. In making sure the criminal justice system operates within the law, the courts are theoretically blind to demands of the general public or changes in cultural and other environmental factors. However, a significant body of research suggests that judges, whether elected or appointed, make decisions congruent with the values they bring to the office. Their decision making often reflects the regional or political values they have acquired more than a strict interpretation of the law (Cole, 1987; Frazier and Block, 1982; Kolonski and Mendelsohn, 1970).

The informal political system comprises sources of pressures and demands that are placed directly on the criminal justice system. These pressures support or oppose existing programs or practices or demand new programs or services. In other words, individuals, groups, or organizations may bypass the formal political system and focus directly on a criminal justice agency—or attack the formal political structure and agency simultaneously—to bring about a desired effect. In the previous section on political environmental factors, examples were given of change imposed on the criminal justice system by direct pressure from such groups.

Informal pressure can also be placed on the criminal justice system by legislative bodies. Legislatures may voice support for or opposition to agency programs or practices short of writing new laws. In short, governmental bodies may interfere with the routine operations of an agency as well as define the agency's official goal or mission (Guyot, 1985). For example, most state legislatures have both House and Senate committees on corrections, police, courts, or the criminal justice system. Such committees may show intense interest in a criminal justice agency program or operation, and voice an opinion on appropriate agency philosophy, policies, or procedures. Such an opinion itself may create a response on the part of an agency without official legislation. In Michigan, for example, the Senate Committee on Criminal Justice argued for the development of a military camp for young inmates. The department of corrections was initially opposed to the "boot camp." However, the camp was eventually established to house 150 inmates—compared with 20,000 in the state prison system—presumably to appease the committee.

The formal and informal political systems faced by the criminal justice agencies are not mutually exclusive. The example given above shows members of the formal political system exerting informal influence. We can return to MADD also to see how the two systems mix or overlap. MADD can consistently pressure police agencies to increase the frequency with which they arrest drunk drivers and pressure judges to give out tough sentences, while lobbying legislators to toughen legislation against drunk drivers and provide increased resources to improve anti–drunk-driving efforts.

Agencies may respond directly to pressure from the public or a particular constituency and plan to effect an operational or programmatic change. They may first, however, approach the formal system for support by asking legislative bodies for additional funding (Cordner and Hudzik, 1983) or statutory support for their plan. In this manner, the formal political system is pressured by the agency to respond to demands from the informal political system. The move to community policing, or the foot-patrol program, is a rich and interesting example of the political interactions, initiated by the police, among the community, the police, and city hall.

In Flint, Michigan, an industrial town that had unemployment rates of up to 23 percent in the 1980s, the crime rate rose rapidly, and community members demanded increased police service. City funds were unavailable because of the economic problems, but the Mott Foundation, a local foundation created to assure the quality of life in Flint, funded the establishment of a foot-patrol experiment. Funds from Mott were used to pay foot-patrol police officers' salaries for a three-year period. The program was evaluated periodically through direct interviews with residents in the foot-patrol neighborhoods. Although the foot-patrol program did not seem to affect crime rates, it provided residents with increased perceptions of safety, and the residents favored the availability of foot-patrol officers (Trojanowicz, 1983). In fact, when the Mott Foundation grant ran out, the community voted overwhelmingly for a tax increase to continue the foot-patrol program as a permanent part of the police force.

The foot-patrol program was not overly popular, however, with many police administrators as well as members of the city government. Although they were pleased with the tax increase, members of both groups continued to struggle to have the monies allocated to the foot-patrol program lumped into the total police department budget rather than earmarked for foot-patrol operations. It was also evident to administrators that the foot-patrol officers were gaining, or had the capacity to gain, credibility and political influence among the constituents in the neighborhoods they served. Hence, administrators were concerned with the possible loss of bureaucratic control over foot-patrol officers (Trojanowicz, Steele, and Trojanowicz, 1986). The foot-patrol officers were, in effect, now capable of being significant figures in the informal political system themselves through the influence and credibility they built within the community.

Clearly, the political environment varies greatly in influence, structure, and form. In small rural communities, for example, criminal justice actors may be subjected to constant community input because they are part of the local social system. Citizens may be able to get something done by attending city council meetings, banging on the police chief's desk, or seeking out the judge at the local restaurant. In large urban communities, criminal justice agencies are shielded from such direct input from community members. Citizen complaints are handled through formal channels with much red tape. Influence is gained only through concerted interest-group effort, which must usually include pressures through the formal political system as well as pressure on the criminal justice system itself (Olsen, 1973). State and federal agencies, especially corrections systems, are large, bureaucratic, and distant from the general public. They are, therefore, protected from the informal political system. To the extent they are vulnerable to political influence, it is likely to be from the formal political system.

Public agencies take their general mandates from the political system and are constrained by the legal and budgetary control of the formal political system. However, they are subject to other pressures, demands, and constraints from clientele and constituencies served, competing and cooperating agencies, and other specific elements of their task environment. In the following section, we attempt to identify these groups.

Task Environment Elements Specific to the Criminal Justice System

The task environment of an agency can be defined generally as the forces in the environment that are related directly to the goal-setting and goal-directed activities of the criminal justice system (Steers, 1977). The task environment includes unions, personnel, other criminal justice agencies, social service agencies, citizens receiving services, criminal offenders, attorneys, and victims. These sources of pressure are common in criminal justice agencies to a varied extent. In effect, these entities attempt to override official goals and reshape the way criminal justice agencies do business as well as what their business is.

Unions and new personnel often criticize established oganizational practices, norms, and ethics. Unions clearly attempt to force a system to alter its practices toward employees (Swanson, Territo, and Taylor, 1988). New personnel bring their own values and beliefs into an organization; and, to the extent their values vary from existing values, they may affect the goals, practices, and decision making within the system (Eisenstein, 1973). It was hoped, for example, that upgrading the educational levels of police officers—i.e., making a baccalaureate degree common—would make officers nonracist and able to relate well to members of the communities they serve (National Advisory Commission on Criminal Justice Standards and Goals, 1973b).

In this regard, affirmative action has also had an impact on particular aspects of criminal justice agencies. Hiring women police and corrections officers has caused agencies to alter physical requirements for recruitment, including physical fitness testing for entry (Booth and Harwick, 1984). More importantly, perhaps, the mixing of genders has forced agencies to provide methods to assimilate female personnel and accord them professional status (Price, 1974). Agencies now, for example, must provide procedures to protect each gender from sexual harassment from the other especially when one has a position of authority over the other.

The type and number of offenders clearly have an impact on the operations of criminal justice agencies. The emergence of street gangs causes police agencies to alter policies, procedures, and resources. Anti-gang units are often formed to respond to gangs as a crime threat or in response to public fears (Center for Assessment of the Juvenile Justice System, 1982). The increased arrest of gang members affects the corrections system, especially large jails and prisons, because gangs tend to coalesce in correctional institutions and attempt to rule them (Irwin, 1980; Jacobs, 1983a).

Increasing the number of arrests, as a result of increased crime, public pressure on police, luck, or skill, will affect operations throughout the criminal justice system. The populations of local jails and lockups will increase, court dockets and caseloads of prosecuting attorneys will expand, and perhaps plea bargaining will favor defendants more than usual as a result of high caseloads. Finally, prison populations may increase.

Changes in the quality and type of criminal activity may affect the operational goals and procedures of agencies. In our example of street gangs, allocating additional law enforcement resources to that problem will take resources away from other activities. Response time to burglaries or accidents may increase, traffic control may be reduced, as resources are taken away from these areas to deal with street gangs. Prison administrators may become more concerned with maintaining order than with treatment or rehabilitation in institutions populated by street-gang members.

A striking example of the vulnerability of the system to specific elements in its environment can be seen in the interactions between state mental health systems and the criminal justice system, especially jails and prisons. Both systems are ultimately involved in social control. Historically, mentally ill citizens were confined in state mental institutions; in effect, they were controlled through incarceration. During the late 1960s and early 1970s, mental health professionals and legislators moved away from confining mentally ill citizens for long periods of time and instituted a program of community mental health, or keeping mentally ill citizens out of institutions unless they posed a substantial danger to themselves or others. This change came about in part in response to the recognition of abuses and arbitrary decision making within mental institutions. In addition, mental health professionals reasoned that individuals suffering from mental problems could be cured only in the community, where they must ultimately live and survive. State mental hospitals were emptied, therefore, during the 1970s, and strict legal constraints have kept mental-hospital admissions to a low level since.

Moving to a community base, however, has created problems for criminal justice agencies, especially jails and prisons. Mentally ill citizens who behave in criminal or antisocial ways now have to be controlled and cared for by the criminal justice system instead of by the state mental health systems (Guy, Platt, and Zwerling, 1985). A growing number of jail and prison inmates across the nation are mentally ill (Steadman, Monahan, Duffee, Hartstone, and Robbins, 1984). In analyzing the data from the Bureau of Justice statistics in the Survey of Jail Inmates, we found that approximately 16 percent of inmates incarcerated in our nation's jails in 1983 reported symptoms of mental illness or prior institutionalization in a mental hospital. In addition, current standards of care for inmates imposed on jails and prisons by the courts require that they be provided with adequate psychiatric and medical assistance (Embert, 1986). In effect, the role of the local jail and prison has been modified by changes within the mental health system. Policies, procedures, and behaviors of the employees of jails and correctional institutions must also be changed to perform the new task imposed by its environment.

We could continue at great length giving examples of how specific factors within an organization's environment can impose their will on an agency and cause it to alter its mission, policies, or procedures. However, a general analysis of the dynamics of an organization's environment can provide an understanding of the general nature of environmental forces. In the next section, we provide this analysis.

Environmental States

The specific environment of an organization can range from simple to complex and from static to dynamic. A *simple* environment is one in which the external forces that affect the organization, or with which the organization must interact, are few in number and are relatively homogeneous. Conversely, an organization that deals with a number of heterogeneous external factors exists within a relatively *complex* task environment (Duncan, 1972). Each state will affect the behavior of an organization differently. Police agencies that work in small communities with stable populations and little demographic change face a limited number of problems, most of which are recurring and predictable. The small-town cop probably knows many of the citizens personally, knows who the troublemakers are and where trouble spots are, can predict the behaviors and expectations of the political leaders, and is in a position to influence aspects of his or her environment.

If such a Sleepy Hollow begins to change demographically, economically, or culturally, the environment becomes increasingly complex. If, for example, a relatively large firm moves into Sleepy Hollow, the population will increase, additional housing will be built, individuals with different ethnic backgrounds may settle there, traffic patterns will change, and crime and interpersonal conflict may increase. The police agency may need to expand, be concerned with the behavior of the new community members (at least initially), and cope with altered traffic patterns, more taverns, and tavern patrons. The environment for small-town cops thus moves from placid and simple to complex and diverse. They will not have personal knowledge of all of those they will be dealing with and will become increasingly formal in their interactions with citizens. If a new firm creates hazardous waste, think of the new expertise and enforcement obligations the officers of Sleepy Hollow will need to acquire.

The most complex environment for criminal justice agencies is to be found in big cities. There are clear differences between big-city and rural policing due to the complex versus simple task environments. Even those with limited imaginations should not have trouble perceiving the profound differences within big-city task environments and small-town police and criminal justice systems. The most complex environment for criminal justice agencies exists within a densely populated industrial county in which a number of cities of varying sizes have police agencies, courts with misdemeanor jurisdiction, and lockups, all of which link to the county or circuit courts of felony jurisdiction and the county sheriff (road patrol and county jail). The members of the criminal justice system must deal with a number of jurisdictions, agencies within and across jurisdictions, and heterogeneous political and cultural systems.

We would expect criminal justice practitioners in such large or densely populated jurisdictions to behave in impersonal and highly bureaucratic ways. In addition, criminal justice practitioners in large jurisdictions have little opportunity for personal contact with influential community members and political figures. Such contact is left to criminal justice administrators, who interact with the political–legal system, interpreting public opinions and demands into criminal justice policy.

An organization's environment may be static or dynamic as well as simple or complex. A *static* environment is one that remains constant or stable over time; it is predictable. A *dynamic* environment is one that is subject to unpredictable change (Duncan, 1972; Steers, 1977). For example, the Sleepy Hollow police department worked in a static environment before the hypothetical economic and demographic changes took place. As demands on an agency become diverse and unpredictable, the environment begins to take on a dynamic nature. An environment can also have both simple and dynamic components. Much of the criminal justice practitioner's work is routine, repetitive, and predictable; yet, some facets are unpredictable. In many respects, the ultimate art of the criminal justice practitioner or administrator is to predict or anticipate as many contingencies as possible, thereby simplifying some aspects of a complex dynamic environment. For example, police agencies attempt to predict crime patterns, traffic patterns, and gang behavior (Kinney, 1984). Parole boards attempt to predict the postrelease behavior of inmates. Inasmuch as certain demands placed on the criminal justice system are routine or can be made predictable, a chunk of the environment of its agencies can be considered stable.

However, criminal justice agencies are often confronted by surprises and new demands from their environment. The influx of mentally ill inmates into the jails and prisons may, in retrospect, have been predictable, but it was not predicted, at least in an operational sense. The smooth flow of cases through a prosecutor's office and the court may be disrupted by a heinous crime that gains a great deal of notoriety. The prosecutor and staff may be forced to spend a great deal of time and energy on the case to satisfy public expectations for successful prosecution.

Urban police work can often be highly complex and unpredictable. An excellent example occurred in New York City in 1967. New York suffered a citywide power outage because of a problem in a utility company generator. In the chaos that followed the outage, looters pillaged retail stores, breaking windows and removing merchandise. The police had to mobilize and deal with this unexpected contingency. The effect of the police intervention was increased arrests, which, in turn, put pressure on lockups, bail and bond systems, prosecutors' staffs, courts, probation departments, and county correctional facilities. An important implication here is that the criminal justice system typically bears the responsibility for dealing with unique situations.

Organizational Response to the Environment

Environmental Uncertainty

More dynamic and complex organizational environments have greater uncertainty associated with them. And the more an organization perceives uncertainty in the cues and demands from its environment, the more difficulty it will have in making effective decisions. The perception of uncertainty in the environment is the result of three conditions: a lack of information about environmental factors important to decision making; an inability to estimate how probabilities will affect a decision until it is implemented; and a lack of information regarding the cost associated with an incorrect decision (Duncan, 1972). Table 2-1 provides a good general description of how environmental states affect certainty or uncertainty.

What is pivotal, as will be expanded upon later in this chapter, is an organization's ability to respond appropriately to its environment. The more uncertainty an organization perceives in its environment, the more difficulty it will have in responding to pressures from its environment. A public agency that fails to maintain successful relationships with its environment will fail to be responsive to demands, will not appropriate

Table 2-1 Characteristics of Various Environmental States

	Simple	Complex
Static	CELL 1: *Low Perceived Uncertainty* 1. Small number of factors and components in the environment 2. Factors and components are somewhat similar to one another 3. Factors and components remain basically the same and are not changing	CELL 2: *Moderately Low Perceived Uncertainty* 1. Large number of factors and components in the environment 2. Factors and components are not similar to one another 3. Factors and components remain basically the same
Dynamic	CELL 3: *Moderately High Perceived Uncertainty* 1. Small number of factors and components in the environment 2. Factors and components are somewhat similar to one another 3. Factors and components of the environment are in continual process of change	CELL 4: *High Perceived Uncertainty* 1. Large number of factors and components in the environment 2. Factors and components are not similar to one another 3. Factors and components of environment are in a continual process of change

Source: Reprinted from "The Characteristics of Organizational Environments and Perceived Environmental Uncertainty," by R. B. Duncan. Published in *Administrative Science Quarterly,* 1972, *17,* p. 320 by permission of *Administrative Science Quarterly.*

adequate resources and support for its activities (Sharkansky, 1972; Rourke, 1986; Wildavsky, 1974), and will be unable to adapt to significant environmental change (Scott, 1987).

Decoupled Organizations

To add to the issue of uncertainty, large organizations tend to become decoupled. As such, they may face multiple environments and interact with each environment at different organizational levels. It is clear that large organizations face multiple constituencies with conflicting demands. This is especially true within complex and dynamic environments. To complicate matters further, an environment may be conceptualized as having two subenvironments that an agency may have to respond to: the political–legal and service-delivery subenvironments.

We can understand this concept by looking outward from organizations as they interact with the environment. Large organizations tend to break into overlapping subgroups, the dominant coalition and the work processors. The dominant coalition is the small group of employees who oversee the organization and dictate policy decisions; the work processors are the bulk of the organizational members, who are directly involved with the primary clientele of the organization (Nokes, 1960). Members of the dominant coalition interact with the political–legal system, administrators of related organizations, organized support and opposition groups, and the news media; they typically become the focal point of public pressure. These policy-level administrators must deal with political and public opinions that reflect the often conflicting views of the organization's multiple constituency. In responding to the variety of pressures from the political environment, the dominant coalition must be concerned with the myths, image, and posture of the agency. The work process group, in contrast, deals directly with the agency clientele and delivers services to them (Meyer and Rowan, 1978; Nokes, 1960). In large systems, members of the work process group become "street-level bureaucrats," who negotiate rules for the allocation of scarce agency resources with clients (Lipsky, 1980). Each subgroup of the organization faces different demands and pressures from different sources. Figure 2-2 shows a decoupled organization interacting with its subenvironments.

Decoupled organizations face a unique set of problems. To begin with, the cues, pressures, and constraints that the dominant coalition faces may be profoundly different from those faced by members of the work process group. For example, elites may demand that wife abusers be arrested more frequently—or policymakers may perceive such demands will be forthcoming—and policy will be directed toward increased arrests of wife abusers. However, street police officers may be reluctant to do so as their past experience with their clientele has convinced them that arresting wife abusers may not be an effective way to deal with the

Figure 2-2   A Decoupled Organization Within Its Environment

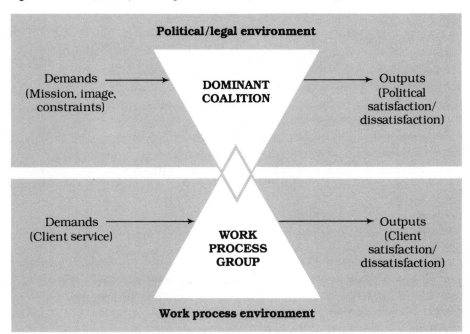

problem (Galliher, 1985). Or administrators may feel they must wage wars on drugs or gambling, while law enforcement officers may understand that certain forms of drug use or gambling are approved behaviors within their community and may actively avoid controlling those types of crime on their beats (Wilson, 1968).

Corrections systems provide fruitful examples of decoupled organizations. Corrections reform has been the concern of concerted political elites since 1870, when the National Congress of Penitentiary and Reformatory Discipline met in Cincinnati. This group called for sweeping reforms and implementation of standards for the maintenance and management of inmates. Since, other meetings of establishment elites (Quinney, 1974) have been convened, and lasting groups, such as the American Correctional Association, have been formed and have prescribed standards for corrections. Courts have intervened and provided inmates with constitutional rights and have examined prison and jail conditions under a constitutional microscope. However, this collective effort for change, while reflected in the written policies and procedures of most corrections systems, has primarily served the function of maintaining and legitimizing the corrections system by updating the language and symbols that explain the system to the public (Kalinich and Banas, 1984). Within the bowels of the system, the work process people—

corrections officers and other staff—work pragmatically with the raw material, the inmates, to keep the system in some semblance of order. The demands of part of the political–legal environment are absorbed and iterated back through language and symbolism by the dominant coalition. However, the day-to-day work is typically based on a series of informal rules negotiated between corrections staff and inmates (Kalinich and Stojkovic, 1985) and may have nothing to do with the prescriptions and standards promulgated by interested elites and pressure groups or by the courts.

The process of decentralizing, or federalizing, large bureaucracies is typically done so that the work process members have enough flexibility to deal with their local clientele or to respond to the demands of their local constituents. Decentralization is, in effect, a recognition that local environmental dimensions may be different at different levels of the organization and that the organization may face more than one environment. Police agencies in large metropolitan areas often are broken into a number of districts that are governed by district commanders, who work with some degree of autonomy from the central bureaucracy. Parole agencies are typically governed loosely by a central office and broken into geographical districts, with each district expected to function with some degree of autonomy. However, the different environments faced by an agency can create friction between central-office staff and field staff even in formally decentralized bureaucracies (McCleary, 1978; also see Pfeffer, 1978, and Selznik, 1949).

McCleary's (1978) interesting organizational study of a parole system describes the impact of different operational philosophies held by the dominant coalition—the central office—and the work process members—parole officers and district supervisors—on fundamentals of parole supervision in a state agency. The central office, for example, attempting to update the system, felt that it was inappropriate for a modern, professional parole system to have its officers carry guns. Parole officers argued, however, that dangers existed within their work environment that made carrying a gun a necessity. The central office, nonetheless, officially decreed that officers would no longer be allowed to carry guns in the field. Parole officers, however, continued to carry guns, and their supervisors supported them by not enforcing the central-office ban on firearms.

In effect, the central office attempted to alter the image of the agency to be congruent with external expectations for professionalism and effecting rehabilitation among its clients. However, the parole officers responded to their perceived environmental constraints. One may argue that the differences of views were based primarily on the personal values of the members of the central office and the field staff. However, many of our job-related values and norms come from our immediate work group, which is affected by the environment it is immersed within (Hall, 1982; Steers, 1977). Basically, each group was responding to what it perceived to be the realities or expectations of their respective environments. However, their perceptions of environmental demands were filtered by their work-group norms, past practices, and personal agendas (McCleary, 1978).

Organizations are not helpless entities, however, that ritualistically respond to environmental forces. Rather, organizations generally have policed their boundaries well and exert some degree of control over the flow of environmental inputs into their systems. In the following section, we discuss the common methods agencies use to manage environmental forces.

Managing Environmental Forces

The important point of this chapter is that almost all organizations are vulnerable to environmental forces, although to varying degrees (Jacobs, 1974). Organizations are open systems and are dependent upon, and constrained by, environmental systems for mandates, authority, and resources, and must produce goods or services for their clients. In effect, organizations must enter into exchange relations across their boundaries with other systems (Scott, 1987). This is an important consideration, as the ability of an organization to develop favorable exchange relations with its environment is ultimately related to its effectiveness (Osborn and Hunt, 1974).

Organizations, however, often do not maintain such relations and instead attempt to behave as rational, or closed, systems. They expend efforts at setting and policing their boundaries in an effort to protect their core from external environmental influences (Thompson, 1967). Organizations are therefore subjected to the task of managing and coping with their environments. Managing environments requires exerting control over environmental forces or creating mechanisms to buffer the agency from inputs. Production organizations stockpile raw materials, accumulate cash reserves, and control their markets with advertising, etc., all in an attempt to make them less dependent on their environments (Blau, 1955). Criminal justice agencies, as public bureaucracies, get their inputs (mandates, resources, support and opposition for programs) from the political–legal and cultural systems. They, like other public agencies, can protect their boundaries by invoking their bureaucratic power in both the formal and informal political system or by conforming or appearing to conform to environmental demands or expectations through symbols and rhetoric.

Influencing Input

It is tempting to think of public bureaucracies, especially criminal justice agencies, as being apolitical or above politics in the performance of their duties. An earlier view that supported this rationalistic view of public organizations posited that the political structure created policy and that public administrators carried out policy (Henry, 1975). However, bureaus have the power to influence policy inputs from the political system (Long, 1949). Legislators who control budgets and create social policy depend on agencies to carry out their programs. In addition, agencies have expertise that lawmakers as a matter of routine depend on when creating changes (Rourke, 1976). Agency administrators are typically called on to provide information and to advise or to state their position to legislative bodies that are proposing legislation that would restrict or broaden the scope of an agency's duties or powers. Legislative committees routinely call on directors of corrections, chiefs of police, and jail administrators, to define problems and solutions, or to respond to questions and issues put to them by the public.

In addition, police, courts, and correctional agencies forward budgets and programs annually to their governing political bodies and argue their positions based on their unique understanding and expertise. The budgeting process is an opportunity for criminal justice administrators to propose programs and legislation that would alter the scope of their organizations' duties as well as expand their resources (Cordner and Hudzik, 1983).

Those criminal justice administrators who understand the political process and are capable of acting as "statespersons" (Downs, 1967; Rourke, 1976) for their agencies can have extraordinary influence and power over political inputs. The Federal Bureau of Investigation under the directorship of J. Edgar Hoover is a testimony to the ability of a criminal justice agency to protect its boundaries through its influence over the formal political process (Powers, 1986). Chiefs of police or corrections administrators who view their function as being above politics and reject the political aspects of their role, or who are simply inept at functioning within the political process, typically fail to protect their agencies from political inputs.

Bureaus may also influence the open political system by gathering support from public groups. A number of groups exist outside the criminal justice system that attempt to constrain, support, or direct the system. Such groups include the American Correctional Association, National Sheriff's Association, American Friends Service Committee, Fraternal Order of Police, American Bar Association, American Civil Liberties Union, and, to some extent for corrections, the American Medical Association (Fairchild, 1981; Stolz, 1985). While their means may differ—e.g., the American Civil Liberties Union brings issues to the public through law suits and public decrees, and the American Correctional Association promulgates standards for corrections operations—the views of such groups can have an effect on the formal political and legal system (Stolz, 1985; Melone, 1985). However, criminal justice administrators also may utilize such groups for support in the open political system because the membership of many of the organizations is made up primarily of criminal justice practitioners and administrators.

The news media act as a conduit between agencies and the environment. A media message can create support for or opposition to an agency or its programs and can also be a vehicle for a bureau to influence key sources in its environment. It is common for agencies at the federal level to exploit the news media to influence their immediate environment as well as the public. Information can be leaked, for example, to test for responses or to bring pressure to bear on other subcomponents or hierarchical levels of a bureau (Halperin, 1978). Using the media's influence to protect agency boundaries is a robust technique that criminal justice agencies seem not to exploit as a matter of course. The opportunity would seem to be available; public interest in "cops and robbers" appears insatiable. Criminal justice agencies have made clumsy ventures at public relations and public influence by using the media, especially with police–community relations (Radelet, 1986) or Officer McGruff ad campaigns encouraging citizens to take steps to prevent crime. Again, the Federal Bureau of Investigation has done an outstanding job of developing contacts with the media and presenting an impeccable image of itself. Also, most elected sheriffs, being political by nature, have typically had a good sense of how to deal with the media.

However, police and corrections agencies have typically received negative press coverage because of the sensationalism of the enterprise and, in part perhaps, because of the lack of motivation a local or state civil servant may have compared with a politically oriented administrator such as an elected sheriff or federal bureaucrat (Siedman, 1976). Our heuristic view is that media information about the criminal justice system has been generally negative and has brought occasional hostile pressures to bear on criminal justice agencies rather than presenting criminal justice practices in a favorable light to the public and the political–legal system (Radelet, 1986).

Using Symbols

An organization can also protect its boundaries by using symbols, slogans, and pithy rhetoric to express its philosophy, policies, and means of operations in abbreviated form. The limited understanding of bureaus by most of those outside the bureaus' boundaries, and the sloppiness of human thinking, causes excessive reliance on symbolism, making it a powerful tool. The symbols, slogans, or rhetoric evoked by an organization become a code representing agency philosophy and lending meaning to entrenched policy:

> To the extent that antagonistic constituencies view them [symbols] as legitimate, or at least acceptable, they [symbols] promote consensus. . . . By communicating easily consumable statements, they link society as a whole

with its institutions by identifying generalizable values. . . . They insulate organizations from conflicting contradictory pressures and help prevent dysfunction [Kalinich, Lorinskas, and Banas, 1985, p. 43].

Organizations spend a significant part of their resources on such window dressing (Wilensky, 1967). Symbols can be seen, for example, in sweeping goal statements that are nonoperational and encompass the needs or demands of a broad constituency. Agencies use general symbolic statements to give them the appearance of conforming to the demands of clients, constituents, and other forces in the environment. When environmental pressures demand changes in an agency's philosophies, scope of duties, activities, etc., the agency will search for the least profound change (Downs, 1967) and do so by first manipulating its symbols (Kalinich, Lorinskas, and Banas, 1985). In other words, bureaus manipulate their symbols to ward off pressures for substantive change. The art of manipulating symbols thus becomes a technique to protect the bureau's boundaries.

The process of evoking symbols is a significant aspect of the criminal justice system because the system is shaped by innumerable symbols and myths (Atkins and Pogrebin, 1982). Examples of the use of symbols in the face of pressures from environmental forces are abundant (Lovell and Stojkovic, 1989). As times changed, the posture of penology has moved from a philosophy of discipline to corrections and rehabilitation. Guards were changed to corrections officers, convicts to prisoners to inmates and finally to clients. In many places, corrections officers wear blazers rather than uniforms and badges. Police no longer fight crime—they "serve and protect" or act as agents for crime prevention. Reform bodies such as the National Advisory Commission on Criminal Justice Standards and Goals (1973a) may have actually inhibited change because it gave the system the appearance of having the capability for change by revising and updating the language through which the system is conceptualized (Kalinich and Banas, 1984).

It can similarly be argued that police–community programs were symbolic responses to protect police agencies from political inputs. Traditionally, police projected the image of crime fighters. When the racial riots of the late 1960s brought hostile pressure on police agencies from minority and liberal groups, the police responded with a temporary measure. Police–community units were created with limited resources and were aimed at promoting shallow public relations. Police agencies avoided expending resources on these programs to avoid structural changes with the police bureaus (Kalinich, Lorinskas, and Banas, 1985).

Responding to Client Demands

Agency boundaries, especially decoupled agencies, are also permeable at the operational level. A very good example of this exists within prisons.

The administrators of corrections systems—the director of corrections, wardens, deputy wardens—promulgate policies, procedures, and rules for corrections officers and inmates to follow in the day-to-day operation of the institution. However, a great deal of leakage of authority exists in a bureaucracy between the hierarchy and the line staff (Downs, 1967)—in this case, the corrections officers. Corrections officers conform to many of the demands of the inmates, their clients, rather than to the formal organizational rules in an effort to keep order in the cellblocks. In effect, an informal system of governance that circumvents many of the formal policies, procedures, and institutional rules is created based to a great extent on inmates' values, needs, and norms (Kalinich and Stojkovic, 1985).

In the police world, line police officers are granted a great deal of discretion to deal with the day-to-day problems they face within the communities they serve. Officers have choices in how and on whom they will enforce the law or implement policy and procedures. In the "watchman" style of policing (Wilson, 1968), the officer is extremely sensitive to community norms and ignores law and agency policy in favor of local norms and behaviors. For example, if gambling is an accepted form of behavior in the community, the officer will not enforce antigambling statutes in deference to community members. The norms of the client in both these instances influence and alter the formal rules of the agency. In the jargon of organizational theory, the agency's boundaries have been penetrated by the norms of the clientele, and the agency has become debureaucratized (Kaufman, 1969; Scott, 1987).

Several examples of boundaries being permeated by nonorganizational norms are given in this chapter; the failure of local law enforcement officials to enforce the Eighteenth Amendment and the politicization of foot-patrol programs are dramatic examples. One can argue that the elimination of the foot-patrol officer in Chicago in favor of putting police in patrol cars was Taylorism in action (Fischer and Sirianni, 1984). Separating police officers from their community constituents was an effective way to seal off the police organization from its immediate environment and to exert control over the rank and file.

Organizations can attempt to protect their boundaries from infringement at the operational level by attempting to control the norms and behaviors of their members. This control can be accomplished by indoctrinating its members in organizational norms, clarifying organizational behavioral expectations through declarations of crisp policies, and enforcing organizational rules and regulations. Control over agency members limits members' responsiveness to demands from external sources and keeps the organization from becoming debureaucratized.

However, organizations have less than complete control over their members. In fact, criminal justice practitioners have a great deal of discretion and power, and routinely make ad hoc decisions in the course of their work (Atkins and Pogrebin, 1982). Making judgment calls on a case-by-case basis—the application of discretion—defines criminal justice practitioners as professionals. In addition, it is difficult for agencies to control subordinates' behavior, especially where the structure of the agency requires that line staff perform their duties without continuous observation by supervisory personnel, which is precisely the structure of most criminal justice agencies. Hence, the operational boundaries of criminal justice agencies are permeable. This phenomenon is found especially in criminal justice organizations that tend to be decoupled.

Decreasing Vulnerability to Pressure

Organizations vary in their vulnerability to environmental pressures (Jacobs, 1974). Goffman (1966) described prisons and mental institutions as "total institutions," suggesting that they were almost closed systems. Historically they were protected from intrusion from environmental forces to a great extent. Prisons were protected from the legal system by federal courts, the legal system itself, and the "hands-off" doctrine, which kept prisons exempt from civil litigation. The hands-off doctrine eroded and prisons are now vulnerable to civil litigation. Large, well-established organizations with sufficient resources to police their boundaries, influence their environments, and function within predictable work environments are the most impermeable agencies. Conversely, those that are dependent on their environments, that have limited resources, and that function within turbulent environments are forced to adapt to environmental conditions and demands or fail (Hall, 1982; Scott, 1987). Also, organizations that do not modify their structures will fail to manage environmental demands (Hannan and Freeman, 1984), while agencies that have inherent flexibility can readily adapt to changes in the environment (Duffee, 1985).

Criminal justice agencies are, for the most part, well established and can be thought of as rather large systems within the immediate community each serves. In urban settings, and at the state and federal levels, the boundary between the criminal justice system and the general community at the policy level may be difficult to permeate, but the boundary between the system and community may be porous at the operational level, suggesting that large criminal justice systems may tend to be decoupled. They face heterogeneous constituencies and a wide range of problems, and function within a turbulent and somewhat unpredictable environment. In small communities, the social exchange between community members and members of the criminal justice system may effectively minimize boundaries, except in symbolic ways, and policies and practices may be based heavily on local values and demands. Criminal justice agencies in these communities usually have homogeneous constituencies and a relatively narrow scope of problems, and function within a stable and predictable environment; administrators need not expend great efforts protecting the agency's boundary.

Implications for Administrators

We have described environmental pressures at length and have discussed the notion of organizational boundaries, which protect organizations from unwanted pressures. We have also provided a general description of methods bureaus typically use to control environmental pressures and to avoid becoming debureaucratized. In this regard, we have discussed the administrator's role as defending the agency against environmental intrusions. We have not explicitly discussed the related yet opposing role of an administrator: to make the agency be responsive to the community or its constituencies. An organization must, on the one hand, survive and maintain some sense of internal stability and protect its established routines in order to deliver services successfully (Nelson and Winter, 1982). On the other hand, it must provide services by means that are congruent with community preferences. Although organizational members may make decisions about what constitutes appropriate services, environmental constituents ultimately judge the value of an organization's outputs. In other words, an agency that develops favorable relations with its environment will likely be perceived as a responsive, productive, and contributing organization.

Administrators bear these responsibilities for an agency's relationships with its environment. Their presentation of the organization as possessing crucial expertise and dedicated members and their dynamic leaderships will have an influence. Agencies that present themselves as "rational" and mission- or goal-directed will typically have status with legislative bodies and be able to compete favorably for resources (Greene, Bynum, and Cordner, 1986). To the extent that demands and pressures from the environment vary, administrators may need to make structural, functional, or symbolic changes within the agency. Administrators who resist change may find themselves out of work or find the formal political–legal system bringing change to the agency.

A reactive posture can be taken, and administrators may respond to altered demands and constraints as they fall on their desks. However, administrators cannot respond to all inputs if environmental demands are contradictory or capricious; they must consider the agency's norms, resources, expertise, scope of authority, as well as turf issues and relationships with cooperating and competing agencies and clientele before meeting new demands. Responding in a knee-jerk fashion to all demands may create chaos within an agency rather than responsiveness.

Ideally, administrators should predict environmental changes and enter into planned change, prepare for future demands, and prepare the members of the organization to be responsive to changes in environmental demands (Weiner and Johnson, 1981). Our previous discussion of the impact that emptying mental institutions has had on the corrections system is an example of a change that could have been predicted and planned for. However, planned change is easier to write about than to implement. Many changes are easy to predict only after they have taken place. Also, although organizations may be able to readily predict future demands on the system, support from the organization's members or the formal or informal political systems may not be sufficient to provide the organization with enough momentum to reallocate resources, change philosophies or policies, or remove the impediments to change.

For example, during the late seventies and early eighties, many public and political figures predicted that the prisons would become overcrowded and argued for facility construction. In fact, a bond issue to build more prisons was put on the ballot in Michigan in 1981. Despite support from the state attorney general, the bond issue failed. Seven years later, overcrowding was a reality rather than a predicted possibility, and prisons were being built at a rapid rate. The uncontrolled input of offenders from the environment overpowered the environmental forces that resisted the construction of new facilities. Change in this case was reactive rather than managed through planning and was created by environmental conditions beyond the control of the corrections system.

We will not provide a crisp set of procedures for a criminal justice agency administrator to apply in dealing with environmental pressures. (These issues will be examined in some detail in chapter 12, which discusses change and planned change.) However, we can offer some general prescriptions. Most importantly, administrators of criminal justice agencies should avoid believing they work in a closed, or rational, system. Enforcing laws, being encumbered by written policies and procedures, working within a classic chain of command, and wearing uniforms and badges can contribute to a myth that criminal justice is aloof from environmental pressures, and its boundaries are sacred. Administrators interact with agency environments whether they accept that fact or not, and they must be prepared to protect the agency from capricious or disabling inputs yet be responsive to legitimate demands. They must be able to interpret legitimate environmental demands to the organization's members and attempt to adapt to these demands in a systematic way. Ultimately, criminal justice organizations receive their mandates, authority, and resources as inputs from the environment. Judgments on the performance and effectiveness of criminal justice agencies and practitioners will ultimately be made by the broad and conflicting range of constituencies they serve.

Summary

Throughout this chapter we have examined the interdependence of the criminal justice system and its environment. In effect, all organizations function within the general environmental conditions that exist within a society. Further, all public organizations are integral to society's formal and informal political environment. Finally, criminal justice organizations function within a specific environment that includes clients, related agencies, and other systems that make immediate demands. Environments may be stable and predictable or turbulent. Regardless, the organization, specifically the administrators, must be in tune with changing environmental conditions. Administrators have a duty to be responsive to legitimate demands and changing constraints, yet protect the organization from capricious, inappropriate demands. Ultimately, an agency will be evaluated on its ability to negotiate its interdependence with its environment.

The ability of a criminal justice agency to negotiate with environmental forces depends on the ability of the agency and its members to communicate effectively with external groups. The next chapter examines the problems of communication in criminal justice organizations. In that chapter, the obstacles agencies encounter in building and maintaining effective communications with exogenous individuals, groups, and organizations are discussed at length. The chapter on communication is, in many ways, an extension of the discussion of environmental forces and provides further insights into the problems criminal justice agencies may have in interacting with the environment.

─────────────── **CASE STUDY** ───────────────
Big Business Invades a Small Town

Norwich is a rural town with a population of 10,478. Almost all the townspeople are second or third generation, and all are white. Most of the inhabitants earn their income from the agricultural industries in the area, while the rest work in adjunct services, shops, taverns, and the local hospital.

Chief of Police Ron Yednock has held his post for over twenty years. Eight full-time and seven part-time police officers and a dispatcher are under his command. The police station is old but well maintained and has a lockup with a capacity of eight.

The city fathers have always respected Chief Yednock's work as well as his judgment. However, some business owners are chronically unhappy with the police department's informal policy toward juveniles who shoplift from their establishments. The business association has approached the city council repeatedly asking that the chief be more formal in his dealings with juvenile offenders so that they may be dealt with more harshly.

Indeed, the chief's major problems have been occasional bursts of juvenile crimes, which he has settled informally whenever possible with the parents and others involved. In addition, Norwich has an occasional drunk driver whom Chief Yednock and his officers almost always handle informally in spite of the national trend and legislative support to put drunk drivers in jail. Chief Yednock has a straightforward attitude: if it ain't broke, don't fix it. His methods have been effective for twenty years.

However, he learns that General Motors is going to begin construction of an engine-assembly plant in Norwich. The plant will employ 1,700 line workers and about 500 supervisory and administrative staff. The plant will be in operation in about sixteen months. A few of the local inhabitants will probably go to work there. But most of the workers at the new plant will not be local.

Merchants, property owners, and the local banker are overjoyed. The chief is not. He shares his views at the city council meeting. The chief points out that the city will have to be prepared for major changes in responsibilities. These changes, he argues, will result from the addition of the rather large plant and the number of new inhabitants who will move to Norwich to work in the plant.

Before he can be specific and discuss the potential law enforcement problems he predicts, other council members attempt to assure everyone present that "things will take care of themselves." They point out that the new taxes generated by the plant and additional housing that will be constructed will generate enough revenue to add the necessary sewers, water supplies, roads, schools, etc.

The chief responds that there is more to running the city than maintaining the school system, building roads, etc. He argues that the city will have to expand police and fire services, and police services will be especially crucial during the period when the plant is under construction. He also points out that a sudden increase in the population will bring a lot of unpredictable problems to the community, which the police department will have to deal with.

Chief Yednock argues that the 21 percent increase in the population will require that the police force be doubled; his officers, old and new, will need extensive training in police–community relations; a larger jail will have to be constructed and staffed; and law enforcement will have to become more formal than it currently is.

Many of the city council members are surprised by the chief's position. The possibility of increased social-control problems hadn't occurred to them. One member thinks the chief is "crying wolf" to increase his power and the size of his agency and challenges the chief to prove his case with statistics and to project a best and worst crime rate for Norwich. Other council members are interested in the chief's opinion but agree that he should support his views with some evidence.

The meeting ends with some antagonism toward the chief's position. However, the council members schedule a special meeting to give the chief an opportunity to prepare a detailed assessment of the problems he sees in the future for Norwich.

Chief Yednock returns to his office and meets with his officers. He discusses the content and tone of the city council meeting and summarizes his situation stating, "What I have to do is prove what we already know." He asks for suggestions. An officer with a graduate degree in criminal justice responds. She suggests that providing hard facts to prove his point is not as important as finding groups of citizens who accept his position and who will support him at the next meeting.

Yednock knows this approach could hurt the good relationship he has built with the city council over the years. He thinks he will first attempt to put together an argument for the council members as they requested but let them know there is probably political support for his position. If that fails he will take a direct political approach and hope he can find community support.

Case Study Questions

1. Why do you think Chief Yednock was alert to the social-control problems that would come with the building of the new plant while the council members were not? What insights do your conclusions provide into understanding why criminal justice agencies are routinely accused of being reactive instead of proactive?
2. Which environmental conditions will change in Norwich as a result of the new plant? Which conditions will change the most dramatically and which will change the least? Is there any way of accurately answering this question?
3. Chief Yednock is preparing to meet the new demands he perceives for social control. How should he go about preparing to deal with the formal and informal political systems that may evolve as a result of the changes the new plant will create in Norwich?

For Discussion

1. In what way do environmental factors contribute to the conflicting goals and priorities of the criminal justice system? How does the bureaucratic structure of criminal justice agencies mitigate some of the conflicting demands and expectations the system faces?

2. Correctional agencies need to protect their boundaries yet be responsive to public sentiment, political inputs, and the needs of their clients. What guidelines would you give to corrections administrators to help them keep a balance between responsiveness and protecting an agency's boundaries?

3. What mechanisms or techniques can a police agency develop to make it sensitive to changing environmental circumstances? Is this more an issue of organizational philosophy than of technique? Explain.

4. How does the status of a criminal justice agency help it enter into favorable negotiations and exchange relations with its environment? Or should the question be does the agency's ability to enter into favorable negotiations and exchange relations with its environment affect its status?

For Further Reading

Cole, G. (Ed.). *Criminal Justice: Law and Politics.* Pacific Grove, Calif.: Brooks/ Cole, 1987.

Fairchild, S., and Webb, V. (Eds.). *The Politics of Crime and Justice.* Beverly Hills, Calif.: Sage, 1985.

Olsen, M. *The Logic of Collective Action: Public Goods and the Theory of Groups.* Cambridge, Mass.: Harvard University Press, 1973.

Rourke, F. *Bureaucracy, Politics, and Public Policy.* Boston: Little, Brown, 1976.

PART 2

THE INDIVIDUAL IN CRIMINAL JUSTICE ORGANIZATIONS

Managers manage people. In the smallest organization or the largest, managers must be concerned with how individuals react to the organization and how they can influence those reactions. In criminal justice these concerns often take on added significance. Here, the work can range from the monotony of lengthy stakeouts or duty in the prison tower to the intense pressures generated by a robbery in progress or a prison riot. It may range from dealing with common misdemeanors to making decisions about the life and death of offenders or members of the public. The work is often stressful, frequently chaotic, and always marked by competing demands and goals. In Part Two we look closely at the role of the individual in criminal justice organizations. Our focus will be on how individuals are affected by their organizations and how managers can influence that process.

CHAPTER 3

Problems of Communication

- ☐ Basic Theory of Communication
- ☐ Communication in Organizations
- ☐ Information and Communication
- ☐ Communication Roles for the Criminal Justice Practitioner
- ☐ Communication Barriers
- ☐ Informal Communication Networks
- ☐ Research on Communication in Criminal Justice
- ☐ Implications for Criminal Justice Management
- ☐ Summary
- ☐ Case Study
- ☐ For Discussion
- ☐ For Further Reading

When we train criminal justice people, we try to sensitize them to the fact that they work in a system, that they don't work in a vacuum. Most practitioners are willing to complain about how other criminal justice agencies won't cooperate with their agency but don't pay attention to the effects of their behaviors on the rest of the system. You would think the relationship between police officers and lockup or county jail correctional officers would be different though. Members of both groups are usually sworn law enforcement officers, they run across each other during the day, at least at booking, and within each group—county deputies and jailers, city police and lockup officers—they work for the same agency. You would think they would talk to each other, know each other's problems, and cooperate as a matter of routine. Unfortunately, that does not seem to be the case.

During training sessions with police officers I ask about sharing information concerning offenders they arrested or were transporting to the local jail with their booking officers. I ask, "If you were taking an arrestee to the jail and he/she said that when he/she got there, he/she would kick a certain correctional officer's butt, how many of you would pass that information on?" They usually all raise their hands. Then: "What if the offender stated that he/she would start his/her mattress on fire?" Most will raise their hands. Then: "What if the offender threatened to assault or 'get' another inmate—for example, his rap partner?" A few might raise their hands. Finally, I ask, "If the offender told you he/she was going to hang himself/herself or commit suicide in some way after he/she was locked up, how many of you would pass this on to the booking officer?" Rarely is a hand raised. But if you asked a jail administrator or booking officer to rank these threats in order of their importance as information, the suicide threat would be their first choice. The first step in cooperation between agencies is a mutual understanding of other agency priorities. Assumptions based upon preconceived ideas and the ideology of one's own little work . . . prevent communication, understanding, and cooperation between agencies. [Statement from Paul Embert, training coordinator, School of Criminal Justice, State University, Michigan, reflecting experiences training police officers and police command staff.]

The literature on both organizational theory and communication refers to communication as the "glue" that holds organizations together. The typical organization—private firm, federal regulatory agency, police or corrections agency—is put together in some logical way, at least on paper. But whether the organization functions logically and productively depends greatly on the quality of its communication. Hence all members of an organization are given "permission," if not training, to communicate within certain limits in order to facilitate coordination among members and among components of the organization.

Throughout this chapter we argue that the effectiveness and productivity of an organization are inexorably linked to effective communications. Most, if not all, organizational members understand the importance of communications. Poor communication, however, is often blamed for problems that occur within an organization. For example, when subordinates disobey directives and are difficult to control, it is often convenient for managers to assume communication is faulty rather than examine more fundamental issues such as the applicability of directives or the willingness of subordinates to follow orders.

Studying the criminal justice system as one unit or as a system places the discussion of communication in an interesting and unique light. The components of the criminal justice system were historically designed to countervail each other to assure the rights of the criminal defendant. Thus, members of different criminal justice agencies have different roles, duties, and perceptions about the purpose and mission of the system. As in the quotation at the beginning of this chapter, members of different agencies have their own preconceived notions and their own languages. The conflicting roles of criminal justice agencies cause most of the day-to-day interactions and communications among practitioners to be adversarial rather than cooperative in nature or intent. Hence practitioners in criminal justice agencies are often denied "permission" to communicate cooperatively with certain of their colleagues. In addition, unlike agencies whose members have a limited number of individuals with whom they interact with some consistency, a criminal justice practitioner interacts and communicates with many individuals and groups within the system and outside the system, and the roles, values, subgroup languages, and desired payoffs of those groups vary greatly.

In this chapter, we apply the basic theories of communication to the individual practitioner in the criminal justice system, considering the unique and varied interactions practitioners have on a routine basis.

Basic Theory of Communication

Interpersonal communication begins with a basic dyad—one individual sending a message to another. If a message sent from Person A fails to get to Person B, no communication has taken place. Communication between two people can be thought of as a sequential process with Person A encoding a message, then transmitting it through some medium, after which the message is received by Person B and decoded. The process is examined in detail here.

Process

Encoding is the first manifestation of the communication process. The sender feels the need to convey a message to another individual or individuals and encodes the meaning of the message into symbols. Words are the most familiar symbol form to us, although communication with nonverbal symbols is rather common. We can think about Morse Code, flag signals, codes used by police dispatchers to briefly describe situations or orders in addition to common words. But the sender's thoughts and meaning must be encoded into some verbal or nonverbal symbolic form before the message can be transmitted.

The next step in the process is to transmit the message through a medium that the sender chooses. The intended receiver of the message must then receive the message and decode it—that is, the receiver interprets the symbols conveyed in the message and gives them meaning. If the communication flows both ways, the receiver responds to the message with communications back to the sender, who now becomes the receiver. Figure 3-1 shows this basic interaction.

Barriers to Communication

Although this appears to be a straightforward and reliable process, we all know from our personal experiences that often simple messages between two individuals are not communicated effectively. The communication process is frequently unreliable, if not convoluted, for a number of reasons. Senders may not formulate their meaning properly in symbols that can be transmitted to the receiver. Stated simply, one must say what one intended to say. Assuming the sender has encoded and transmitted the message to the receiver with some accuracy, a series of communication barriers may intervene to block the communication or alter the meaning of the message. These are the major communication barriers (DuBrin, 1978):

1. Preconceived ideas
2. Denial of contrary information
3. Use of personalized meanings
4. Lack of motivation or interest
5. Noncredibility of the source
6. Lack of communication skills
7. Poor organizational climate
8. Use of complex channels

A message sent through such barriers can be impeded or re-formed.

Preconceived ideas. "People hear what they want to hear" describes this phenomenon. If we have a preconceived idea about information being transmitted to us, we tend to receive and understand the message

Figure 3-1 The Basic Communication Process

Encoding ------- Transmitting ------- Medium ------- Receiving ------- Decoding
    (Message)   (Channel)   (Message)

as that idea. For example, if someone is giving us information about the stock market, we may hear the first sentence or two and then assume that the balance of the information matches our own prior assessment of market conditions. In this example the complete message has not been received.

Denial of contrary information.   Messages that conflict with information we have already accepted as valid are often denied or rejected. For example, after assessing the message, we may reject information about the stock market based on prior information. This is a prudent or rational communication decision. However, the message may conflict with our personal beliefs or values, in which case we reject it or deny its validity without any deliberation or thought. This process, referred to as cognitive dissonance in the psychology literature, is the kind of denial of information that creates a communication barrier. Individuals who are addicted to drugs or alcohol often deny feedback from their friends about their addiction. They may reply, "I use drugs daily because I like it, not because I need it."

Use of personalized meanings.   The words chosen by the sender may have different meaning for the message receiver. Professional jargon or legal terminology may have little, no, or a different meaning to those outside the profession or legal system. Words and sentences that convey images of pleasure for one party may convey contrary images for another. A young person may refer to an experience with enthusiasm and say it was "really bad," meaning it was very good. Guilt is based on fact in the criminal justice system, but in psychiatry it is the state of one's conscience.

Lack of motivation or interest.   Motivation in communicating and interest in the message must exist for both the sender and receiver, at least to some reasonable extent, if a message is to be communicated effectively. Memo writing in organizations is a standard method of communication. However, if memoranda become excessive, personnel may lose interest in spending their time reading them. If such a situation exists, a motivated communicator may supplement memos with a fresh or unique medium to get the attention of receivers.

Noncredibility of the source.   The sender of a message may not be believable for a number of reasons. Individuals who, for example, have given out inaccurate information in the past lack credibility, while individuals who have a history of providing reliable information are considered highly credible senders of messages and get the attention of prospective receivers. Individuals with relatively greater status in an organization have more credibility than those with little or no status.

Lack of communication skills. Poor communication skills can be attributed to an individual's lack of proper training, educational level experience, and cognitive capacity as well as personality traits. Practitioners in the field of criminal justice must master the art of receiving, collecting, recording, and disseminating information. This can be accomplished through formal education, academy training, and experience throughout the practitioner's career. A "streetwise" education is also important for developing a full range of communication skills. Understanding of and fluency in street language is necessary to achieve maximum delivery of services to clients and the public.

Poor organizational climate. An organization that promotes openness and trust among its members encourages active communication. Very formal organizations may discourage all but formal and approved communications among their members. This insistence on formality often promotes an active, informal "grapevine," which often creates a suitable climate for gossip.

Use of complex channels. The more gates communication must pass through, the more likely the message will pass slowly and be altered. Highly complex channels of communication, which are endemic to large complex organizations, make communicating inefficient and ineffective. Such organizations tend to create red tape and usually become rigid because important information cannot be transmitted readily from clients or to policymakers.

Communication gap. These barriers to communication can create a communication gap: the difference between the message the sender intended to communicate and what the receiver understands the message to be. The existence of a communication gap between individuals in an organization becomes an organizational problem and impedes effective management and operations.

Communication in Organizations

As we can see from the discussion of barriers to communication, simple messages between individuals can be inadvertently filtered or even lost. We can also see that when the individual is a sender or receiver within an organization, additional factors—organizational climate and complexity of communication channels—can make the communication process even more difficult. Both the formal organizational structure—the chain of command and hierarchy—and the informal social system within the organization affect the organizational climate and the complexity of communication channels.

Chain of Command

Scholars concerned with organizational behavior have pointed out that the innate weakness of the communication process in a large bureaucracy can lead to a weakening of administrative power or to leakage of authority (Downs, 1967). This conclusion is somewhat ironic as the traditional chain of command provides a clear set of communication paths for its members. An agency's policies and procedures, as well as traditionally accepted practices, direct members' official communications rather explicitly. Directives from top management are usually sent down through the chain of command, and subordinates are required to routinely report to superiors. However, each level of a chain of command through which messages must pass can filter and alter information. Each level in a typical agency's hierarchy thus becomes a gate that imposes control over the communication flow.

Messages can be filtered intentionally or unintentionally. Subordinates can intentionally avoid putting forward information that will make them look inept. Similarly, supervisors can avoid communicating directives to subordinates that they feel will create problems in productivity or lower their status. Messages may be filtered unintentionally as they pass through the chain of command because of the personal barriers to communication—preconceived ideas, use of personalized meanings, lack of motivation or interest. Memos sent upward or downward through the chain of command may stack up on the desk of a middle manager. Thus, individual efforts at effecting official communication through formal channels can be a challenge rather than a matter of routine. For the new organizational member who lacks experience or credibility, effective communicating may be elusive.

Organizational Rules for Communication

Every organization has a set of rules for communication, which may be spelled out clearly in written policies and procedures. For example, subordinates are typically required to give particular information to their supervisors, and supervisors are expected to provide direct instruction and guidance to their subordinates. Routine reports that discuss production status, arrest rates, etc., are often required. Often, rules are unwritten but traditional. For example, it is usually unacceptable for a supervisor to chastise a subordinate who is not under the supervisor. Standard courtesies such as calling a superior by title also fall into this category (Cushman and Whiting, 1972).

In addition to well-established and explicit communication procedures and protocols, rules may be subtle and be based on the organization's social system. "Informal rules that exist within the organization, e.g., rules governing when to meet face-to-face rather than send a memo, or which topics are appropriate and which are not" are far more common than formal rules (Farace, Monge, and Russell, 1977:134). Communication rules are content rules, which govern standard word usage or consensus on the name of a concept, or procedural rules, which deal with the actual ways that interactions take place.

New members of an organization typically learn communication rules through trial and error or informal training (Farace, Monge, and Russell, 1977). Failure to understand or conform to these rules impedes successful communication. In a complex system such as the criminal justice system, which comprises many interacting agencies and diverse work environments, members face a complex and diverse set of communication rules.

Communication Networks

Every organization has its formal or official structure, as well as its informal work groups. Each has its channels of communication, which overlap to some extent. The communication between individuals within and between the official and informal subsystems can be viewed as a communication network. A simple definition of communication network is "those interconnected individuals who are linked by patterned flows to any given individual" (Hellriegel, Slocum, and Woodman, 1986). If these communication networks have been developed purposefully by management, they are considered formal networks. Whether formal or informal, a communication network can be a production network, an innovation network (where messages about new ideas and concepts are shared), or a maintenance network (through which members learn about social roles and power relationships and links between work groups) (Book, 1980). Likert (1961), in his classic study of medical organizations, found that organizations with individuals who communicated across subgroups and who thereby linked them together were highly productive.

Individuals may also be part of "kinship networks" within organizations. These social groups are formed more for personal than for professional motives. The reasons individuals join together in such networks may not have much to do with the goals of their agency. Such networks are called Old Boy groups, and they may comprise old college friends or people with the same political views or other significant personal similarities (Book, 1980). Police and corrections officers often meet socially at the local tavern after their shifts. At these meetings, a great deal of discussion about work-related problems—shoptalk—goes on and strengthens the bonds of the group. Entry into a kinship network is typically restricted. It is difficult for an outsider to be a communicator within this type of network.

In a system like the criminal justice system, the basis for a kinship network can be the uniqueness of one's task role or the prescribed role of the agency itself. Each component of the criminal justice system has different roles: police fight crime, courts protect the rights of the accused and distribute justice, and corrections controls and treats offenders. Those differing roles create commonalities for members of each agency. But within each agency, the role is subdivided. Police, for example, do road patrol, walk beats, investigate crimes, and administer the agency. Officers who work in the streets have a great deal in common with each other and much less in common with administrators. Thus, kinship networks form within the criminal justice system as a natural consequence of its differing structures and functions, in addition to those factors that typically help develop networks in the workplace.

Nonverbal Communication

Nonverbal symbols are a significant part of the communication process for an organization and its individuals. However, verbal communication has been studied by scholars at far greater length than nonverbal communication. As a result, our discussion of nonverbal communication will be brief. Capital punishment is a strikingly clear example of a nonverbal message sent to would-be perpetrators of certain crimes about the potential consequences. In effect, criminal deterrence is premised on the symbolic message evoked through punishment of the criminal offender.

Nonverbal symbols may stand on their own but are usually integrated with verbal messages. Organizations may intentionally use nonverbal symbols to represent them. For example, police officers wear distinct uniforms and wear guns to make an authoritative statement. Judges wear black robes and sit at an elevated bench to set them apart and above everyone involved in the process. The nonverbal behaviors of administrators may send messages that describe the agency. These messages may be congruent or incongruent with the organization's written or stated purposes or philosophy. For example, criminal justice administrators who give the appearance of being corrupt or inept may reduce the credibility of their agencies' stated purposes. Internally, bosses who advocate participative management but who pay no attention to feedback from subordinates give a nonverbal message that is incongruent with their stated message.

Individuals convey nonverbal messages through facial expressions, hand gestures, and other physical language. Messages may also be conveyed through one's dress, hair style, tone of voice, or actions (Book, et al., 1980). Reading nonverbal messages is an important part of interviews, interrogations, and even polygraph exams (Inbau, Reid, and Buckley, 1986). Again, using nonverbal messages that are congruent with verbal messages or the substance of the intended message is important for clear communication. Conversely, the recipient of nonverbal symbols needs to understand the nonverbal repertoire of the sender in order to decode a message accurately. Limited understanding of nonverbal codes can be an additional communication barrier.

Information and Communication

The terms *communication* and *information* are often interchangeable. However, they are distinguishable concepts if one thinks of communication as the process of passing on information. In other words, information is the substance that we attempt to share through symbols in communication. Communication becomes, then, the exchange of symbols that represent the information. Borrowing freely from Farace, Monge, and Russell (1977), we will briefly look at the relationship between information and communication, considering communication load, absolute versus distributed information, and environmental, motivational, and instructional information.

Communication Load

Load is the rate and complexity of communication inputs to an individual. Rate is the number of pieces of information that are received and resolved per time period. Complexity is the number of judgments that must be made or factors that must be taken into account while dealing with communications. Overload occurs when the flow of messages exceeds an individual's or system's capacity to process them.

There are three major determinants of load for an individual or system. The first of these determinants is the environment. A stable and predictable environment provides a less complex set of messages than an unstable environment does. In addition, the extent to which a person or system depends on elements in the environment affects the input of messages. Second, the capacity of the individual or system to assimilate messages plays a key role in determining overload. Third, the individual's or system's desire for information affects information load. Computer technology can greatly increase the criminal justice system's capability to collect and store information. This capacity can expand the communication load at the input end. However, because the ability to process and utilize the information is a function of organizational intellect, not of computer technology, an information overload may be created.

These three determinants of communication load affect the management of information and communication within an organization. Criminal justice agencies, traditionally structured along traditional bureaucratic lines, provide stable working environments, although a great deal of uncertainty exists within those environments. At the same time, limited resources and old habits help keep criminal justice agencies from being able to process information efficiently.

Absolute Versus Distributed Information

Absolute information is an idea or piece of knowledge expressed in recognized symbolic terms. Distributed information is an idea or piece of knowledge that is dispersed through a system. In other words, "what is known in an organization and who knows it are obviously very important in determining the overall function of an organization" (Farace, Monge, and Russell, 1977:27). In criminal justice organizations, information is often tucked nicely into a policy and procedures manual—when such a manual exists—where no one ever sees it. The rationale for training is, in part, to assure the distribution of absolute information.

Forms of information.   We can say that information, or communication, takes on three forms that are important for the well-being of an organization or its members. First, *information can be environmental*—that is, it describes the environment that surrounds the organization or its members. Here, recipients of the communication are getting information that describes actions, events, constraints, or processes in the world in which the individuals exist. For example, corrections officers are instructed that inmates must be given due process before being punished for an infraction of a prison rule.

Second, *motivational communications* provide information about organizational or personal goals or values. Corrections officers may dislike the fact that inmates must have a hearing before they can be punished for violating a prison rule. Therefore, officers must be told that they will be held accountable for punishing inmates without giving them the benefit of a hearing. Or they may be sold the idea that giving inmates a hearing will increase the system's credibility with inmates and make their job easier.

Third, *instructional information*, or communication, tells individuals how to proceed or what course of action to take to reach a goal. Continuing with our example, corrections officers must receive instructions about how the hearing will proceed and what their role is in it.

What we have described briefly here is the notion that individuals in organizations must be provided with information about the environment of the organization, the expectations of the organization, and how to perform their role in it. Cogent communication on these three topics is, therefore, the most basic step of policy and program implementation and the basis of training in organizations.

Communication Roles for the Criminal Justice Practitioner

In this section, we briefly discuss communication networks in the criminal justice system. To expand our earlier definition of a network, we are referring to a group of individuals who are connected over some time period by communication that has purpose and that is common to all the members. A network is a dynamic rather than static concept as members may enter or leave the network system.

We can apply this concept most readily by examples. A corrections officer in a large prison may be part of four or five networks simultaneously. He or she is part of the formal network—the chain of command—by decree. Also, as the literature has established, the experienced officer builds working relationships with pro-order inmate leaders. Because of the high turnover rate of corrections officers, those who remain for any length of time probably have formed their Old Boy network of both officers and inmates. In addition, an officer may be an active union member, thus being a part of that network. An officer who is respected by the administrative staff may be a member of the organization's dominant coalition. These networks are not mutually exclusive but overlap. Where these subsets of networks merge, another network is created with membership from all subsets. We do not wish to imply that corrections officers are the only focal point of networking in a corrections system. Middle managers may network with those above and below them in the agency's hierarchy. Top managers may network with community members or political figures. Figure 3-2 diagrams the interlocking of the networks just described. The street police officer may be the focal point of an even more diverse subset of networks. Figure 3-3 explores the possible links. Prosecuting attorneys may be the locus of a network that is shown

Figure 3-2 Multiple Networks for Prison Corrections Officers

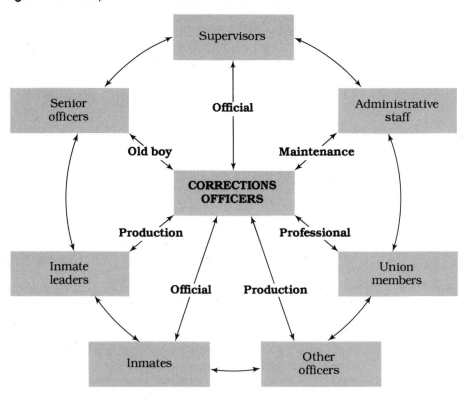

Figure 3-3 Multiple Networks for Line Police Officers

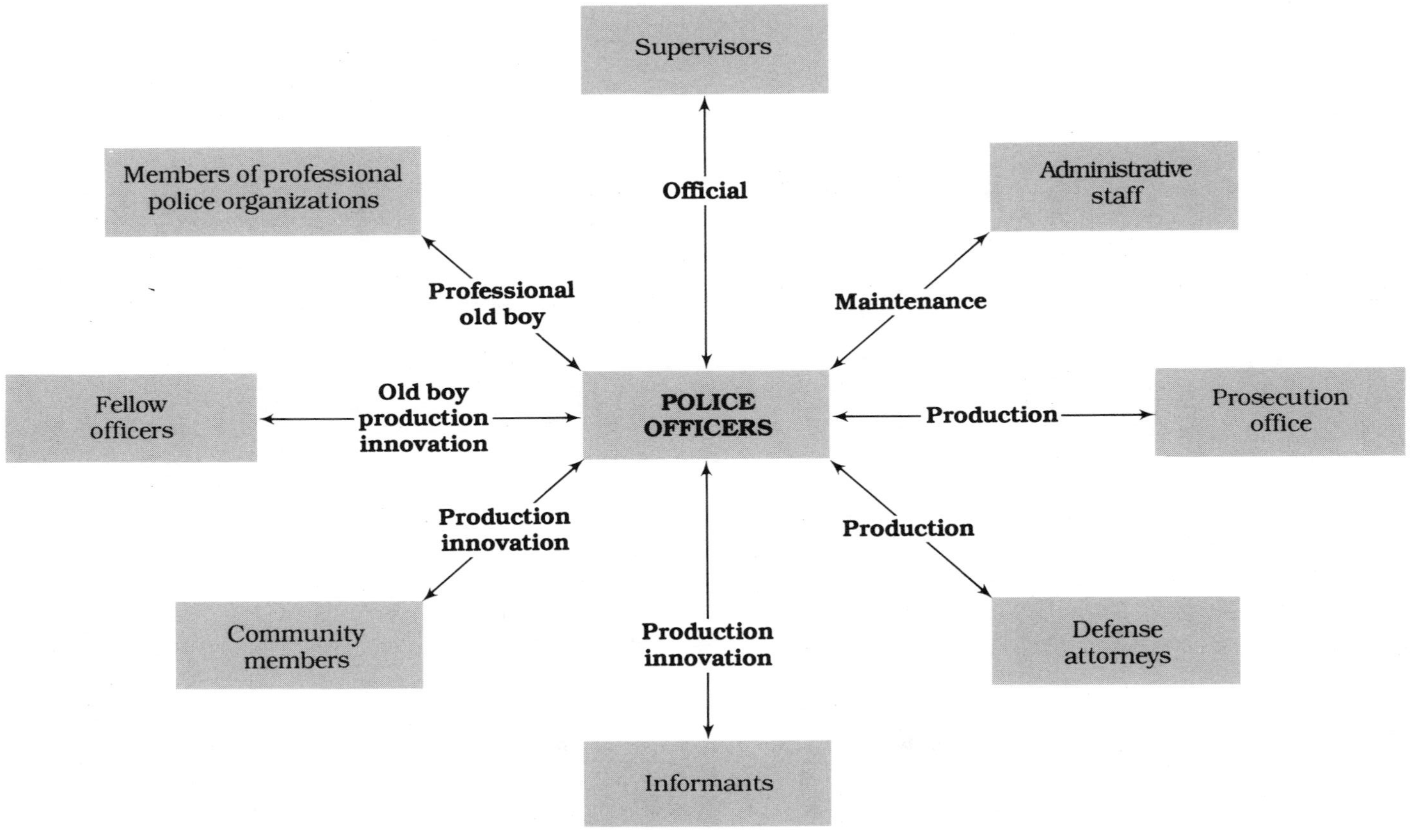

in figure 3-4. To meet the demands of managing a modern jail, jail administrators may attempt to build a network that includes personnel at the jail, local courts, probation departments, police agencies, and community social service agencies, as well as key members of the community. Figure 3-5 depicts such a network.

We could continue to design hypothetical networks within and across criminal justice agencies, as well as networks that link members of criminal justice systems to exogenous political forces, community members, and public and private agencies. The number of official, kinship, and informal networks that can be conceived is potentially endless. The important point is that, for efficient operations, both formal and informal communication networks that focus ultimately on results and productivity must exist. Agencies put little effort into the development of informal networks with such a focus. Concepts like team policing, for example, are implicitly based on networking. However, rather than nurturing productive informal networks, bureaucracies expend resources to thwart their development in an effort to protect hierarchical authority. Such quasi-military efforts are naive and counterproductive.

Figure 3-4 Multiple Networks for Prosecuting Attorneys

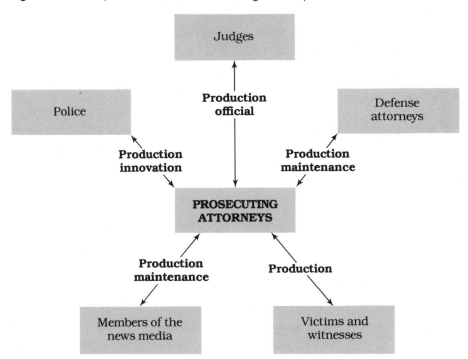

Figure 3-5 Multiple Networks for Local and County Jail Administrators

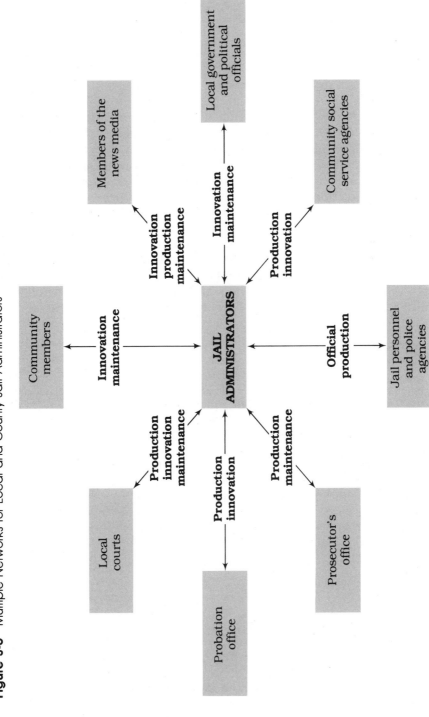

Communication Barriers

More pronounced communication barriers exist in the criminal justice system than in other systems because criminal justice has historically been organized so that its agencies check and balance each other. In theory, the police make arrests of offenders whom they view as probably being guilty, while the court system assumes the offender innocent until proven guilty. Although plea bargaining makes this proposition questionable, conflicts in roles and priorities do exist between police and court personnel. The conflict becomes even more pronounced in the interactions among police, prosecutors, and defense attorneys. The murky role of corrections, including the probation systems of local courts, is often seen as providing services for convicted offenders. This role is often viewed negatively by police, prosecuting attorneys, and even local judges. One can begin to see that communication among criminal justice agencies is carried out by individuals who have different views on how criminal offenders should be treated and processed, as well as divergent views on the role and purpose of the criminal justice system. Thus, communication networks that include individuals from different agencies must begin by overcoming *preconceived ideas* about the treatment of offenders and different perceptions of the role of the criminal justice system in general.

We can see how other communication barriers can become exaggerated because of basic differences in perceptions. For example, if a parole officer suggests to a police officer that many offenders change, the police officer may be inclined to *deny this information* by thinking or saying that criminals just get more skilled at crime and therefore don't get caught.

The *personalized meaning* of words and phrases varies from agency to agency. Police have official codes and abbreviations, courts and lawyers rely heavily on legal language, and corrections has its own professional jargon relating to the sentencing and processing of offenders. A criminal justice practitioner from any agency may become familiar with the unique language of another agency. This language must be learned and used in proper context for good communication to take place.

At the official level, the *motivation* for and *interest* in communicating certain information from one criminal justice agency to another may vary greatly. Police provide evidence on a case to the prosecutor, and after conviction both agencies pass that information on to the corrections system. But there is reluctance to pass information on to other criminal justice agencies. The police are not open with defense attorneys about a case; defense attorneys by oath do not provide information about a criminal defendant that will harm the defendant; corrections agencies are often reluctant to open their files to police agencies, fearing police will use the information to the detriment of a corrections client. In addition, police agencies with similar functions in the same jurisdiction may not be willing to share information because they view themselves as competitors. Thus, agencies are motivated to conceal information because of their conflicting perceptions of the function of the criminal justice system. As we will see later, however, information is often readily exchanged among agencies and individual practitioners as networks are developed that are based on an exchange model; this model provides inducements to trade information that ordinarily might be withheld.

It is easy to understand how the conflicting roles of criminal justice agencies and the differing perceptions of their practitioners can create an *organizational climate* that is not conducive to ongoing and open communication. Clearly, the credibility of a communicator from another agency or even one's own agency can be suspect.

It is also important to consider the *complexity of formal communication channels* in the criminal justice system. Large criminal justice organizations and their component agencies have many hierarchical levels, many specialized subunits, and much isolation of members from one another. Channels of communication in such an organization will be much more complex than those in a smaller criminal justice organization.

In addition to communicating with others in the criminal justice system, the practitioner may come into contact with victims, suspected or convicted offenders, witnesses, members of public interest groups, news media representatives, employees of public social service agencies and private security companies, and even elected officials. These individuals have differing values, nonverbal codes, subgroup languages with personalized meanings, motivations for and degrees of interest in entering into communication, and communication rules and skills. The barriers to communication will be different for each set of individuals that the criminal justice practitioner must deal with, and these barriers can confound the communication process with harsh regularity.

Informal Communication Networks

We have suggested that communication networks can be important for efficient and effective operations in criminal justice agencies and the criminal justice system. Unofficial or informal networks within and between agencies that evolve in the search for efficient methods to achieve the goals of the system—at least as perceived by the network members—are often based on the exchange principle or depend on a "linking pin."

Exchange

The basis of exchange theory is relatively simple. Worker A assists Worker B, and B pays for the assistance by helping A in some way. The shared assistance may be in the form of effort, or labor, but typically is information or assistance in cutting bureaucratic red tape. The exchange is based on bargaining among actors in the criminal justice system over time and is a product of the social system in which it functions (Marsden, 1981). Exchanges may be random or ad hoc. It is common, however, for exchange systems to be somewhat stable and to include a cadre of participants who link up with peripheral members when appropriate.

It is difficult for some to understand that such a system exists. It would seem that if everyone performed duties as prescribed, there would be no need to trade effort for effort. However, such a system exists for several reasons. First, large bureaucratic systems tend to pass work and information on slowly, and a relatively high number of transactions are required. By forming exchange networks that circumvent the formal structure, workers can economize on effort, time, and resources by cutting down the number of transactions (Williamson, 1981). In effect, through exchange systems, the work of the organization can be done with relative efficiency.

Second, the rules that govern practitioners' work efforts and territories are not rigid, and an individual worker may shift resources, efforts, and priorities for some external motivation or reward. In an exchange network, the reward may be an implied promise of extra effort on his or her behalf in the near future. For example, a police officer may forward information to a parole officer on the conduct of parolees if the parole officer will reciprocate. The information may be exchanged by phone or over lunch rather than through formal communication links.

Third, the exchange of information helps both parties perform their legitimate functions and contributes to the attainment of the overriding goals of the criminal justice system. The system exists for the mutual good of the participants. If the participants are seeking legitimate agency goals, it will serve the goals of the criminal justice system. "Continued exchange relationships generate a sense of trust between the system's participants, which in turn promotes a cooperative attitude that is strengthened by the organization's reward structure" (Cole, 1983:112).

The glue that links exchange systems together is communication. Thus, exchange systems become communication networks that enhance the productivity of their members. Because the members' motivation for and interest in communicating are based on self-interest, the normal communication barriers are overcome by the network participants.

However, exchange networks and informal communication systems aren't always created to enhance an organization's efficiency. The traditional agency grapevine may carry false or inaccurate information. Networks may be created to facilitate personal rather than organizational goals. In addition, well-intended workers may pursue their own interpretation of their agencies' goals when working together in exchange networks. Their view of the goals of the system may often be different from those of the system's policymakers, who presumably are attuned to public demands through the political system. And although information may flow freely within a network, members may intentionally or unintentionally withhold crucial information. As we discussed in chapter 2, most large public service agencies are decoupled, with policymakers and workers responding to demands from separate environments. Exchange mechanisms may further decouple the administrative arm of an organization from the work-processing sector.

Linking Pin

Likert (1961) found that productivity in industry was highest in companies that were coordinated by a hierarchy of interlocking groups rather than by a traditional chain of command with its directed policies and procedures. The interlocking groups are bound together by *linking pins*, persons who serve as members of two or more groups or are part of the social system of two or more groups. Linking pins are individuals who make a concerted effort to have credibility and influence in their own units as well as in other units that affect the efficient operation of their units. The linking pin acts as an informal coordinator, making ad hoc efforts to smooth the work flow between units. We can surmise that the person acting as the linking pin could overcome the barriers of communication between units and probably establish an exchange system between units.

Research on Communication in Criminal Justice

Although the literature on public administration discusses communication directly, criminal justice literature is not rich in this area, at least not expressly. One finds works in which communication in criminal justice organizations is discussed even though it is not the major topic. Here, we cover some of the literature in the field of criminal justice that clearly focuses on communication in spite of the authors' proposed issues.

Making Communication an Efficient Tool

In the police area, Waltmen (1983) focuses on the use of nonverbal communication techniques in interrogation. In the area of corrections, social skills training, of which communication is a significant part, has become popular. Such training is considered therapeutic for young adult and juvenile offenders. Although it is difficult to measure the efficacy of such treatment (Henderson and Hollin, 1983), it is felt that improvement of such skills, including communication skills, will improve offenders' ability to adjust to their environments. In the area of courts, Chapper (1983) has shown that the efficiency of the civil appeals process could be increased by requiring oral rather than written arguments in specific cases. Craig (1983) argues that juries can be more flexible in their findings if the instructions from the judge are altered so that juries have more discretion. The present format of instructions inadvertently restricts most juries by limiting their decision alternatives. Finally, Katzev and Wishart (1985) discuss methods of judicial instruction to jurors to avoid false testimony of eyewitnesses.

Confidentiality

We recognized previously in this chapter that there are some restrictions on the flow of information and communication in the criminal justice system. In the 1980s, expunging criminal records became standard. The Search Group, Inc. (1982), found that most states require that juvenile records be sealed or expunged after an offender has reached the age of majority. These records are available to the courts only if the juvenile is subsequently convicted as an adult for a major felony. Private agencies typically do not have access to sealed records.

Along this line, exclusionary rules in a criminal trial prohibit the communication of evidence that has been obtained in ways that are considered illegal—a coerced confession, for example. In effect, this purposeful communication barrier sometimes creates a difference between "real" facts and "legal" facts—facts that can be presented in a court.

Conflict

To a great extent, conflict between individuals or groups may be a result of communication barriers. For example, Kagehiro and Werner (1981) show that county-jail inmates and corrections officers hold stereotypical views of each other, are defensive toward each other, and tend to blame the other group for problems. Such stereotyping leads to a misunderstanding of violations and applications of jail rules. In a similar vein, Cole, Hanson, and Silbert (1982) suggest that the implementation of inmate mediation within a prison system precludes full-blown formal litigation, saves time and resources, and achieves amicable solutions.

Ryan (1981) examined conflict levels between police and probation officers. He showed that the quality and quantity of contacts between police and probation officers had an impact on their level of conflict. For officers with a great deal of work-related and personal contact, conflict was extremely low. Such contacts may minimize inaccurate stereotypes and communication barriers between the two groups. Finally, Pindur and Lipiec (1982) found that a system that required continual and immediate contact between arresting police officers and members of the prosecuting attorney's staff improved the relationship between the two agencies.

Communication with Citizens

The literature discussing community crime control focuses expressly or implicitly on communication. A major attempt to communicate the problem of crime and encourage citizens to take personal action to protect themselves was titled "Take a Bite Out of Crime." The campaign utilized the media and provided public service ads that encouraged citizens to take standard precautions to protect themselves from crime. Follow-up studies by the Center for the Study of Mass Communications Research (1982) and by O'Keefe and Mendelsohn (1984) showed that community members had seen or heard the crime-prevention ads and were motivated to take some anticrime steps in their communities. Almost all the literature on community crime prevention includes prescriptions for team policing and foot patrols and discusses the importance of having police and community members interact and improve communication between themselves (Trojanowicz and Banas, 1985). It is interesting to note that communication is not often cited as a fundamental problem in such literature, and the barriers to communication described in this chapter are rarely addressed directly.

W. J. Brown (1983) discusses procedures for dealing with citizens' complaints against police, while E. Scott (1981) investigates the links a metropolitan police department creates between the community members who contact the police and other public service agencies. Recommendations are given for an improved referral system for the police, who are often the first to deal with or identify problems. Also, Tullar and Glasser (1985) and Missonellie and D'Angelo (1984) recommend improved use of technology to strengthen police communications with the public.

An interesting article by Kohfeld (1983) reminds us that creating a deterrent effect by arresting and punishing offenders is premised on communication of the fact that offenders are arrested and punished to the population as a whole. Kohfeld looks at the belief that robbers are informed and rational and will lower their criminal activity as police activity increases. From statistical evidence, he claims that there is no real causal link. Robbers may be rational but not informed.

Relations between corrections and the public can sometimes lead to conflict. In an effort to improve the information flow between corrections and the media, the National Jail Coalition (1984) produced a short manual that briefs reporters on complex jail issues. Tully, Winter, Wilson, and Scanlon (1982) present recommendations to assist corrections with community relations. They observed a case in which a corrections department was attempting to build a facility in a resistant community. Basically they recommend that speakers from corrections who are trying to sell programs to the public know how to communicate with the public and have credibility with them rather than be administrators or public relations people.

Dealing with the public through the news media to produce favorable police–community relations may be fraught with deep and fundamental problems. For example, Selke and Bartoszek (1984) found through surveying criminal justice and journalism students that a great deal of suspicion and distrust exists between the two groups even before they enter the field. Hence, both sender and receiver in the police–media dyad have preconceived notions about the information being communicated, and the communicator typically lacks credibility.

Let us not forget the usually forgotten victim. Hagen (1983) suggests that victims need to be made active participants in their cases by being kept abreast of progress and having procedures explained to them. After extensive interviews with six hundred victims, Hagen found that those who were kept advised of the progress of their cases and who understood the criminal justice process as it applied to their cases were typically satisfied with the outcomes. Conversely, those who were not given information were typically unhappy about the outcomes of their cases.

Intraorganizational Communications

Several articles about intraorganizational communication focus on organizational climate and complexity as inhibitors of communications. Nuchia (1983) admonishes law enforcement agencies that police officers have a First Amendment right to be critical of their departments. Archambeault and Wierman (1983) recommend that police bureaucracies move away from the traditional chain of command to the so-called Theory Z approach, which encourages teamwork rather than adversarial and competitive relationships among agency staff. Similarly, Melancon (1984) argues that police agencies should institute quality circles, which are similar in concept to management Theory Z and which facilitate the participation of line staff in management.

Dickinson (1984) argues that prisons should radically change communication policies toward inmates and allow them much more contact with the outside world than they now have. In inmate rehabilitation, Jacks (1984) recommends an eclectic approach to interacting with inmates called Positive Therapeutic Intervention. The approach requires simply that corrections staff be trained to be good listeners and pay constant attention to inmates when they discuss their problems.

All forms of participatory management tend to increase the frequency and quality of communication among organization members. Although such improved communication is at the core of most modern management or human relations approaches to management, the process and theories of communication are rarely an explicit part of criminal justice research. Only three of the articles cited focused directly on communication; and communication is underrepresented in the research on organizations in general (O'Reily and Pondy, 1979). It seems that much

more attention should be given to the "glue" that holds organizations together.

Implications for Criminal Justice Management

It is easy to conclude that communication in organizations is linked to efficiency. If individuals within and among organizations communicate poorly, it is difficult for them to coordinate their work and link their tasks. If directives and orders are communicated ineffectively, programs, plans, and changes in routine tasks are difficult to implement. Managers and practitioners would agree to this conclusion, at least in principle. And current research suggests that, indeed, there is a link between effective communication and efficiency in human services (Snyder and Morris, 1984).

Therefore, managers and practitioners in criminal justice agencies should actively seek to improve communication and should not take it for granted. If it is the glue that holds organizations together, improving channels of communication and individual communication skills should be standard procedure. Typically, improving communication is ignored or is relegated to occasional training seminars that do not teach that art in the context of the organization. This situation is unfortunate because a great deal has been written on improving individual communication skills, and training programs to develop effective communication skills are abundant. Assisting organizational members to improve their skills through ongoing training could significantly decrease communication barriers. But most criminal justice practitioners are left without such training and usually pick up the values, priorities, and jargon of their agency in short order as they are socialized into their work groups. However, they are rarely given any direct or formal training about the values, priorities, and jargon of those outside their organization, and therefore communication is often stymied. To the extent that formal training in communication is provided to criminal justice practitioners, it focuses on law, agency rules and protocol, the chain of command, and other formal aspects of communication. Report writing may be offered to new recruits, but comprehensive training in interpersonal communications is not a common part of training agendas.

Some criminal justice agencies do have training for their professionals in communications however. The Michigan Department of Corrections, for example, provides extensive human relations training for their corrections officers. They are taught how to recognize and deal with communication barriers between staff and inmates and about the psychological games some inmates play. They then learn effective communications skills to overcome these barriers and problems. Taking this approach, other agencies could teach their members the values, priorities, and language sets of groups they routinely deal with as part of their training programs.

Not all communication problems in criminal justice agencies are simply interpersonal. Communication between members of different components of the system is often limited because of conflicting goals. To the extent that members perceive interagency relationships as more conflicting than negotiative, interagency communication will be limited, formal, and closed rather than informal and open. Agencies can improve interagency communication simply by making clear to their members which issues involve legitimate goal conflict and which allow for negotiation and cooperation. This procedure would give agency members permission to interact and communicate with some openness in many areas.

In addition, in those criminal justice agencies that are large enough to organize bureaucratically—with formal hierarchies, chains of command, rules and regulations guiding tasks—formal communication is channeled vertically, limiting the extent to which members can communicate laterally or among subcomponents. Small agencies that attempt to organize in a quasi-military manner probably also insist on vertical channels of communication. Such attempts limit the range of communication for the organization's participants. However, we have seen that members break out of such restrictions by forming networks and entering into exchange systems with information as the commodity of trade. It would seem wise, therefore, for agencies to promote or openly sustain innovation or production networks and beneficial exchange arrangements. In other words, large organizations should seek to promote and control lateral communication within and between agencies by establishing formal lateral links and promoting informal socialization between pertinent members.

Summary

The administration and management of the criminal justice system are authoritarian in nature. In such an authoritarian, bureaucratic system, information is viewed as flowing downward. It is often assumed that poor communication is simply a problem of subordinates' not getting the message because of some defect on their part rather than being an ongoing problem that needs constant attention. The assumption ultimately underlying bureaucratic mentality is that if everyone knows and follows agency policy and procedures, the work will get done. If policy and procedures are not followed, it is because members do not read directives or because they read them and ignore them. For the classic bureaucrat or authoritarian administrator, therein lies the basis of all major communications problems. The solution to the problem is to tighten controls and to reestablish authority at the top (Downs, 1967). A breakdown in communication is typically interpreted by administrators as an authority gap or leakage of control.

Hence, the first step to improved communication in criminal justice agencies and within the criminal justice system is for policymakers, administrators, and managers to start moving away from boss-centered management toward subordinate-centered management. This prescription is certainly not new. The literature on criminal justice management is rich with discussions on the value of participatory management, Theory Z, management by objectives, etc. Proposals such as team policing, foot patrol, and therapeutic community corrections environments have active and open communication as fundamental elements. These concepts are discussed and written about with much greater zeal than they are utilized. The authoritarian values within criminal justice administrations persist.

The following chapter applies theories of motivation to the criminal justice system. The discussion in that chapter reveals the importance of effective communication in motivating agency personnel. Effective communication between administrators and subordinates is the vehicle by which subordinates can be given an opportunity to participate in the mission of the organization.

CASE STUDY
Communications at the Courthouse

Centerville is a semi-industrial town in the Midwest with a population of over 200,000. The local court comprises eight circuit court judges, a court administrator, and his staff. The presiding judge, Ramon Murphy, a loyal Democrat, has served for several terms. The chief prosecutor, Beatrice P. Bargin, is serving her first term, is a Republican, and believes in applying sound management principles to her office. She fought for the addition of a court administrator to the staff. Judge Murphy was opposed to adding a court administrator, but he now plans to utilize the court administrator to help solve a rather typical problem for courts. Cases are backlogged, and Judge Murphy plans to take action.

Judge Murphy calls in the court administrator, Dennis Hamilton, and tells him to set up a meeting of all judges for the following week to discuss the problem. Hamilton writes a memo to the judges and the prosecuting attorney advising them of the staff meeting. Bargin responds to Hamilton by asking that he further research the problem and recommend solutions before a meeting is convened. Two of the other judges— Republicans—respond by stating that Hamilton does not have the authority to call a meeting of judges. Two other judges respond that they approve of such a meeting but can't fit it in their calendars as scheduled. The remaining judges do not respond, but Hamilton hears through the grapevine that they don't think they have backlogs and will not waste their time for Hamilton or Murphy.

Hamilton reports to Murphy and apprises him of the bad news. Murphy is outraged. He tells Hamilton that he was supposed to check with all parties to see whether they could schedule a meeting in the near future, not to try to convene one. He further advises Hamilton that all memos that give judges any direction are to be signed by him, not some "idiot without a law degree." Murphy orders Hamilton to personally apologize to all parties for his inappropriate behavior and try to establish possible times for a judicial staff meeting.

Hamilton makes his rounds beginning with Prosecutor Bargin. She tells him to forget the meeting until the problem is thoroughly defined. The other judges accept his apology graciously but tell him to tell Murphy that they don't have a problem, except for attending meetings. Taking Prosecutor Bargin's advice, Hamilton returns to his office and begins examining the extent to which the case flow is backlogged for each judge. He also tells Murphy what the other judges told him to tell Murphy.

Murphy is really mad now. He shouts, "Hamilton, you go back and tell all of those other judges and Miss Uppity Prosecuting Attorney that when I say. . . ." Hamilton is now at the center of a contest. The original intent—examining the case-flow problem—has been forgotten because of the procedural problem of who calls staff meetings. Hamilton is being used as the transmitter in this contest. He knows he cannot transmit Judge Murphy's sentiments, but he can become the translator for the parties in the conflict. He may be able to exert some influence because he has some control over the flow of communication. He also knows that if he is later viewed as misrepresenting parties in the debate, he may be looking for a new job. He believes that Prosecutor Bargin is correct in her advice and that a factual assessment of the problem may be a sound beginning, even though Judge Murphy has expressed a negative opinion of Bargin's input.

A simple and fundamental problem in the court system has been blown out of proportion. Communication on case-flow matters ceased because other agendas, including professional independence, political affiliation, status, and personal feelings, all swamped the single channel of communication, the hapless court administrator.

Case Study Questions

1. What barriers to communication have come into play at the courthouse?
2. What networks exist and what actors are excluded from the existing networks? Why?
3. What could Hamilton, the court administrator, have done at the beginning of the process to enhance communication between the pertinent parties? Now what can he do?

For Discussion

1. How can the different work environments of police, courts, and corrections inculcate in personnel ideas that will become barriers to cross-agency communications?

2. The professionalism of police officers can create immense barriers to communication between police officers and members of the general public. Do you agree or disagree with this statement? Think of the different ways a professional can be defined as well as the traditional structure and hierarchy of police agencies.

3. What, in your opinion, are the major barriers to communication between components of the criminal justice system? What steps can be taken to eliminate the barriers you have identified?

4. How does organizational decoupling affect interorganizational communications? How does decoupling facilitate communications between practitioners and the clients and interest groups being served?

5. Can a criminal justice organization develop a linking-pin position in its formal organization? Or does a linking pin naturally evolve into that role? Discuss how a criminal justice agency can develop linking pins. Where should they be placed in your hypothetical agency? How will you select and recruit them?

For Further Reading

Book, C., Albrecht, T., Atkin, C., Bettinghaus, E., Donohue, W., Farace, R., Greenberg, B., Helper, H., Milkovich, M., Miller, G., Ralph, D., and Smith, T., *Human Communication: Principles, Context, and Skills.* New York: St. Martin's Press, 1980.

Farace, R., Monge, P., and Russell, H. *Communicating and Organizing.* New York: Random House, 1977.

Inbau, F., Reid, J., and Buckley, J. *Criminal Interrogation and Confessions.* Baltimore: Williams & Wilkins, 1986.

Likert, R. *New Patterns of Management.* New York: McGraw-Hill, 1961.

CHAPTER 4

Motivation of Personnel

- ☐ Motivation Defined
- ☐ Theories of Motivation
- ☐ Prescriptions for Criminal Justice Management
- ☐ Summary
- ☐ Case Study
- ☐ For Discussion
- ☐ For Further Reading

Even though [corrections] officers can now bid on the institutional assignments they perform, it is not the specific duties that are involved in a particular job that seem to be the officer's primary concern. The motivations for working on a particular job assignment are, for the most part, a reflection of individual attempts to relate meaningfully to their work environments, rather than attempts to find positions from which they will be able to make meaningful contributions to the correctional task [Lombardo, 1981:45].

Since the pay raise my people get is tied to the ratings I give them, there is a strong incentive to inflate ratings at times to maximize their pay increases to help keep them happy and motivated, especially in lean years when the merit ceiling is low. . . . Conversely, you can also send a very strong message to a nonperformer that low ratings will hit him in the wallet. . . . There is no doubt that a lot of us manipulate ratings at times to deal with the money issue [Longenecker, Gioia, and Sims, 1987:185].

From these two quotes, we can begin to see that the process of employee motivation is often puzzling and difficult to understand. Different incentives are needed for different people. Moreover, differing job tasks may require an array of motivational techniques to get the employee to accomplish them. In some instances the provision of increased monetary rewards may be satisfactory for getting employees motivated; in other instances, employees may require attention to their personal needs and increased emphasis on their input in producing a product or service. From the first quote, it is apparent that some corrections officers expect meaningful structuring of their tasks. For example, being autonomous or being able to contribute to the well-being of the prisoner is of importance to many corrections officers. Research has demonstrated that proper motivation of criminal justice employees reaches far beyond purely monetary incentives; criminal justice administration must therefore develop and advance other methods of motivating personnel.

The purpose of this chapter is to examine the subject of motivation and how it applies to the criminal justice process and its personnel. We review the major theories of motivation, as developed by work in the field of organizational behavior, and, more importantly, apply these theories to the various components of the criminal justice system. Because of the dearth of material in this area that refers to criminal justice personnel, it is necessary to review the major findings from other fields and attempt to apply these results to criminal justice. In short, our goal is to answer the following questions: What are the major theories of motivation? Which theories of motivation are able to explain the behavior of criminal justice personnel? How can we restructure existing criminal justice bureaucracies to motivate employees to work efficiently and effectively? Before we attempt to answer these questions, however, it is important that we provide a definition of motivation.

Motivation Defined

Motivation can be viewed in two ways. First, one can view motivation as a psychological concept, examining the state of mind of the individual and why he or she exhibits a certain type of behavior. For example, it has been said that American culture values the work ethic. Much of this attitude can be traced to personal values that are transmitted to children in their formative years. Learned values, therefore, play a critical role in whether a person is motivated to perform various tasks. (Later in this chapter we will discuss those factors that lead or cause one to act in a certain fashion, from both a human and an organizational point of view.) The psychological definition of motivation depends on how the individual perceives the world and on the "psychological contract" between the individual and the work environment (Schein, 1970). With respect to criminal justice, one could ask, for example, what factors motivate people to become police officers, or, more importantly, what factors in the police environment motivate individuals to do their jobs? Even more telling would be an examination of those structures in the police organization that promote the fulfillment of individual needs while at the same time motivating people to do their jobs.

Second, motivation can be examined from an organizational point of view, exploring the kinds of managerial behavior that induce employees to act in a way consistent with the expectations and demands of the organization. This organizational way of examining motivation enables one to explore motivational strategies that promote the best interests of both the individual and the organization. A sense of congruence between the employee and the organization is sought, and the responsibility of management is to provide mechanisms that enable employees to be highly motivated and moved to do the work expected of them. In criminal justice agencies, one could ask, for example, how the administrator of a police organization or a correctional institution motivates employees or what the best strategies for motivating rank-and-file police officers or corrections officers are.

In the remainder of this chapter, we attempt to provide answers to these questions. Our discussion focuses on those theories of motivation that have guided criminal justice research. Because there has not been much research on motivation in the criminal justice system, we review pertinent theories and studies that address issues fundamental to criminal justice. In addition, we provide some prescriptions for criminal justice systems based on our understanding of motivation. To begin, we examine several different theories of motivation.

Theories of Motivation

A number of theories have been developed to explain motivation. We need to review them here and use them to understand criminal justice systems and their employees. It is important that we highlight those approaches most relevant to the criminal justice system and grounded in empirical literature. Five such theories can be identified:

1. Need theory
2. Theory X and Theory Y
3. Achievement–power theory
4. Expectancy theory
5. Theory Z

Need Theory

The most recognized theory of motivation comes from the work of Maslow (1943). He argued that one can examine motivation as one result of various physical and psychological needs. The central theme of need theory is that all people have needs, both physical and psychological, which affect their behavioral patterns. Maslow argued that human beings have five basic needs.

Physiological needs assure the basic survival of the individual. Included in this need category are food and water. Physical well-being must be assured before any other needs can be fulfilled.

After physical needs are met, there is a *need for safety and security.* Human beings require that they be safe in their environments and free from any threat of attack by aggressors. In addition, people need to know that there is a secure and certain environment in which they can act as social beings.

Belonging needs are reflected in the desire to be loved and to belong to a group. In addition, people need to have and show affection toward other human beings. This need may be expressed either in joining groups or by receiving support from one's family, friends, and relatives.

In addition to being loved, other needs of individuals center around *self-esteem*—one's self-image and how one is viewed by peers. Individuals seek prestige and recognition from their loved ones and their fellow workers. Self-confidence is intricately tied to this perception of self-worth.

Self-actualization needs center around one's potential to grow and to do one's best in endeavors. According to Maslow, these needs are different for every individual, which is why it is difficult to develop a motivational strategy that is able to meet the self-actualization needs of all employees.

Figure 4-1 displays the need hierarchy as described by Maslow. As can be seen, the hierarchy is divided into higher-order needs and primary needs. Higher-order needs are belonging, esteem, and self-actualization, while primary needs are physiological and for safety and security. What does the research evidence show about need theory? Tosi, Rizzo, and Carroll (1986:221) conclude that there is support for need theory and, in particular, Maslow's conceptualization of need theory. They believe research has demonstrated that when lower-level needs are not met, concern for higher-level needs decreases; that when an individual need is satisfied, it becomes less important, except in the case of self-actualization; and, finally, that there is a difference in need orientation among occupational groups. Rank-and-file workers, for example, consider lower-level needs to be more important in work situations than do managers. Managers perceive higher-level needs to be more important than lower-level needs.

In addition, some research indicates that age is a critical factor in need orientation. Research suggests that older police officers and those with higher levels of education perceive control of their environments and some autonomy as critical to job satisfaction. Moreover, older police officers seek self-actualization through the completion of tasks (Griffin, Dunbar, and McGill, 1978: 77–85). Providing these officers with control of their jobs through structural changes in the police department may be a way to retain and satisfy them.

Support for need theory has also been documented in the field of corrections. For example, research suggests that many corrections officers leave their positions because of the inability of the organization to meet their needs for improved working conditions. "Intrinsic working conditions," such as degree of autonomy, perceived variety of tasks, amount of authority, and learning opportunities, are all critical to turnover (Jurik and Winn, 1987: 19–21).

Managerial behavior, therefore, requires attention to the various levels or stages of development of workers and how to motivate them to

Figure 4-1 The Need Hierarchy. (From *Movitation and Personality* by Abraham H. Maslow. Copyright © 1954, 1987 by Harper & Row, Publishers, Inc. Reprinted by permission of the publisher.)

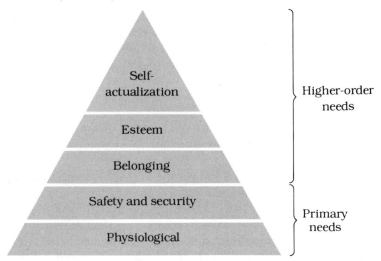

meet higher-level needs as they travel up the need hierarchy. This seems to be a dilemma for current managers of organizations, including criminal justice, because it is somewhat problematical as to how these needs are not only identified but also met within an organization (Witham, 1980). Police organizations, as an example, are composed of such a wide variety of personalities, it would be difficult to identify motivational strategies for all the differing levels. Ideus (1978) addresses this issue with respect to institutional corrections, suggesting that the importance of motivational theory lies in its ability not only to identify these needs but, more importantly, to match the individual needs of employees with the demands of the job. Ideally, efficiency and effectiveness could be enhanced if corrections organizations were able to match individuals to clearly identifiable tasks.

Bennett (1981) goes further and suggests that because of the structuring of the police role, it is difficult for some needs to be met. Specifically, he suggests that many lower-order needs, such as physiological ones, cannot be adequately met because of the long hours and waiting associated with the job. Of greater significance is the police organization's inability to deal with the self-esteem needs of officers. He argues that the leadership within many police departments does not promote a sense of belonging among officers. This lack of belonging usually manifests itself in conformist behavior, which inhibits an open atmosphere of trust and recognition. Because recognition is infrequent, many officers become cynical. Although Roberg (1979) has identified this problem in relation to police management, little has been done to prescribe for police managers, or for that matter other criminal justice managers, how they are to function given the needs of their employees.

Obviously, the motivational process is complex, and it is often difficult to discern which of the many variables are the most critical. Yet it does become apparent from research conducted in criminal justice organizations that the fulfillment of needs is crucial to how employees are motivated. Cordner (1978) suggests that many public service employees, particularly police officers, have their lower-level needs met by the organization. It follows, as a result, that higher-order needs require attention by the organization, in particular the need to be recognized, to participate in decision making, and to be given responsibility. At present, this is not a possibility within many public service organizations; and criminal justice agencies are no different in this regard.

What is of value to criminal justice managers is to be able to recognize those needs that require attention so that job tasks can be completed. For example, for a police officer, patrolling the same area day after day may not be the most self-actualizing activity, yet it is a job that must be done by the police organization. Providing attention to basic needs, such as ensuring the safety of the officer, may be enough for this task. In similar ways, other needs of police officers must be understood in light of the tasks of the organization. In addition, it may be that many tasks associated with the police role, at least at the line level, cannot fulfill the higher needs of the rank-and-file police officer. For middle managers, the issue of higher needs is more critical than for line officers. Presently, this type of issue has not been addressed by administrators in criminal justice organizations.

Theory X and Theory Y

The second theory of motivation is composed of two parts—Theory X and Theory Y—and is based on the work of McGregor (1978). In his seminal article entitled "The Human Side of Enterprise," McGregor describes these two approaches to human behavior and management. These approaches are based on a number of assumptions about human behavior. Theory X is derived from three fundamental beliefs; McGregor (1978:13) considers these beliefs the "conventional view" of management.

1. Management is responsible for organizing the elements of productive enterprise—money, materials, equipment, people—for economic ends.
2. With respect to people, management directs their efforts, motivates them, controls their actions, and modifies their behavior to fit the needs of the organization.
3. Without active intervention by management, people would ignore— even resist—organizational needs. They must therefore be persuaded, rewarded, punished, controlled; their activities must be directed. This is management's task. We often sum this process up by saying that management consists of getting things done through other people.

Theory X is also based on a number of ancillary beliefs about individuals in organizations: they are lazy, lack ambition, are predominantly self-centered, are resistant to change, and on the whole are not too bright.

This carrot-and-stick approach to management works to the detriment of meeting the higher needs of employees. As McGregor (1978:16) states:

> The carrot-and-stick theory does not work well at all once man has reached an adequate subsistence level and is motivated primarily by higher needs. Management cannot provide a man with self-respect or with the respect of his fellows or with the satisfaction of needs for self-fulfillment. It can create such conditions that he is encouraged and enabled to seek such satisfactions for himself, or it can thwart him by failing to create those conditions.

As a result of the inadequacy of this approach for meeting higher human needs, of which McGregor believes ego needs, social needs, and self-fulfillment needs to be the most important, he proposes an alternative view of management—Theory Y, which views the human condition in an optimistic way. Theory Y is based on the following assumptions (McGregor, 1978:16–17):

1. Management is responsible for organizing the elements of productive enterprise—money, materials, equipment, people—for economic ends.
2. People are not ignorant of or resistant to organizational needs. They have become so as a result of their experience in organizations.
3. Motivation, potential for development, capacity for assuming responsibility, and readiness to direct behavior toward organizational goals are present in people. Management does not put them there. It is a responsibility of management to make it possible for people to recognize and develop these attributes themselves.
4. The essential task of management is to arrange organizational conditions and methods of operation so that people can achieve their own goals by directing their own efforts toward organizational objectives.

As can be seen, this approach to management is based on assumptions about humans and their functioning in large organizations that are different from the assumptions of Theory X. Fundamentally, management has a crucial role to play in motivating employees. More importantly, this approach to motivation suggests that there is a definite relationship between job satisfaction among employees and management style. This management approach has been supported by many in the police field who argue that the Theory Y style is more conducive than Theory X to helping police deal with the demands of competing groups in today's society. Furthermore, they argue that a system of supportive management is the most effective because it provides a satisfying work environment for the individual officer (Cordner, 1978). Many, like Roberg (1979), have suggested that a Theory Y approach may be more applicable than Theory X to a complex task such as policing.

This conclusion seems to be equally applicable to prosecution, courts, and criminal corrections. But additional research on motivation and criminal justice operations needs to be conducted. Although Theory X has been the norm in traditional criminal justice organizations, it deserves increased attention both by those interested in explaining motivation in these systems and by those who seek advice on how to motivate criminal justice employees.

Moreover, we do have some insight into the motivation process among administrators. For example, Downs (1967) suggests that the motives of employees are not always consistent with those of administrators. His model of motivation in public organizations is tied to aspects of both Theory X and Theory Y. According to Downs (1967:84–85), public administrators, like those in the criminal justice system, have two types of motivations that are manifested in a number of goals. Power, money, income, prestige, convenience, and security are all manifestations of *self-interest* (Theory X), the motivating factor for many public administrators. Additionally, public administrators may be motivated by *altruism* (Theory Y), where the goals of loyalty, pride, desire to serve the public interest, and commitment to a specific program of action take precedence over self-interest goals.

Achievement–Power Theory

The achievement theory of motivation was originally developed by McClelland (1965). In addition, attention is now being paid to the power motive. It seems appropriate to discuss these two motives (achievement and power) together. We begin by examining achievement. Individuals can be led toward specific behaviors because these behaviors produce feelings of achievement.

McClelland (1965:322) suggests that people with high achievement values do the following:

1. Seek to achieve success through their own efforts and not have their success attributed to other factors.
2. Work on projects that are challenging but not impossible.
3. Receive identifiable and recurring feedback about their work and avoid situations where their level of achievement is in question.

This last proposition was tested by Stoller (1977) in his analysis of the effect of feedback on police performance. He examined the relationship between feedback and increased police productivity as measured by issued citations. Increased performance was achieved by forty-eight of the fifty-four officers who received the feedback. This seems to be a recurring theme in much police research: consistent feedback from upper-level managers can promote increased productivity among line officers (Roberg, 1979:114).

Other research done on police has indicated that there is a need on the part of many officers to increase their level of responsibility and participation in decision making. Hernandez (1982) found in the Mesa, Arizona, police department that a "professional model" of policing, which involved participation in problem solving and decision making, increased the officers' level of commitment to the department and their level of motivation.

The second motive associated with this theoretical position is the power motive. A growing body of literature attempts to document the role that power plays in organizations, particularly in decision-making processes (see Salancik and Pfeffer, 1977; Porter, Allen, and Angle, 1981; and Pfeffer, 1981). Our goal, however, is to examine power as an aspect of motivation. The power motive can be defined as a person's need to have some type of influence over another's behavior.

The power motive can be expressed in two ways. First, it may be in the form of *personalized power,* as manifested through an adversarial relationship; person-to-person competition is emphasized, and domination is a by-product. People are viewed simplistically as winners and losers, with the main goal being the achievement of power over others. Second, *socialized power* is impersonal and is expressed through a concern for others; it is employed by individuals who are sensitive to the fact that someone's gain means another person's loss. This type of power orientation is humanistic and is employed by those in leadership roles in social organizations (Tosi, Rizzo, and Carroll, 1986:228).

This presentation of the achievement–power theory of motivation enables us to see how the factors of achievement and power are instrumental to the motivation of individuals. Surely we can say that individuals are motivated by the quest for either achievement or power or both. Little research supports either of these positions completely; however, we do know, for example, that achievement, as defined by promotion, is important in the police field. Gaines, Tubergen, and Paiva (1984) concluded that promotion is extremely important in meeting the needs of police officers. In particular, they found that for some officers higher needs were more important than lower needs and that promotion was, in part, related to the satisfaction of those needs. In effect, the officers' desire to achieve, in this case through promotion, was crucial to their levels of motivation.

With respect to the power motive and criminal justice personnel, research has been done primarily within correctional institutions. Stojkovic (1984) documents the types of socialized power within inmate social systems and how they affect the operation of a prison. Socialized power among corrections officers was also explored by Hepburn (1985) and by Stojkovic (1987). Specific bases of socialized power were employed by both inmates and officers to complete their respective job assignments and tasks. For example, corrections officers considered the use of legitimate power—reasonable instructions and rules—as a useful tool in motivating prisoners to do what is expected of them. Additionally, the use of coercive power or force was not rated highly by corrections staff as a way of gaining compliance among prisoners. Power as a motivational tool has also been documented by research on corrections administrators (Stojkovic, 1986).

Understanding the social bases of power within the prison is crucial not only for motivational reasons but also for exploring the organization itself. Chapter 8 examines the concept of power in the context of criminal justice organizations.

Expectancy Theory

Expectancy theory is based on the belief that if a certain amount of effort is put forth, a calculated outcome will result. It is a rational approach to motivation. It posits that police work, for example, relies on an *expectation* among police officers that their efforts will produce a reduction in crime. The individual officer's motivation to perform depends, in part, on reduced crime rates. From an idealistic perspective, rational activity on the part of the police officer should reduce crime and increase the officer's satisfaction.

Figure 4-2 depicts some key concepts in expectancy theory. We summarize these concepts here (Tosi, Rizzo, and Carroll, 1986:240).

A basic concept is that *performance equals motivation plus ability.* Performance is a function of the ability of the individual to complete the task along with the motivation to do the task. More importantly, if either motivation or ability is not present, then there will be no performance.

An *expectancy* is the likelihood that an event or outcome will occur. Expectancies take two forms. First, there are effort–performance expectancies, where the person believes that a specific level of effort will result in a particular performance. The police officer, for example, may believe that there is a connection between the level of patrol activity and the crime rate in the precinct. In short, there is a correlation between the amount of work done and the end result, which in this example is the amount of crime in a specific area.

Second, there are performance–outcome expectancies, where there is an "expectation about the relationship between a particular level of performance and attaining certain outcomes" (Tosi, Rizzo, and Carroll, 1986:243). In this form of expectancy, the police officer may believe that there is a relationship between activity and a positive evaluation from superiors that is ultimately expressed in some type of reward, e.g., a promotion. However, the relationship between police activity and crime rates is somewhat problematical. If, for example, there is a low probability that police activity will lead to an actual reduction in crime, then it is difficult to see how one can reward individual police officers to produce the desired performance, e.g., reduced crime. In addition, if it is unlikely

Figure 4-2 Some Key Concepts in Expectancy Theory. (From *Managing Organizational Behavior,* by H. L. Tosi, J. R. Rizzo, and S. J. Carroll. Copyright © 1986 by Pitman Publishing Company. Reprinted by permission of Harper & Row, Publishers, Inc.)

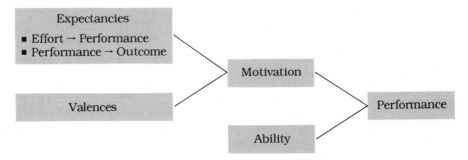

that the officer will gain any reward from the activity, he or she will not be motivated to do the activity. As a result, we would expect that the motivational levels of individual officers would be low because there is a low probability that their work activity produces the desired performance. Therefore, it may be that the individual officer would not choose crime reduction as an outcome. More importantly, the officer may desire other outcomes more, and typically those are attainable and rewarded consistently by the police organization.

Valences are the level of satisfaction or dissatisfaction produced by various outcomes. In brief, they are the individual's estimate of the advantages or disadvantages of a particular outcome. In the police example, if the effort required to produce a reduction in crime among officers does not lead to a satisfactory level of reward from the organization, this activity has a low positive valence; it is not worth the effort to pursue the activity knowing the low level of reward attached to the effort.

These principles taken together are represented in figure 4-3. We can see from this figure how the various expectancies operate to produce the outcomes or payoffs.

Tosi, Rizzo, and Carroll (1986:243–244) discuss how expectancy theory can be expanded to include other factors that affect the motivational level of employees. They argue that motivation is a function of expectancies and valences; ability is a function of performance potential and organizational factors; performance results from motivation and ability and leads to both intrinsic and extrinsic rewards; the level of performance affects the effort–performance expectancies; the rewards

Figure 4-3 Effort–Performance and Performance–Outcome Expectancies. (From *Managing Organizational Behavior.* by H. L. Tosi, J. R. Rizzo, and S. J. Carroll. Copyright © 1986 by Pitman Publishing Company. Reprinted by permission of Harper & Row, Publishers, Inc.)

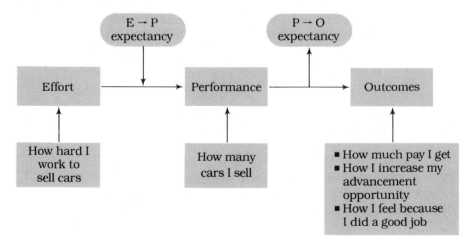

received for performance affect performance–outcome expectancies in later periods; and rewards also affect satisfaction. Figure 4-4 depicts this expanded expectancy model.

Interpreting and applying this model to police officer motivation, we can say that, first, the individual motivational levels of police officers are a function of what they expect and what valence they assign to their various activities. Second, the ability of an officer to do the job is a function of the officer's performance potential or the range of skills used in the achievement of objectives (Tosi, Rizzo, and Carroll, 1986:244). These skills may be limited by structural factors such as job descriptions, policies, and technology. Arresting all known criminals, for example, would be impossible for the police officer because of the limited resources of police organizations and the policies of the organization toward full enforcement of the law (Goldstein, 1984).

Third, when police activity leads toward some performance and that performance is a function of motivation and ability, then we would expect that a reward would follow. If an increase in arrest activity leads to an increase in pay or a promotion, then the officer receives an extrinsic reward for the performance. Additionally, if arresting individuals provides the community with a safe environment and gives the officer a good feeling about doing the job, the officer receives an intrinsic reward; this reward is typically self-administered by the individual.

Many have suggested that a clearly identified reward structure within police departments is what is needed to properly motivate officers (for example, Gaines, Tubergen, and Paiva, 1984:265–275). However, others have argued quite persuasively that these rewards are far and few between and are limited by the structure of many police departments. Conser (1979:286) contends that motivation is difficult in police organizations because the opportunities for advancement and promotion are limited. He recommends a number of mechanisms that would raise the motivational levels of officers, including merit pay packages, extra vacation leaves, and extra pay for education. Nevertheless, some research suggests that extrinsic rewards, such as increased pay and promotion, are only a small part to the motivation of police officers. Intrinsic rewards, e.g., achievement (Baker, 1976), are just as valuable. More importantly, it seems that proper motivation of specific officers requires a multitude of management strategies. Figuring out the most appropriate strategy within a certain context and with the right officer is the responsibility of managers.

Fourth, when an officer perceives that a level of performance will consistently produce a similar positive outcome from the organization, e.g., a reward, this perception will affect future expectancies; this process is nothing but learning by the officer and reinforcement by the organization through the reward structure. As the police officer learns that ticket writing, for example, is positively rewarded by the organization, the

Figure 4-4 An Expanded Expectancy Model. (From *Managing Organizational Behavior,* by H. L. Tosi, J. R. Rizzo, and S. J. Carroll. Copyright © 1986 by Pitman Publishing Company. Reprinted by permission of Harper & Row, Publishers, Inc.)

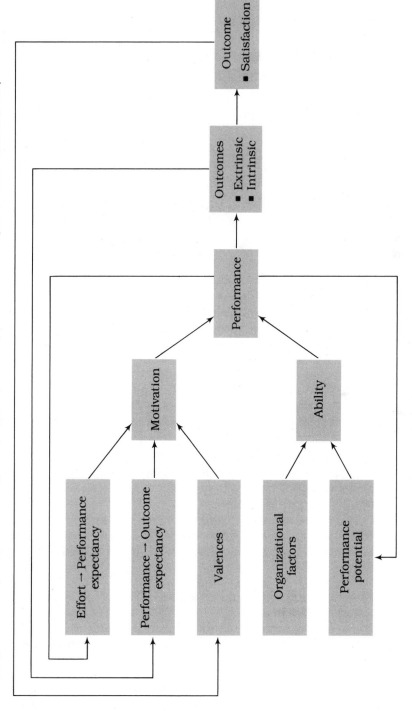

officer will continue to perform the activity until rewards are discontinued by the organization. In effect, the performance expectancy is a function of reinforcement and feedback by the organization (Stoller, 1977:57).

Finally, if the police officer is consistently being rewarded, both extrinsically and intrinsically, then we can say that he or she has a high level of satisfaction with the organization. Conversely, if rewards are not being received by the police officer, then we can expect that dissatisfaction is high and will continue to stay at this level until modifications are made. Criminal justice managers need to be aware of and sensitive to the level of dissatisfaction if organizational objectives are to be met (Witham, 1980:10–11). In fact, it may be accurate to discuss organizational deviance within criminal justice bureaucracies as a function of dissatisfaction among employees (see Manning and Redlinger, 1977).

Theory Z

Earlier in the chapter we discussed the differences between Theory X and Theory Y. Here we present an extension of Theory Y. This new theory, referred to as Theory Z, suggests that management must come to grips with the fact that organizations, either private or public, can no longer exist in a social vacuum; they not only function within a larger context but are also expected to effectively deal with the needs, desires, and problems of their employees in creative and diverse ways.

As a result, proper management and administration of contemporary organizations must consider the needs of the employee and, more importantly, how those needs can be met within the context of both the organization and society as a whole. For this reason Theory Z is viewed as a holistic approach to management and administration. With respect to employee motivation, Theory Z recommends broad changes and reforms. Before we discuss these changes and how they would affect criminal justice administration, we need to examine the basic tenets of Theory Z.

Theory Z has had many proponents, but Ouchi (1981) is probably the most notable. He suggests, along with others, that Theory Z is based on three beliefs:

1. There is among management a concern for production, a position expressed in Theory X.
2. There is among management a concern for the well-being of workers as productive employees. This position is similar to a basic assumption of Theory Y.
3. Finally, and the belief that distinguishes Theory Z from Theories X and Y, the organization cannot be viewed independently of the larger social, economic, and political conditions in society. More impor-

tantly, the work setting must be understood along with other institutions in society, such as family and school.

What distinguishes Theory Z from both Theory X and Theory Y is that it attempts to integrate the concerns of both of these theories while simultaneously reaching beyond the organizational structure into the very fabric of society. It holds that organizations cannot be isolated from other social forces. Therefore, Theory Z offers a synthesis of the previous theories and a macro orientation with respect to employee motivation. It suggests that motivation is not only organizationally determined but also influenced by broad and powerful influences in society.

A number of advantages follow from applying Theory Z to the administration of criminal justice agencies. Theory Z has had limited application in public organizations, including criminal justice. Nevertheless, there has been support for such an application. Archambeault and Wierman (1983), for example, argue for the application of Theory Z to policing. They suggest several changes that have to occur in the management of police organizations in order for police to become more responsive than they now are to their employees and their communities.

First, there must be shared decision making in police organizations, with individual officers having increased input on matters that affect them, although management would still be the final authority on key administrative issues. Although intuitively the approach is appealing, it would not be honest to suggest that such an arrangement would be easily accepted by older and more experienced officers. The traditional structure of police organizations would have to be drastically changed in order for Theory Z to have a chance of being implemented and followed. As suggested by Archambeault and Wierman (1983:427), there has to be a serious commitment by top administrative officials in police organizations to such a radical approach before implementation occurs. Without such a commitment, Theory Z would have a low probability of succeeding.

Second, supporters of Theory Z suggest that there be a team approach to policing, with the emphasis on the collective responsibility of officers. The idea here would be to get police away from the traditional notion of individual responsibility and individual work. Theory Z envisions officers working together toward the attainment of collectively defined goals, even though final responsibility would still lie with police administrators.

Third, police officers would have a clearly identified career path, with attendant rewards and promotional opportunities laid out in advance. There are some disadvantages to this idea. It seems to assume infinite reward opportunities and promotional paths. In some periods of time, this may be the case, yet, on the whole, promotional opportunities are often few and far between in many criminal justice organizations. What if the rewards and career opportunities are just not available? What is to be done with the police officer, for example, who has become "cross-trained" in a number of specializations, yet is never able to get a promotion? As fiscal constraints increase, it is not clear how Theory Z will resolve these thorny issues. This is not to suggest that nothing can be done, but, at a minimum, proponents of Theory Z are going to have to offer concrete answers to some of these practical concerns.

Fourth, Archambeault and Wierman (1983:427) suggest that the police organization must be more "holistic" in its dealings with police officers by appreciating the fact that officers exist in society. They have needs beyond the work setting, which include but are not limited to, for example, educational, personal, and family needs. Although it would be unrealistic to expect criminal justice organizations in this country to provide for all of the needs of employees, as is done in Japan, it is reasonable for administrators in criminal justice to be sensitive to the needs of workers, and, in return, employees have to make a personal and professional commitment to the organization. The result of this arrangement is loyalty to the goals of the organization by subordinates and a smoothly run organization.

Although such an approach is desirable in criminal justice, again we must question its feasibility. It is not clear how administrators would be able to provide a structure that deals with the many needs of subordinates. Clearly, criminal justice managers and administrators need to be attuned to their workers, but what are the most effective approaches for attaining that objective? It is likely that Theory Z may require more than can be realistically expected from those who administer our criminal justice systems.

This is not to suggest, however, that there is no room for the application of Theory Z to criminal justice management. Its most positive aspect is the belief that there is a relationship between organizational structure and the motivation of employees. Our contention in this chapter has been that employee motivation cannot be understood independently of organizational structure. Theory Z posits that management has a responsibility to structure a work environment that promotes the highest level of employee motivation. If Theory Z enables managers and administrators to rethink their roles in shaping and influencing their subordinates, then it has begun a movement of real value to the administration of criminal justice systems. Presently, it needs to be critically examined. No theory is flawless; only through future critical evaluation will we see the benefits of the application of Theory Z to criminal justice.

Prescriptions for Criminal Justice Management

It is quite apparent that the motivation process is complex. In addition, the application of existing theoretical models to the various criminal justice systems is problematical because no single theory of motivation is going to explain the many factors that affect the motivation of criminal justice personnel. Nevertheless, we can provide some suggestions to criminal justice managers about the approaches and programs most suited to their employees.

With respect to the theoretical positions on motivation examined previously, one key element links all these differing approaches to employee motivation: the needs, perspectives, and viewpoints of employees are instrumental not only to their individual growth but also to organizational effectiveness. More directly, it would be accurate to conclude that effective criminal justice management recognizes that the motivation of employees requires the growth and maturity of those employees through proactive and flexible management strategies. Without such flexible approaches to employee motivation, employee development is stymied, and organizational effectiveness is reduced. Lynch (1986:53) states:

> The present challenge to police managers is to provide a work climate in which every employee has the opportunity to mature, both as an individual and as a member of the department. However, the police manager must believe that individuals can be essentially self-directed and creative in their work environments if they are motivated by the management.

While cognizant of the fact that the management of criminal justice systems is different from the management of private companies or other public institutions, we still believe that a number of programs can be taken from these other sectors and applied effectively to criminal justice processes. We review and interpret two of these programs here: quality circles and Management by Objectives. An examination of other useful programs with respect to job design is provided in chapter 5. The student is encouraged to review these programs also because they too are applicable to the motivation process.

Quality-Circle Programs

Quality-circle programs are based on two fundamental assumptions. First, interactions among employees should provide for the maximum growth of the individual. Quality circles are meant to enhance the ability of workers to improve themselves, both personally and professionally. Second, by providing conditions for the growth of employees, the organization will become increasingly effective. In short, it is in the best interests of the organization to promote the well-being of workers. Operating on these two assumptions, quality-circle programs are defined as small groups of employees, typically nonmanagement personnel from the same work unit, who meet regularly to identify, analyze, and recommend solutions to problems relating to the work unit (Hatry and Greiner, 1984:1). Additionally, management must support these groups of subordinates.

Within the police subsystem of the criminal justice process, researchers have strongly recommended this approach. Having conducted probably the most exhaustive study to date of the implementation of quality circles and other participatory-management programs in policing, Hatry and Greiner (1984) suggest that the use of quality-circle programs greatly enhances the potential for producing small-scale service improvements and improving work-unit morale among officers. These improvements are crucial, in our opinion, to the motivation of police officers.

Moreover, this approach to improving the motivational levels of police officers is also applicable to other workers in the criminal justice process, e.g., corrections officers, counselors, and court personnel. Although many of the prescriptions currently being made concern the improvement of police, the application of these quality-circle programs to the other components of the criminal justice system is sorely needed. Brief, Munro, and Aldag (1976) describe the applicability of such approaches, particularly job-enlargement programs, to correctional institutions. And although Saari (1982) is cautious to accept management practices that he defines as fads, he does see the value of providing more information about management programs to those who run and manage our court systems.

Although the research literature has been generally supportive of quality-circle programs, it would be naive to suggest that they can be applied to all situations in criminal justice. Understanding the motivation process requires an analysis of the tasks of the organization. To suggest, for example, that quality-circle programs be adopted by corrections administrators faced with increased militancy among both prisoners and staff may be inappropriate. We do suggest, however, that the quality circle be considered as a possible alternative to increase the motivation levels of criminal justice employees, even though it may not be a panacea for all motivation problems.

Management by Objectives (MBO)

Probably no other innovation within management circles since the 1950s has had as much influence on organizations as Management by Objectives (MBO). MBO can be defined as a process whereby individual managers and employees identify goals and work toward their completion and evaluation within a specific time period. Much research evaluates the effectiveness of MBO programs within organizations (Carroll and Tosi, 1973). And, in addition, there has been wide application of MBO to the various components of the criminal justice system (Angell, 1971; Sherman, 1975; More, 1977; and Archambeault and Archambeault, 1982). However, the efficacy of the model for the various components of the criminal justice system remains unproven. Some believe its application to criminal justice can make the system effective, and can help improve the level of motivation among criminal justice employees. Others, how-ever, do not consider MBO to be universally applicable in criminal justice. A review of some of the research on this topic is required.

Beginning with research that supports the application of MBO to criminal justice operations, the police field has the greatest number of advocates for this view. Angell (1971) was the first to suggest that the implementation of MBO in policing would be of great benefit. In particu-lar, Angell sees the democratization of the police field as a step toward improving the delivery of services. Opponents, such as Sherman (1975), suggest that this democratic model, as conceived by Angell, would be deleterious to police organizations because it grants decision-making authority to teams of police and diminishes the power of middle man-agers in the traditional police hierarchy. In fact, Sherman argues quite persuasively that his own research on team policing indicates that mid-dle management will resist the efforts of higher-echelon personnel to democratize police organizations. Essentially, he believes that any planned change within police departments must include all members of the department. Anything short of total involvement will be viewed by the rank and file as just another one of "the boss's pet projects" (Sherman, 1975:377).

More recent research, however, supports the application of MBO to police departments and suggests that it is critical to effective manage-ment. Hatry and Greiner (1984) employed multiple research methods to assess the effectiveness of MBO programs in a number of police de-partments. In addition, they evaluated motivational programs in more than seventeen police departments and reviewed materials provided by an additional thirty police departments. From this evaluation, they con-cluded that "MBO systems have considerable potential for motivating management employees to improve service outcomes and service delivery efficiency" (1984:130). More importantly, they suggest that much can be done to improve the operation of MBO systems in police departments if proper attention is given to them by administrators.

Archambeault and Archambeault (1982:92–93) suggest that for MBO to work in correctional institutions a number of conditions have to obtain. First, as others have stated, administrative personnel have to be committed to the MBO program. A lack of commitment only breeds contempt for and disapproval of the program in lower-level employees. Second, administrative staff must be able to receive criticism and sugges-tions from employees. Otherwise, management will not be attuned to the workings of the organization. Third, any MBO program must take into consideration the power structure in the organization. It is often difficult for managers to share power with subordinates; this has been a recur-ring problem in many MBO programs—administrators deny that power to make decisions must be shared with all workers. But the empower-ment of employees and the subsequent enrichment of their jobs are implicit in the MBO approach. Chapter 8 examines how this empowerment process can work in criminal justice organizations. Fourth, workers as well as management must believe that the MBO process is worth pursuing. In many organizations, lack of commitment has led to the demise of MBO programs.

Summary

The purpose of this chapter was to explore theoretical models of motivation and apply them to the criminal justice process. We found that a number of theories of motivation were applicable to criminal justice, yet no one model was able to explain the diverse and complex motivation processes of all criminal justice personnel. One recurring theme did run through many of the theories, however: management needs to recognize that subordinates have needs, abilities, and opinions that are crucial to the effectiveness of the organization. Whether we were discussing policing, courts, or corrections, this requirement still applied.

In addition, we reviewed in this chapter two models for improving the motivation level of criminal justice employees: quality-circle programs and MBO. We proposed that criminal justice management and administration can be improved through the proper use of these models. Furthermore, our recommendation of these programs was based on the empirical literature. Clearly, additional research needs to be done on these programs and their applicability to criminal justice operations.

An understanding of the motivation process cannot be divorced from other relevant aspects of an organization. Subsequent chapters, starting with the following chapter, on job design, address important issues that also affect the motivation of criminal justice workers. Leadership, power, and socialization all have an impact on how police officers, court personnel, and corrections workers are motivated.

CASE STUDY
Motivating the Police Officer

Officer James LeGrange, an experienced member of the St. James Police Department, has just completed a rigorous day in which he has trained and broken in a new recruit. He began with a lecture about how all the rules and regulations are "bullshit" and how real policing is learned on the streets. The young officer, David Jones, listened intently, yet he felt overwhelmed by the information he was receiving. He could not believe what he was hearing, so somewhat cautiously he asked Officer LeGrange why he felt the rules were not important to the performance of an officer's job. Officer LeGrange responded, "Because there is no incentive for the good officer to do his job." He added, "All the stand-up cops are the guys who are busting their butts every day to do the things that are important to them. Things like dealing with the real dangerous criminals on the street; that's what's important, but the captains, lieutenants, and even the sergeants, the guys who you know the best and probably respect the most, they don't even care about you. The only guys who get the rewards around here are the real loser cops who bitch and whine when everything is not going their way. The guys who do the job don't get any rewards. Like I said, kid, there is really no incentive for us to kill ourselves when you don't get squat for it."

Officer Jones thought that LeGrange was burned out by the job, the kind of guy the training officer described in academy class. He responded, "If you feel that way, why don't you talk to the sergeants and the other administrators about your feelings?" Quickly, Officer LeGrange responded angrily, "What the hell do you think cops like me have been trying to do for the last few years? The reason we don't get anywhere is that the bosses can't even figure out we don't have any motivation to do this job anymore. All they care about is that no problems are caused by the troublemakers in the department. I wish that sometime the sergeant would pat me on the back for just being a good cop and doing a decent job. In my twenty years of being a cop, I have never heard any supervisor tell me that I am O.K. and doing a good job."

Officer Jones saw that Officer LeGrange was upset about the issue, and he wondered why this guy was even training him. He tried to make things better by saying, "Well, it seems that what the department needs is an incentive program that keeps the good officers interested in their jobs while getting rid of the guys who don't do anything or are a detriment to the department." "Uh-ha kid," Officer LeGrange responded cynically. "But you are missing the point. Having an incentive program means the bosses have an idea about what a good cop is and then they can reward him. Hell, the biggest problem with the department is that they don't have a clue as to what being a good cop means and how to reward him. That's why they spend all their time worrying about the guys who are worthless to the department. They know what a bad cop is and how to deal with him, but they don't know how to recognize the good one, and that is why so many guys quit the job."

"Well, that's it kid. The shift is over. We'll see you tomorrow." "I hope you are in a better mood then, Jim," stated Officer Jones. "Yeah, I hope so too, but don't bet on it," replied Officer LeGrange. Walking away, Officer Jones hoped that he would never become as cynical and frustrated a cop as Officer LeGrange, yet he feared that he would.

Case Study Questions

1. If you were an administrator in the St. James Police Department, what would you do to motivate Officer LeGrange? In addition, what type of strategy do you think would be the most useful in keeping Officer Jones motivated?
2. Do you think that Officer LeGrange believes police officers are motivated primarily in the way Theory X assumes or in the way Theory Y assumes?
3. Would an MBO program deal with the frustrations expressed by Officer Le-Grange?

For Discussion

1. It is often said that criminal justice employees are unmotivated. Comment on this assertion and discuss possible ways in which the

motivational levels of criminal justice workers can be raised. In addition, examine what you believe to be the role of criminal justice managers in the motivation of subordinates.

2. Discuss a particular theory of motivation and apply it to one of the components of the criminal justice system. Cite both advantages and disadvantages of the approach in motivating subordinates.

3. Invite a police chief to class to discuss specific strategies he or she employs to motivate officers. Examine these strategies and suggest both positive and negative aspects. Finally, discuss approaches you think will improve the motivation of police officers.

4. Examine quality-circle programs and MBO models in criminal justice organizations. What are both the prospects for and problems with these types of programs in criminal justice? Go to the library and review the recent literature on the effectiveness of these programs in both private and public organizations. Discuss with the class how you think these types of programs would benefit the various organizations of criminal justice.

For Further Reading

Herzberg, F., Mausner, B., and Snyderman, B. B. *The Motivation to Work.* New York: Wiley, 1959.

Likert, R. *New Patterns of Management.* New York: McGraw-Hill, 1961.

Maslow, A. *Motivation and Personality.* New York: Harper & Row, 1970.

McClelland, D. C. *Assessing Human Motivation.* Morristown, N.J.: General Learning Press, 1971.

Job Design

To me, when I was a kid, the policeman was the epitome—not of perfection—was good and evil in combination, but in control. He came from an element in the neighborhood, and he knew what was going on. To me a policeman is your community officer. He is your Officer Friendly; he is your clergyman; he is your counselor. . . . Now all we are is a guy who sits in a squad car and waits for a call to come over the radio. We have lost complete contact with the people. They get the assumption that we're gonna be called to the scene for one purpose—to become violent to make an arrest. No way I can see that. I am the community officer. They have taken me away from the people I'm dedicated to serving—and I don't like it [Officer Vincent Maher, quoted in Terkel, 1974:188].

[For the corrections officer assigned to the tower, the job is a] residue of the dark ages. He requires 20/20 vision, the IQ of an imbecile, a high threshold for boredom, and a basement position in Maslow's hierarchy [Toch, 1978:20].

We give too little thought to work itself. Work must be more than congenial: it must be absorbing, meaningful, and challenging. There just isn't any work as inherently rich in these qualities as police work. Yet, in many cases we have done such a successful job of strangling and stifling the juices of the "work" that we now find ourselves searching for ways to make it interesting [Reddin, 1966:12].

We are at work for much of our lives. This is true whether you examine the duration of our careers or the amount of time we spend on the job every day. For many of us, also, work is not only a place where tasks are accomplished but also an experience that adds to the value and meaning of our lives. Although we have many work-related personal goals, our jobs also fulfill organizational goals. Our efforts may contribute to the control of crime, the processing of offenders, or the treatment of those convicted.

In this chapter we examine the interplay of these personal and organizational goals. We focus on how the structure of work can satisfy or fail to satisfy these goals. After reviewing some of the criteria for a "good job," we consider the technological aspects of the design of jobs and the influence of Frederick Taylor in industry and in the human services. We also examine some of the undesirable consequences of poorly designed work. The chapter then turns to advancements made in theoretical approaches to job design and finally to examples of job design and redesign in criminal justice.

What Is Job Design?

In criminal justice the design of jobs is often taken for granted: police officers police, corrections officers guard, probation officers manage their caseloads, and judges deliberate. It is often assumed that these tasks govern the design of work. Both theory and research in industrial set-

Engineering and Efficiency in Job Design

The task-force report was most critical of jobs characterized by "dull, repetitive, seemingly meaningless tasks" and traced these impoverished jobs to the "anachronism of Taylorism" (1973:XV). Throughout most of this century, technological criteria or concern with the efficient completion of tasks has dictated the design of most industrial jobs. Frederick Winslow Taylor and his associates are properly credited as the major influence behind this trend. Increasing the efficiency of labor through the fragmentation of work, the use of time and motion studies, and the motivation of workers with pay incentives was the main component of Taylor's Scientific Management (1947). From the marriage of task and technology emerged such innovations as the "science of bricklaying," worked out in detail by Frank Gilbreth.

> He developed the exact position which each of the feet of the bricklayer should occupy in relation to the wall, the mortar box, and the pile of bricks, and so made it unnecessary for him to take a step or two toward the pile of bricks and back again each time a brick is laid. . . .
>
> Through all of this minute study of the motions of the bricklayer in laying bricks under standard conditions, Mr. Gilbreth has reduced his movements from eighteen motions per brick to five, and even in one case to as low as two motions per brick. . . .
>
> With union bricklayers in laying a factory wall, . . . he averaged, after his selected workmen had become skillful in his new methods, 350 bricks per man-hour; whereas the average speed of doing this work with the old methods, in this part of the country, was 120 bricks per man-hour [Taylor, 1947:81].

Taylor's influence on the design of jobs cannot be fully appreciated without examining his underlying assumptions. Throughout his works Taylor presents unflattering views of human nature. In his often-cited description of a highly trained pig-iron handler, Taylor refers to him as being "as stupid and phlegmatic as an ox" (1947:62). In Taylor's view most people are unmotivated by work itself but are motivated by leisure and increases in pay. Close supervision by college-educated, highly trained managers and financial incentives in the form of increased wages for increased production will counteract the natural tendency toward laziness.

Taylorism in the Human Services

Scientific Management formed the foundation of industrial engineering and technology and has remained a principal influence in the engineer's design of job content in industrial settings. Taylor, however, was careful to distinguish the "mechanisms" of Scientific Management, which may tings, however, question such assumptions. The term job design has been used to describe the "deliberate, purposeful planning of the job including all of its structural and social aspects and their effect on the employee" (Hellriegel and Slocum, 1979:431).

There are many approaches to job design and many lists of criteria for a good job. Although efficiency was once the chief concern, a wide variety of other goals have been recognized. One popular list of "psychological job requirements" includes the following factors (Emmery and Emmery, 1974:47):

1. *Adequate elbowroom.* Workers need a sense that they are their own bosses and that except in unusual circumstances they will not have a boss breathing down their necks. But they don't want so much elbow-room that they don't know what to do next.

2. *Chances to learn on the job and go on learning.* Such learning is possible only when people are able to set goals that are reasonable challenges for them and to know results in time for them to correct their behavior.

3. *An optimal level of variety.* Workers need to be able to vary the work so as to avoid boredom and fatigue and to gain the best advantage from settling into a satisfying rhythm of work.

4. *Help and respect from work mates.* We need to avoid conditions where it is in no one's interest to lift a finger to help another, where people are pitted against each other so that one person's gain is another's loss, and where the individual's capabilities or inabilities are denied.

5. *A sense that one's work meaningfully contributes to social welfare.* Workers do not want a job that could be done as well by a trained monkey or an industrial robot machine. They also do not want to feel that society would probably be better served by not having the job done, or at least not having it done so shoddily.

6. *A desirable future.* Workers do not want dead-end jobs; they want ones that continue to allow personal growth.

These qualities of a good job reflect a common concern in the literature and can be traced to the warnings of Karl Marx, who said:

> What do we mean by the alienation of labor? First, that the work he performs is extraneous to the worker—that is, it is not personal to him, is not part of his nature; therefore he does not fulfill himself in work but actually denies himself; feels miserable rather than content; cannot freely develop his physical and mental power but instead becomes physically exhausted and mentally debased [cited in Josephson and Josephson, 1975:87].

These concerns were echoed in a 1973 federal government task-force report entitled *Work in America.* The conclusion of the report begins with the words of the existentialist philosopher Albert Camus: "Without work all life goes rotten. But when work is soulless, life stifles and dies" (Special Task Force to the Secretary of Health, Education and Welfare, 1973:186).

have limited applicability outside the machine shop, from the "essence" of Scientific Management, which would have much wider utility:

> Scientific Management is not an efficiency device, . . . not a new system of figuring costs; it is not a new scheme for paying men; it is not a time study; it is not a motion study. . . . These devices are useful adjuncts to Scientific Management. . . . In its essence, Scientific Management involves a complete mental revolution on the part of working man [Taylor, 1919:68–69].

In the human services, the essence of Taylorism has been a potent influence, but the mechanisms have not been ignored. Time and motion study has been used to determine the best location of instruments for dentistry, the need for mechanized hospital beds, and even the advantages of rhythmic movements for surgeons. Beyond these studies, however, Taylor's concern with increasing efficiency through the fragmentation of work and close supervision has found wide application in the "people work" industries.

Unlike managers in production industries, however, managers in the human services can rarely define their workers' roles with reference to the requirements of an assembly line or machine. In a review of policing, public welfare, and other street-level bureaucracies, Lipsky (1980:14) notes that most human services work is characterized by considerably more discretion and variety than are jobs in a factory. These differences, however, have not insulated human services work from tight bureaucratic control. For example, Karger (1981:42) notes the similarities between the alienating features of industrial and human services work.

> The routinization of public welfare is complemented by increased specialization and the creation of continually narrower job descriptions. . . . Accountability is achieved through daily logs, regular breaks, and performance objectives. The assumption is that workers are selling their labors rather than their skills. . . . Even in private welfare we see "numbered contact hours"—a designation referring to quantity rather than quality. . . . The workplace in a large public bureaucracy—with its large rooms filled with long rows of cubicles—appears more like a bureaucratic assembly line than a private environment in which to discuss personal matters. The client is objectified as a problem that must be processed as the line grows longer.

Taylorism in Criminal Justice

In the field of criminal justice, policing has been described as a "Taylorized occupation" (Harring, 1982). Concern with productivity has led administrators to fragment the role of the police officer. Automobile-based patrolling and the use of nonsworn personnel for traffic control, bus monitoring, and other tasks have taken away from regular line officers the "Florence Nightingale" duties that Harring argues provided a broad, humane role for the police. He concludes that the Taylorization of police institutions is important to study because it can undermine the notion that the police are immune from the dehumanizing experiences of other workers.

This trend toward decreased discretion and increased control has been referred to as the deprofessionalization syndrome (Stone and Stoker, 1979; Sharp, 1982). The irony behind the syndrome is that as management has increased its professionalization through increased accountability and bureaucratization of work life, the status of front-line personnel has diminished. Hahn (1974:23) notes:

> The professionalization of police departments, therefore, acts to undermine the professional stature of individual police officers by limiting their personal discretion in handling the problems of "clients" in the community.

Similar concerns about deprofessionalization are seen in the areas of probation and parole. Because probation offices generally come under the jurisdiction of the courts, Lawrence (1984) argues that they have traditionally been uncertain of their professional status. He reports that "many probation officers see themselves more as judicial servants caught in the civil service malaise than as professionals" (1984:1). The revolution in technology in the field of community supervision may further erode the autonomy and discretion of front-line workers. The introduction of standardized classification instruments is an example. The instruments frequently use information about an offender's criminal history and other background variables to establish a numerical score reflecting the appropriate security level. These devices not only restrict the judgment of probation and parole officers in assessing their cases but also dictate the amount of time they can spend on cases regarded as requiring maximum, medium, or minimum supervision.

The development of electronic monitoring systems for offenders also appears to be altering the jobs of probation and parole agents. Such devices track the offender's location through an electronic device generally strapped to the ankle. A review of these and other changes in the processing of information in probation and parole offices suggests that they are likely to have a major impact on the nature of probation and parole jobs. The devices will accentuate the clearly defined law enforcement role of probation and parole officers and diminish the discretionary aspects of their work, which are generally associated with their treatment function (Moran and Lindner, 1985).

In corrections, jobs have frequently been described by highly circumscribed responsibilities. Civil service job descriptions in New York State list the corrections officer's duties this way:

> Correctional officers supervise the movement and activities of inmates; make periodic rounds of assigned areas; conduct searches for contraband; and maintain order within the facility. They advise inmates on the rules and regulations governing the operation of the facility and assist in solving problems.

In 1967 the President's Commission on Law Enforcement and the Administration of Justice described corrections officers as the "employees who man the walls, supervise living units, escort inmates to and from work, and supervise all group movement around an institution." These responsibilities were clearly distinguished from the professional role of other corrections staff. Such descriptions reify the corrections officer's job by ignoring the discretionary human relations aspects of the role.

Parallels between criminal justice and industrial work can be overemphasized however. As Toch and Grant (1982:85) suggest, "no matter how badly off human service workers are, their fate is less circumscribed than that of the men and women who serve machines and are constrained by their technology." Lipsky (1980) makes a similar point when he remarks that police, judges, and probation officers continue to exercise considerable discretion because of the way their jobs are designed.

Responses to Job Characteristics

Much of the recent interest in the design of jobs has grown out of concerns raised in studies of worker satisfaction. Although more than 85 percent of American workers report general satisfaction with their jobs, detailed inquiry has revealed sharply declining levels of satisfaction with specific aspects of the work environment (see Hackman and Oldham, 1980). Discontent among hourly and clerical workers has risen to the highest level since those measurements began to be made in the 1950s. Other research has identified young workers as the most dissatisfied and the most likely to be concerned with job-design issues (Sheppard and Herrick, 1972). The discontent of workers was dramatically illustrated in the early 1970s at a strike in a Lordstown, Ohio, automobile plant. Workers there did not protest low wages but instead voiced opposition to routine and boring labor. A Lordstown employee described the frustration workers felt:

> You have to . . . break the boredom to get immediate feedback from the job because the only gratification you get is a paycheck once a week, and that's too long without any kind of gratification from the job [quoted in Kreman, 1973:173].

In criminal justice we lack the longitudinal data necessary to indicate changes in levels of job satisfaction. Still, the literature is suggestive about employees' expectations of their work. A study of police officer satisfaction, for example, paralleled findings in industrial settings when it revealed that many officers described themselves as generally satisfied with the tangible benefits of their jobs but concerned about such issues as opportunities for advancement and opportunities to improve their skills. Only about half the officers reported that they would recommend police work to a friend, and many reported that their enthusiasm for the job had diminished over time (Buzawa, 1984).

Patterns of job satisfaction appear to be similar for police and corrections officers. Attitudinal changes appear to occur following training. During the initial years on the job, satisfaction decreases and cynicism increases (Niederhoffer, 1969; Van Maanan, 1973). Researchers have also described an inverted, U-shaped curve in which negative attitudes are highest in the middle of careers and lowest among officers with the least as well as the most seniority (Poole and Regoli, 1980; Toch and Klofas, 1982). Education levels have also been found to be negatively correlated with job satisfaction among police officers. Evidence indicates that a disproportionate number of the more educated police officers voluntarily leave their jobs before retirement (Buzawa, 1984). It has been suggested that this turnover is due to the frustration of working in a rigid setting. One study, however, suggests that this turnover may be the result of increased job opportunities (Buzawa, 1984).

In human services occupations, reactions to work also include stress and burnout. Both of these concepts refer to physical and psychological reactions to the work environment. After reviewing the available literature, Whitehead and Lindquist (1986) argue that chronic, intense stress may lead to burnout, which has been defined as "a syndrome of emotional exhaustion and cynicism" (Maslach and Jackson, 1981).

Although much of the literature on burnout in the human services has focused on issues surrounding client contact (see Maslach, 1976), some researchers have examined organizational causes. Cherniss (1980) suggests that burnout may arise from boredom, excessive demands, and such job-design problems as role conflict, role ambiguity, and lack of participation in decision making. In criminal justice research, organizational factors have been identified as the major causes of stress and burnout. In studies of corrections officers in New Jersey, Pennsylvania, Illinois, and Washington, Cheek and Miller (1982, 1983) found that "administrative sources" were the primary reasons for stress on the job. Administrative sources included lack of communication from management, lack of clear guidelines, and lax or inconsistent administrative practices. The researchers argue in favor of a redesign of the corrections officer's job. Whitehead and Lindquist (1986) came to similar conclusions from their multivariate analysis of burnout among corrections officers. Using a standardized instrument developed by Maslach and Jackson (1981), these authors found that not only was inmate contact not a cause of burnout, but such contact was positively associated with feelings of accomplishment. However, administrative policies and procedures were identified as sources of stress. This finding was also replicated with a sample of federal corrections officers (Lasky, Gordon, and Srebalus, 1986). Whitehead and Lindquist suggest that these findings may support the view that managerial control efforts conflict with officers' desires for autonomy and discretion.

Whitehead (1985) also studied burnout among probation and parole officers. Using the Maslach Inventory (Maslach and Jackson, 1981) with a sample of nearly 1,500 probation and parole officers in four states, he found that respondents scored higher than other human services workers on most of the burnout dimensions. In considering causes, Whitehead argues that his data do not support theories that link burnout to emotionally charged contact with clients. Instead, burnout among probation and parole agents was tied to the officers' need for efficacy and a sense of providing competent service to clients. These findings support theoretical perspectives that view job-design factors as important sources of burnout.

Job-Design Theory

Ten years after Taylor first published a description of Scientific Management in 1911, the Hawthorne studies at the Western Electric Company in Chicago began to demonstrate the importance of nontechnological considerations in job design. In these studies, researchers, under the direction of Elton Mayo, tested the effects of experimentally induced conditions on worker fatigue and monotony. Set up as standard engineering experiments, the research focused on independent variables that were physical or technological in nature. Researchers found, however, that productivity increased regardless of increased or decreased illumination and regardless of the timing of work breaks or the length of the working day. The researchers soon abandoned concern with the technological variables and focused on social and psychological explanations (Roethlisberger and Dickson, 1939).

Although workers performed dull, repetitive tasks that required little skill and afforded little status, productivity and job satisfaction increased under the attention of the investigators. One explanation for the increases became known as the Hawthorne Effect, which suggested that the novelty of having research conducted and the increased attention from management could lead to temporary increases in productivity. To explain persistent increases, the researchers focused on the informal interpersonal relationships of the workers. From these findings developed the human relations school of management, which became associated with the work of Mayo (1946), and Roethlisberger and Dickson (1939).

The human relations school replaced Taylor's portrait of the workers as motivated by money and leisure with a view of them as motivated also by social attachments. Contemporary job-redesign theories have built on these models and have also incorporated increasingly complex theories of motivation. Much of modern job-design theory can be traced to the motivational sequence proposed by Maslow (1943) and applied to management by McGregor (1978) (see chapter 4) and to the empirically based theories of Herzberg (1966). Although some have argued for the redesign of jobs as a response to changes in society, most contemporary theories have been described as "classical theories of job redesign" with a foundation in the works of Maslow and Herzberg (Kelly, 1982:37).

Job enrichment can be traced to the work of Herzberg, beginning in the 1950s. Motivation–hygiene theory was developed by Herzberg from critical-incident research in which he asked workers to describe the high and low points in their work lives. The research uncovered two sets of factors involved in motivation at the workplace (Herzberg, Mausner, and Snyderman, 1959; Herzberg, 1966). "Hygiene factors" are external to the work being performed. These include pay, supervision, physical conditions at the work site, and interpersonal relations. Contentment with these factors does not motivate workers however; it simply prevents dissatisfaction. Herzberg labeled a second set of factors "motivators." These factors are intrinsic to the work itself. They include responsibility, recognition, and opportunities for achievement and growth. (One study replicated Herzberg's finding regarding hygiene factors and motivators with a sample of corrections officers (Hayslip, 1982)). Job-enrichment models, which Herzberg calls "orthodox job enrichment," build on motivation–hygiene theory by assuming that workers will be motivated only after hygiene needs are met and sources of intrinsic satisfaction are built into jobs. Job design according to this theory is concerned not simply with improved efficiency but with motivating employees by meeting their higher-order needs.

Some research (Hackman and Oldham, 1980:58), however, has not supported the original dichotomy between hygiene factors and motivators and suggests that the findings may be an artifact of the particular interview techniques used by Herzberg. The substantive issue flowing from this criticism concerns the relationship between satisfaction with extrinsic factors and motivation. For instance, some theories argue that motivated employees need not be satisfied with the contexts of work (Morse, 1973). A related criticism of motivation–hygiene theory is that it pays too little attention to differences in workers' responses to jobs. Workers may attach different interpretations to job situations, and they may respond differently to jobs with varying levels of enrichment (Hackman and Oldham, 1980:57). Some workers may thrive in enriched jobs, while others may respond with confusion, resentment, and inability to cope with the new demands.

Enrichment theory and research have expanded to accommodate criticisms of the motivation–hygiene theory, and other theoretical orientations have been incorporated into job-design efforts. One popular approach to job enrichment has been developed by Hackman and Oldham (1980). This model has the virtues of being empirically based and attentive to individual differences. For Hackman and Oldham, job redesign involves increasing certain core job dimensions that influence the psychological states of workers, which in turn affect personal and work outcomes. This sequence can be moderated, however, by certain variables: an individual's level of knowledge and skill, need for accomplishment and growth, and satisfaction with pay and working conditions. The complete model is shown in figure 5-1. This theoretical perspective recognizes the importance of matching individual workers with their jobs. Under the model, job enrichment is inappropriate and is likely to have negative consequences if workers have a low need for growth and jobs are relatively high on the core dimensions. However, when jobs are low on the core dimensions and workers are satisfied, have appropriate knowledge, and possess high needs for accomplishment and development, the potential for job enrichment is great.

As part of their theory, Hackman and Oldham (1980:77) describe the job characteristics that they regard as most significant for employee motivation. These characteristics can also be combined into a single measure of the motivating potential of a particular job. These are the core job dimensions:

1. *Skill variety*—the degree to which jobs require a variety of different activities, skills, and talents.

Figure 5-1 Job-Enrichment Model. (From J. Hackman/Oldham R. *Work Redesign.* Reading, Mass.: Addison-Wesley, © 1980, p. 83.) Adapted by permission.

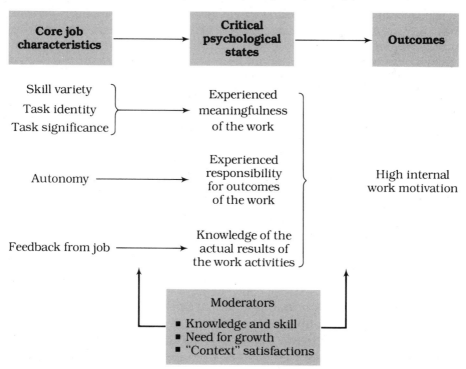

2. *Task identity*—the degree to which a job requires the completion of a whole task rather than bits or pieces of a project.
3. *Task significance*—the extent to which a job has a meaningful impact on others; the importance of the job.
4. *Autonomy*—the degree of freedom, independence, and discretion provided by a job.
5. *Feedback*—the extent to which workers get direct and clear information about the effectiveness of their performance.

Job-design efforts have frequently incorporated a process known as job analysis: the study of work assignments with the goal of specifying the precise skills and training needed for the work. Most often, job analysis is limited to the technical dimensions of jobs and is used in the production of job descriptions (Ghorpade and Atchison, 1980) or to identify appropriate levels of compensation.

Hackman and Oldham's model takes a broader view than job analysis of the kinds of information needed in job-redesign efforts. The authors have developed an instrument, called the Job Diagnostic Survey, that allows managers to measure all the variables in the theory and to assess both jobs and workers with regard to the need as well as the potential for job enrichment. The Job Diagnostic Survey provides measures of the core job dimensions as well as measures of the worker-related variables. Considerable research has been done with the instrument, and Hackman and Oldham have published averages for all the variables for nine separate job families. The Job Diagnostic Survey has also been used to study criminal justice occupations. Brief, Munro, and Aldag (1976) used the instrument as the foundation of a data-based argument for redesign of some corrections officer tasks. The researchers found that the most satisfied corrections officers were those whose jobs had the highest variety, task identity, feedback, and autonomy. They also found, as the theory predicts, that these relationships tended to be moderated by individual needs for growth.

Job-Redesign Programs

Since IBM first began to experiment with job redesign in 1943, programs have been implemented in numerous work settings. In reviewing much of the literature on these programs, Kelly (1982) suggests that three approaches to the redesign of work have emerged. In mass-production industries, often characterized by fragmented jobs on assembly lines, job-redesign efforts have sought to reduce or eliminate assembly lines. In continuous-process industries, such as chemical production, jobs have been enriched through the creation of autonomous work groups. In service industries, Kelly argues that enrichment has occurred principally through the combination of work roles from different parts of the job hierarchy. Other authors have distinguished job enlargement, which involves the addition of tasks to job descriptions, from job enrichment. Still others have characterized programs as involving additions along the horizontal dimension, as in job enlargement, and strengthening the vertical dimension, as in job enrichment.

Many redesign programs have included combinations of strategies. In a well-known redesign of assembly-line tasks, AB Volvo of Sweden incorporated a variety of approaches (Gyllenhammer, 1975). In one auto-assembly plant, managers turned to job enlargement by adding variety to workers' tasks. Some 1,600 workers rotated their jobs, often making several changes a day. In another plant, Volvo rotated assembly-line jobs within teams of twelve to fifteen members. Workers themselves decided how to rotate jobs within the groups and also met regularly with management to discuss how the work could be improved. In the production of trucks and buses, which was considered slower and more complex than the auto assembly line, Volvo formed smaller work groups with increased autonomy. Within these groups some workers performed specialized assignments, while others opted to alternate tasks. In their new plants Volvo eliminated assembly lines and replaced them with work teams, each operating out of separate sections of the shop floor and responsible for completed parts of the final product.

In another well-known redesign project, managers at Texas Instruments sought to enrich the jobs of building janitors and matrons. The program began with training in managerial techniques, including those derived from McGregor's (1978) Theory X and Theory Y. Early program recruits later hired additional staff and chaired regular meetings, which included training in management concepts as well as discussions of work-related problems. Teams of workers became responsible for redesigning the maintenance tasks as well as for quality control. The results of the program included improved cleanliness at reduced costs, reductions in worker turnover, and other improvements, including the following worker-originated innovations (Toch and Grant, 1982:78):

1. Teams eliminated cleaning carts, installed supply cabinets, and took responsibility for their own inventories.
2. Work groups divided and controlled their own work, including scheduling the closing down of washrooms to minimize unpredictability for other employees.
3. Matrons, unhappy with a disinfectant that had corrosive effects and caused dermatitis, negotiated with a vendor who developed a new chemical to their specifications. Cleaning time was cut in half when the new chemical was packaged in spray form.
4. Janitors and matrons took responsibility for inspections of facilities.
5. The workers also became concerned with preventive maintenance.

They embarked on an ingenious campaign to educate and involve the users. For example, matrons spoke to new hires as part of the company's employee-orientation sessions to explain their cleanliness goals and to solicit cooperation. In another approach, matrons and janitors photographed areas that were particularly untidy or dirty. These photos were circulated on production lines in an attempt to elicit cooperation from factory, laboratory, and office employees.

The Texas Instrument program is cited for disconfirming the assumption that the higher reaches of the Maslowian hierarchy have been reserved for skilled workers. As Toch and Grant (1982:79) point out, "if toilet bowls can acquire motivating potential, any job is more enrichable than we first suspect."

Job Redesign in Criminal Justice and Other Human Services

Although few job-redesign efforts in human services have incorporated the specific types of data called for by Hackman and Oldham, considerable research supports the efficacy of such efforts. Sarrata and Jeppensen (1977), for example, found that the job-design features that Hackman and Oldham identified as producing satisfaction in blue-collar workers functioned the same way for child-care workers.

Research has also shown that human services workers often value the most enriched aspects of their work or even take steps to enrich their own jobs. In a classic job-design study of psychiatric aides, Simpson and Simpson (1959) found that the attendants reported intrinsically rewarding tasks involving patient care as their main reasons for staying on the job. The same aides reported originally being attracted to the job for extrinsic reasons, including job security and pay. In a study of corrections officers, Toch (1978:19) found that 20 percent of officers were independently experimenting with nontraditional enriched roles, which included "the officer as dispenser of mental health services, as a person who resonates to adjustment problems of inmates in crisis." Lombardo (1981) and Johnson (1977) also identified diversity in the way corrections officers perform their tasks.

Apart from the efforts of individual innovators, numerous formal programs have also involved the redesign of work in the human services. In mental health settings, aides' jobs have been enriched through the addition of treatment responsibilities (Ellsworth and Ellsworth, 1970). In criminal justice, the jobs of front-line workers have been redesigned through a variety of approaches including job enlargement, vertical loading (job enrichment), and the creation of autonomous work groups.

One of the earliest documented job-redesign efforts in corrections occurred under Howard Gill, superintendent of the Norfolk Prison Colony in Norfolk, Massachusetts, between 1931 and 1934 (Doering, 1940). Under Gill's grand scheme for creating as normal a community setting as possible, a new kind of prison guard was required. While the officers who patrolled the perimeter and stood watch in the towers played the traditional role, inside the colony, house officers performed additional tasks that included casework and counseling as well as facilitating inmate self-government within the housing units.

Lindquist and Whitehead (1986) report on a more recent experiment in job enlargement involving corrections officers. In the Alabama Supervised Intensive Restitution (SIR) program, corrections officers supervised inmates in the community as a solution to the problem of prison overcrowding. The officers managed caseloads of approximately thirty-five and acted much the same as probation and parole officers. The SIR officers experienced a greater sense of personal accomplishment and higher levels of job satisfaction than a sample of regular corrections officers and a sample of probation and parole officers.

Several efforts have also been made to enrich criminal justice jobs. Rather than add tasks to the job description, these programs generally increase responsibilities of front-line staff, a process known as vertical loading. One example is Carter and Wilkins's (1976:394) caseload-distribution program in probation and parole. In the Work Unit Parole Program begun in California in 1965 and later introduced in Wisconsin, cases are assigned a weight based on the amount and type of supervision needed, and caseloads are determined by equal distribution of weighted cases. This program has allowed staff to spend time in the treatment and custodial supervision of cases, where the need is greatest.

A different approach to the vertical loading of jobs is seen in the work of Toch and Grant (1982). They added responsibilities often reserved for management to the tasks of both police and corrections officers by involving front-line staff in examining and resolving significant work-related problems. Although Herzberg (1978:40) argues that such participation is not part of the work itself and is, therefore, a hygiene factor rather than a motivator, Toch and Grant argue that participation is a necessary part of job enrichment in the human services because of the wide discretion human services workers have. As they point out, "enriching a guard's or police officer's job means expanding the prison's or police department's human services involvement, a task that cannot be accomplished by edict" (1982:133).

In a program with the Oakland (California) police department, Toch and Grant used groups of officers with records of violent confrontations with citizens to study and resolve problems of police violence. The groups collected and analyzed data (tape recordings of confrontations) and devised innovations, including peer-review panels, specialized training, and mediation units to deal with family crises and landlord–tenant disputes. In a project with New York State corrections officers, group participants were selected on the basis of their interest in job enrichment as determined by a questionnaire. The groups at four separate prisons analyzed the corrections officer's job and suggested alterations. The project resulted in blueprints for training, increased involvement of officers in treatment and classification, and mechanisms for increasing communication with management.

In a replication of the Toch and Grant method, Klofas, Smith, and Meister (1986) used groups of jail officers to plan the operation of a new jail in Peoria, Illinois. In a program lasting two years, front-line officers wrote policies and procedures for the facility. Included in the products of their planning were innovations in classification and programming and a revision of the shift pattern and job assignments. Job satisfaction increased over the course of the program, particularly with regard to perceived support from supervisors and opportunities to contribute new ideas.

Perhaps the best-known restructuring of the traditional police role is offered in Angell's (1971) model of team policing, which parallels autonomous work groups in industry. Linking police morale problems to the practices of classical management, Angell provides an alternative to the traditional police hierarchy. The core of his democratic model of policing is teams of police generalists, who provide services to designated neighborhoods. Teams are composed of officers of equal rank who are assigned to relatively small geographical areas for extended periods, which gives them a chance to become familiar with the culturally homogeneous neighborhoods and to work closely with residents. The team initiates all investigations and may call in specialists if they are needed. Evaluations of team policing have highlighted its potential but have also called attention to forces within the organization that are resistant to change (Sherman, Milton, and Kelly, 1973).

In a review of recent innovations in policing in six American cities, Skolnick and Bayley (1986) also elaborate the benefits of team policing. They argue that while the old professionalism leaned toward "legalistic" styles of policing, the new professionalism is marked by a service-oriented style. They illustrate their arguments with a review of changes in several cities (1986:214): Detroit's ministations exclusively organize community crime prevention; and Santa Ana's substations function as community . . . meeting areas as well as locales for disseminating crime-prevention information." The programs thus benefit the community as well as the participating officers.

In their discussion of a Houston program that integrates patrol, investigation, and intelligence collection, Skolnick and Bayley (1986:95) highlight another advantage of decentralization:

> To be successful this kind of teamwork among patrol officers and specialists requires a radical change in the traditional management style. Decisions must be made from the bottom up rather than the top down. The supervisor's

job is not to produce conformity with a preordained plan but to help develop a plan out of the insights of the many people doing the work on the street. . . . Not only will policing become more purposeful this way, but, it is hoped, officers will develop greater enthusiasm for their work. No longer are they spear carriers in someone else's drama; they become responsible directors in their own right.

Revitalization of community policing is also being advocated by members of the Executive Session on Policing, which is associated with Harvard University's Kennedy School of Government (Kelling, 1988). Sometimes referred to as "problem-oriented" policing, the approach calls for police to work closely with citizens in identifying and solving problems before crimes occur. Officers and citizens resolve problems such as broken windows, local bullies, and other disruptions that make neighborhoods look and feel unsafe. As its supporters note "The resourcefulness of police officers . . . can at last be put to the service of the department" (Sparrow, 1988:4).

Programs creating autonomous work groups have also been initiated in correctional institutions. Under the unit management system, pioneered in the Federal Bureau of Prisons, an alternative to the traditional prison hierarchy is established (Levinson and Gerard, 1973). Large institutions are divided into architecturally distinct housing units, which typically have from fifty to one hundred inmates. Inmates can be assigned to the units based on similar treatment or security needs. A group of corrections officers and counseling staff has ongoing contact with a small group of inmates in their unit. Frequently headed by a corrections officer, the teams are responsible for all decision making in the unit. Although the distinction between custodial and treatment staff remains, officers and counselors share some duties. The roles of the team members are thus changed in both the horizontal and vertical dimensions.

In probation and parole, the Community Resource Management Team (CRMT) has been developed as an alternative to the traditional caseload model (Clear and O'Leary, 1983:126). Based on the assumption that "no one person can possess all the skills to deal with the variety of human problems presented by probationers" (Dell'Appa, Adams, Jorgensen, and Sigurdson, cited in Clear and O'Leary, 1983:126), the model creates specialists in skill areas. Probation officers act as advocates concerned with the purchase of services or referrals in specific areas such as employment, counseling, legal assistance, and drug abuse. CRMT staff thus have "duty areas" or functional responsibilities rather than caseloads.

Clear and O'Leary (1983) describe a project that gave probation officers functional rather than caseload responsibilities. The project directors discovered that some officers naturally adopted functional approaches:

One officer, regarded as especially skilled in intensive counseling activities, had in fact stopped seeing some of her caseload so that she could see a minority of cases more intensively. Other areas of officer interest and knowledge included drugs, the military, and language problems. One officer had developed a system of mail reporting for a large noncontact caseload. The problem facing the supervisor was to make the best use of these existing officer skills and interests in the supervision of clients [Clear and O'Leary, 1983:127].

Probation officers in the large urban department involved in the change project altered the organizational structure to accommodate officer interests as well as the existing classification scheme. A two-person team became responsible for intake and initial case analysis. One of the intake officers also handled low-risk cases on a low-reporting basis. Medium-level cases were handled by a team divided by functional interests, and high-risk cases were handled in small caseloads by single officers with counseling interests. Clear and O'Leary make the important observation, however, that this model may not be appropriate for other agencies or even for some other big-city agencies. They call for the direct involvement of staff and for flexibility in the redesign of probation officer tasks so that each organization can take advantage of its own resources.

Summary

In this chapter we have attempted to integrate knowledge about task design from the fields of general management and criminal justice. Human services appear to lag behind industry in the design of jobs. Human services managers, including those in criminal justice, however, are showing increased concern with the nature of the tasks performed by front-line staff. Research on job satisfaction and burnout has contributed to this concern. At the same time, technological changes and increased bureaucratization in criminal justice threaten to limit front-line discretion and impoverish job tasks in much the same way that Scientific Management has had negative consequences in industry.

One response to the deprofessionalization syndrome is to carefully reconsider the design of jobs in criminal justice. Theory and research in industrial settings can guide these efforts. Design theories now incorporate concern for individual differences with measures of task-related variables. A substantial record of job redesign in industrial settings can guide the criminal justice manager, and a valuable body of research and practical experience is developing within the field of criminal justice itself. Existing efforts range from enlarging jobs by adding tasks to completely restructuring organizations in order to enhance jobs as well as increase effectiveness.

In the next chapter we focus on the final topic in the discussion of the role of the individual within criminal justice organizations. Concerns with communication, motivation, and job design all rely heavily on leadership within organizations, the topic we tackle next.

CASE STUDY

A Program of Job Redesign in Corrections

A year ago a bitter strike rocked the department of corrections. For nearly three weeks national guards replaced striking corrections officers in prisons throughout the state. What was unusual about this job action was that it wasn't over money or fringe benefits or even working conditions as we usually think of them. At the bottom of this strike was the feeling among the corrections officers that their contributions were not valued, that they had lost status over the years, and that administrators didn't care about them.

As is usual in a labor strike, there were no real winners. The kinds of things the officers wanted didn't fit neatly into the contract. Administrators also had no reason to smile. The strike had revealed how disaffected the corrections officers were and called into question the quality of management in the department. The inmates, too, lost. Not only was their regimen restricted by the strike, but when it was over, they faced a further embittered and frustrated guard force. An uneasy tension pervaded the state's prisons.

The administration and the union leadership knew things couldn't continue in the same way. Something had to be done to resolve the issues underlying the strike, issues that didn't fit neatly into collective-bargaining agreements and issues that didn't go away just because the officers were back at work. After discussions with university faculty, administrators and union leaders settled on a model for addressing work-related problems that had been developed in the auto industry. There, Quality of Work Life programs were cosponsored by the United Auto Workers and auto manufacturers to address problems that were not covered in contracts. In the program, workers participated in assessing work-related problems and in developing solutions to those problems through collaborative efforts between the union and the company and between the workers and the managers.

An outside consultant was brought in to manage the program in the department of corrections. The program was to be data-based and to involve groups of officers studying work-related problems and proposing solutions. The data for the program came from a survey of corrections officers that tapped levels and sources of dissatisfaction on the job as well as interest in enriching jobs. The job-enrichment items focused on officers expanding the human services aspects of the work. The survey revealed the disaffection among officers in the department. The officers felt buffeted by policies developed in the central office without their input. They felt their ideas were ignored and that administrators cared little about them. Many officers also felt their jobs provided few opportunities to pursue their interests and use their skills in dealing with inmates. They felt constrained by limited custodial roles.

Volunteer groups of corrections officers at the maximum security prisons, under the direction of the consultant, reviewed the data from the survey, studied problems at their particular institutions, and proposed solutions. The groups produced formal proposals, which included an elaborate statement of the problem to be addressed, a description of the proposed program, and a budget for the program, as well as an analysis of the resources and obstacles affecting implementation. The problems ranged from conflicts with the central office to difficulties with particular types of inmates. The variety of problems reflected differences across as well as within the state's prisons. Here are some of the programs developed by the officers:

- A program for on-the-job training of new officers using experienced officers. The aim was to improve training as well as to utilize officers' experience. The proposal detailed procedures for training new recruits in assignments throughout the facility and for evaluating the training efforts.
- A program to provide special training in counseling for officers with high inmate contact. The program included continuing in-service training, liaison arrangements with social service staff, and a record-keeping process for handling inmate problems.
- A program to provide front-line officers with opportunities to evaluate and comment on noncontractual policies that affect their jobs. The proposal spelled out the logistics for providing written feedback from line officers to prison wardens and central office on the problems created by or the advantages of new policies and procedures.
- A program of peer support for officers having problems connected with work. The proposal established training procedures for peer counselors, who would be available to assist officers with work-related problems such as abuse of sick time, unusual conflicts with inmates, or emotional problems.
- A program to involve officers in the classification of inmates and the assignment of inmates to jobs. The program built on officers' knowledge of facility resources and needs and provided for frequent exchanges of information between officers and civilian classification and placement staff.

The programs developed were tailored to the needs of the institutions where the volunteer groups of planners worked. They did, however, have some things in common. The programs recognized a variety of work-related problems experienced by officers; they provided input by officers into the management of the prisons; and they created opportunities for officers to expand their roles.

Case Study Questions

1. Consider the causes of the corrections officers' strike. In what ways do these seem related to the design of jobs? How do officer proposals address these design issues?
2. What theoretical approach or approaches underlie the job-redesign project?
3. What roles do you think management and organized labor and front-line workers can play in work redesign? Do you think collaborative efforts can be successful in the long run?

For Discussion

1. The argument has been made that Scientific Management has been influential in criminal justice and that, as managers have become

more advanced professionally, front-line criminal justice jobs have become more impoverished. Is the deprofessionalization syndrome an inevitable consequence of improvements in the technology of criminal justice? How would you suggest that jobs such as those in probation and parole be designed to provide opportunities for enrichment while still utilizing risk-assessment instruments, electronic monitors, and other technological advances?

2. Consider a specific job within the criminal justice system. What characteristics of that job are sources of motivation and what characteristics may lead to dissatisfaction or burnout? How would you redesign the job to emphasize the first set of characteristics and de-emphasize the others? Do you think others would agree or are there important individual differences to take into account?

3. Examine the job-characteristics model of Hackman and Oldham. How well does that model account for motivation in workers in criminal justice? Describe the core job characteristics of a particular job. How do they relate to important psychological states? What specific kinds of knowledge and skill, needs for growth, and satisfactions with pay and working conditions can influence the outcomes of your particular job?

4. There is some disagreement about the importance of participation in the redesign and enrichment of human services jobs. Do you feel that such participation by front-line staff is desirable? What level of participation do you support? What benefits and problems might be associated with worker participation in job design in criminal justice?

For Further Reading

Chernis, C. *Staff Burnout: Job Stress in the Human Services.* Beverly Hills, Calif.: Sage, 1980.

Hackman, J. R., and Oldham, G. *Work Redesign.* Reading, Mass.: Addison-Wesley, 1980.

Skolnick, J. H., and Bayley, D. H. *The New Blue Line: Police Innovation in Six American Cities.* New York: Free Press, 1986.

Toch, H., and Grant, J. D. *Reforming Human Services: Change Through Participation.* Beverly Hills, Calif.: Sage, 1982.

Leadership

One is tempted to say that the research on leadership has left us with the clear view that things are far more complicated and "contingent" than we initially believed and that, in fact, they are so complicated and contingent that it may not be worth our while to spin out more and more categories and qualifications. . . . At the extremes, we can be fairly confident in identifying good or bad leaders; but for most situations we will probably have little to say. We may learn a great deal about interpersonal relations but not much about organizations [Perrow, 1986].

When I am asked what leadership means to me, the first thing that comes to mind is getting the job done the way I think it should be done. That is why I always believed being an effective leader or warden in a prison really means convincing the public, the politicians, the inmates, and the correctional employees that my way of doing things is the best possible way of doing things. If I can convince people of that reality, then, I think, I am a good leader.

[Warden of a maximum security prison in the Midwest, 1986].

Many interested in the administration of criminal justice today have addressed the issue of leadership. The contemporary criminal justice administrator is expected to be an effective leader, an expectation that fits with the general demand for competent leaders in all organizations, both public and private. Although a great deal of prescriptive material describes for the criminal justice administrator how to lead an organization effectively, little empirical evidence shows what effective leadership entails. More importantly, few of the existing theoretical models of leadership created in other disciplines, which may be useful to the criminal justice administrator, have been applied to this area.

In this chapter, we provide a review of the relevant aspects of leadership and apply our understanding of the leadership process to the components of the criminal justice system. Our review, however, is not prescriptive. Instead, we offer an analytical framework for understanding the process of leadership in criminal justice organizations. This framework is rooted in empirical research and theoretical models of leadership. In this way, we hope not only to provide increased understanding of this process but in addition to suggest what can and cannot be expected from criminal justice leaders.

To accomplish these objectives, we explore several areas. First, we define leadership and argue that because criminal justice administration is fundamentally politically driven, it is useful to understand leadership within the political arena.

Second, the chapter reviews the major theories of leadership that have been developed in research on organizational behavior. Our discussion in this section integrates what we know about leadership research done in other organizations and applies these findings to the criminal justice system. Our review in this section includes an analysis of both behavioral and contingency theories of leadership. Both show promise for explaining the leadership process in criminal justice organizations.

Finally, the chapter explores the criminal justice research that addresses the issue of leadership. Although much of this literature is overly prescriptive and does not reflect the realities of criminal justice organizations, we provide an overview of those few pieces of research that empirically test theoretical models of leadership. We then make some recommendations for future research on leadership in criminal justice organizations.

Leadership Defined

Four distinct, yet not separate, ideas about administration guide our definitions of leadership. *First, leadership is a process that effectively accomplishes organizational goals.* One cannot conceptually separate leadership from organizational effectiveness (Tosi, Rizzo, and Carroll, 1986), from the accomplishment of objectives. For example, the effective police chief can lead a department to attain objectives set by the organization.

Second, leadership can be learned by people in administrative positions in organizations. Much of the literature in criminal justice management assumes that effective leadership can be taught. Millions of dollars have been spent since the 1960s by criminal justice organizations, especially police, to develop training modules that help administrators accomplish organizational goals. Although there may be little or no value to criminal justice managers in knowing the "correct" style of leadership, the characteristics of good leaders identified by empirical research can be the basis of suggestions and recommendations to criminal justice administrators about the leadership process. But these characteristics are constrained by and contingent on the tasks, functions, and objectives that the organization expects to accomplish. Even though this process of leadership is complex, we believe it can be learned and applied to the effective administration of criminal justice organizations.

Third, the leadership process is a group process. To accomplish organizational objectives, leaders must influence a number of people. In short, no group, no leader. The process of leadership must thus be examined in light of how leaders get people to achieve the tasks necessary for organizational existence and survival. Ostensibly, we may be talking about methods of compliance and power in organizations. Chapter 8 examines these topics in criminal justice organizations. For now, we want to know the kinds of techniques that are used in the relationship between a leader and subordinates. Yukl (1981:12–17) suggests eleven different techniques of influence that affect the leadership process:

1. *Legitimate request.* A person complies with an agent's request because the person recognizes the agent's "right" to make such a request.

2. *Instrumental compliance.* A person is induced to alter his or her behavior by an agent's implicit or explicit promise to ensure some tangible outcome desired by the person.

3. *Coercion.* A person is induced to comply by an agent's explicit or implicit threat to ensure adverse outcomes if the person fails to do so.

4. *Rational persuasion.* A person is convinced by an agent that the suggested behavior is the best way for the person to satisfy his or her needs or to attain his or her objectives.

5. *Rational faith.* An agent's suggestion is sufficient to evoke compliance by a person without the necessity for any explanation.

6. *Inspirational appeal.* A person is persuaded by an agent that there is a necessary link between the requested behavior and some value that is important enough to justify the behavior.

7. *Indoctrination.* A person acts because of induced internalization of strong values that are relevant to the desired behavior.

8. *Information distortion.* A person is influenced, without being aware of it, by an agent's limiting, falsifying, or interpreting information in a way that is conducive to compliance.

9. *Situational engineering.* A person's attitudes and behavior are indirectly influenced by an agent's manipulation of relevant aspects of the physical and social situation.

10. *Personal identification.* A person imitates an agent's attitudes and behavior because the person admires or worships the agent.

11. *Decision identification.* An agent allows a person to participate in and have substantial influence over the making of a decision, thereby gaining the person's identification with the final choice.

Any one or a combination of these techniques can be used. Think how administrators in criminal justice use these techniques to influence their subordinates and lead their agencies. For example, the prison warden, who rules his institution with an iron fist is employing coercion as a method of leadership, while the police sergeant is employing rational persuasion with the beat officer when he suggests that cordial interactions with citizens are essential to effective police work. Regardless of method, however, effective leaders are able to get subordinates to work toward the stated objectives of the organization.

These techniques are different from styles of leadership. A style of leadership consists of all the techniques a leader uses to achieve organizational goals. The prison warden who employs coercion, information distortion, and indoctrination as techniques of influence with inmates and corrections officers is exhibiting an autocratic style of leadership. Later in the chapter we explore other styles of leadership, some of which are more effective than others in criminal justice administration.

Fourth, leadership in public bureaucracies like the agencies of criminal justice is inherently political and must be examined within the political arena. Leadership in organizations is often discussed with an internal focus. Little is said about the external nature of leadership, even though an external view is critical to a complete understanding of how public agencies are run. A common criticism of applying research findings on leadership in private organizations to public organizations has been its limited value given the political contexts within which public organizations operate. In fact, some would say that the lack of attention in the research to the external and political nature of leadership makes many of the existing theories on leadership of little or no value to those who operate public bureaucracies.

Our position is that existing theories of leadership are relevant to understanding the leadership process within the criminal justice system, but some consideration must be given to how criminal justice administrators, as public bureaucrats, lead their agencies. In other words, we need an examination of the leadership phenomenon within the political arena.

For example, take the career of former FBI Director J. Edgar Hoover. It has been said that he employed charismatic and legitimate forms of authority (techniques of influence) to lead the FBI. This characterization, however, does not describe the political relationships that over a fifty-year period made him an effective leader of a large public bureaucracy. Leadership must thus be understood as a process that reaches well beyond the formal boundaries of the organization. As the quote at the beginning of the chapter states, leadership in criminal justice agencies involves convincing both subordinates and those outside in the political arena that a particular method (usually the leader's) is the best one for accomplishing organizational objectives.

Many leaders of criminal justice bureaucracies understand the political nature of their positions, but it is equally important that they be aware of the vacillations in public interest in and concern about their agencies. Thus, leadership of a criminal justice agency requires flexibility, but, as Selznick (1957) reminds us, public agencies must also clearly define their mission, structure this mission into their hierarchy, maintain the values of the organization that give it its identity, and control conflicts among competing interests in the organization. In short, criminal justice administrators must operate their organizations in tune with the political realities of the external environment while simultaneously maintaining their identities. Because of the tension between changes in the external political environment and the desire of the criminal justice administrator to keep control of the organization, leadership becomes a crucial and critical process. Dealing with this tension makes criminal justice administration difficult today.

In sum, then, we can define leadership as being tied invariably to the effectiveness of an organization; as being able to be learned depending on the tasks, functions, and objectives of the organization; as being carried out in a group setting; and, probably most importantly in criminal justice agencies, as having political and public foci.

Theories of Leadership

Much of what we know about leadership has been derived from research that takes one of three approaches. The first approach, and probably the oldest, is based on the instincts of the leader. It is assumed that a leader is born and not made. This approach tends to emphasize inherent personality traits of the individual. In addition, it assumes that leadership can be evaluated on the basis of the personality characteristics of the leader. Much research, however, questions whether these personality traits actually exist or, more importantly, can be viewed separately from the situational context (Tosi, Rizzo, and Carroll, 1986:553; Bass and Stogdill, 1981). Thus, it is difficult to know whether the leader's personality makeup is critical to the leadership process or whether particular traits of a leader are required for a goal to be achieved. For example, an authoritarian police sergeant may be successful in a situation that requires a clear, concise, and immediate response, e.g., a hostage situation, yet this style of leadership may be totally ineffective in a situation that requires deliberation and patience, e.g., police officer training. Because of a number of difficulties associated with this approach, it has been largely abandoned by those interested in studying the leadership process.

Much of the contemporary research done on leadership takes one of two other approaches. The behavioral approach emphasizes the behaviors of individual leaders. Much of the criminal justice research on leadership tends to use this approach. As suggested by Tosi, Rizzo, and Carroll (1986:554–557), behavioral approaches fall into two distinct areas: the distribution of influence and the task and social behaviors of leaders.

The final approach to examining the phenomenon of leadership is referred to as the contingency method. Compared with the other two methods, this approach is relatively recent and tends to emphasize multiple variables, particularly situational variables that constrain leadership. These situational variables include characteristics of subordinates, the organizational context, and the style of leadership.

Our review of behavioral and contingency models in this chapter provides us with insight into how the process of leadership has been explored by those interested in this phenomenon from the perspective of organizational behavior. Our goal is to see how and whether these theories fit the leadership process in criminal justice. We begin our review with an examination of the behavioral approaches.

Behavioral Models

Because of the many problems associated with the trait approach to understanding leadership, researchers have focused on the behaviors of leaders. This approach suggests that effective leadership depends on how the leader behaves and acts with subordinates. More importantly, the behavioral approach accentuates how leaders initiate interactions with subordinates to get them to accomplish organizational tasks. This process is known as initiating structures. For example, with a behavioral approach, we would be interested in knowing how the warden of a prison interacts with administrative staff, treatment specialists, and corrections officers so that the tasks essential to the prison's mission are completed.

In addition, behavioral approaches are concerned with how the employee is able to achieve personal goals within the organization while simultaneously accomplishing the central tasks of the organization. In our example, we would be interested in what the prison warden does to accommodate or consider the opinions, ideas, and feelings of the staff about the day-to-day workings of the prison. Do the corrections officers feel supported? Do treatment personnel feel they have a central role? Is there room for advancement in the prison's hierarchy?

These concepts of *consideration for subordinates* and *initiating structure* guide the behavioral approaches to leadership. They evolved from two separate sets of leadership studies done in the 1940s, 1950s, and early 1960s: the Ohio State Studies and the Michigan Studies. In addition, a popular model of supervision was created at this time; it is known as the *managerial grid.*

Originally devised by Blake and Mouton (1964), this grid was based on two dimensions of behavior—"concern for people" and "concern for production." These dimensions are similar to the concepts of consideration and initiating structure. Fundamentally, according to Blake and Mouton, the most effective manager is one who is both concerned with high levels of production among employees and sensitive to their needs. There has been considerable application of the managerial grid to criminal justice (see Duffee, 1986). Here, however, we do not focus on the grid but instead present the original ideas and work from which it was derived. We begin with the Ohio State Studies.

The Ohio State Studies, which began in the late 1940s, concluded that leadership could be examined on the two dimensions of consideration and initiating structure. *Consideration* is the leader's expression of concern for subordinates' feelings, ideas, and opinions about job-related matters. Considerate leaders are concerned about employees, develop trust between themselves and subordinates, and more often than not develop good communication between themselves and workers. *Initiating structure* is the leader's direction of himself or herself and of subordinates toward specific goals. The role of the leader is to make sure that an adequate structure is available for employees so that organizational objectives are accomplished. The Ohio State Studies concluded that effective leadership is present in an organization when the levels of consideration and initiating structure are high among leaders.

However, as suggested by Hellriegel, Slocum, and Woodman (1986), the central limitation of the Ohio State Studies was a failure to recognize the importance of the situation in the leadership process. The police sergeant, for example, who heads a tactical unit does not need to be considerate of employees when faced with an emergency situation. Instead, it would seem appropriate that the delineation of roles and duties be made clear to patrol officers in the unit. In this example, a high degree of initiating structure is critical. Thus, effective leadership may depend on the situation.

The Ohio State Studies seem applicable only to specific situations where both consideration and initiating structure are appropriate. Our second set of studies emphasizes one of these dimensions over the other in the leadership process.

The Michigan Studies sought to dichotomize the leadership process into two dimensions of supervisory behavior: the production-centered supervisor and the employee-centered supervisor. We know that not all supervisors behave the same with respect to their outlook toward their jobs, the employees, and the tasks required to meet the organization's objectives and goals. Some police sergeants, as immediate supervisors, are interested in high activity by subordinates, whether that be ticket writing, arrests, or some other police performance measure. Other police sergeants are concerned with the perceptions of rank-and-file officers about their roles in the organization. These supervisors care about how officers fit into the organizational hierarchy and about their level of satisfaction with their work.

According to the Michigan Studies, the effective leader, on the whole, attempts to be employee centered, which in turn engenders productive subordinates. In fact, however, it is questionable whether the phenomenon of leadership can be understood as being either employee centered or production centered.

Regardless of which approach is the more credible, both have serious problems that limit their application to criminal justice organizations. First, it is not clear that either the Ohio State Studies or the Michigan Studies adequately assessed the concept of leadership. We are concerned here with the methodological problem of construct validity. Do these studies actually measure the notion of leadership? Distinctions must be made, for example, between leadership and power. Does the prison guard who befriends an inmate and is respected by the inmate exhibit some type of leadership or what is known as referent power? How do we know what is occurring in this relationship? How can we separate the two processes both conceptually and practically? Much of the behavioral research has not made distinctions between these concepts and, as a result, it is not evident that leadership is being explored. The same point can be made about distinctions between leadership and authority. (For further discussion of the concepts of power and authority, see chapter 8.)

Second, a related concern is that much of the leadership research within the behavioral framework is based on convenient but limited conceptualizations of the leadership process. By viewing leadership in a dichotomous fashion, we are creating for ourselves, as researchers, an easy method for exploring the process of leadership, yet we may be limiting our overall understanding of the concept. Dichotomies are convenient, yet they do not always provide us with an explanation that is both testable and comprehensive. Take, for example, a police sergeant. Can we understand his leadership behavior simply by stating that he is either an employee-centered supervisor or a production-oriented supervisor? Isn't it realistic to say that he could be both? For that matter, could he not exhibit other leadership behaviors besides these two?

More importantly, isn't his leadership approach highly influenced by the tasks he has to accomplish, along with the technology available to him? He may have a task that requires subordinates to follow a predetermined set of policies and procedures, which may be the only acceptable or the only tested way of accomplishing the task. For example, the sergeant of a tactical unit may need a production-oriented style of leadership because of the nature of the work—many dangerous tasks and highly uncertain situations. Thus, to suggest that one approach to leadership is more applicable than the other in criminal justice organizations is simplistic and not sufficient for explaining the intricacies of the leadership process in those organizations.

Third, our concern with external validity revolves around the application of research findings done largely in private organizations to public organizations like criminal justice. Is it possible for the police sergeant or the corrections manager to be employee centered? In addition, what does employee centered mean in the context of the expected role of both the supervisor and the subordinate in criminal justice organizations? How are the dimensions of leadership identified by this body of research affected by the tasks of the organization? In attempting to be employee centered, is the police sergeant constrained by the tasks required? In short, is leadership affected by the situation and the tasks of the supervisor and the subordinate?

With these three criticisms in mind, we have to be cautious in applying the findings from either the Ohio State Studies or the Michigan Studies to the workings of middle-level managers or administrators in the criminal justice system. Instead, we can say that these behavioral studies were the first to address the concept of leadership in an accessible way. Much of the research in criminal justice leadership has been rooted in these studies. Although we are somewhat critical of this research, we believe that the application and testing of these theoretical models in criminal justice organizations have provided the incentive to view the leadership process in a comprehensive fashion. Recent leadership research has been in the direction of understanding the situation in criminal justice organizations. This research is rooted in contingency theories of leadership, which we discuss next.

Contingency Theories

Contingency theories of leadership differ from both trait and behavioral theories in that they emphasize the situation or context. An examination of various situational variables is important and central to an understanding of leadership in organizations, according to contingency theorists. We can see how this approach is useful for studying leadership in criminal justice organizations. The lieutenant in a prison, for example, is constrained by situational aspects in dealing with both corrections officers and prisoners. It has been well documented that prison officials cannot exercise total power. Depending on the organizational structure of the prison, there are limits to what can be done to lead groups toward the accomplishment of organizational objectives. The leadership style employed is therefore contingent on the situational aspects of the prison and the nature of the relationship between keeper and kept.

The two contingency theories we examine in this chapter are Fiedler's contingency model and the path–goal theory. Each has distinctive elements that contribute to our understanding of leadership in criminal justice organizations. In addition, from each model we can draw different implications for the management and administration of the systems of criminal justice.

Fiedler's contingency model According to Fiedler (1967), the leadership process is constrained by three major situational dimensions. First, leader–member relations are the level of trust and the degree of likeness that the leader has with subordinate groups. According to Fiedler, how well a leader is able to guide immediate subordinates is contingent on their relationship. For example, it is easy to see in police organizations that some supervisors are better liked by rank-and-file officers than other supervisors. The leader who is not liked or well received by subordinates is constrained by this situation and can be ineffective in guiding and influencing workers to accomplish organizational tasks.

Second, the task structure of the organization is, in Fiedler's (1967:53) words, "the degree to which the task is spelled out . . . or must be left nebulous and undefined." Routinized task structure has clearly defined procedures for accomplishing organizational objectives. The machine-based factory has clear directions for running the machine. It is easier to lead when the task structure is clearly defined and open to direct monitoring by the supervisor. The organization with an undefined task structure or uncertainty as to how a certain objective is to be achieved presents problems.

Most of the activities of criminal justice organizations have uncertain task structures even though these agencies have relatively stable policies and procedures because it is not all that certain that the tasks accomplish the goals professed. It is one thing to say, for example, that officers patrol the streets of the city (task), yet it is another to say that this task accomplishes the goals of crime prevention and societal protection. This uncertainty about the relationship between task performance and goal accomplishment produces agencies that, more often than not, are unstructured and loosely coupled. As a result, effective leadership becomes problematical and difficult for both administrators and immediate supervisors.

Third, the position power of the leader is the ability of the leader to exercise power in the organization. Fiedler's test of position power is the ability to hire and fire subordinates. A leader with high position power is able to hire or fire at will. A leader with low position power has limited authority to dismiss someone or bring an individual into the organization.

Here again, we can see how criminal justice administrators are constrained because they have limited authority to hire or dismiss someone. Many organizations of criminal justice, being public agencies, are governed by civil service or independent commissions that regulate, monitor, and control all personnel decisions. Administrators cannot dismiss someone without going through an elaborate process of review, typically by an external group or agency. Moreover, immediate supervisors—for example, police sergeants—have no power to make such critical decisions. In fact, much of the position power in the immediate supervisory positions of criminal justice has been limited by legal decisions, an environmental constraint over which administrators have little control. Although it would be inaccurate to state that administrators and frontline supervisors have no position power, that power is limited and is relatively weak when compared with the position power of comparable groups in the private sector.

Given these situational dimensions—leader–member relations, task structure, and position power—we can match the proper leadership styles with the right situations to produce the most effective form of leadership. Leadership style can be determined by asking leaders to describe, either favorably or unfavorably, their least-preferred co-worker. This is known as an LPC score. According to Fiedler, the leader who describes a least-preferred co-worker in a favorable manner tends to be permissive and human relations oriented. The leader who describes a least-preferred co-worker in unfavorable terms is concerned with task production and getting the job done. Moreover, Fiedler suggests that task-production leaders tend to be more effective in structured situations, while human relations–oriented leaders are more effective in situations that require a creative response on the part of supervisors and subordinates. This is not always the case, but it is generally true, according to Fiedler.

In addition, high situational control exists for a leader when there are good leader–member relations, a high task structure, and the leader has high position power. Low situational control exists when the opposite conditions are present: poor leader–member relations, low task structure, and the leader has little or no position power. Finally, moderate situation control means the situational characteristics are mixed. Some characteristics work to the advantage of the leader (for example, high leader–member relations) while others do not (poor position power) (Tosi, Rizzo, and Carroll, 1986:503–504).

By matching the degree of situational control with differing LPC orientations, we can determine the most appropriate leadership approach. The low-LPC leader would be the most effective in situations where there is low situational control (the leader–member relations are poor, low task structure, and the leader has little or no position power). In this example the low-LPC leader would be most effective in situations that required situational control and specific directions to employees. In this case, the workers may believe that their own success in accomplishing the tasks of the organization is related to the guidance of the leader. The human relations–oriented leader (high LPC) will be the most successful where the group has structured tasks and a dislike for the leader. Additionally, the human relations–oriented leader is effective in a situation where the group likes the leader and has an unstructured task.

Within criminal justice organizations, we can see how leadership style can be effective depending on situational aspects. For example, the sergeant who directs a tactical unit in a police organization may be more effective if employing a task-oriented rather than human relations–oriented leadership style because many of the tasks are structured, leader position power is relatively high (the sergeant often has direct input into who is in the unit and how they function), and strong identification with the leader is critical because of the nature of the tasks being performed. We would not expect the sergeant in this unit to ask for input from subordinates on how the unit is to be run because the sergeant has to give orders and directives to achieve the goals of the unit.

However, the situational aspects of being a supervisor of corrections officers may require a different type of leadership style. If the supervisor is well liked by the officers, tasks are only vaguely related to the goals of the organization, and he has weak position power, it may be advantageous to the supervisor to be human relations oriented. In fact, in institutional corrections today, it has been said that the uncertainty about the relationship between the tasks being performed and organizational objectives and the weak position power of both supervisors and administrators requires leaders to be more human relations oriented. In effect, corrections supervisors need to be open and flexible with subordinates if organizational goals are going to be accomplished. Yet, it can equally be argued by task-oriented leaders that if the leader–member relations in correctional institutions are poor, tasks unstructured, and leader position power weak, an autocratic management style would be the most effective.

Two basic criticisms can be leveled against this theory of leadership. First, it seems that Fiedler treats LPC as a dichotomous and unidimensional variable, implying that leaders are either task oriented or human relations oriented. The theory does not admit the possibility that leaders could be equally high on both dimensions. Our understanding of administrative behavior intuitively suggests that this is not the case, and that managers do exhibit both styles of leadership depending on the situation.

Second, there is an implicit assumption in this theory that task structure and leader–member relations cannot be modified or changed by the leader's style. Although Fiedler has argued that situational dimensions can be altered by the leader, the theory rides on the assumption that leadership style cannot be altered. More directly, Fiedler argues that it is easier to alter situations within the organization than to alter the style of leadership exhibited by the leader. For example, if leader–member relations are not good, it may be more appropriate to spend time rearranging this situation than trying to change the leader's style. There may be much truth in this statement, yet there is no reason to believe that style of leadership cannot be modified as easily as the situational dimensions. In fact, it can be reasonably argued that some situational dimensions can be affected by leadership style and changed for the good of the organization. Is it not possible, for example, that the leader can modify his or her style so that an unstructured task is more structured?

Two implications of this theory for criminal justice management can be drawn. First, if effective leadership is the goal in criminal justice organizations, then matching the right leader with specific tasks becomes critical; yet this luxury may not be possible. Given that many administrators and supervisors in criminal justice organizations are not chosen because of ability to lead but rather because of years of service, scores on tests, and loyalty to the organization, to mention a few criteria, it is not clear how leaders can be placed in specific situations. Although private organizations may have the luxury of removing and replacing ineffective leaders, such is typically not the case in criminal justice organizations. Surely, administrators attempt to identify good leaders in criminal justice agencies and promote them to positions of authority, but the selection of these administrative officials is not based solely on their leadership qualities.

Second, if Fiedler's ideas on leadership are to be applied to criminal justice agencies, then administrative officials and those in supervisory positions need training to become aware of their personality orientations and how these orientations are expressed. Such training is severely lacking, although officials have been requesting it for many years (Geller, 1985).

Path–goal theory. While Fiedler's theory of leadership attempts to isolate the situational characteristics and the orientation of the leaders in order to understand the leadership process, path–goal theory suggests that the interaction between leader behavior and the situational aspects of the organization is important (House and Mitchell, 1985). Additionally, this theory argues that leadership is linked to an expectancy theory of motivation (see chapter 4), which posits that the leader's behavior has a direct impact on the actions of employees if it is a source of satisfaction for them. In other words, leader behavior is viewed as effective if the leader is able to make satisfaction for employees contingent on good or positive performance.

Moreover, effective leadership is tied to the degree of direction and guidance that the leader can provide in the work situation. This guidance and direction can be tied to four styles of leadership. The styles of leadership are viewed as independent, yet they can all be exhibited by a leader in different situations. In short, effective leadership, according to path–goal theory, is situational, and the belief in one correct theory of leadership is invalid.

Directive leadership emphasizes the expectations of the leader and the tasks to be performed by subordinates. The leader instills into subordinates the importance of the rules and regulations of the organization and their relationship to task performance. Under this style of leadership, the leader provides the necessary guidance to subordinates to motivate them to accomplish the tasks required by the organization.

Supportive leadership stresses a concern for employees. This type of leader is friendly with employees and desires to be approachable. The primary concern of the leader is both to accomplish the tasks of the organization and to meet the needs of the workers.

Participative leadership emphasizes collaboration of the leader and subordinates. The leader employing this style attempts to involve subordinates in the decision-making process of the organization and to assure them of their importance in the organization.

Achievement-oriented leadership is concerned with having subordinates produce results. Such a leader expects that workers will attempt to do their best, and that if goals are set high enough and subordinates are properly motivated, they will achieve those goals. The leader thus has confidence that employees will achieve the stated goals and tasks.

Two contingency factors shape subordinate performance and level of satisfaction in this theory. *Subordinate characteristics* are aspects of the worker, most of which are rooted in personality. According to House and Mitchell (1985:494), three characteristics determine which leadership style will be most effective with subordinates. These are *locus of control*, where internally focused individuals are receptive to a participative leadership style and externally controlled individuals are comfortable with a directive form of leadership; *authoritarianism*, where individuals with high authoritarianism react positively to directive leadership, and those who are low in authoritarianism are receptive to participative leadership; and *ability*, where employees who are highly competent in their jobs do not need to be led or directed and benefit from a participative style of leadership, while those who are not so competent need directive leadership.

Environmental factors are characteristics of the work situation. According to path–goal theory, three environmental factors affect a subordinate's ability to perform the tasks required; these factors intervene between the subordinate and the leader. *Task* is the structure or level of uncertainty that enables the employee to accomplish the task or prevents the employee from accomplishing the task. The directive style of leadership may be appropriate when the subordinate does not understand how to do the task. Without proper leadership, the subordinate will never be able to clear the path necessary to accomplish the task; proper leadership style is critical here. The *formal authority system* of the organization may be a critical factor in the environment. If, for example, the worker perceives the formal structure of the organization as a barrier to the accomplishment of goals and thereby to the rewards associated with the accomplishment of those goals, the leader must remove the barriers so that the worker can effectively meet the stated objectives of the organization. Finally, the *primary work group* may prevent the worker from achieving organizational tasks and objectives, which in turn affects the number of rewards the worker will receive from the organization. The leader, therefore, makes sure that the task expected of the worker is clearly stated and defined, that goals of the organization are attainable and have rewards, and that there are no barriers to performance. Under optimal conditions, the leader provides the atmosphere where uncertainty about the relationship between task performance and organizational rewards is low. The leader thus clears a path through these environmental factors primarily by increasing the value of tasks and rewards, removing barriers to the accomplishment of organizational goals, and reducing uncertainty so that tasks can be achieved by subordinates.

Figure 6-1 diagrams path–goal theory. From this representation, we can see how specific leadership styles are effective given the contingent factors in both the worker and the environment of the worker. It becomes quite clear that directive leadership is the most effective (effectiveness

Figure 6-1 Summary of Path–Goal Relationships. (From R. J. House, and T. R. Mitchell, "Path–Goal Theory of Leadership," in *Organizational Behavior and Management* (4th ed.), edited by H. L. Tosi and W. C. Hamner. Cincinnati: Grid, 1985, p. 496. Reprinted by permission of the authors.)

Leader behavior	and	Contingency factors		Cause		Subordinate attitudes and behavior
1. Directive		1. Subordinate characteristics: Authoritarianism Locus of control Ability	Influence	Personal perceptions		1. Job satisfaction Job → Rewards
2. Supportive		2. Environmental factors: The task Formal authority system Primary work group	Influence	Motivational stimuli Constraints Rewards		2. Acceptance of leader Leader → Rewards
3. Achievement-oriented						3. Motivational behavior Effort → Performance Performance → Reward
4. Participative						

being defined by the degree of satisfaction expressed by workers) in situations where the task is ambiguous and uncertain, whereas this leadership style produces lower levels of satisfaction among workers when the task is relatively clear and the workers are easily able to complete the task. Supportive leadership is best employed when the tasks being performed by subordinates are stressful, dissatisfying, and frustrating. Finally, participative leadership may be the most effective when the individual is highly involved in the task or when the task is relatively nonroutine and somewhat ambiguous. In this situation, the leader provides the necessary platform for the subordinate to express concerns about how the task can be accomplished and rewards maximized. Once again, the theory suggests that the primary role of the leader is to provide the paths by which subordinates' rewards can be maximized while simultaneously meeting the objectives of the organization.

Path–goal theory can make three contributions to criminal justice administration. First, criminal justice administrators need to spell out clearly the types of rewards that subordinates can receive if and when they follow specific paths designed and structured by the organization. Quite simply, if, for example, Officer Jones is told that she will receive a promotion or a positive evaluation from her supervisor if the tasks assigned are accomplished, there must be a reward system that promotes and reinforces that behavior. All that path–goal theory suggests is that subordinates will follow and accomplish tasks defined and assigned by the organization if there are rewards attached to the accomplishment of those tasks. If leadership cannot develop and promote such a structure, then leadership is at fault.

Such may be the case in many criminal justice organizations. Take police organizations as an example. If the principles of path–goal theory were followed, administrators would have as a primary goal the removal of obstacles to officers so that they would follow the rules and regulations of the organization with the hope of being promoted some day. By applying the various styles of leadership, contingent on the personal characteristics of subordinates and the environmental characteristics of the work situation, leaders would clear the path for subordinates to accomplish the goals of the organization while simultaneously meeting their own expectations and enhancing their rewards, e.g., a promotion.

Yet, police organizations often cannot provide the rewards sought by police officers. Supervisors have little control over reward distribution, and therefore the style of leadership exhibited by the supervisor is somewhat meaningless. If, for example, a court orders a police department to hire and promote minority candidates over majority candidates because of past practices of discrimination in the department, the police supervisor may have limited control over who gets promoted and, more importantly, may have a difficult time convincing subordinates that there actually is a "clear" path to promotion or mobility in the organization.

Second, path–goal theory suggests, quite correctly, that no one style of leadership is sufficient for all the situations faced by criminal justice administrators and supervisors. This point cannot be stated too often. In many instances, good administrators in criminal justice organizations have recognized that proper leadership requires a correct assessment of the situation. Additionally, it becomes clear that leadership is an ongoing and proactive process that demands constant evaluations of multiple situations. More importantly, leaders have to constantly reevaluate the situations faced by subordinates and how paths can be cleared for the attainment of both organizational objectives and the goals of the employee.

Third, path–goal theory requires that criminal justice administrators design paths and goals for criminal justice employees that are reasonable and attainable. Path–goal theory assumes active leadership on the part of supervisors. Criminal justice administrators who do not clarify paths for subordinates only create confusion for themselves and much alienation and disillusionment among employees. Such ineffective leadership places obstacles between supervisor and subordinate that may be difficult to overcome.

Leadership Research in Criminal Justice

We stated in the beginning of the chapter that there has been little empirical testing of the theoretical models of leadership in criminal justice organizations. The theoretical testing that has been done, in addition, is still rooted in some of the positions of researchers in the 1950s (the Ohio State Studies and the Michigan Studies). This situation may be caused by slow application of current theoretical models of leadership to criminal justice organizations or the limited number of reliable instruments to test these rather new theoretical positions. Regardless, we do have some research, particularly in the police field, that can tell us about leadership in criminal justice agencies and from which implications for management can be drawn.

Research by Kuykendall and Unsinger (1982) suggests that police managers have a preferred leadership orientation. Employing an instrument created by Hershey and Blanchard (1977), the researchers found that police managers are likely to use styles of leadership known as selling (high task and high relationship emphasis), telling (high task and low relationship emphasis), and participating (high relationship and low task emphasis), with very little concern for delegating (low relationship and low task emphasis). These styles of leadership are similar to those discussed previously. Of these the most preferred is the selling style. The researchers suggest that police managers are no less effective than managers in other organizational settings and that the selling, telling, and participating styles lead to organizational effectiveness.

Similar findings were generated by Swanson and Territo (1982) in their research involving 104 police supervisors in the Southeast in the late 1970s. Using the managerial grid, the researchers found that their sample of police supervisors showed high concern for both production and people, and emphasized team management in their organizations. Additionally, employing other measures, the researchers found that police supervisors used a style of communication that emphasized the open and candid expression of the manager's feelings and knowledge to subordinates rather than a style of communication that emphasized feedback from subordinates to managers about their supervisory capabilities. This research suggested that police managers had an open communication style with subordinates and supported the idea that police managers were indeed democratic in their leadership styles. (At least they professed to be.)

Later research, however, suggests that such a participative and democratic leadership style is not as ubiquitous in police organizations as previously indicated. Auten (1985), for example, found in his sample of police supervisors and operations personnel in state police agencies in Illinois that the dominant managerial model was the traditional paramilitary one, with one-way communication. In addition, these police supervisors and operations personnel strongly believed that they had no meaningful role in organizational decision making. The researchers suggest that there were communications breakdowns between the supervisory and operations personnel and the administrative heads of the agencies.

Not only is there limited consensus as to what type of leadership styles predominate among police managers and administrators, but when police supervisors are asked to think about a leadership style as opposed to acting out a style in a specific situation, they tend to change their approaches to leadership (Kuykendall, 1985). It is quite apparent that what one thinks is an appropriate style of leadership may not be in agreement with what one actually does in a given situation.

Nevertheless, much of what we know from leadership research done in police agencies suggests that police managers and administrators usually employ a style of leadership that is both task centered and employee centered. Although we would like this style to also be that of police administrators, other kinds of evidence suggest that maybe the high degree of concern for employees expressed by police administrators in our leadership research is not totally accurate. Current research, for example, on occupational stress, high turnover, absenteeism, and substance abuse in the police field suggests that the traditional paramilitary structure of police organizations, with its emphasis on an autocratic style of leadership, creates and perpetuates these problems. These problems may be traced to other factors in the police role, e.g., the danger associated with the job, yet it is important to examine how specific leadership styles contribute to many of these problems. Much leadership research in policing is lacking in this area.

With regard to corrections, much of what we know about leadership is rooted in highly prescriptive material, which limits our understanding of the process. However, many of the problems experienced in police organizations are experienced equally in correctional organizations; hierarchical structure, limited and often rigid communications systems, and centralized decision-making authority in correctional organizations produce many of these problems (Archambeault and Archambeault, 1982). Like police research, leadership research in corrections is not only limited but offers little information that is useful to corrections administrators.

Given the current state of research in both police organizations and correctional organizations with respect to the leadership process, we recommend that the following issues be addressed by those interested in understanding leadership in these organizations in the future. First, we need additional research on how criminal justice administrators actually lead their organizations. From this data, prescriptions for policy can be increasingly informed and useful to the criminal justice manager. Much existing research is out of date and tells us little about the increasing complexities of the leadership process.

Second, there needs to be increased awareness of the contemporary models of leadership offered by organizational behavior theory. For example, it would seem critical that contingency approaches be examined in relation to criminal justice organizations, along with refinement of instruments to test these theories in the criminal justice environment. The situational aspects that influence the leadership process must be examined in the operations of criminal justice systems. Too often research in criminal justice organizations has been set up to ascertain whether administrators are participative or autocratic in relation to their subordinates. Maybe it is time to stop searching for the perfect criminal justice manager and to begin examining situational aspects of the work environment that constrain administrators in their leadership functions.

Third, to fully understand the leadership phenomenon in criminal justice organizations it is imperative that new methodologies allow us to look at the intricacies associated with the leadership process. Traditional survey methods in criminal justice organizations have yielded some valuable information, yet field methods would provide information about the actual leadership mechanisms used by criminal justice administrators. To understand the leadership process, it would be helpful to watch and document what criminal justice leaders do and, more importantly, to be able to distinguish effective criminal justice leaders from ineffective ones. In this way, prescriptions for administrators would be informed by data and useful in their day-to-day interactions with subordinates.

Finally, we need to discuss how much we can expect of our criminal justice managers in the way of leadership. It is common to blame the poor performance of subordinates on ineffective management or leadership. We have heard this complaint often in criminal justice organizations. Yet, it is shortsighted to suggest that all problems in criminal justice can be attributed to faulty leadership. Criminal justice administrators have limited or no control over some aspects of the work of their organizations. As a result, requesting a new leader "to set the organization back on path" is probably, in the words of Hall (1982:158), "little more than a cosmetic treatment."

For example, an uncertain and unstable political environment makes multiple demands on a police chief. Not being able to appease all groups all the time, the chief is constrained in decision making. On many occasions, because the chief has limited resources and multiple demands, all the expectations of everyone in the community for police services cannot be met. Too often the chief is viewed as being an ineffective leader when leadership has little to do with this problem. To be effective a leader must provide some degree of control over the external environment. But we need to be realistic about how much a police administrator can control. Perhaps, for this reason, many experts recommend that incoming police chiefs develop clear and stable relations with local political groups so that expectations can be spelled out on both sides (Murphy, 1985).

Summary

This chapter began with an examination of criminal justice leadership in a political context. Our purpose was to suggest that the criminal justice administrator more often than not has to be politically astute. Additionally, it must be understood, however, that only so much can be expected of the criminal justice administrator and that the charge of ineffective leadership is often incorrect and unfair.

The chapter, moreover, reviewed the theories of leadership offered in the literature on organizational behavior. From this review, it is apparent that leadership is an important process in organizations. All the models can provide us with some information about leadership in the organizations of criminal justice. Clearly leadership is a complex and often misunderstood process. Understanding the styles of leadership, the contingent factors that affect the leadership process, and the paths that enable employees to accomplish both personal and professional goals is valuable in understanding criminal justice administration and offering prescriptions to managers in these organizations.

Although the theoretical insights are available to us, we have not fully applied or tested many of these approaches in criminal justice. Much of the literature has been prescriptive and not data informed. Moreover, most of the theoretical testing that has been done in criminal justice organizations has been limited and exclusively applied to police organizations. We called for additional research and suggested that contingency approaches be examined in the organizations of criminal justice. Only through critical research can we comprehend how the leadership process operates and, more importantly, offer valuable insights to those people who administer and manage our criminal justice organizations.

CASE STUDY

Supervising the Police Officer: The Leadership Factor

The Ragsdale Police Department had a long history of operating under the traditional paramilitary model, with a clear chain of command and discernible lines of authority. More often than not, police officers understood and legitimized this structure. However, the common council demanded that the department alter its method of operation and become receptive to the demands of the community. A number of incidents had involved police officers and members of the minority community; in one such incident, the police were accused of employing heavy-handed tactics with the patrons of a local bar owned by a prominent black politician. This incident, along with some minor altercations with other minority citizens, led the Fire and Police Commission to demand changes in the department. Under pressure, the conservative, long-time police chief resigned.

In came an outsider from a large, urban department who had a progressive philosophy toward policing. In particular, he emphasized openness and flexibility when interacting with the public. The first thing newly hired Police Chief Beckworth instituted was a democratic management style in the department. Officers were encouraged to question and discuss the policies of the department and to make suggestions. Initially, the officers were somewhat hesitant about the new police chief. Why did he feel it necessary to change the old ways of doing things in the department? Many officers expressed the opinion that the chief was only playing into the hands of all the citizen groups. One of those officers was Michael Jeske.

Jeske was a veteran with more than twenty-five years in the department and a cynical attitude toward new policing ideas. "All this talk about opening up the department to the public is a bunch of baloney. What the hell do citizens know about policing anyway?" Spouting his views at a local union meeting, he received a lot of support from fellow officers. "And another thing," he shouted, "all this bullshit about how the department is going to be more open to the officers and listen to their input is dangerous. I have seen this in the past, and it never worked. It's like your honeymoon; after the first couple of weeks, it's all downhill." Knowing that the officers were somewhat hesitant to accept some of his progressive ideas, the chief decided to meet with the recognized leaders of the department, those who were respected by other officers and wielded much power among them. Because the department had only 500 officers, Chief Beckworth was able to identify the informal leaders among the officers through their sergeants.

Chief Beckworth met with twenty officers whom his lieutenants and sergeants had identified as the leaders among the troops. Chief Beckworth began the meeting by saying, "My goal here is to get to know you guys better and to discuss any suggestions that you have about running this department." Officer Jeske sat in the back of the room and listened intently as other officers asked superficial questions. "Is there any way we can get warmer jackets for the winter months?" Knowing that the meeting wasn't going anywhere and getting somewhat frustrated, Chief Beckworth decided to end it when Officer Jeske jumped in and shouted, "Pretty damn frustrating isn't it?" Chief Beckworth looked toward the back of the room where Jeske was sitting and replied, "Yes it is, and what are you going to do to relieve my frustrations here?" Jeske quickly responded, "Now you know how the officers feel about the leadership in this department." Chief Beckworth, realizing that he had an opening with the men through this incident, jumped on it quickly. "What do you mean and what can be done to improve the leadership in the department?"

Officer Jeske leaned back and looked at Chief Beckworth while the other officers sat in their chairs motionless. "The first thing you administrators have to realize is that we are not dummies and can figure out when we are getting snowed. You say that your ideas are going to open up the department and make it more flexible. You say that you are going to listen to the men more than in the past. The one thing you did not ask before this all started was whether we were even interested in your ideas. You talk about having us participate in the organization, but you didn't even ask us if we wanted to. I think that a number of us officers believe that leadership in the department starts with the chief being honest with the troops from the beginning. You have got to remember that a lot of chiefs have come and gone in this department and almost all of us have experienced the changes. We know a good leader; it starts with honesty up front and concern for the officers' welfare. Right now we don't know if you're an honest chief or another political hack from city hall."

Chief Beckworth was amazed by the openness of Officer Jeske and promised to be honest to the men. "I guess we are going to have to see your honesty and leadership in action. We'll then make a decision about you," replied Jeske. Chief Beckworth could only hope that he would be the leader his officers expected. He left the informal meeting knowing that effective leadership was going to exist only if a commitment to it was shown by the administrators at the top of the organization, starting with himself.

Case Study Questions

1. Given the climate of the Ragsdale Police Department, what recommendations would you give Chief Beckworth about leadership?
2. How should Chief Beckworth approach Officer Jeske about his cynical attitude toward the department?
3. Can you suggest a career path model to Chief Beckworth that would improve the morale of officers in the Ragsdale Police Department?

For Discussion

1. Discuss the limitations of leadership in criminal justice organizations. Do the best individuals become criminal justice administrators or managers? If not, why not? In addition, are many of the problems associated or attributed to criminal justice leadership really leadership problems? Discuss prison overcrowding, for example. Can we expect a prison

warden to effectively manage an overcrowded prison? Is overcrowding in prisons a corrections problem that administrators can address, or is it a societal problem? Explore this issue with respect to the role of leaders trying to deal with this complex problem.

2. Explore the findings of the Ohio State Studies and the Michigan Studies as they apply to the agencies of criminal justice. Are they applicable or not? What about participation in leadership in criminal justice systems? Should criminal justice managers be concerned with the personal aspects of employees' lives? Will this concern necessarily translate into effective leadership and productive criminal justice employees? Why or why not?

3. Suggest a specific path–goal model that can be employed by a criminal justice manager. Discuss the implications of your path–goal model for effective leadership in that organization of criminal justice. Finally, examine possible obstacles that would prevent the attainment of goals by subordinates under this approach to leadership.

4. Offer some concrete suggestions about leadership to a police chief, using one of the theories of leadership examined in this chapter as a model. Ask for feedback from the chief on the feasibility of your proposals and their effectiveness in a police organization.

For Further Reading

Bass, B. M. (Ed.). *Stodgill's Handbook of Leadership.* New York: Free Press, 1981.

Fiedler, F. A. *A Theory of Leadership Effectiveness.* New York: McGraw-Hill, 1967.

Geller, W. A. (Ed.). *Police Leadership in America: Crisis and Opportunity.* Chicago: American Bar Association, 1985.

Ouchi, W. *Theory Z: How American Business Can Meet the Japanese Challenge.* Reading, Mass.: Addison-Wesley, 1981.

PART 3

GROUP BEHAVIOR IN CRIMINAL JUSTICE ORGANIZATIONS

An organization is more than a collection of individuals. Organizations influence the people within them in both formal and informal ways. The interactions of individuals of equal status within the organization, communication along hierarchical lines, and contact between workers in criminal justice and offenders or the general public all contribute to the culture and ethos of criminal justice organizations. In this field, theory and research have looked beyond the individual to group influences to explain such problems as conflict, corruption, and the abuse of power. In Part Three we examine the role of the group within criminal justice organizations. We consider how groups shape what goes on and how managers can influence that process.

CHAPTER 7

Occupational Socialization

- [ ] What Is Occupational Socialization?
- [ ] The Socialization Process
- [ ] Problems in the Socialization Process
- [ ] Socialization and the Police
- [ ] Socialization in Corrections
- [ ] Strategies for Socialization
- [ ] Summary
- [ ] Case Study
- [ ] For Discussion
- [ ] For Further Reading

Becoming a federal judge is like being thrown into the water and told to swim [a federal judge quoted in Carp and Wheeler, 1972:372].

When the recruits first come to the academy, each staff member is introduced to the recruits and allowed time to say a few words to them. When it is my turn, I tell them in no uncertain terms that I am there to train them and that they are there to do what they are told. When I am done with my speech, I make every one of them get out of their seats and do twenty push-ups. I don't care if they're in a suit or in a dress, they do the push-ups. I want them to know right off who the boss is [a police academy trainer quoted in Charles, 1986:34].

And I walked in the first day and an officer threw a big bunch of keys down on the table and walked out. Didn't tell me nothing. But there was an inmate who broke me in. His daddy and my daddy used to work in the mines together. He broke me in, the inmate did [a corrections officer quoted in Roszell, 1987].

Stanley Kubrick's film *Full Metal Jacket* vividly portrays the process of changing young recruits into marines trained and willing to fight and die for their country. All organizations have processes (usually less dramatic than those used by the marines) for converting people into organizational members with appropriate attitudes and behaviors. In this chapter we examine the process by which recruits into the occupations of criminal justice become seasoned. We examine the socialization influences on judges, parole officers, and other criminal justice professionals from both a theoretical and practical perspective. We also consider difficulties in the socialization process that may contribute to such problems as stress or misconduct. In particular, we review the research on the socialization of the police and the socialization of corrections officers. We focus on recruitment as well as formal and informal training practices. Finally, we consider the ways in which managers influence the process of socialization in criminal justice organizations.

What Is Occupational Socialization?

Occupational socialization is the process by which a person acquires the values, attitudes, and behaviors of an ongoing occupational social system. It is a continuous process and includes both intentional influences, such as training, and unintentional influences, such as the locker-room or work-group culture. The attitudes, values, and behaviors acquired as a result of occupational socialization can include those regarded as appropriate and legitimate for the job as well as those that are illegitimate and even illegal. Thus judges may learn appropriate sentence lengths for offenders, but judges convicted in the 1986–1988 Greylord investigations in Chicago argued that they also learned to accept bribes because of the shared view that they were underpaid compared with their lawyer peers. Similarly, police learn to implement the law of arrest, but even "good" cops learn to bend the rules on the job. When Officer Robert Leuci (whose story was told in the movie *Prince of the City*) was collecting evidence on police corruption in New York for the Knapp Commission in the early 1970s, he testified also to giving drugs to addicted informants in exchange for information, and some believe he committed many more serious crimes (Dershowitz, 1983).

Behavior in organizations remains remarkably stable despite frequent turnover of personnel. Organizational behavior persists as long as the attitudes, beliefs, perceptions, habits, and expectations of organizational members remain constant. This consistency is particularly evident in criminal justice organizations. The practices of police officers and prison staff often seem unchanging and even resistant to change efforts. One common assessment of legal efforts to change criminal justice organizations is that the courts seem more efficient at bringing about procedural than substantive change. Prison discipline hearings, for example, continue to be characterized as dispositional rather than adjudicatory despite case law requiring impartial, trial-like hearings. How can we account for the fact that almost all inmates are found guilty by prison disciplinary boards? Although inmate behavior is probably most important, part of the explanation may also be found in the concept of organizational role. Katz and Kahn (1978) give the social–psychological concept of role a central place in their theory of organizations. For them, organizations are best understood as systems of roles. These roles link the individual to the organization and assure its continued stability.

Katz and Kahn define *role behavior* as the recurring actions of an individual that are appropriately related to the repetitive activities of others so as to yield a predictable outcome. In addition, they view role behavior as a function of social setting rather than the individual personalities of people in organizations. Role theorists, therefore, suggest that workers engage in both formal and informal learning processes to become aware of and committed to behavioral norms that are seen as appropriate for their job.

This socialization hypothesis, however, is not the only explanation for the shared sets of behaviors that appear to be associated with some occupations. Some researchers have suggested that occupational behaviors are a function of personality rather than socialization. That is, some occupations may attract certain types of people. Research on the working personality of the police has been influenced by this perspective. Some researchers have argued that the personality traits of individual police officers differ from those of the general public prior to their entering the police field (Rokeach, Miller, and Snyder, 1971). Police work has been said to attract recruits who are more authoritarian, more cynical, and more oriented toward excitement than the public at large.

This explanation of police behavior is currently out of favor, however. A number of studies have failed to find significant differences in the attitudes of police officer recruits and the general public, and the original research has been criticized for methodological shortcomings (see Bennett, 1984). Researchers continue to utilize the socialization model, which focuses on the nature of police work itself and the process by which novices are recruited from the general public and become experienced officers.

The Socialization Process

A study of judges illustrates the process of socialization within the federal judiciary. Through in-depth interviews with federal judges, Carp and Wheeler (1972) were able to describe the process by which a lawyer becomes an experienced trial judge. Legal training itself is a lengthy and intense socialization experience. Still, the authors found that novice judges were ill prepared for the problems they faced.

The problems encountered by new judges fell into three categories: legal, administrative, and psychological. The first of these problems arose because of the limited legal experiences of the judges. Most had come from firms dealing primarily with civil suits, and the most common problem of these judges was ignorance of the criminal law. The second complaint was heavy caseloads and difficulty in preventing backlogs. Finally, the judges complained of the psychological stresses of loneliness, of maintaining judicial bearing on and off the bench, and of local pressures in decision making.

The research described a variety of formal and informal mechanisms for addressing these problems. The most conspicuous source of formal socialization is the New Judges' Seminars sponsored by the Federal Judicial Center in Washington, D.C. Although the purpose of these seminars is formal education through speakers and workshops, the judges noted that their primary benefit was informal discussions with other judges. Although less obvious, the most potent source of socialization for new judges was practicing judges in the same court as well as court staff. Carp and Wheeler highlight the distinctive local nature of judicial socialization and its resulting perpetuation of local and regional differences in the judiciary. Senior judges perpetuated local procedures and attitudes by providing their junior colleagues with legal information, administrative advice, and personal reassurances. Likewise, local attorneys with particular specialties often influenced novice judges with limited knowledge in these areas.

One judge described the net result of the socialization process as membership in a fraternal organization characterized by mutual respect and a feeling of brotherhood. (There were no female judges in the study.)

The power of socialization can be overstated, however. The fact that socialization is not perfect is illustrated in the case of Federal District Judge Harry Claiborne. The judge refused to resign his post and continued to collect a salary while imprisoned for income tax evasion. The Senate ultimately voted to impeach the judge to remove him from office.

Stages of Socialization

The case of judicial socialization calls our attention to several factors important in the transmission of organizational roles. In particular, socialization is a process. A model of socialization, therefore, must deal not only with the substantive dimension of the roles but also with change over time and the nature of the influences producing change.

The socialization literature generally divides the process of change into three distinct stages: anticipatory, formal, and informal. The socialization process begins prior to the entry of an individual into an occupation. In this *anticipatory stage,* those considering a particular field begin to anticipate the demands and expectations of their future job. They begin to adopt attitudes and values they believe are consistent with the occupation, and they come to view themselves as members of a group. During this stage, individuals are influenced by two main reference groups. First, those tangential to the occupation, such as friends and family, may transmit their views of the job. For example, a lawyer seeking to join the judiciary may be influenced by family members' views of the status of the job. Second, members of the occupation may directly transmit information about the job. Lawyers working with judges gain insight into what is perceived as appropriate or inappropriate behavior for a member of the judiciary. Along with these sources of influence, both the amount of time in the anticipatory stage and the accuracy of information received affect the adoption of organizational roles.

When a person joins a particular occupation, the second, or *formal, stage* in socialization usually occurs. This is generally a period of formalized training. For judges the formalized training period is shorter and less powerful than that for many other occupations within criminal justice. The New Judges' Seminars are the primary means of formal socialization. In police work and corrections, the training academy immerses recruits into an occupational role. Aside from providing important information about doing a job, the formal training process serves a variety of other functions through exposure to experienced veterans. This reference group provides normative prescriptions for the attitudes and behaviors of the recruits. In doing so, it also creates feelings of belonging and acceptance. The New Judges' Seminars are valued not only for imparting technical knowledge but also for fostering relationships that provide membership in a group. Here the origins of the judicial fraternity can be found.

The third and ongoing phase of socialization is the *informal stage.* In this stage the relevant reference group is peers, managers, and even clients to whom a worker is exposed on a daily basis. Here the routine of the job shapes the role of the criminal justice worker. For judges, daily associations with their staffs and with lawyers influence the uniquely local nature of their roles. For some police and corrections officers, the positive values gained at the academy may give way in the informal stage to cynicism, alienation, and even corruption.

A Model of Influences

Although the stages of socialization illustrate the process of change, a specific model is needed to explain the manner in which socializing influences affect the individual. A theoretical model of the process of taking organizational roles has been detailed by Katz and Kahn (1978). Their social–psychological model relies on four key concepts, as shown in figure 7-1. *Role expectations* are the standards by which the behavior of an organizational member is judged. Different and even conflicting expectations may be held by supervisors, peers, clients, and even the general public. The *sent role* refers to the communication of those expectations

Figure 7-1   A Theoretical Model of Factors Involved in the Taking of Organizational Roles. (From D. Katz, and R. L. Kahn, *The Social Psychology of Organizations,* 2nd Ed. Copyright © 1978 by John Wiley & Sons, Inc. Reprinted by permission.)

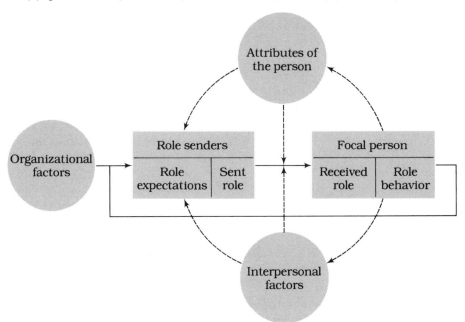

to the member. The *received role* is the person's perceptions and understanding of the sent role. Finally, *role behavior* is the person's response to the complex information received. According to this model, then, the behavior of an organizational member is the result of expectations communicated by significant others and filtered through his or her own psychological processes. The role-taking model thus calls our attention to key variables that may help explain role behavior.

The model also indicates that a person's behavior affects expectations through a feedback process—that is, conformity or lack of conformity to role expectations may influence the sent role over time. In her study of parole, Studt (1978) describes "escalation episodes," in which parolees dramatically altered the role of parole officers. Ordinarily parole officers viewed their role as one of helping within a context of casual surveillance. This role was sustained by the lack of information about a parolee's misbehavior. When, however, officers did receive information about even minor transgressions, they escalated their surveillance role. In one example, an agent arranged for the release of a parolee who had been arrested for an unpaid traffic ticket. The agent set up a meeting with the parolee that afternoon, but the parolee was late.

> The common-law wife was at home with her new baby; she took this occasion to tell the agent she was considering leaving the parolee because he was sometimes physically rough with her. The rest of the afternoon was largely devoted to activities that ranged from searching the extensive case record for evidence of previous violence to investigating the possibility that the parolee's aged parents could provide housing for him temporarily, pending the results of further investigation. By the end of the afternoon, although the parolee had not yet been interviewed, the agent and the supervisor were outlining the case for revocation [Studt, 1978:80].

Katz and Kahn also point out that the process of role taking does not occur in isolation and is shaped by several other factors in the model including organizational, interpersonal, and individual factors. Studt points out, for example, that organizational concerns are a strong factor in the decision to revoke parole. The important question in this case was the extent to which the parolee's conduct could expose the organization to criticism. Other organizational factors that may affect role taking include organizational size and level of bureaucratization. Large, bureaucratized organizations, for example, may support impersonal attitudes among staff. Finally, evidence indicates that position in the organizational hierarchy influences role taking. Even when supervisors are recruited from the front lines, they may take on new roles widely different from those of their former colleagues. Some managerial orientations are a result of position rather than individual character, as was illustrated in a study of corrections staff by Duffee and O'Leary (1980). Front-line officers viewed their activity as centering on order maintenance and restraint, but supervisors were supportive of rehabilitation goals.

Another moderator of the role-taking process is interpersonal relationships. The relationship between parole officer and parolee, for example, appears to affect the parole agent's role. It takes time for a parolee to understand an officer's expectations. Once those expectations are understood, surveillance may be deemphasized. Even a "good" relationship, however, can be disrupted by an incident that triggers an escalation episode.

Finally, roles are also influenced by individual differences in approach to the job. Studt found that some agents were "just doing the job," while others seemed most interested in catching offenders for rule violations. Some emphasized treating parolees with a modicum of respect; some emphasized predictability in their supervision relationships. Such individual orientations can still be accommodated by the general model of role taking.

Problems in the Socialization Process

Evidence for the power of the role-taking model can be found all around us in the patterned behavior of organizational members. Still, there is abundant evidence that the process of role taking is not as straightforward as the model may imply. In criminal justice the most often discussed problem is that of role conflict. In the model, *role conflict* is the occurrence of two or more role expectations such that compliance with one makes compliance with another difficult or impossible. Conflicting expectations may come from two or more role senders or may emanate from a single role sender. These problems are endemic in all street-level bureacracies and particularly in criminal justice. Lipsky (1980), for example, argues that one of the defining characteristics of all street-level bureaucracies is competing goals. This competition is expressed in the conflicting expectations of front-line workers. Police officers are charged with controlling crime as well as meeting due process constraints. Probation and parole officers must provide surveillance of their caseload to prevent crimes and assure compliance with rules, but they must also provide a supportive atmosphere and services to assist in adjustment to the community. In addition to conflicts over substantive goals, all human service workers are sent conflicting messages about the process of their work. Although the importance of providing custodial or helping services is stressed, these services are to be provided to large caseloads of clients. Probation and parole officers may supervise an average of seventy clients. Demands on time thus accentuate conflicts in the role.

Perhaps the literature on institutional corrections best illustrates the problem of role conflict. In his study of a maximum security prison in Rhode Island, Carroll (1974:52) described the basis for role conflict.

Prior to 1956, the officers were "guards" and their role was precisely defined. The sole functions of the guard were to maintain security and internal order. . . . Today the official title of the custodial staff is "correctional officer," a title that both incorporates and symbolizes the conflicting and ambiguous definitions of their current role. As the term *officer* connotes, the custodians remain organized in a military hierarchy, the function of which is to ensure security and order. But the adjective *correctional* connotes an additional expectation of equal priority [—that of changing offenders].

In his study of corrections officers at Auburn (New York) penitentiary, Lombardo (1981) found a similar sort of role conflict. Although the security role of officers required high degrees of social distance from inmates, the informal counseling roles adopted by some officers demanded low social distance. About a third of the officers studied found conflict between these roles. One officer provided the following illustration of the conflict.

There's been times I could have done something for a guy, but I couldn't because of the rules. In one situation where they'd gassed a whole section, the guys [inmates] were vicious. They [other officers and supervisors] wouldn't help them. I opened the windows and turned on the water. One guy was vomiting. I called the medical authorities. The guy wanted air, and I wanted to give him a cup of milk. The medical personnel says no. So there was nothing I could do [Lombardo, 1981:138].

Research into the effects of role conflict indicates that it results in low job satisfaction and poor performance. Role conflict has been found to be a principal cause of stress among corrections officers. It has also been suggested that the conflict "immobilizes" officers and makes them ineffective in both their roles. Other research suggests that conflict over roles causes staff to emphasize their most clearly defined tasks. In their study of Illinois prison guards, Jacobs and Retsky (1975:27) found that "guards are most likely to fall back on their security and maintenance role because it is the only role on which they can be objectively evaluated."

Related to role conflict is the problem of *role ambiguity*. With role ambiguity there is uncertainty about what the occupant of a particular office is supposed to do—that is, the sent message is unclear. This problem often manifests itself in the lack of clear performance criteria, a common complaint among police and corrections staff and a major source of stress on the job (Terry, 1983:162). Wilson (1968), for example, notes that the police have been given tasks that cannot all be performed to the satisfaction of society. Police are destined to be viewed as either ineffective or overly repressive. In their maintenance function, for example, differing expectations about what constitutes a just resolution of a dispute between two parties often leave police officers with great discretion and little direction.

In his classic essay, Gresham Sykes (1971) describes the ambiguity in the role of the corrections officer. He points out that the goals of punishment and rehabilitation provide little direction. Questions of what is appropriate punishment remain unanswered, and the technology for changing offenders' behavior is uncertain. The corrections officer is, therefore, left with an uncertain mandate. The officer must gain compliance from inmates and maintain control within the prison. This mandate is accomplished through accommodations, which Sykes describes as the corruption of the guard's authority. Officers allow inmates to violate some minor rules to gain cooperation "when it counts." Others also note that the corrections officers who are regarded as good by their superiors are the ones who get the best compliance without having to resort to formal disciplinary procedures.

General performance prescriptions provide little concrete advice for officers. As with role conflict, officers may seek additional direction. After a survey of maximum security guards, Poole and Regoli (1980) concluded that role stress, defined as perceived uncertainty about job expectations, was positively associated with custodial orientation—that is, those officers experiencing role ambiguity were most likely to define their job in narrow custodial terms.

Lee and Visano (1981) discuss a special case of role-related problems in criminal justice. These authors focus on the concept of *official deviance,* which they define as "actions taken by officials which violate the law and/or the formal rules of the organization but which are clearly oriented toward the needs and goals of the organization, as perceived by the official, and thus fulfill certain informal rules of the organization" (1981:216). Thus official deviance does not benefit the individual as corruption may but is aimed at furthering the perceived goals of the organization. In most cases role incumbents regard official deviance as expected and thus as part of their job. This was the case when Lieutenant Colonel Oliver North and Admiral John Poindexter testified in the Iran–Contra hearings that they originally misled Congress to avoid disclosure of aid to the Nicaraguan Contras.

Criminal justice provides numerous examples of official deviance. Blumberg's (1967) study illustrates official deviance among public defenders. Defense lawyers and particularly public defenders are expected to maintain ongoing relationships with judges and prosecutors. Relationships with most clients are transitory. As a result, defense attorneys often pressure clients to plead guilty in order to process cases efficiently. They may even conspire with other courtroom actors to increase punishments for seemingly guilty clients who insist on going to trial.

The pressures supporting official deviance were also revealed in investigations of the security service of the Royal Canadian Mounted Police (RCMP).

[Members of the RCMP] are formally bound through law and the rules of the RCMP organization to uphold the laws of Canada. But they are informally instructed that they must engage in such "dirty tricks" as illegal break-ins and wiretappings, kidnapping, theft of documents, faking of documents, and even arson. Superior officers of the RCMP have admitted to a federal inquiry on RCMP "wrongdoing" that members of the security services who refused to engage in dirty tricks because they were illegal would be punished by transfers, denial of promotions, and so forth. At the same time, Mounties were warned that if caught, the RCMP would deny any knowledge of their activities and leave them to defend themselves as best they could [Lee and Visano, 1981:218].

The cases of public defenders and Mounties clearly show differences in the severity of official deviance but both reflect responses to conflicting demands in criminal justice. Neither example can be explained by viewing individual actors as bad apples; instead, all are responding to role expectations.

The bad-apple theory has also been rejected as a useful explanation for *corruption*, which does result in personal gain. In fact, in its investigation of police corruption in New York, the Knapp Commission (1972:114) went so far as to note that the elimination of bad apples was a "proven obstacle to meaningful reform." The explanation of corruption as the product of a few aberrant individuals ignores organizational structures and operational codes that establish norms and expectations that permit corruption to grow and spread through organizations. As the Knapp Commission (1972:114) noted, "even those who themselves engage in no corrupt activities are involved in corruption in the sense that they take no steps to prevent what they know or suspect to be going on."

No aspect of criminal justice is immune to corruption. Investigations into corruption in the Cook County (Illinois) courts between 1986–1988 resulted in nearly sixty federal indictments for case fixing and payoffs. Probation officers have been known to exact sexual favors from clients who sought to avoid revocation; corrections officers have been prosecuted for smuggling drugs into prisons and even for aiding in prison escapes. Most of the research on corruption, however, has focused on the police.

Studies of police corruption have investigated behavior ranging from accepting an occasional free meal to participating in burglary rings. Much of the research has examined the sources of support for corrupt practices. Sherman (1974), for example, argues that a rookie police officer's work group exercises considerable influence. The likelihood of new officers' accepting bribes is related to the extent to which such practices already occur in the work group. In fact, failure to indulge in corrupt practices may not be sanctioned by an officer's peers. Sherman reports that officers who rejected peers' invitations to receive payoffs to overlook illegal gambling often transferred to different jobs. Rejection of solidarity left officers isolated from their peers.

Aside from the influence of peers, there may also be supervisory support for corrupt practices. In 1967, the President's Commission on Law Enforcement and the Administration of Justice pointed to administrators as having a direct influence on the ethical standards of front-line officers. Police executives can contribute much to a department's tolerance of or intolerance for corruption and the establishment of departmental norms for behavior through their influence on organizational roles.

Corrupt police officers, however, do not view themselves as corrupt, and the sent role is viewed as one of nondeviance. Thus corruption is shared with other officers who provide open support for each other (Reiss, 1971:171), and such support is accomplished through the legitimization of corruption. Wilson (1968) points out that police justify some types of corruption by pointing to declining moral standards in the general community. They note the hypocrisy in the desire to have police officers who will not take bribes when even prominent citizens may wish to bribe them. Skolnick (1966) also explains that police officers legitimize some corrupt practices by distinguishing between practices that will or will not harm the public. In the study, graft associated with bookmaking was regarded as acceptable in a West Coast police department, but bribes associated with drugs were not.

Others have also indicated that the same role-sending process that supports corruption also sets its limits. Thus officers may differentiate between clean graft (acceptable) and dirty graft (unacceptable) (see Sherman, 1974) or may distinguish between accepting a bribe and extorting money from someone. Extreme forms of corruption appear to be rare and require an explanation that looks at factors beyond the occupational-socialization model.

We have discussed both the stages in which socialization occurs and the specifics of the process itself. In the following sections we examine the content of socialization, which differs for different occupations. We look at socialization among the police and among corrections officers. In these areas there is sufficient research to describe occupational socialization. These generalizations, however, are not meant to downplay the significance of the moderators of role taking, which we discussed previously.

Socialization and the Police

The suggestion that large numbers of recruits are attracted to police work because they have authoritarian and violence-seeking personalities has not been supported by the research. Instead, novice police officers seem drawn to the task by a variety of motives. One early study found that nearly a third of recruits were "always interested in being a policeman"; others were attracted by prestige, working with people, and the variety in the work (Reiss, 1967). For these officers anticipatory socialization was a powerful influence. These interests, however, have not generally been confirmed in other studies. Although most recruits may possess an accurate impression of police work prior to selection, the nature of the job is not necessarily what draws them. Motivations are complicated, but the stability of civil service employment and economic benefits attract a significant number of officers (Niederhoffer, 1969; Harris, 1973). Female officers, however, are likely to be attracted to the job by the "interesting" nature of the work (Ermer, 1978).

Regardless of motivation, anticipatory socialization leads a police officer candidate to certain expectations about the job. Veteran officers also have expectations of the candidates. In a study of the Fort Wayne, Indiana, police, Charles (1986) discovered that in the past officers in the department were given a list of potential police candidates and asked to vote on whether an applicant should be accepted or rejected. Now objective and subjective exams define whether a candidate is "good" police material, but that assessment still depends heavily on the candidate's image of police work as gained through anticipatory socialization. "Good police material" in general "portrays an individual who is propolice, highly motivated to become a police officer, willing to remain in the department for at least twenty years, accepting of an authoritarian atmosphere, and interested in fighting crime" (Charles, 1986:37).

Anticipatory socialization determines the ease with which the recruit fits into the social systems found in the formal and informal stages of socialization. The formal socialization process is perhaps more elaborate in policing than in any other occupation within criminal justice. Academy training can last sixteen weeks, with candidates living together and spending only weekends at home. Life at the academy is characterized by "absolute obedience to departmental rules, rigorous physical training, dull lectures devoted to various technical aspects of the occupation, and a ritualistic concern for detail" (Van Maanen, 1985). Although the curriculum includes subjects from report writing to hand-to-hand combat, the lessons of the academy go far beyond the technical information imparted by instructors. Bennett (1984) summarizes four main functions of academy training for the police. First, it provides prescriptions for attitudes, values, and behaviors. Second, it provides opportunities for recruits to evaluate their own behavior and performance against the behavior and performance of their peers. Third, the academy reference group provides a sense of belonging, acceptance, and being rewarded by the group. And, fourth, the reference group acts as a controlling influence by withholding acceptance in the face of inappropriate attitudes or behavior.

The basis for identification with the police reference group was examined in a study of a training academy. Harris (1973) found that three structural factors strengthened the ties between individual recruits and the police peer group. First, police work is depersonalizing. Officers are stereotyped by administrators and by the public, and their views are oversimplified. They find themselves stripped of individuality. Behavior that was previously accepted is no long permitted. Drinking in public may bring criticism from the public and from police officials. Similarly, interactions with the public are often molded by the officer's newly acquired authority. The police officer finds that his or her social identity is equated with the occupation. In or out of uniform, a cop is a cop. Thus isolated from the community, the recruit turns to peers for support. In fact, a study of resignations from a police academy found that recruits were most likely to resign when they felt police solidarity did not adequately compensate for social isolation (Fielding and Fielding, 1987).

A second factor in police solidarity can be found in the drive toward police professionalism. Harris argues that this drive is in some ways an effort to cover feelings of isolation, fear, and disappointment with the hostile reaction of the public. Professionalism assumes that only other police are qualified to judge police behavior, and thus there is support for secrecy, distance from the public, and close bonds to one's peers. A third source of solidarity is the ambiguous nature of police work. The unpredictable routine and lack of appreciation from politicians, the press, and other groups breed defensiveness and contribute further to the in-grown nature of police groups.

The informal and continuing stage of socialization involves learning to cope successfully in the real world. In policing this initiation into reality is done through Field Training Officers (FTOs), who supervise the novice officers on the street. Experienced veterans, including the FTOs, often provide an insightful summary of the academy experience for the new officer. One mentor cautioned a new officer:

> I hope the academy didn't get to you. It's something we all have to go through. A bunch of bullshit as far as I can tell. . . . Since you got through it all right, you get to find out what it's like out here. You'll find out mighty fast that it ain't nothing like they tell you at the academy [quoted in Van Maanen, 1985:208].

The rookie's evaluation of the academy is thus confirmed, and the new officer continues to learn that peers are the people who can and must be trusted.

The FTO or other experienced officers provide continuous coaching of the novice. Westley (1970:157–158) vividly describes it:

> Eight hours a day, six days a week, . . . they talked with their partners. Long hours between action have to be filled; and the older men, hungry for an audience, use them to advantage. Here the experienced man finds an opportunity to talk about himself as a policeman, about his hardships and happiness. Here is someone to whom he is an expert. . . . Thus, amidst an increased barrage of warnings as to silence, the recruit is initiated into the

experience of the man, the history of the department, the miseries of police work, the advantages of police work, and the gripes and boasting of a long series of men. . . . This is the training and the initiation.

A critical moment in that training and initiation is what Van Maanen has identified as the enforcement encounter. The first enforcement-related contact of an officer's probationary period demonstrates the hostility between police and the public. Continued encounters make for a reality shock, which highlights the discrepancy between "idealistic expectations and sordid reality" (Niederhoffer, 1969:52).

Perhaps the most extreme description of informal socialization of the police is presented in a study of a Midwestern police department by Westley (1970). The officers he studied formed a distinct subculture marked by clear norms of conduct. These norms included secrecy—a strong prohibition against discussing police business with outsiders—and the use of violence. Many of the officers supported the use of violence in the form of roughing up suspects simply when disrespect to the police was shown or to obtain information. The roots of this morality, this subcultural ethos, lay in the perception of hostility from the public. In response to public criticism, police solidarity grew, and officers protected their comrades even to the extent of excusing beatings and graft.

Such extreme cases are unlikely today, and the adoption of subcultural values is clearly moderated by individual variables. At the minimum, however, police officers seem to resolve their conflict with the public and with police administration by relying on advice to "lie low, hang loose, and don't expect too much" (Van Maanen, 1985:212).

Socialization in Corrections

Although the reasons for taking up any occupation are complex and varied, the attraction for corrections officers seems less complicated than that for the police. In a study of new corrections officers in Canada, Willett (1977) described the motivations of recruit officers as "prosaic." Lombardo's (1981) study of New York guards came to a similar conclusion. Most of the new recruits were attracted to the job mainly by the promise of regular pay and job security. Many officers come to corrections from periods of unemployment or insecure jobs. For these officers the nature of the work is not the attraction; in fact few recruits know much of the nature of corrections work prior to entry into the field.

Anticipatory socialization for corrections officers is thus marked by incomplete and inaccurate information. Potential recruits acquired their images of prison from the popular media long before they decided to become guards. Stereotypes from James Cagney movies and television portrayals of prison violence mingle to create the impression that the job of corrections officer is one of watching (at a distance) over a mélange of dangerous subhumans. As one recruit put it, "I thought a prison guard was like a turnkey, and inmates were fierce monsters standing around looking at you" (quoted in Willett, 1977:430). Even recruits who have friends and relatives working in the prison may have little accurate information about the job. One officer in Lombardo's (1981:23) study noted:

> I had some help having a cousin down there. He got me a copy of some old rule books and some other things. Even these didn't give a full understanding of what you're getting into. Again, just ideas from the movies. Guards, not pushing inmates but still the bad guys. But I knew some guards and knew they weren't like that. I was willing to take a chance.

Just as the rookie police officer may be jolted on first contact with a hostile public, the rookie corrections officer experiences a significant reality shock on first contact with inmates. New officers learn that they will be in close contact with inmates, and the stereotype of the dangerous con dissolves. Officers begin to see inmates as a diverse group with many being "no different from the run of guys on the street" (quoted in Willett, 1977:433). As anticipatory socialization dissolves under the weight of real experience, the informal and formal processes begin.

Corrections officers often attend the training academy only after weeks or even months of on-the-job training at an institution. This schedule is due more to necessity than design. Officers are usually available and needed in the institutions well before a training academy class is scheduled. This arrangement does, however, expose the recruits to the reality of prison work, and many officers quit shortly after this exposure. In Jacobs and Grear's (1977) study of officers who were fired or quit at Stateville Prison in Illinois, 41 percent of resignations and 60 percent of terminations occurred during the first six months on the job. Such high rates of turnover so soon after initiation are indicative of the power of the socialization process. Officers who are not responsive to it leave.

The informal socialization process for new guards is often marked by mistrust and often hostility from their experienced peers. At the same time that recruits are learning that inmates are human like anyone else, their preconceptions of other officers as "pretty good guys" dissolve. This change in perceptions usually relates to strong prohibitions against normalizing relationships with inmates. Although the rookies are taught to be firm but fair, only formal contact with inmates is expected. In fact, the informal socialization process in some institutions has been described as going so far as to support and even demand unnecessary violence against inmates (Marquart, 1986b). Older officers seem particularly concerned that recruits maintain considerable social distance from inmates. The irony is, however, that such distance is difficult to maintain in light of the constant contact between officers and inmates and is generally not maintained by the older officers.

The FTO programs common among the police are generally not as formally organized in corrections. Although there is some effort to pair rookies with experienced officers on job assignments, these efforts often break down because of staff shortages. Not infrequently, new officers find themselves alone on job assignments, surrounded by inmates and poorly supervised. In such cases rookies often turn to inmates for help in carrying out assignments. Lombardo (1981) points out how inmates provide some of the most significant training for officers. They even offer instruction on procedures such as searches and shakedowns. One officer noted:

> An inmate broke me in. Inmates trained officers. Really! He told me to stand back and he showed me how and where to frisk. He hit the table to sound it out. Rap the bars to see if they were solid [quoted in Lombardo, 1981:32].

As the informal socialization process for corrections officers begins, then, conflicting role expectations are sent to the rookie. Veterans and supervisors emphasize the guard's formal role, while at least some inmates send expectations of reasonableness, dependence, and friendship. The officers thus see themselves caught in the middle. Such confusion is often accentuated by the formal training process. Whatever the curriculum, the corrections academy is often viewed much as the police academy, and experienced guards counsel recruits to "listen carefully, give it back at the exams, then forget it and do as we do. Treat the course as a good holiday from the real work" (quoted in Willett, 1977:433).

The first corrections academy opened in 1859 with the goal of training guards who would have a good influence over inmates (Sellin, 1934). It was not, however, until the 1960s, with financial incentives from the Law Enforcement Assistance Administration (LEAA) and the urging of the Joint Commission on Correctional Manpower and Training (1969), that academy training gained wide support. That support has continued from the Commission on Accreditation for Corrections, which has established minimum training requirements.

The length of academy training fluctuates from as few as four to as many as sixteen weeks. The curriculum generally includes technical information, such as firearms training and emergency procedures, and a smattering of behavioral sciences. As with the police, however, the informal lessons of the academy are also significant. Corrections academies often employ the same model of regimentation as the police in an effort to create unity and professionalism among the recruits. Without the anticipatory socialization characteristic of the police and with constant manpower shortages, however, corrections academies often have difficulty enforcing regimentation. In Lombardo's (1981) study, the academy's failure to dismiss rule violators increased recruits' cynicism. The novice officers' expectation that the academy experience is of little relevance to the actual work may also be confirmed. Officer cadets often complain that subjects are too academic, and even instructors are sometimes seen as teaching one thing while believing another (Willett, 1977:438).

Frequently the impression of the academy as irrelevant is reinforced once a new officer is back in the institution (Liebentritt, 1974). The informal socialization process then continues throughout an officer's career. Studies suggest that this process involves changes in officers' attitudes over time. New officers tend to be relatively naive, with low levels of cynicism and generally positive attitudes. The oldest officers show a similar disposition, perhaps accepting their fate. In the group between these two, however, negative attitudes are high.

Although the concept of a subculture has been useful in studies of the police, its appropriateness in describing corrections officers is debatable. Evidence indicates that officers share some basic concerns about security and appropriate social distance from inmates (Crouch and Marquart, 1980), but studies indicate too that corrections officers vary considerably in their attitudes toward inmates. Lombardo (1985) also notes that the processes needed for the formation of a subculture are not present among corrections officers: corrections officers are not attracted to the field by some shared sense of mission; they generally do not work together; they do not share in the decision-making process; and there is limited communication among them. Relations among officers are often characterized by suspicion rather than solidarity.

Rather than describe corrections officers as a subculture, some authors have used the concept of pluralistic ignorance. Under conditions of pluralistic ignorance, individuals falsely believe that their own opinions are not widely shared. Thus Klofas and Toch (1982) found that corrections officers reported themselves as being less punitive and less custodially oriented than their peers. Some officers were effective opinion leaders and convinced the majority that their view was widely shared. In reality the officers greatly exaggerated the punitiveness of those peers and only a small group of officers could accurately be described as primarily custodially oriented. The subculture was a myth.

Strategies for Socialization

The process of socialization is not immutable. By deliberate design or by their failure to design, managers continuously influence the socialization process. In this section we examine the ways in which managers affect the process of socialization in criminal justice.

As discussed, the socialization process begins with the anticipation of occupational roles. A manager's impact at this stage is generally limited and indirect. At best, managers can support what they regard as desirable images of the occupation. When the television show "Miami Vice" portrayed corrections officers as sadistic and corrupt in one episode, for example, the American Correctional Association sought and received an apology with the hope of deterring any such portrayals in the future. Police community-relations programs provide a similar function. When police officers escort McGruff, the crime dog, on tours of elementary schools and shopping malls, they are spreading an image of police professionalism.

A direct influence on socialization occurs during recruitment and selection. The determination of job titles and qualifications is the first step in this process. Some communities, for example, use the title of police agent rather than police officer to convey a sense of professionalism. The change in title from prison guard to corrections officer was also meant to connote a different role for front-line prison staff. Likewise, campus security carries a different set of expectations than campus police, and state trooper conveys its own images.

Job qualifications also directly influence socialization. Experience, education, and even fitness requirements determine the paths candidates must take. In 1969 the Joint Commission on Correctional Manpower and Training noted that age requirements affected organizational roles by creating a generation gap between workers and clients in criminal justice. At the time, the gap was regarded as detrimental. Presidential commissions have long been concerned with educational requirements (National Advisory Commission on Criminal Justice Standards and Goals, 1973a, 1973b). In the 1960s and 1970s the Law Enforcement Education Program provided funds for the education of criminal justice employees. A college education, now required for most social service positions, is regarded as beneficial for almost all entry-level positions in criminal justice (Waldron, 1984).

An obvious influence on organizational roles is exerted in the selection process itself. During this process a variety of criteria, often intuitive, sometimes systematic, is used to weed out candidates. A common approach was described by Willett (1977) in his study of Canadian corrections officers. The selection procedures involved informal and unstandardized interviews. The interviewers possessed no particular skill and were given no particular instructions but focused on maturity and intelligence, ability to supervise, ability to organize, and ability to communicate. In policing, hiring practices are often elaborate and include required civil service tests, physical-fitness evaluations, character investigations, and even polygraph examinations in addition to oral interviews.

Efforts to introduce psychological assessments into the selection process are still more sophisticated but not necessarily more successful at discriminating good and bad employees. Standardized tests, such as the Minnesota Multiphasic Personality Inventory and the Cattell 16PF, have been used, but a review of the research determined that, for corrections officers, the empirical studies are not of sufficient quantity or quality to warrant conclusions (Wahler and Gendreau, 1985). Research continues, however, and psychological screening has become common in policing (Territo, Swanson, and Chamelin, 1985) and is beginning to be utilized in corrections. New York State requires psychological screening of all corrections officer candidates (Morgenbesser, 1984). These tests are used in the hope of identifying highly unusual psychological profiles rather than making subtle distinctions between candidates.

A different approach is found in behavioral-skills assessments as a basis for selection. These assessments are based on job analyses and focus on the ability to perform specific tasks or the potential to acquire necessary skills through training. Some criminal justice organizations are developing assessment centers that use simulations of on-the-job performance (see Byham and Thornton, 1982).

The formal stages of training provide significant opportunities to influence socialization. Here the process as well as the training content influence role taking. Van Maanen (1982) describes some variables or strategies in the training process that influence socialization. Managers should be aware of the ways in which manipulation of these variables can affect socialization.

The *degree of formalization* is the extent to which training is segregated from the ongoing context of work. In criminal justice the police academy represents a highly formalized process, while most probation officers undergo a much less formalized process of on-the-job training. Formalization has several important consequences. The more formalized, the more the training will stress adoption of appropriate attitudes and beliefs and the more new employees will be stigmatized in the organization, usually by segregating them in a rookie class. At the same time, formalized training is often technical in nature and its relevance for day-to-day work is likely to be questioned by both rookie and experienced employee regardless of content.

Collective socialization strategies involve the training of new members as a group. *Individual strategies* involve an apprenticeship approach to socialization. Collective strategies inevitably create feelings of comradeship and peer support as trainees experience being "in the same boat." Among the police, for example, collective strategies may be useful because officers often must depend on each other in the field. The cost, however, may be that these strategies create distance from supervisors and enhance subcultural supports. Individual strategies depend on the affective bonds between individuals and breed dependence on mentors or on established ways of doing things. The new probation officer who shares a mentor's caseload may get individualized attention but be slow to gain autonomy. In probation, where close supervision of front-line staff is difficult, this dependence in the training phase may be desirable.

In *sequential socialization* a trainee passes through discrete stages on the way to becoming a fully accepted member of an organization.

Police, for example, go through a sequence of academy training, field training, and a probationary period, while corrections officers frequently begin with on-the-job training prior to entry into the academy. When training is divided into these relatively separate steps, coordination of those stages becomes important. Lack of coordination may mean that material is contradictory or that trainees can disregard material learned in one stage, as is often the case in the transition from training academy to on-the-job training. This lack of continuity can lead to cynicism among the recruits.

Serial socialization relies on experienced veterans to groom newcomers in organizations. Criminal justice organizations frequently rely on serial practices. Experienced police officers, for example, often get academy instructor assignments and FTO jobs. Similarly, novice judges turn to experienced judges for advice. Such practices assure that organizations will change only slowly. Established attitudes and practices are passed on, and new ideas gain little support. Such stability may not always be beneficial, however, and *disjunctive practices* may be useful in introducing change. University faculty, for example, may be called on to discuss police–community relations or offer training in new procedures for classifying probationers.

Investiture strategies make membership in organizations easy by accepting the recruit's credentials as the major entrance requirements. Education and the practice of law gain one entry to the judiciary and form the foundation for a professional identity. However, *divestiture processes* strip away certain characteristics before permitting entry. Academy training requires regulation haircuts, special uniforms for the novitiate, and separation from friends and family. Although perhaps mild compared with the experience of a marine recruit, this experience is designed for similar reasons—to dismantle the identity of the newcomer and to replace it with an appropriate organizational identity. This process binds the rookie to the organization and promotes a strong sense of fellowship among those who have traveled the same path.

Socialization is more prevalent during the early than the later stages of a career (Schein, 1971), and thus recruits are more susceptible than experienced workers. Nonetheless, managers must be aware of the socializing influences that continue to confront staff. Personnel practices such as shift assignments or bidding procedures for job assignments may influence socialization. For example, Klofas and Toch (1982) found that anti-inmate attitudes among young corrections officers received support when the rookies were clustered on the 3-to-11 shift. The officers lacked the seniority to bid on assignments that would have integrated them with their experienced peers on desirable shifts. Assignment to vice divisions or repeat-offender programs may expose employees to additional subcultural influences. Technological changes may also influence socialization. Continued training may alter expectations or relationships between employees and clients. And the new generation of correctional architecture with its emphasis on direct supervision of inmates may alter assumptions about inmates (Menke, Zupan, and Lovrich, 1986). Although socialization influences may be most prominent at the beginning of careers in criminal justice, those influences should not be neglected at any time.

Summary

In this chapter we have examined the process by which the novice employee in a criminal justice organization is transformed into a seasoned veteran. The process includes a variety of influences beginning before an employment application is filed and continuing throughout a career. Role expectations are sent from organization outsiders and insiders. Those expectations are filtered by an individual to produce attitudes and behavior regarded as appropriate for a member of the occupation. The consistency of these attitudes and behaviors in all individual employees provides stability for the organization.

In search of stability, criminal justice organizations have designed elaborate processes to affect the attitudes and behaviors of their members. From image-building programs to apprenticeship and academy training, criminal justice workers are molded by their organizations. Each step transmits not only technical knowledge but also the ethos of the organization. The product, however, is not an organizational automaton. The roles sent to workers are complex and varied and often conflicting. Such demands may foster a range of undesirable outcomes from cynicism to stress and from official deviance to corruption.

Understanding occupational socialization is thus fundamental to management in criminal justice. Here we have closely considered the processes for both police and corrections officers. These processes reveal the influences, both positive and negative, on criminal justice staff. Through planning, management can gain some control over these influences and consciously affect the occupational-socialization process.

In the next chapter we consider another topic central to the management of criminal justice organizations. The mandate of these organizations necessitates possessing the authority to deprive individuals of their liberty and even their life. This makes the analysis of power in criminal justice organizations uniquely important.

———————————————— **CASE STUDY** ————————————————
Reflections on a Career

Yeah, when I got into this business I thought it was a noble profession. I still think maybe it is for most guys. I thought the cops were helping people. We busted the bad guys and that made society safe. You needed cops around to keep things safe and to help people out. That's what first attracted me to the job, the idea of doing something useful, that and the security.

Back then there were none of these tests, no psychological exams or fitness tests. Back then, what you had to do is want it bad enough and be accepted by the rest of the cops. The academy was just getting started then. I think I was in the third or fourth class to go through.

I remember thinking that that was really some experience. We were all going to be professionals, the GI Joe model, you know, sharp and crisp. The law was laid out clearly. I could recite the legal definition of an assault. The lines were clear. We were recruits and the instructors were the gods; there was never any question of our status. We were the ones running the obstacle course, and they were the ones doing the yelling. We even had classes in due process of law. Those weren't so clear, and even the instructors snickered a little. One of them even called it the "cover-your-ass class."

The day I left the academy I was still convinced that being a cop was important. We were sharp; we were professional; and we were going to make a difference. Especially us. You see, that was the late sixties, and there was a lot of trouble. Some of the old guys couldn't handle the protests, mostly college kids screaming obscenities, and the cops were just supposed to take it. In my class, we were the same age as a lot of those kids. Hell, I went to high school with some of them. If anybody could take it, understand it, and maybe fix it, it was gonna be us.

Some things about being a cop grind you down and some hit quick and knock you down. Years of seeing pushers get out and drive away in their fancy cars grinds you down. But my first week on the job, well that knocked me down. I was out with my training officer. We were downtown when a protest quickly changed into a riot. Some guy smashed a window right in front of us. My partner grabbed him; he started cursing the cops up and down. It was "pig this" and "pig that" when, all of a sudden, the training officer crowned him with his stick and then beat the crap out of him. I remember thinking, this was one of those older cops who couldn't take it, but what was I supposed to do? I mean, should I report it or what? I even thought it might be a test, and they expected me to report it. After the arrest, the training officer never mentioned it; the low life never reported it, and neither did I.

I guess it wasn't a test. Or, maybe it was. My training officer and I got along pretty well after that. And I guess I started to learn that things weren't as clear as they once seemed. Maybe that's when the grind set in. Pushers with nice cars, creeps yelling "pig." You'd pull some guy over, and he would hand you a twenty with his driver's license. You know damn well next day he'd be in some bar bitchin' about how all the cops are corrupt. He might even turn out to be IA (internal affairs). You couldn't trust anybody except maybe the officer next to you in the car and the ones you were in the academy with. I started to hang around a lot with those guys.

It didn't take long to resent all of the hassles. Pretty soon you realized it might cost them more if you cleaned out some of those pushers before dragging them downtown, and if a guy were guilty or disrespectful, an occasional whack wouldn't do any harm. Maybe everybody didn't feel that way, but nobody ever talked about it.

Pretty soon you think it's going on all around you. I remember once we had a legal wiretap on a store where we thought they were selling drugs. I'm listening in when a caller asks if he can store a load of hot TVs in the back room. Twenty minutes after the TVs are delivered, cops from the 53rd (precinct) raid the joint. They had it staked out for a receiving-stolen-goods bust. Well, suddenly the phone gets busy as hell. The cops are calling their buddies to tell them to come down and pick up a TV. Pretty soon cars are lined up outside and people are putting TVs in their trunks. Some guys even brought their squads. Well you see, problem is, I got all these calls on tape. I ended up destroying the tape. Had to. When some of the guys heard about it, the tape and all, well, pretty soon a guy shows up at my house with a nineteen-inch color set. That was years ago.

I don't know how we got into this thing, but I don't make any excuses. When my buddies and I started to get some seniority, we could pretty much name our own assignments. Somebody had the idea of pulling this job on a weekend. Jim was the desk sergeant in charge of assignments so he could keep the other cops out of the downtown area. We went in the drugstore next to the bank, broke down the wall, and walked out with almost 500 grand. Too bad Jim rolled over on us when he got caught passing some of the money. I never thought he would. We were in the academy together.

I don't know how we got into this, but I don't make excuses. Somehow I wound up here, in protective custody, sharing a cell with a rapist.

Case Study Questions

1. In what ways can we see the officer's situation as the result of a socialization process rather than of individual weakness?
2. How would you describe the formal and informal socialization of the officer in this case study?
3. How do the role-taking model and subcultural perspective apply in this case?

For Discussion

1. Describe the content of the role of a probation officer. What are the norms and values associated with this work? Include those that can be regarded as legitimate as well as those regarded as not legitimate. What are the sources of these norms and values? How do education, training, and the work experience influence them?

2. How can you distinguish between corruption and official deviance in policing? What socialization processes support each of these? Design an in-service training program whose chief goal is to combat the organizational processes you describe.

3. If you were selecting volunteers to work in a maximum security prison what attitudes and values would you find desirable and why? What attitudes and values would you like to see transmitted in the formal socialization process and in the informal stage of socialization?

4. Your job is to develop a program for training corrections officers for a special internal-affairs unit. They will investigate problems of contraband and violence in prison while working as regular officers. Whom would you recruit, and how would you structure the process of training?

What would the content of training be? What problems with the socialization process do you anticipate?

For Further Reading

Charles, M. T. *Policing the Streets.* Springfield, Ill.: Charles C Thomas, 1986.

Katz, D., and Kahn, D. *The Social Psychology of Organizations.* 2nd ed. New York: Wiley, 1978.

Lombardo, L. X. *Guards Imprisoned: Correctional Officers at Work.* New York: Elsevier, 1981.

Terry, W. C. (Ed.). *Policing Society.* New York: Wiley, 1985.

Power

The sentencing power is so far unregulated that even matters of a relatively technical, seemingly "legal" nature are left for the individual judge, and thus for whimsical handling, at least in the sense that no two judges need be the same. . . . The point is, I hope, sufficiently made that our sentencing judgments splay wildly as results of unpredictable and numerous variables embodied in the numerous and variegated inhabitants of our trial benches [Frankel, 1973:25].

The nature of the work supervised, including the technology involved, the nature of the enforcement pattern, the spatial context in which it is carried out, the occupational cultural norms of the subordinates, the type of group structure involved, environmental constraints affecting the definition of the crime, the constraints of the definition of legitimate intrusion as defined by subordinates, the nature of the citizens in contact and their specific roles, the uniqueness of discretion involved in their work, and the task demands and superior expectations demanded, all interact to constrain and define the position of the [police] sergeant in each specific organizational context vis-à-vis other, alternate, organizational control mechanisms [Tifft, 1978:104].

Those who got it in with them officers got connections. They got drugs with them coming into the place. . . . Everybody need some satisfaction, so you go to the man. In here, it's the white boys. They got the drugs and power cause they give what you want. . . . Nobody has real power in here except them people with stuff [marijuana]. If you be running it, well you got what you want and what others want. . . . That makes you king, so you try to get some. . . . If you got connections on the outside, you can get it in and make money. Them officers and visitors bringing it in, . . . and that's what is done [inmates quoted in Stojkovic, 1984:520].

From these descriptions, it is clear that the concept of power is expressed in different forms within the various components of the criminal justice system. Whether it be the sentencing judge, the police sergeant, or the prisoner, all rely on power to gain compliance from others. A police supervisor may wish to exercise control over the beat cop, or a prisoner may desire to control another prisoner. Expressions of power are ubiquitous in criminal justice organizations. In addition, who has power and how that power is acquired vary within the different components of criminal justice.

Police organizations, for example, employ different types of power to gain compliance from officers. The types of power used depend on the tasks and functions of the particular unit. Supervisors in the vice unit do not use the same types of power as those in the detective unit because each unit has its own duties and responsibilities. In correctional systems, the types of power used by supervisory personnel are often constrained by a number of factors inherent in the prison structure. As an example, we know that pure coercive power rarely works in prison, in part because inmates significantly outnumber staff. As a result, we see others types of power used by corrections administrators and officers to gain compliance from prisoners.

Our purpose in this chapter is to review the literature on the concept of power and apply this material to criminal justice organizations. As some scholars suggest, the investigation of power in organizations is not new, yet few studies have examined the complexity of the issue (House, 1984). Furthermore, many researchers have suggested that measuring power is extremely difficult (Podsakoff and Schriesheim, 1985). More importantly, we have few studies of the exercise of power in the organizations of criminal justice. Nevertheless, a major goal of this chapter is to ascertain the types of power and authority employed in criminal justice bureaucracies by examining the major research that has been done in the criminal justice area.

In addition, this chapter discusses the consequences of power relations in organizations and emphasizes the political nature of power in organizations and the strategies criminal justice officials can employ to maintain their power positions. We begin, however, with a definition of power and distinguish it from authority.

Power Defined

Power is one of the most difficult concepts to define, and, as a result, the organizational literature contains multiple definitions of it. Hinings, Pugh, Hickson, and Turner (1967), for example, believe that it is analogous to bureaucracy. Some authors have viewed power in only one dimension, i.e., as purely coercion (Bierstedt, 1950; Blau, 1964). Dahl (1957) defines power in this way: "A has the power over B to the extent that he can get B to do something B would not otherwise do."

Although this somewhat simple definition has been accepted by many interested in power in organizations, others have seen power as being much more complex and have defined it more broadly. They look at power at the organizational level and include the role of social systems in organizations (Emerson, 1962; Dubin, 1963; Crozier, 1964; Lawrence and Lorsch, 1967)—that is, the interactions of people and units. If we view organizational power as a product of exchange relationships in organizations, we can see how the interdependent nature of organizational tasks creates power for some people.

Perrow (1970) has demonstrated that sales departments within industrial firms are much more powerful than other units within the organization. He argues that specific units within an organization are able to exhibit what is known as "interdepartmental power" and that any investigation of power must be able to discern those units, which are critical to the operation of the organization. If some sectors of an organization are more powerful than others, what within these units makes them powerful and central to the organization? One possible answer is that these units are effective in dealing with uncertainties in the organization's task environment. In effect, they are able to absorb the uncertainty created by an often turbulent and unstable environment (March and Simon, 1958).

Criminal justice organizations, however, often do not operate in unstable environments, and they are not influenced greatly by market concerns. They generally operate in consistent and predictable ways. Power acquisition, therefore, among subunits in these organizations is typically not based on how well they can deal with uncertainties in their task environments. What is important to criminal justice organizations is that they accomplish their tasks in an efficient manner while simultaneously meeting the demands of the public.

Thus, some have suggested that it is not the interaction with the environment that is important to understanding organizational power. More critical is how units operate to accomplish tasks that are crucial to the organization's survival. Hickson, Hinings, Lee, Schenck, and Pennings (1973) have demonstrated that organizational units that cannot be replaced in an organization (substitutability), that have a pervasive and immediate relationship to the workflow of the organization (centrality), and that deal with contingencies effectively are usually powerful in organizations.

This assertion is borne out by much evidence gathered in institutional corrections and in police organizations. Early research by Sykes (1958) demonstrated how the help of inmates is required to run prisons. In the words of Sykes, there is a "defect of total power" in our correctional institutions among custodial staff. Because inmates are crucial or central to the operation of the prison, are not likely to be replaced by other workers, and can deal relatively well with the various contingencies of prison life, it is easy to see how they would have power within the institution. This observation is equally applicable to police officers. Research has documented how certain police positions are more powerful than others and that the types of power used by police are constrained by the task required and the police hierarchy (Tifft, 1978:104–105).

Sergeants in tactical units, for example, have high reward and coercive power available to them. They make the determinations, in most cases, of who will come and go into the unit. Moreover, many sergeants have high expert power. Their knowledge of the activities of the unit makes them hard to replace and critical to the police organization.

Before we continue, however, we need to summarize the key aspects of power in organizations. First, power denotes that "a person or group of persons or organization of persons determines, i.e., . . . affects, what another person or group or organization will do" (Tannenbaum, 1962:236). Second, power exists among the units of an organization as well as at the interpersonal level. Much of the research has emphasized the interpersonal aspects with little regard for the organizational level, thus obscuring the importance of departmental power in the organizational setting. Third, power in an organization depends on how subunits deal with uncertainty and on whether they meet the criteria of substitutability and centrality. A hypothesis in the literature is that units that meet these criteria are able not only to influence the direction of the organization but also to solidify themselves in power positions (Michels, 1949).

Finally, we must differentiate between power and authority. Many have considered these terms interchangeable, yet, as Pfeffer (1981) suggests, doing so is not helpful to an understanding of the process of power acquisition in organizations. He posits, therefore, that the two can be best understood by examining the extent to which employees "legitimize" their use. He further argues that the use of authority seems legitimate to those being supervised or controlled in an organization. Power, however, especially purely coercive power, is not a form of compliance that sustains organizational life. Power that is legitimized over time becomes characterized as authority. This view of power and authority has many ramifications for organizations. Ultimately, organizations seek the expression of authority rather than power. Pfeffer (1981:4) states:

> By transforming power into authority, the exercise of influence is transformed in a subtle but important way. In social situations, the exercise of power typically has costs. Enforcing one's way over others requires the expenditure of resources, the making of commitments, and a level of effort which can be undertaken only when the issues at hand are relatively important. On the other hand, the exercise of authority, power which has become legitimated, is expected and desired in the social context. Thus, the exercise of authority, far from diminishing through use, may actually serve to enhance the amount of authority subsequently possessed.

For our purposes here, we want to know the types of power and authority employed in criminal justice organizations. In addition, it is equally important to match types of power and authority with tasks. Police, for example, may require specific types of authority or power or both to perform their jobs. The same is true for corrections. As a result, the issue becomes identifying those types of power or authority that enhance the ability of a component of criminal justice to successfully complete its objectives. Some types of power and some types of authority are more suitable than others.

Types of Power and Authority

Any discussion of the types of authority must begin with the work of Weber (1947). From his earliest writings, Weber distinguished authority and power, with authority denoting compliance to particular directives essential for achieving a common or shared goal. Power is based on coercion, not compliance, and is used in organizations that emphasize strict obedience, e.g., slave-labor camps and some prisons.

Weber delineated three types of authority: traditional, charismatic, and legal. *Traditional authority* is authority that is vested in the position a person holds and that has a long tradition in a culture or organization. This type of authority can be found in countries with traditional monarchies. Within organizations, one can say that old and well-tested methods of operation are part of the organization's tradition or, equally important, may reflect the interests of those who run the organization in maintaining the status quo. As Hall (1982) suggests, traditional authority is expressed in the saying "the old man wants it that way."

The second type of authority is *charismatic authority.* This type is founded in the personable attributes or actions (or both) of a particular individual in an organization. President John F. Kennedy, for example, wielded tremendous amounts of charismatic authority, largely because many people found attractive qualities in him. An example in the criminal justice field is the veteran police officer. Many officers who have spent a long time on the streets adopt a "police personality" that they are able to turn into charismatic authority. The flamboyant police officer described in many novels expresses this type of authority.

Finally, there is *legal authority.* This type of authority is based on an appeal to the formal rules and regulations of an organization. In addition, this type of authority is rooted in the hierarchy of the organization. It is predicated on the belief that subordinates are expected to follow the orders and commands of those above them in the formal chain of command. Much of the authority exercised within criminal justice agencies is of this type. Corrections officers are organized in a chain of command, and officers assume that those above them in the institutional hierarchy have the right to impose rules and regulations. We will see how this type of authority breaks down under the strain of day-to-day activity in later chapters in the book.

Although Weber's ideas about authority have been widely accepted by people seeking to explain compliance mechanisms in organizations, his concept of power has not found as much acceptance. Current research has fostered an increased awareness of power in organizational settings, but most of this research has focused on power at the interpersonal rather than organizational level and, in addition, is open to criticism on the grounds of validity and reliability. This is equally the case for research done on power distribution in criminal justice settings. These problems aside, we can still identify bases of power found in organizations and discuss them in light of what we know about criminal justice administration.

According to French and Raven (1968), there are five bases of power in all organizations. These bases (or types) of power are used to gain the compliance of subordinates. We will see that some are akin to the types of authority described by Weber. Others, however, match the traditional definition of power given previously in this chapter. The five types of power are reward, coercive, legitimate, referent, and expert. Although these bases of power were originally meant to explain the behavior of subordinates and supervisors at the interpersonal level, they may also be used to analyze power at the organizational level (Hall, 1982:135). Moreover, these concepts of power are meant to be explored on the basis of the interactions and relationships of individuals in organizations. In short, there is no power unless it is expressed by someone and received by another. The person who expresses the power is referred to as a power holder, while the receiver of the power is referred to as a power recipient.

Reward power is based on the perception of the power recipient that the power holder can grant some type of reward or remuneration for compliance to orders or commands. An example of this type of power is the piecework system found in many factories. The worker does what the supervisor says to do in order to get paid. Without the reward by the supervisor or the company the supervisor represents, the worker would not perform as ordered to. It is the reward, in the form of a salary or hourly rate, that makes the worker comply with the directives of the supervisor.

A second type of power is *coercive power.* Coercive power is based on the belief of subordinates that if they do not do as they are told they will be either threatened with punishment or punished directly. This type of power has been associated with traditional prison structures. It is widely believed that if the inmate, for example, does not comply with the wishes of corrections officers, the inmate will be punished. This is not always the case, and the belief in coercive power as the primary compliance mechanism in prison organizations remains somewhat problematical given the nature of institutionalization today and the other forms of power available to corrections officers.

Legitimate power is exercised when a power holder is able to influence a power recipient to do something based on some internalized belief of the power recipient. This type of power is most closely aligned to Weber's concept of authority. The internalized norm can be traced to many sources: cultural values, social structure, or a designated and legitimized informal leader. French and Raven suggest that an individual in an organization may follow the directives of a superior because the superior's power is legitimized by another, informal, leader in the organization. Police officers may follow the commands of the shift sergeant not totally because of the traditional authority the commander has but because an informal leader, e.g., a veteran police officer, who is viewed as a legitimate representative of police, follows those commands. In this way, legitimate power can be expressed not only by those in the chain of command of the organization but by those in the informal sector of the organization. Problems are created for criminal justice administration when orders and commands made by those in the formal sector of the organization (police sergeants, for example) are not consistent with the expectations and demands of leaders who exhibit legitimate power at the informal level and are respected by rank-and-file workers (police officers). This problem is a direct consequence of power relations in organizations, which we address in another section of the chapter.

Power that is based on the identification of the power holder with the power recipient is labeled *referent power*. This fourth type of power is predicated on the attractiveness of the power recipient to the power holder. French and Raven state: "In our terms, this would mean that the greater the attraction, the greater the identification and consequently the greater the referent power" (1968:265). This type of power can be seen in correctional institutions. In many instances, officers are viewed in a positive light by inmates, and an inmate may even attempt to emulate an officer's attitudes and beliefs.

An important difference between this type of power and reward and coercive power is the mediation of rewards and punishments. In reward and coercive power, the power holder is able to control rewards and sanctions. Referent power is contingent on the identification of the power recipient with the power holder, regardless of the consequences of the relationship, positive or negative. An individual, for example, may have an opinion on a subject but will go along with the group because of a desire to be like members of the group. The group in this case is exhibiting a strong form of referent power over the individual.

The police-socialization literature is replete with examples of individual officers who because of intense peer pressure go along with the demands of the group even though their behavior goes against police rules and regulations. Research on this topic has suggested that to understand the power of the group we must understand the socialization process of police officers and how it reflects the expectations of society (Manning and Van Maanen, 1978; Stoddard, 1983). Chapter 7 discusses occupational socialization within criminal justice organizations.

The final type of power offered in the French and Raven typology is *expert power*. Expert power is based on the power recipient's belief that the power holder has a high level of expertise in a given area. This type of power is based on the "cognitive structure" of the power recipient and fosters the dependence of the power recipient on the power holder, although this dependence may lessen over time. Within the courts in this country, there is a strong belief that attorneys, both defense and prosecuting, exercise tremendous amounts of expert power over their clients. A defendant, for example, relies on the knowledge of the defense attorney and complies with the attorney's wishes when in the court social system.

Although the French and Raven typology offers five distinctive types of power, other forms of power have been identified in the research literature and are applicable to criminal justice administration. Bacharach and Lawler (1980) discuss information as another source of power in organizations. Individuals or groups may have power because of their ability to control the information flow in the organization. Most important is the ability to control information that is essential for maintaining the operation of the organization (Pfeffer, 1977a). This power can be distinguished from expert power because it is derived from one's position and not from one's knowledge. For example, inmates who understand the legal system may exhibit a form of expert power, while inmate clerks have access to information that allows them to manipulate the prison structure to their advantage, e.g., knowing whose cell will be searched by corrections officers.

A final type of power that has received attention by the research community is based on the ability to acquire and provide needed organizational resources. Research (Salancik and Pfeffer, 1974:453–473) has shown how certain subunits in organizations become powerful because of their ability to acquire critical resources. Another work by Pfeffer and Salancik (1974) suggested that subunit power is contingent largely on the ability of the subunit or department to gain outside grant and contract funds. This ability enables the subunit to have more prestige than the other subunits and to gain a lasting position of power in the organization (Lodahl and Gordon, 1973).

Consequences of Power Relations

The research on the effects of varying types of power in organizations is plentiful (see Hall, 1982:136–139). Using the French and Raven typology, Warren (1968) has shown that on the dimensions of "behavioral conformity" (conformity without any internalization of norms) and "attitudinal conformity" (conformity and internalization of norms) schoolteachers showed high levels of attitudinal conformity when they were subject to expert, legitimate, and referent power, while reward and coercive power were related to behavioral conformity. The relevant point is that differing kinds of power exist in organizations and that the behavioral output is noticeably different when different types of power are employed.

This interpretation is further supported by the work of Lord (1977), who analyzed the relationship between types of social power and leadership functions. Lord concludes that legitimate power is highly related to the leadership functions of developing orientation (providing direction to employees), communicating, and coordinating, whereas coercive power is most highly related to facilitating evaluations, proposing solutions, and total functional behavior. He maintains that various types of power have differential impacts on the organization and its members.

Julian (1966) concludes that, depending on the type of hospital, different types of power are utilized. For example, he describes how voluntary hospitals rely on a legitimate power system with talks and explanations to patients. In contrast, he found that veterans' hospitals employed methods of coercion in gaining compliance. Through the use of sedation and restriction of activity, workers were able to get compliance and at the same time fulfill their primary organizational goal: control of patients. An implication from this research is that differing organizations use diverse types of power to accomplish their organizational goals, and the type and amount of power used are variable and contextual.

The same is true in criminal justice organizations. Tifft (1978:90), in his analysis of control systems and social bases of power in police organizations, attempted to examine the "structural conditions" that affect the location of power. In addition, he was interested in exploring how these conditions affect the exercise of power, how they can be altered to increase organizational control, and what the consequences of these structures are on the people within the organization. He concludes (1978:104–105) that there are structural factors within police organizations that contain the bases of power available to the police sergeant. He further suggests that differing policies would have to be implemented within different police units for the effective exercise of police sergeant power. Detective units, for example, would be best suited if sergeants had previous experience in the unit since expert power or knowledge is critical to the sergeant role. A knowledge of the methods and operations of burglars and robbers provides the sergeant with requisite knowledge that is respected and valued by subordinate detectives. Because expert power is so critical to the sergeant's role in a detective unit, it would be prudent for police administrators to place people in the unit who have had some experience as detectives. In this way, organizational control is enhanced. The consequence of such a policy would be greater effectiveness and efficiency within the unit.

Tifft further states that the various functional units of a police force allow differing types of power to be developed. He mentions that a patrol sergeant has coercive and legitimate power because of the tasks of that particular unit, whereas a tactical unit exhibits high levels of referent, legitimate, and expert power because of the structural design and activities of that unit. Traffic sergeants are not able to develop referent and expert bases of power because of the nature of the tasks of the unit, the rather rapid rotation of officers out of the unit, and the minimal types of expertise required to conduct routine traffic investigations. Thus, one would expect that legitimate, reward, and coercive power are the primary tools of compliance available to the traffic sergeant. In addition, as stated by Tifft (1978:100), even coercive and reward power may be circumscribed by the ideology, intraorganizational conflicts, and size of the unit.

Stojkovic (1984, 1986) reports similar findings with respect to the expression of power in correctional institutions. He found among prisoners five types of social power: coercive, referent, legitimate, provision of resources, and expert. Coercive power was employed by prisoners in the inmate social system to gain "respect"; referent power was the mechanism of compliance used by various religious groups; legitimate power rested with those inmates who were older and had longer periods of confinement; provision-of-resource power was exhibited by those inmates who could distribute contraband materials, often illegal narcotics; and expert power was seen among those prisoners who were knowledgeable about the legal system and could provide legal assistance to other prisoners.

Stojkovic concluded that the social bases of power are much more circumscribed for corrections administrators than for inmates. He found only three types of power among corrections administrators: coercive, reward, and access to information. These bases of power were easily eroded, however, and were limited in gaining the compliance of inmates and corrections officers. Access-to-information power, for example, was perceived by prisoners to be the result of active "snitch" recruiting on the part of corrections officials and thus was pernicious and destructive to the institutional environment. This finding obviously raises questions as to which types of power are more conducive to organizational stability than others.

Both Stojkovic (1987) and Hepburn (1985) report interesting findings concerning the power of corrections officers. Hepburn (1985) found that because of significant changes in the administration of prisons and the demographics of prisoners, corrections officers are required to do their jobs much differently today than in the past. Interestingly enough, he does not picture prison guards as being solely concerned with punitiveness or coercion of prisoners. He found that both legitimate and expert power were used by corrections officers. He also found that referent and reward bases of power were weak, and that although it was not as prevalent as other types of power, coercive power was used by some guards.

These findings contrast with those of Stojkovic (1987:6–25) in his analysis of power among corrections officers. Although Hepburn (1985) found reward power to be weak among the officers he surveyed, Stojkovic found the reliance on reward power to be strong among corrections officers in his study. This finding is consistent with previous research that suggested that "accommodative relationships" are at the core of the relationship between corrections officers and prisoners (Sykes, 1958:40–62; Sykes and Messinger, 1960). In addition, although Hepburn found coercive power to be less relied on than other forms of power by many corrections officers he studied, later research suggests that, at least in some parts of the country, this method of gaining compliance among prisoners is still strong (Marquart, 1986b). Future research will have to be conducted to accurately assess the bases of power among corrections officers.

In summary, we have seen that the social bases of power vary from organization to organization and that certain structural characteristics affect the types of power within an organization. The important question becomes, Under what conditions and with what tasks are specific types of power more appropriate than others? We have found that, depending on the police unit and function, different types of power are required. With respect to institutional corrections, we have seen how the bases of power differ from group to group. For criminal justice administration, then, the key issue is to recognize the correct type of power for the situation, while being aware of the structural constraints of the organization. Obviously, certain types of power are not going to be useful within many criminal justice organizations. Gaining compliance in correctional institutions, for example, through purely coercive methods is doomed to failure because of the nature of the institutional groups. In fact, this type of response was attempted and failed miserably in many correctional institutions (Jacobs, 1977).

This same argument can be applied to the police field. Employing coercive methods of compliance among rank-and-file officers, usually through strict rules and regulations, is no longer satisfactory because many officers are averse to such strategies. In fact, many have called for a loosening of the police organizational structure to make it receptive not only to the changing nature of the police officer but more importantly to the nature of the police role in society. External groups and demands from these groups have also had a tremendous impact on the operating methods of police departments.

In essence, some traditional methods of compliance in criminal justice agencies may not be perceived as legitimate by many criminal justice employees and the general public. Such legitimacy is crucial to effective criminal justice administration. As a result, several important management questions remain: What types of power are perceived to be legitimate by those who perform criminal justice functions? If improper types of power are being employed by criminal justice administrators, what are the end results? These questions lead us to the topic of the final section of this chapter, the connection between the legitimacy of power and political behavior in criminal justice organizations.

The Legitimacy of Power and Political Behavior

According to Tosi, Rizzo, and Carroll (1986:527), "when legitimate authority fails, political behavior arises." Political behavior is any action of the criminal justice worker that promotes individual goals over organizational goals. In their opinion, political behavior exists in organizations when there is (1) a lack of consensus among members about goals, (2) disagreement over the means to achieve goals, or (3) anxiety about resource allocation. Each one of these problems exists within many criminal justice agencies, and, as a result, political behavior among criminal justice employees is inevitable. Let us examine these three problems within correctional institutions, beginning with the lack of goal consensus among corrections staff.

Research in correctional institutions since the 1950s has indicated how disagreement over goals among corrections staff has created not only political behavior but also ineffective operations. This disagreement is essentially over treatment versus punishment. Is it the purpose of correctional institutions primarily to punish offenders or to rehabilitate them or both? This debate not only has created conflict as to what the purpose of imprisonment is but, in addition, has raised the issue of whether such conflicting goals can, in actuality, be met within the prison setting. Current research has clearly indicated the variability of attitudes among corrections employees as to what the purpose of imprisonment should be (Klofas and Tech, 1982). This research has also questioned whether there is any agreement among the public as to the primary purpose of our correctional institutions. Lack of agreement, both internally and externally, has created a situation conducive to political behavior. Without the legitimacy engendered by agreement on goals among corrections workers and acceptance of these goals by the public, prescriptive recommendations as to which types of power should be employed in these organizations are of little or no value. The only value to suggesting specific types of power within criminal justice organizations is if they are able to create legitimacy and acceptance among those who work in these organizations.

A similar issue arises when one discusses the proper means to achieve the goals that are agreed on. Police organizations, for example, for years have debated what types of patrolling are the most appropriate, efficient, and effective in achieving the generally accepted goals of crime prevention and societal protection. Whether the debate is over foot patrol versus motorized patrol or one-man cars versus two-man cars, the lack of agreement among police administrators, the general public, and officers on the beat as to the appropriate means to achieve these goals has created a climate in which political behavior flourishes. Once again, prescribing proper methods of obtaining compliance within criminal justice organizations becomes pointless when legitimacy is absent.

Finally, administrators of criminal justice agencies rely on political behavior when they are not certain what their budgets will be in the future. Because criminal justice agencies rely on the public budgeting process and must compete with other social service agencies for funds, it is inevitable that political behavior results. Political behavior, in this instance, may not be bad in and of itself because of the necessity of acquiring resources for the organization. In fact, political behavior may be expected as a requisite skill of an effective criminal justice administrator. In this case proper political behavior may be viewed as legitimate by not only employees but also others in the political arena. When this expression of political power is viewed as illegitimate by employees, the public, and significant political figures in the community, it can have a deleterious effect on the organization.

Our purpose in this section is not to speak pejoratively about political behavior in criminal justice organizations, especially as it relates to budgeting. Our purpose is to propose some bases of power that are conducive to the development of legitimate authority in criminal justice organizations and that prevent the perpetuation of political behaviors that do not contribute to the effective and efficient operation of these agencies. We begin with an examination of the political processes of criminal justice organizations.

Dalton (1959) suggests that with the diffusion of types of power in organizations there is a concomitant rise of powerful cliques or coalitions. These cliques defend their members in response to various threats to organizational autonomy. Pfeffer (1981:36) points out that such cliques and coalitions are highly political, relying on various strategies to advance their own purposes and causes over those of other coalitions in the organization. This political nature of coalitions and their power configurations are relevant to decision-making processes in organizations (March, 1962; Kaufman, 1964; Allison, 1969; Pandarus, 1973). More importantly, these political behaviors erode employees' sense of legitimacy and may lead to a number of dysfunctional behaviors in the organization.

Such results are not any more true than in the agencies of criminal justice. Institutional corrections, for example, has been fragmented along interest-group lines for many years, both internally and externally (Stastny and Tyrnauer, 1982). Inmates, corrections officers, and administrators have been traditionally alienated from one another, and, as a result, the prison has been ineffective in accomplishing many of its goals. This observation is consistent with our previous observation that the lack of consensus among groups in an organization reduces legitimacy and engenders political behavior. Only by obtaining consensus can the issues of means to achieve goals and resource allocation be resolved.

This issue is not only one for prison organizations. Many similar observations can be made in police systems. Much research has been done since the 1960s on management models for effective police supervision. Volumes of research have discussed how police supervisors should manage their subordinates; yet there is much basic disagreement as to what police should be doing and what methods are the most effective for the accomplishment of their goals. We can speculate that because of a lack of consensus on goals, disagreement over what means should be applied to achieve those goals that are agreed on, and uncertainty over resource allocation, police organizations are prime places for political behavior on the part of employees. In fact, much of the research on police socialization is, in effect, research on the political actions or behavior of police officers, e.g., police corruption.

Effective Types of Power

The critical question becomes, What are the types of power that criminal justice employees are most likely to consider legitimate? Borrowing from the work of Tosi, Rizzo, and Carroll (1986:540–542), we can identify the psychological effects of specific types of power on individuals, as represented in figure 8-1. In this model, the five bases of power correspond to the French and Raven (1968) typology, examined previously in the chapter. (Charismatic power is analogous to French and Raven's referent power.) There are three possible effects of these types of power. The exercise of legitimate, charismatic, and expert power leads to *acceptance* on the part of the employee; reward and coercive power may lead to acceptance if the power is used for some legitimate purpose or may lead to two dysfunctional effects—*learned helplessness* and *resistance*—if the power is used for illegitimate purposes. For example, when a police sergeant employs coercive power to motivate an officer, this use of power is perceived as having a legitimate purpose and therefore is accepted by the officer.

This model also stresses ancillary effects of power exercised in organizations, all of which are relevant to criminal justice administration. Although legitimate, charismatic, and expert bases of power lead to acceptance on the part of employees, acceptance leads to the rationaliza-

Figure 8-1 The Psychological Effects of the Use of Power in Organizations. (From H. L. Tosi, J. R. Rizzo, and S. J. Carroll, *Managing Organizational Behavior.* Copyright © 1986 by Pitman Publishing Company. Reprinted by permission of Harper & Row, Publishers, Inc.)

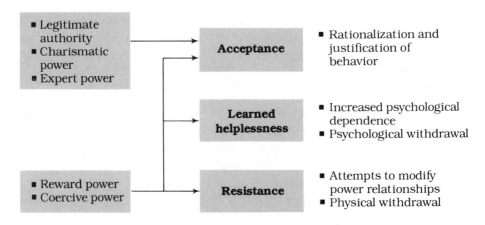

tion and justification of the behavior. In short, the power recipient legitimizes, understands, and accepts the directives of the supervisor. When learned helplessness and resistance are the effects, there is increased psychological dependence, psychological withdrawal, attempts to modify power relationships, and possible physical withdrawal from the organization. These effects may be manifested through appeals to reason by the power recipient to the power holder, minimal compliance, sabotage, development of a counterforce, and leaving the organization. All are common reactions to power expression in criminal justice organizations, and their frequency may decrease the efficiency and effectiveness of these organizations.

Many have suggested that prisons are prime candidates not only for the political behavior mentioned previously but for the dysfunctional behaviors associated with coercive and reward types of power. It is all too common in the research literature on prisons to see how both inmates and corrections staff, suffering from learned helplessness, ultimately withdraw from the institution in either a psychological or a physical sense. In fact, stress among corrections employees and prisoners is now being researched. Many of these characteristics may be, in part, reactions to the exercise of coercive power by supervisors in these organizations. More directly, much of what we know about social systems in prisons can be tied to the illegitimacy of the current types of power being exercised by both corrections administrators and officers. The inmate social system may represent a "counterforce" to the power of those in command of the organization.

These effects of the use of power are seen equally in police organizations. Much current research has explored the problems associated with the traditional police structure. We are arguing here that the types of power traditionally associated with that structure are, in part, the cause of resistance, most notably the development of a police counterforce and of departures from the organization. The research literature has documented the development of subcultures in police organizations that may oppose the formal structure or may be mechanisms for adapting to the formal structure and its methods of gaining compliance among officers. In addition, the high turnover in many police departments can be tied to the types of power exercised by supervisors.

However, if legitimate, charismatic, and expert bases of power lead to acceptance among employees, as shown in figure 8-1, then it would seem logical to attempt to employ these in our criminal justice organizations. A body of research supports this position. Etzioni (1961) suggests that organizations have a high level of commitment by members if they are involved in the organization, which they cannot be if coercive and reward power are used. Current research reports similar findings. The amount of control exhibited by employees in their organization is directly related to compliance to organizational rules and regulations (Houghland, Shepard, and Wood, 1979; Houghland and Wood, 1980; Styskal, 1980). In effect, as the organization is legitimized by subordinates, it gains compliance from them.

Much can be said about the value of instilling a sense of legitimacy in criminal justice employees. As stated before, political behavior tends to surface in organizations where legitimacy is not present. Such seems to be the case in many criminal justice organizations and to suggest otherwise would be naive. The future of criminal justice administration hinges to a great degree on how legitimacy will be gained from both subordinates and the general public. The use of other methods of compliance in these organizations is just one avenue that deserves attention by those who administer our agencies of social control. The traditional types of power employed in these agencies no longer promote effective administration. Other bases of power would seem to be conducive to criminal justice management. We can only speculate about what these other bases would be. It is easy to say that legitimate, expert, and referent bases of power need to be developed, yet this assumes that we have goal congruity, methods to achieve goals, and certainty as to budget allocations in these organizations. Attention must be given to these problems if effective compliance structures in criminal justice organizations are to be created. We can then develop bases of power that are consistent with our objectives and, more importantly, are perceived as legitimate by the lay public and by those who perform the day-to-day tasks in criminal justice agencies.

Summary

The purpose of this chapter was to describe the types of authority and power in organizations and how they produce specific consequences for organizational members. The discussion suggested that the types of power found in many criminal justice organizations produce effects that are, in the long run, dysfunctional. We further suggested that certain types of power may be more useful than others to administrators of criminal justice organizations. These types of power were legitimate, expert, and referent. But they can be effective as compliance mechanisms only when other key issues of goal consensus, means to achieve goals, and resource allocation are addressed.

Finally, we suggested that because these issues have only recently been examined by criminal justice administrators, a proper compliance structure may not yet exist for many agencies of criminal justice. Criminal justice management must decide on proper compliance structures for their organizations given the nature of their tasks and the expectations of society. Without a proper examination of these pivotal issues, criminal justice agencies will remain in conflict. Conflict in organizations is the topic of the following chapter, which concludes our examination of group behavior in criminal justice organizations.

CASE STUDY

The Corrections Officer's Dilemma: Who Has the Power in the Joint?

Nantucket Prison was built well before the beginning of the nineteenth century. It was the end-of-the-line prison in a state correctional system that was overcrowded and underfunded. Besides housing some 200 inmates above its rated capacity, the prison was run by gangs with such authority that corrections officers often feared for their lives and did not have any ideas on how to interact with them effectively. This situation changed when veteran Robert Stones was transferred from the state's small camp system to the prison. Stones had been in corrections for almost twenty years and understood how to deal with inmates or, in his words, "deal with the inmate mentality." He was viewed by Warden Johnson as someone who could train the corrections officers how to deal effectively with inmates.

The corrections officers were hesitant and somewhat uncertain about what Stones could teach them that they did not already know. Stones agreed that his real value to the institution would be training the new officers. Warden Johnson agreed that Stones should work with the young corps of officers who were receptive to his ideas of dealing with inmates. The first corrections officer assigned to work with Stones was a new recruit named James Bowers. Bowers had a background in community-based corrections and knew about how former inmates, those on parole, reacted to authority. Because much of what he knew was community oriented, Stones wondered whether Bowers understood what prison life was about, even though he had been to prison transporting parolees who had their paroles revoked. Knowing that what Bowers learned he would tell the other officers, Stones was methodical in his training.

"The first thing you have to remember, Bowers, is that prisoners run the joint," said Stones. "Even more important is the fact that inmates could take over a prison any time they wanted, and that is why you have to understand where the powerful inmates are coming from." Bowers was somewhat bewildered by Stones's statement. He asked, "If inmates run the prison, what the hell kind of role do corrections officers have in this process? What are we, just babysitters for these guys?" With a smile on his face, Stones responded, "Well, to a degree, and with some inmates we are nothing but babysitters. But the important point is that you have to recognize that inmates do have a say about their incarceration. Forget the idea that we have total power here. Most of what we do is compromising. You got to compromise." Bowers did not know how to respond, but he remembered Stones's suggestions and thought them over.

Three months later he had his first chance to use them. It was an ordinary day in cellblock C when Officer Bowers noticed three inmates cornered in the maintenance room. His initial response was to go over and break up the inmates. Seeing what Bowers was going to do, Stones stopped him and suggested that he make sure other inmates in the cellblock were ready for lunch. Later in the day Bowers asked Stones why he prevented him from breaking up the inmates. Stones responded, "Those three inmates were making a deal for some marijuana, and the white guy was the dealer. He has a lot of power in here, and I respect him and his position." He added, "He distributes the dope, and I let him, while at the same time he controls the disruptive inmates in the block. We have our little deals that keep this place running. Now I want you to know that it's not a lot of dope, just enough to keep the prisoners happy." Bowers could not believe what he had heard. He angrily responded, "How can you let such things go on in the prison? We have to have greater control." With a grin on his face, Stones replied, "We have control because of what I do. It gets back to what I said earlier, that you have to respect the fact that some inmates have power in this prison and that pushing dope is one type of activity that gives them power." Bowers responded that he thought this type of dealing with inmates was in the long run dangerous because it caused fights and violence among prisoners. But Stones reaffirmed that his dealing with powerful inmates who distributed marijuana was essential to the stability of the prison. He added that control problems with inmates in the past were related to the inability of officers to recognize the power that prisoners have in the prison and that power can be expressed in a number of ways, including the selling of dope.

"Now I don't want you to get the wrong idea," said Stones. "I don't think that we should let these guys do whatever they want in here, but there has to be a recognition by the officers that dope peddling gives some guys a lot of power and that it has been in prison for a long time and will continue to be around. The fact is that we can't get rid of all of it; we can only hope to control it. The same is true of those religious leaders in here. Do you think those Muslim leaders get what they want from these other inmates and officers? You bet they do, and it's all because they are respected by a lot of the inmates. To do our jobs, we have to deal with the realities of the prison." Officer Bowers responded, "Is it the same way with the gang leaders in here?" "Now you are catching on kid. It's like the inmates say, you have to give a man respect if you want respect from him," answered Stones.

Officer Bowers went home that night and thought through what Officer Stones had said to him. He concluded that prison stability may depend not only on the power of inmates but also on how officers use their own power among inmates. Later that night a statement Stones had made to him three months earlier rang through his head: "Remember, Bowers, inmates run the joint."

Case Study Questions

1. What types of power do you believe would be the most effective in gaining control of Nantucket Prison?
2. Do you think Stones is effective as a corrections officer in his interaction with prisoners? If so, why? If not, why not?
3. What are some problems with negotiating with prisoners to maintain control of a prison? Will negotiating give corrections officers increased legitimacy among prisoners? Is that good or bad for the prison? Why or why not?

For Discussion

1. Of the types of power described in this chapter, which do you think is the most relevant to a specific agency of the criminal justice system? Are the types of power exhaustive, or can you think of others outside of the French and Raven typology presented here? Describe the strengths and weaknesses of this typology in criminal justice organizations.

2. What do you believe is the role of power in criminal justice administration? Is power important to agencies of criminal justice? What kind of power? Is it critical to have power as a criminal justice manager, and, if so, should this power be internally or externally based? Finally, describe instances where criminal justice administrators have abused their power, and offer suggestions as to how we can control these individuals.

3. Distinguish between power and authority. Do you believe the foundation of criminal justice organizations is power or authority? Why? Give examples in everyday criminal justice life that reflect the differences between these concepts.

4. Discuss the role of politics in criminal justice organizations. Is politics critical to these organizations, and if so, how should it be controlled? Is it true, as Long said years ago, that "politics is the lifeblood of administration" (1949:257) in public agencies like criminal justice organizations? Comment on the relevance of power to criminal justice administration and the survival of criminal justice organizations.

For Further Reading

Culbert, S. A., and McDonough, J. J. *Radical Management: Power Politics and the Pursuit of Trust.* New York: Free Press, 1985.

Kotter, J. P. *Power and Influence.* New York: Free Press, 1985.

Mintzberg, H. *Power in and Around Organizations.* Englewood Cliffs, N.J.: Prentice-Hall, 1983.

Pfeffer, J. *Power in Organizations.* Marshfield, Mass.: Pitman, 1981.

Srivastva, S. (Ed.). *Executive Power: How Executives Influence People and Organizations.* San Francisco: Jossey-Bass, 1986.

Organizational Conflict

Once the conflict began, the spiteful and invidious nature of the interpersonal and intergroup behaviors created an organizational paranoia that was very contagious and difficult to treat. What makes this case even more serious is that it is not atypical in its dynamics when compared to other cases of conflict in correctional institutions. However, there is very little information about how to deal with such conflict. Until more is known about this kind of organizational problem in human service organizations, a great deal of public employee time, energy, and commitment, in addition to taxpayers' dollars, will continue to be wasted on inefficient and ineffective programs [Duffee, 1986:270].

Conflict is frequently, but not always, negatively valued by organization members. To the extent that conflict *is* valued negatively, minor conflicts generate pressures toward resolution without altering the relationship; and major conflicts generate pressures to alter the form of the relationship or to dissolve it altogether. If inducements for participation are sufficiently high, there is the possibility of chronic conflict in the context of a stable relationship [Pondy, 1985:389].

This chapter addresses a subject that many academics, practitioners, and policymakers interested in criminal justice find perplexing—the process of conflict in criminal justice organizations. We have all worked in organizations and have experienced conflict, whether it be disagreement with the boss about our work assignment or about the overall direction of the organization. Conflict is endemic to all organizations, including the organizations of criminal justice. This chapter examines conflict in criminal justice organizations by exploring several topics.

First, we provide a definition of conflict in organizations, along with an examination of the stages of a conflict episode. We describe what conflict in criminal justice organizations means and, more importantly, the process of conflict. We should then be able to understand why conflict exists in the organizations of criminal justice and the many dynamics associated with the conflict process.

Second, we explore the types of conflict behaviors exhibited by people in organizations. In this section of the chapter, our discussion focuses on existing knowledge from organizational-behavior literature about the process of conflict in organizations and applies these ideas to the operations of criminal justice organizations.

Third, we examine the topic of conflict management. Various interventions are suggested, and various dimensions of the outcome of a conflict are explored. We suggest also that a proper analysis of conflict and its resolution must consider how conflict reaches well beyond the borders of the individual organizations of criminal justice.

Finally, the chapter concludes with a discussion of the role of conflict in criminal justice organizations and how conflict management can enhance the effectiveness of these organizations.

Conflict Defined

Like other topics this book has explored, the idea of conflict is one that is intuitively understood yet technically difficult to assess or measure. For this reason researchers interested in conflict in organizations often employ a number of different conceptualizations. Conflict is defined as a dynamic process in which two or more individuals in an organization interact in such a way as to produce "conflict episodes" that may or may not lead to hostile behaviors (Pondy, 1985:383). Pondy, for example, suggests four ways in which conflict can be understood in organizations. First, the *antecedent conditions of conflict* are often explored by researchers. These types of investigations typically examine the conditions that are precursors to conflict, such as resource scarcity and policy differences. When, for example, a corrections officer does not agree with an immediate supervisor on how to supervise inmates, the disagreement may lead to conflict between subordinate and supervisor. This policy difference thus may be viewed as a precursor to some type of conflict in the future.

Second, conflict can be understood as producing *affective states* within individuals. An example is the presence of stress, hostility, or anxiety among workers because of conflict in their organizations. In our example, if the corrections officer is upset by what she perceives as an incorrect policy choice by the immediate supervisor, she may create much stress for herself and become dysfunctional to the organization in the long run. Much of the research on stress in criminal justice organizations may reflect the inability of the worker to deal effectively with a conflict situation in the workplace. And, therefore, the examination of stress among criminal justice employees may require an exploration of the conflict process in those organizations. For this reason perhaps, many organizations of criminal justice have introduced conflict-management seminars for their employees.

Third, conflict can be viewed from the *cognitive states* of the individual employee. Once again, in our corrections officer example, the officer may or may not be aware of the conflict she has with the supervisor. Researchers interested in conflict processes in organizations have examined employees' awareness of conflict in their organizations and the degree to which it influences their behavior. We may, for example, survey corrections officers and ask them whether they perceive conflict situations in their work and how they deal with these situations. Corrections officers are in fact good at adapting to or accommodating the conflict inherent in their roles. As Lipsky (1988) suggests, much of what street-level bureaucrats, such as police officers and corrections officers, accomplish is achieved through a series of accommodations. We would add that these accommodations may be in reaction to the conflict situations they face.

Fourth, conflict in organizations has been examined by exploring the *actual conflict behavior*, whether it is passive resistance or outright confrontational or aggressive behavior. Many researchers interested in correctional institutions can understand this form of conflict research because of the voluminous material on the nature of disturbances or riots in correctional institutions. Much of the research has examined the etiology of these riots (Barak-Glantz, 1985).

Types of Conflict

We can identify four types of conflict in organizations, each of which requires a different adjustment mechanism. The four types of conflict are personal conflict, group conflict, intraorganizational conflict, and interorganizational conflict.

Personal Conflict

This type of conflict exists within the individual and usually is some form of goal conflict or cognitive conflict. Typically, this form of conflict is a result of not meeting one's expectations. For example, a young police officer who holds certain ideals about the police profession may find that many of them are not consistent with the demands of the police role or the police organization. He may feel much personal conflict as a result of not being able to reconcile his expectations with the expectations of his superiors. In short, he may feel what Festinger (1957) refers to as "cognitive dissonance."

To deal with this conflict, he may change his expectations to bring them in line with the organization's expectations, or he may seek to understand the conflict and thereby reduce its impact on him. Whatever his decision, it will affect his future behavior. In the extreme case, the officer may decide to leave the organization because he cannot deal with the personal conflict. For this reason, conflict-management programs, which we discuss later in the chapter, are critical to the organizations of criminal justice.

Group Conflict

Group conflict occurs in organizations when individual members disagree on some point of common interest. The resolution of the conflict is essential to the survival of the group and may even enhance the effectiveness of the group in the long run. Take, for example, a group of police officers who work in a patrol unit. A conflict arises because of a disagreement over ticket writing. The department has formal expectations as to how many tickets are to be written by the group. However, the officers have their own norms for the number of tickets that are to be written by each officer. The conflict occurs because some officers in the group believe that the expectations of the superior override the informally derived expectations of the group. The ensuing conflict can improve the coordination and communication processes of the group by forcing the group to be cohesive and coordinated in determining an acceptable level of ticket writing. Obviously, if the conflict escalates too far, possibly because proper conflict-resolution techniques are not employed, then the group may disintegrate. Group conflict can also be healthy and productive if handled properly by the immediate supervisor. In our example, the sergeant can use certain techniques to benefit the group in the long term.

Another form of group conflict is intergroup conflict, in which groups within an organization compete for valuable and limited resources. If we look at police organizations and examine the multiple groups within them, we can see why intergroup conflict exists. Many police departments are composed of functional units, which perform the tasks of the organization. Some examples are patrol, detective, vice, juvenile, and traffic. Each has its own objectives and tasks.

Given the differing tasks and the fact that resources are finite in police organizations, it is common for conflict situations to arise. If, for example, the detective unit is favored by the chief and given more resources than the other units, conflict is likely to ensue. The units may perceive the chief's favoritism toward the detective unit as an unfair advantage and request increased allocations for their units. In this example, the chief may resolve the conflict by justifying giving more resources to the detective unit than to the other units. However, if the other units believe that the explanation is inadequate, the conflict may escalate.

If the conflict among the competing units does escalate, the police chief can use the competition among the groups as a mechanism to engender improved performance. Thus, intergroup conflict may be healthy for the organization. It must be mentioned, however, that if intergroup conflict escalates too far, it can be counterproductive. In our example, the competition among the different police units must be monitored so that it remains effective and beneficial. An example of this type of administrative use of competition was documented by Schlesinger (1958) in his analysis of the presidency of Franklin Delano Roosevelt. Roosevelt was able to use the conflict generated by competing governmental units to control information about the workings of the federal bureaucracy while simultaneously generating improved levels of performance among subordinates. This method of conflict management may be effective, but if particular units continually fail in the process, they may become demoralized and assume a defeatist attitude that will be detrimental to the organization in the long term.

Intraorganizational Conflict

While group conflict deals with the relationships within and between groups in organizations, intraorganizational conflict is generated by the structural makeup of an organization—that is, by formal authority in the organization and how it is delegated. There are four major types of intraorganizational conflict: vertical conflict, horizontal conflict, line–staff conflict, and role conflict (Hellriegel, Slocum, and Woodman, 1986).

Vertical conflict. This type of conflict exists between those at different levels in an organizational hierarchy. Within a department of corrections, for example, corrections officers sit beneath sergeants and sergeants sit below lieutenants and so forth. This paramilitary model makes vertical conflict an inevitable event as superiors try to control the behavior of officers. The relationship between corrections officers and prisoners is so tenuous that conflict usually ensues whenever superiors try to tell officers how to relate to inmates. This perceived encroachment by supervisors on officers' jobs is the antecedent condition for conflict. In fact, a body of knowledge about corrections work supports the vertical nature of conflict in correctional institutions not only between supervisor and subordinate but also between inmate and officer (see Lombardo, 1981). Whatever the location, it would be fair to say that vertical conflict is ubiquitous within correctional institutions. Similar research findings support widespread vertical conflict in police organizations (Angell, 1971:19–29).

Horizontal conflict. This type of conflict is exhibited by units that are at the same hierarchical level in an organization. Our previous example of conflict among the various units in a police department can also be understood as an example of horizontal conflict. If the multiple police units are of equal rank, then the conflict is horizontal. If, however, they are not at the same hierarchical level in the organization, then we would say that the conflict among them is vertical.

Horizontal conflict is most evident when there is too much concern for task accomplishments within one unit. If the juvenile unit, for example, seeks increased resources for its investigation of gang-related activities and the arrests of gang members, granting the request may work against the larger purpose of the unit and the department—to maintain order in society. This overemphasis on gang-related activity may produce conflict with other units because they perceive the activities of the juvenile unit to be counter to their own goals—e.g., the public relations unit or the crime prevention unit may be trying to establish positive ties with gang members—or because they feel the activity wastes finite departmental resources.

Line–staff conflict. This type of conflict is readily apparent in private organizations, where staff personnel are used to augment and supplement the work of line managers. Agencies of criminal justice also have support personnel who work with the line managers to accomplish the objectives of the organization. Such people as legal advisors in police organizations or treatment and medical personnel in correctional institutions are good examples. The line–staff distinction in correctional institutions is a noteworthy one because it has generated much conflict between traditional security personnel and those whose goals are treatment and physical care. Like correctional institutions, police organizations have much conflict between line personnel and staff. The most notable causes of these conflicts are the perception of line personnel that staff workers try to assume authority over basic line functions, the inability of the two groups to communicate effectively, the claim that staff people take the credit for successful programs yet are quick to point the finger of blame at line personnel when something goes wrong, and the claim that line personnel do not believe that staff people see the "big picture" of a specific program (Swanson, Territo, and Taylor, 1988).

Role conflict. This type of conflict is probably the most common in criminal justice organizations. Role conflict occurs when an individual is not able to comprehend or accomplish assigned tasks. The source of the conflict may be faulty communication between subordinate and supervisor, disagreement between the subordinate and the supervisor about the tasks required, conflicting expectations from differing supervisors, or differing expectations among the groups the subordinate belongs to as to the role of the subordinate. Regardless of its causes, role conflict as a form of intraorganizational conflict has been documented extensively in the criminal justice literature. (See Philliber's (1987) review of the literature on role conflict among corrections officers.)

We should note here that role conflict and role ambiguity are not the same thing. *Role ambiguity* occurs when a subordinate perceives that information about the required tasks of the job is unclear and inconsistent, while *role conflict* occurs when a subordinate perceives incompatible expectations about how the tasks should be performed. In other words, role ambiguity denotes inconsistencies in the knowledge needed to complete a job, while role conflict denotes inconsistencies about what is expected of the subordinate. It would be fair to say that criminal justice employees experience a great deal of both role conflict and role ambiguity in their jobs.

Finally, we must comment on the effects of role conflict in the organizations of criminal justice. Research has suggested that role conflict in both correctional institutions and police departments not only is widespread, but may in addition lead to many other problems experienced by both these organizations, including high turnover, absenteeism, and low morale. (See Alpert and Dunham (1988) for a good review of these problems in police organizations.) In particular, role conflict can be traced to much of the stress found in these organizations. We know, for example, that people can react in a number of ways to role conflict, including being aggressive toward superiors, attempting to reduce the conflict by communicating effectively with superiors, and withdrawing from the organization. Withdrawal is seen too often in organizations of criminal justice. Thus, future research is going to have to provide concrete suggestions as to how role conflict can be reduced.

Interorganizational Conflict

Interorganizational conflict occurs when there is a common purpose among different organizational units but disagreement as to how that purpose will be achieved. This type of conflict arises when a separate organizational unit (such as one component of the criminal justice system) perceives its goals and objectives to be in conflict with those of other units. Take, for example, the jail and its links to other components of the criminal justice system. The jail has as its central task the control of two offender populations: pretrial detainees (people awaiting trial because they could not make bail and those who have committed serious crimes and are being preventively detained) and those who have already been convicted of a crime and are serving a sentence.

Although these are the two primary groups housed within the jail and its central purpose is to maintain a safe and secure environment for them, the jail, in addition, is used by prosecutors, police, and probation and parole personnel for other purposes. Prosecutors use the jail to coerce recalcitrant inmates to plea bargain. The threat of staying in jail encourages the defendant to "cop a plea" and relieves the pressures of the prosecutor's overcrowded caseload. The jail thus serves the organizational interests of prosecutors in that it ensures a smoothly operating system of plea bargaining and caseload reduction. The jail serves similar interests of both the police and probation and parole personnel. The police use the jail as a repository for the "rabble" (Irwin, 1986) who are found on the streets of our major cities and as an inducement for defendants to confess to a crime or to serve as witnesses against other suspects (Rottman and Kimberly, 1975). Probation and parole officers use the jails as a convenient place for offenders who are suspected of committing either a technical violation or a new crime. In many large urban jails, a sizable number of people are awaiting revocation hearings, and the jail in this case gives probation and parole personnel control over their clients. In short, the jail serves all these components of the criminal justice system and helps these differing organizational units meet their goals.

But, while the jail can be critical for the accomplishment of these goals, it can equally be a place of interorganizational conflict. We can examine, for example, the links between jails and other correctional agencies. It has been relatively common for jails to house offenders who cannot be placed in state prisons or detention settings because they are overcrowded. Data from the Bureau of Justice Statistics (1988) indicate that of the 614 large jails in this country (those housing more than 100 inmates) 22 percent are holding inmates for federal, state, and local authorities. This situation creates much conflict between the jail and correctional institutions. Typically, the conflict is resolved through a feedback process between the jail and other correctional institutions. In effect, jails have communicated directly to correctional institutions that they will not or cannot receive more state prisoners into their facilities. In many cases this interorganizational conflict can be resolved only by the jail's refusing to take inmates from other jurisdictions until the over-crowding problem is resolved.

As another example, jail overcrowding can be caused by the refusal of judges to implement rational bail guidelines for those suspected of a crime. Many jails are overcrowded with individuals who could be bailed out and pose no threat to the community. The question becomes, Why won't judges institute rational bail guidelines if overcrowding is a prob-lem in the jail? The answer lies in the fact that the jail is not of primary importance to them. What is important is that some type of punishment be given to people who have violated the laws. A little jail time reminds the suspect that the court is serious about the crime committed. Judges may feel even more strongly about using the jail in this way when the in-dividual has been before the courts in the past and behavior has not changed. In this example, the judge may have goals that differ from those of the sheriff who runs the jail, and the disagreement about the relative importance of each goal leads to interorganizational conflict in the system.

This same type of interorganizational conflict can be seen in correc-tional institutions with respect to the delivery of services such as educa-tion and medical attention (see Duffee, 1986:274–276), specifically when the provision of these services is the responsibility of another state bu-reaucracy, such as a state department of public health or education.

The important point here is that interorganizational conflict is com-mon in criminal justice. The resolution of such conflict depends on the ability of separate organizational units to coordinate their efforts and increase their level of communication to ensure long-term preservation of their links. It may even be suggested that the resolution of interorganiza-tional conflicts both among the components of the criminal justice sys-tem and between those organizations and other state bureaucracies is the single most important issue facing administrators of the criminal justice system today.

Stages of a Conflict Episode

Although this typology helps us define and categorize conflict in criminal justice organizations, Pondy (1985:382) believes that it does not add to our understanding of the process of conflict. To understand the conflict process, he suggests that research must consider conflict episodes. More importantly, Pondy (1985) emphasizes that not all conflict situations lead to overt aggression or hostility. In other words, the conflict situation may never come to fruition. In fact, the purpose of conflict-management programs in organizations is to prevent the escalation of events that lead to actual aggressive or hostile behavior by employees. In addition, however, it should be pointed out that not all conflicts are resolved through conflict-management techniques; some, for example, may disappear because one of the parties does not perceive the situation as a conflict situation. It is critical, therefore, to identify the various stages of a conflict episode, as Pondy (1985:383–386) suggests.

The five stages of a conflict episode are presented in figure 9-1. The stages are: latent conflict, perceived conflict, felt conflict, manifest conflict, and conflict aftermath. These stages are affected by both environmental and organizational factors, as figure 9-1 shows. Consistent with the idea that a conflict episode is dynamic, we can see that the entire episode evolves from the aftermath of a preceding conflict episode. In this

Figure 9-1 The Dynamics of a Conflict Episode. (From Pondy, L. R., "Organizational Conflict: Concepts and Models," *Administrative Science Quarterly*, 1967, *12*. Adapted by permission of *Administrative Science Quarterly*.)

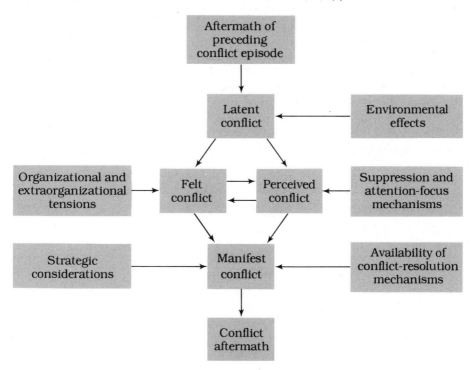

way, all conflict episodes are interrelated and have a degree of continuity. Conflict in organizations must thus be understood beyond the immediate situation.

Latent Conflict

This stage of the conflict occurs when the conditions that are the underlying sources of the conflict are present. According to Pondy (1985:383), latent conflict is typically rooted in competition for scarce resources, drives for autonomy, or divergence of subunit goals. Each one of these roots can be seen in the organizations of criminal justice. In the typical police department, scarcity of resources produces fierce levels of competition among the various subunits when, for example, the juvenile unit demands increased resources to combat gang activity or the vice unit seeks additional officers to arrest drug dealers. Drives for autonomy can also create conflict in police organizations. When immediate supervisors attempt to control the behavior of officers, and the officers, as a group, seek autonomy or control over their work environments, conflict is inevitable. Finally, divergence of subunit goals occurs "when two parties who must cooperate on some joint activity are unable to reach a consensus on concerted action" (Pondy, 1985:383). Patrol officers, for example, who must work together and cannot agree on how to complete their tasks will have much latent conflict.

All three components of latent conflict are present in prison settings. Scarcity of resources is evidenced by limited space, overcrowding, and minimal attention to such areas as treatment programs. Subunits in the prison organization—e.g., treatment personnel and security personnel—compete for these limited resources, each believing that its goals are more critical to the prison. And we see drives for autonomy in correctional institutions among both corrections staff and prisoners. Corrections staff seek additional input into how institutions are run, while prisoner groups demand control over their lives and prison conditions.

Perceived Conflict

This stage of the conflict episode occurs when at least one of the two parties recognize that a conflict situation exists. When they do, they may seek to escalate the conflict episode or choose to deflect it. A police officer, for example, may have a perceived conflict with her partner; she can decide to suppress the conflict because she doesn't believe it to be a major issue, or she can decide that the issue is important to her. The officer may decide to suppress the perceived conflict between herself and her partner over who is going to drive the squad car, yet she may want to push the perceived conflict to the next stage over the issue of handling recalcitrant suspects. The important point is that once we consciously recognize the conflict between ourself and another individual we have control over whether the conflict episode will proceed into the next stage.

Felt Conflict

Felt conflict occurs when a party personalizes the conflict situation. For example, Officer A may be aware or perceive that there is a conflict between herself and her partner, but she doesn't allow the conflict to upset her. However, Officer B may be so upset by a perceived conflict that it now affects his relationship with his partner. Once personalized, the conflict not only is felt but, in addition, may become dysfunctional for the organization. This stage of the conflict episode is critical to organizations; proper handling of the conflict situation in this stage is extremely important to the long-term stability of any organization, including those in the criminal justice system.

Manifest Conflict

After the conflict situation has been perceived and felt by a party, we may move into manifest conflict. This stage of the conflict episode is characterized by overt or covert behavior to bring out the conflict. In prisons, for example, manifest conflict may be expressed in riots or disturbances. These types of overt situations, however, are rare, even for prisons. More often than not, manifest conflict takes the covert form of deliberate blockage by one party of the other party's goals.

Going back to our police officer example, if Officer B knowingly frustrates his partner in such a way that she cannot attain her goals, then manifest conflict is surely present. At this point tension between the two may be the greatest. More importantly, at this juncture managers must step into the conflict situation to diffuse it before it becomes dysfunctional to the organization. As a result, the recognition of manifest conflict among subordinates by immediate supervisors is critical.

The supervisor must recognize, in addition, that he or she may be the source of manifest conflict in the organization. In fact, it is all too common in criminal justice for front-line supervisors to be perceived as the facilitators of manifest conflicts instead of the diffusers of them. Even worse, often the conflicts in criminal justice organizations are not among the employees but between the employees and their supervisors or administrators. In all these cases, it is imperative that the superior not escalate the manifest conflict but facilitate its resolution.

Conflict Aftermath

At this point in the conflict episode, if the antecedent conditions (competition for scarce resources, drives for autonomy, and divergent subunit goals) are dealt with in a satisfactory manner, the conflict will dissolve. Such a resolution is the hope of those who are interested in keeping organizational conflict to a minimum and want to learn from the conflict episode. If, however, the antecedent conditions are not addressed but are only suppressed for the short term, then the conflict will continue to surface as does a wound that has not been properly attended to. If the conflict continues, we enter the aftermath stage. The danger of this stage of the conflict episode is that it may become serious or, worse yet, so weaken the relationship between the two actors that it can never be fully repaired in the future. In this way, conflict episodes become part of a dynamic process. We can see how the conflict aftermath occurs in the components of the criminal justice system. In prisons where the antecedent conditions of conflict (as described previously) are never resolved, for example, the conflict is allowed to fester until a disturbance occurs.

Conflict Behaviors

Awareness of conflict behaviors is important to our understanding of the role conflict plays in criminal justice organizations. Moreover, it enables us to develop and implement effective conflict-management programs in these organizations.

Conflict behaviors can be understood by examining a model proposed by Thomas (1985). The model has two dimensions, each representing an individual's intention with respect to a conflict situation. The two dimensions are *cooperativeness*, attempting to satisfy the other party's concerns, and *assertiveness*, attempting to satisfy one's own concerns. Different combinations of these two dimensions, according to Thomas, can create five conflict behaviors, as shown in figure 9-2. Each one of these behaviors reflects an individual's attempt to deal with a conflict situation.

Competing behavior (assertive, uncooperative) occurs when one is willing to place one's own concerns above the concerns of the other individual. Typically, force and even violence occur in this conflict situation. In addition, the competing type of conflict behavior seeks the resolution of the conflict in a fashion that maximizes one's own interests.

Accommodating behavior (unassertive, cooperative) satisfies the concerns of the other individual rather than one's own concerns in a conflict situation. This behavior may be quite rare in organizations because it is difficult to understand why one would neglect one's own interests and maximize another's, yet we all know this does happen in everyday life.

Avoiding behavior (unassertive, uncooperative) neglects both one's own concerns and the concerns of the other individual. People who exhibit avoiding behavior want a minimal amount of friction in their

Figure 9-2 A Two-Dimensional Model of Conflict Behavior. (From Ruble, T., and Thomas, T. K., "Support for a Two-Dimensional Model of Conflict Behavior," *Organizational Behavior and Human Performance*, 1976, *16*, p. 145. Copyright 1976 by Academic Press. Adapted by permission of the author.)

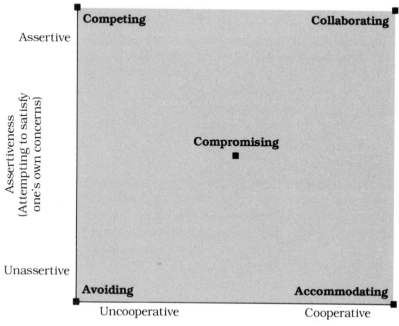

interactions and do everything in their power to make sure no problems occur between themselves and others.

Collaborating behavior (assertive, cooperative) attempts to satisfy the demands and concerns of both parties in a conflict situation; it is a type of conflict behavior that few possess yet many desire.

Finally, *compromising* behavior (intermediate in both assertiveness and cooperativeness) seeks the middle ground. People who exhibit this type of conflict behavior realize that you cannot always get what you want and, in addition, recognize that for the conflict to be resolved there must be some give and take by both sides. Sacrifice, in other words, is part of this type of conflict behavior.

Individually, no one conflict style is bad or good. Whether a conflict behavior is appropriate depends on the context and situation. Accordingly, Thomas (1985:399) suggests that in some situations specific conflict behaviors are better than others. For example, it has been said that conflict management is at the heart of running a modern police department. How chiefs respond to various conflict situations is critical to perceptions about their effectiveness as leaders. When chiefs believe that their way of doing things is correct, it might be appropriate for them to take a stand and compete on the issue. When an emergency arises and a quick response is needed, the competing form of conflict behavior may also be the most appropriate, but we do not want to say it is always the best.

As another example, a citizen group that demands a different form of patrolling in its neighborhood has an understanding of and perspective on the allocation of police officers within the community. In addition, the group may have some knowledge of how and when police resources can be used to combat crime in its neighborhood. This type of information may be valuable to the chief in a number of ways, from creating positive relationships with the community to getting important feedback from residents on how police resources can be distributed in the community. If the police chief's intention is to gain from the community ideas about crime control, then the collaborating style of conflict behavior may be the most appropriate.

If, however, the chief believes that this issue of community input into police operations is trivial or unimportant to the department, he or she may perceive that avoiding the conflict is the appropriate response. If this perception is incorrect however, this type of conflict behavior may prove to be deleterious to the department. For this reason, selecting the correct conflict behavior given the situation is critical to organizations today, in particular criminal justice organizations.

This example describes a conflict situation between a police chief and a group external to the police organization. Conflict situations, however, can also occur within organizations, and selecting the correct conflict behavior in such situations is of equal importance to administrators of criminal justice organizations.

Conflict Management

Thomas (1985:405–411) identifies two types of interventions to deal with conflict situations: process interventions and structural interventions. Each attempts to deal with conflict situations in such a way that the conflict can be resolved. By using both, we can deal with conflict in criminal justice organizations. Although each is an attempt to deal with intraorganizational conflict, some of the ideas presented under each type of intervention can be applied also to interorganizational conflicts. Both are designed to resolve the conflict episode. Process interventions attempt to "become directly involved in the ongoing sequence of events" (Thomas, 1985:405) that result in the conflict. Structural interventions attempt to alter the conditions in an organization that influence the direction of conflict episodes.

Process Interventions

These types of interventions fall into two categories. First, *consciousness-raising interventions* attempt to change the "internal experiences of the parties" that shape their behaviors. This type of intervention requires that the manager or supervisor intervene indirectly in the conflict, suggesting how the competing parties can reconceptualize their perceptions and thus remove the conditions that created the conflict. Second, *interaction management* occurs when a supervisor intervenes directly in the conflict situation between two subordinates, suggesting how the two parties can change their behaviors to resolve this conflict and avoid future conflicts. Both these types of process interventions thus require active participation by supervisors in order for the conflict to be reduced. We review next some of the conditions in organizations that can be altered by process interventions by administrators and managers. Our examination of these conditions includes criminal justice examples.

Personal characteristics. It is quite apparent that conflict episodes in organizations are a result of multiple factors, including the personalities of those involved in the conflict. Our personalities affect how we deal with conflict. As Thomas (1985:406) puts it, individuals in organizations have "repertoires" in dealing with conflict that are rooted in their personalities. These repertoires are difficult to deal with. Sometimes we cannot alter an individual's position in an organization even though we feel that he or she has a poor conflict repertoire. More often than not, we try to adapt to this type of personality with the hope of minimizing conflict. For example, if a police sergeant has a competitive repertoire, we often tell subordinates that they are going to have to live with this person and learn to accept the situation. Obviously, if the situation becomes nonproductive, then actions have to be taken by those supervisors above the sergeant to deal with the conflict. In this example, interaction management has been a tool used by police managers to deal with personality differences among subordinates. Usually the police manager attempts to get the conflicting parties to focus on job responsibilities and how those cannot be hindered by personality differences. This is a rare situation in most police organizations, yet it is important to understand how personalities may contribute to conflict episodes in police organizations.

Informal rules. All organizations have written and unwritten rules about how people are to behave. These rules are critical to the operation of the organization. For example, going to the sergeant or the lieutenant may not be approved by the informal code among officers when there is a conflict between officers. Dealing with conflict episodes in police organizations, therefore, may require an understanding of the role the informal code plays in such situations. Reasonable attempts by police administrators to resolve the conflict may be accepted by the informal code. Though such activities as serving as an arbitrator or "referee" between two disputants might prove to be helpful, the police administrator always must be aware that such an interaction management strategy could be limited by the informal code and should proceed cautiously.

Constituent pressure. In all organizations there is often pressure and competition among groups. This competition typically forces cohesiveness among the groups. Examining a correctional organization highlights this concept. The treatment-versus-custody debate that has raged for years is a good example of how groups become cohesive when they feel they are being threatened. Prison administrators have been unable to deal with the conflict that ensues from constituent pressures but they could do so by using process intervention. One example of an effective process intervention would be to get both groups to realize the benefits to the organization by resolving their conflicts. In our example, the prison administrator could show how the dual functions of treatment and custody serve the purpose of maintaining the order of the prison and also help each group accomplish their goals. In this way, the administrator is trying to raise the consciousness of members in both groups.

Conflict of interest. According to Thomas (1985:407), this precursor exists in organizations when the concerns of two parties in an organization are incompatible. Such conflict is escalated when both parties are competing for limited resources. In prisons, for example, we know that limited funds are available for all programs, particularly treatment programs. Satisfying custodial concerns invariably leads to a reduction in resources for those groups in the prison who are interested in treatment. Unless there is some "organizational slack," as Thomas (1985:407) states, it will be difficult for the prison organization to meet the objectives of both groups, thereby increasing the likelihood of conflict. This conflict episode in prison organizations has existed for many years, and unless further resources are granted these organizations, it is unlikely that the conflict will be reduced. If nothing else, this situation has forced prisons to define the objectives and purposes of their organizations given their limited funds and resources. Moreover, it may not be apparent how process interventions resolve conflicts due to conflicts of interest. Actually, interactive management can resolve the conflict between treatment workers and custody personnel by clearly stating the central purpose of the prison. Once parties recognize that, for example, custody concerns are *supposed* to override treatment goals, the conflict could be resolved. Treatment employees may recognize that the demands, and therefore more resources, should be given to the custody function.

Thomas (1985:408) states that the degree of competition among conflicting interests in an organization is determined by the stakes involved (the degree to which the issue at conflict is important) and the *in-*

terdependence among the competing parties (the relative connection between the groups when competing for high stakes). For example, the corrections officer staff may compete with the treatment staff for scarce resources in the prison independently *(parallel striving)* or seek to block the possibility of the treatment group's achieving its goals *(mutual interference)*. As Thomas (1985:409) suggests, parallel striving may increase the efforts of groups to work toward organizational goals, while mutual interference disrupts each group's attempt to accomplish organizational goals.

Power and status. Power and status play an important part in the conflicts that occur in organizations and their level of intensity. Obviously, a police officer does not seek to enter into conflictual relationships with an immediate supervisor because of a power differential between the two. In fact, avoidance as a conflict behavior is common in situations where there are great power differentials between the parties. Moreover, some units in organizations have greater status and levels of power than others. As a result, departments have to be conscious of their relative power and status before making requests of other departments. Although treatment personnel in prisons, for example, do not have much power, they may believe they have higher status than guards in both the prison and society. This belief may be part of the reason for the high level of conflict between treatment staff and custodial staff. One would not want to reduce the explanation of all conflict between the two groups to status differentials, yet it may be one factor that exacerbates the conflict between them. Another possible process intervention would be the prison administration's making both treatment personnel and custodial workers aware of their relative importance to the prison. Indeed, proper prison administration is to educate workers in what role they play to achieve organizational goals. This awareness in both groups may lead to the reduction of conflict between them.

Organizational policy. An organizational policy is often created to minimize a conflict. However, if rules are nothing but the result of "political struggles" (Thomas, 1985:410), then one would expect that rules and organizational policies are only a short-term response. Opinions among groups in police departments on what type of enforcement action should be taken may vary considerably; therefore, we may make a policy that states when and how an arrest will be made. This policy, however, will not resolve the issue but will only take it temporarily out of the forefront of organizational business. We would therefore expect that once the issue arises again, another rule will be created to deal with the situation and appease the competing parties. Making a new policy that attempts to eliminate conflict between two parties in an organization can be perceived as a process intervention.

Structural Interventions

While process interventions are concerned with conflict episodes, structural interventions are designed to reduce conflict by examining and altering the conditions of the organization that promote conflict. These conditions are ongoing and part of the structure within the manager's system. It is presumed that ongoing conflicts in organizations can be traced to the various structural features of the organization. Thomas (1985:410–411) describes two types of structural interventions that can be employed: selection and training interventions and contextual-modification interventions.

Selection and training interventions. Selection interventions use screening procedures to choose the people who would be best for the organization and the job. Both police organizations and corrections departments attempt to select the most favorable candidates for positions within their organizations. They hope that they have gotten the people who can perform the tasks of the job and whom they can work with. In addition, they attempt to train people to work in the way they believe is most conducive to accomplishing organizational objectives. Organizations hope that through such interventions they can minimize conflict and increase the effectiveness of the organization.

Contextual-modification interventions. These types of interventions attempt to change the context within which parties interact. Such changes typically require forceful management and leadership in the policy-development process. For example, the conflict of interest in correctional organizations between treatment staff and custodial groups can be reduced, in part, through a reduction of competition for scarce resources between the groups. Therefore, if a manager can acquire increased resources for both groups, there is then no reason for competition. Through this contextual modification, the manager has increased the likelihood that each group will be able to meet its own needs while fulfilling the needs of the organization. Yet accomplishing this modification is easier said than done. In fact, our position here is that contextual modifications in criminal justice organizations require great awareness of interorganizational conflict, a topic we examined previously in the chapter.

Limits to Conflict Management

Although conflicts requiring contextual modification may be resolved, other conflicts are more intractable because managers have even less control over their resolution. For example, conflicts escalate in correctional settings when there is limited space for the housing of prisoner populations. Overcrowding produces conflict between both inmates and staff. Yet, corrections administrators do not have the resources to add space. A possible solution to the conflict is to build additional prisons, yet this may be a short-term solution because further resources are not going to be available when prison space again becomes limited.

Instead, a satisfactory solution to the problem may require attention to nonincarcerative mechanisms for dealing with offenders. Given the reality of limited resources in prison settings, the conflict may require solutions that reach well beyond the boundaries of the organization, including solutions on both the interorganizational and the societal level. Many organizational conflicts in criminal justice are thus not satisfactorily addressed because it is beyond the scope of these organizations to resolve the latent conditions that perpetuate these conflicts.

Administrators have to accept that sometimes they will not be able to handle a conflict situation. Sometimes we fail in our attempts to deal with conflicts both internal and external to the organization. This failure, however, does not relegate us to doing nothing. The reasonable position is to learn from our mistakes and to go forward and resolve similar conflicts in the future with the knowledge gained from our past experiences.

Is Conflict Management Possible in Criminal Justice Administration?

According to Thomas (1985:412–415), successful conflict management deals with all the dimensions of conflict outcomes. There are three such dimensions. The first is goal attainment by conflicting parties. In the conflict between treatment staff and custodial personnel, there has to be some type of goal attainment by either one group or the other or both. In an optimal sense, we would like both parties to gain something from the conflict. Although desirable, such an outcome is highly improbable in this case; and Thomas even states that you would not want to grant every party equal weight in the conflict. Custodial functions, for example, may be more important to the prison organization than treatment programs or vice versa. If the conflict does resolve anything, it may be the priority of one function over the other. For this reason effective criminal justice administration requires communication of the priorities in an organization. Once subordinates understand these priorities, the number of conflicts in the organization may decrease. This same line of reasoning can be extended to conflict at the interorganizational level. Clear communication among the components in the criminal justice system will reduce the likelihood of long-term conflict among them. If, however, an administrator perceives that the parties in conflict are of equal value, then the optimal strategy is some type of compromise so that each feels that it received a portion of what it sought in the conflict.

Second, it would seem imperative that administrators in the criminal justice system be aware of the consequences of a conflict episode for the people involved. If, for example, treatment staff feel that they have been treated unfairly by the administration of the institution in resolving a conflict, this perception may adversely affect their productivity and outlook toward the job. Such long-term effects on performance can also be the result of interorganizational conflict. Because the parts of the system are so interdependent, it is crucial that administrators understand the importance of maintaining stable relationships with each other (see the case study at the end of the chapter). These relationships may be the most pivotal aspect of effective criminal justice administration today. Here, collaboration seems to be the best possible method for dealing with conflict. The collaboration strategy enables conflicting parties to see that their concerns are being recognized even though they may not get what they want.

Third, conflict management in the criminal justice system must be economical of time and effort. An administrator of a state corrections system once said privately that his job entailed keeping the conflicts down in the department and keeping his name out of the newspapers. This example indicates the tremendous amount of effort put into dealing with conflicts both within the organizations of criminal justice and outside their boundaries. Energy used to deal with conflicts could be used for constructive activities within the organization. Good criminal justice administrators understand, therefore, the importance of efficient conflict management in their organizations.

This point leads us to the question, Is conflict management possible in criminal justice organizations? We think that it not only is possible but is essential to the operation of the criminal justice system. The key lies in improving communication both within the components of the system and among them. At present, communication is fragmented at both levels. For conflict management to work, this problem of poor communication is going to have to be resolved. Improving communication will require some structural changes, including more specific lines of communication in the organization. At the interorganizational level this would mean raising the consciousness (process intervention) of criminal justice administrators to help them see that improved communication is essential to their effectiveness.

The Role of Conflict in Organizations

A number of views have been espoused over the years concerning the role that conflict plays in organizations. Our position here is that conflict in criminal justice organizations can be both beneficial and harmful. Much of the conflict that occurs in the components of the criminal justice system is good in the sense that it promotes change in those organizations. Conflict makes the system responsive to the demands of a changing environment. An example from the police field highlights this point of view. Assume that a police organization is having problems with the external environment. It is viewed as being nonresponsive to demands from the community for changes in the way police services are delivered. In this situation, conflict may arise not only between community groups and those who run the department but also between the department and the officers. If the department does become responsive to the community, rank-and-file officers may feel that the department is trying to appease the community groups to their detriment. Conflict in this situation may be good for the department because it forces the department to rethink its relationship with both the community and its own officers, a task that can be beneficial to the organization's operations and delivery of services. The ultimate goal of conflict management in the system of criminal justice should be an increase in organizational effectiveness.

Conflict can also be harmful. If, in the previous example, conflict between the officers and the department escalates over the role of the community to the point that the functioning of police units is jeopardized, then conflict has become detrimental to the long-term operation of the department. Management has failed to control the escalation of conflict, and, as a result, the effectiveness of the organization may be diminished.

Conflict in criminal justice organizations is, however, a normal process, and elimination of it is not only unrealistic but also counterproductive to the long-term health of these organizations. In short, conflict serves a useful function. Although long-term and deeply entrenched conflict is of no value to any organization, conflict enables an organization to grow and adapt successfully to its environment.

Conflict in criminal justice organizations seems inevitable given the fact of frequently incompatible goals. It is quite apparent that managers have to learn how to live with, adapt to, and cope with such conflict. Conflict-management programs need to be developed to train managers and administrators how to do so effectively.

Summary

The purpose of this chapter was to discuss the concept of conflict and to apply it to the criminal justice system. We have found in our review that there are stages in the conflict process and various ways of understanding conflict behaviors. It is somewhat trite to state that conflict is endemic to the organizations of criminal justice, yet our review indicated that conflict is an intricate process. In addition, we tried to impress on the reader the value of viewing conflict beyond the organization and to see it as an interorganizational phenomenon. Administrators of criminal justice systems today are constantly dealing with conflicts that arise among them as system actors. System interactions produce conflicts among the components, and it is the responsibility of administrators to deal with such conflicts.

Our call for conflict management in the organizations of criminal justice was predicated on the belief that effective criminal justice administration demands the proper management of conflict. We believe that one cannot discuss conflict management without talking about increased interaction and communication among the components of the criminal justice system. Although improved communication has been recommended for years by many people, today, more so than in the past, the criminal justice system is being called on to be efficient in its delivery of services. We see this goal as possible only if the issue of conflict is addressed directly by those who manage and administer the system.

--------------------------------- CASE STUDY ---------------------------------
Prosecutorial Conflict: Who Decides the Charge?

Mary Beth Boland knew that being a prosecutor was going to be challenging, yet it was her dream to be one since her early college days when she watched the television series "Hill Street Blues." She was apprehensive when she arrived at the district attorney's office to start her new job. When she walked into the office, her immediate supervisor, Carl Groves, shouted, "Boland, get over here and begin working with the intake workers on the cases that are going to be handled today."

Not knowing what was expected of her, she compliantly walked over to the station where an intake worker was located. Nervously, she asked, "What do I do?" The intake worker responded, "Well, I guess the first thing to do is to separate the cases into the good ones and the bad ones." "How do I do that?" asked Boland. "Just look for the ones that are the most serious. Forget about the petty misdemeanor cases. Those go down to Newman over in the misdemeanor division. We deal only with felonies up here." Boland began processing the cases, but wondered when she was going to do some real prosecution in the courtroom. She figured that she was just paying her dues until she had the needed experience.

After six weeks, she began to wonder whether she would ever get out of the intake division. Shortly thereafter, the district attorney assigned her to the misdemeanor court group. Finally, she thought, I am doing real prosecution work. The first case she handled was one of disorderly conduct and resisting arrest. The evidence was very weak. After reviewing the evidence, she decided to recommend a diversion program. Her decision was based, in part, on the fact that the suspect was a first-time offender and had a serious alcohol problem. Diversion seemed to be the best alternative.

Shortly after her decision, the police lieutenant at the local precinct called her to discuss the decision. He told her that the police department for years had always had a "smooth working relationship" with the prosecutors of the county when it came to suspects who resisted arrest and fought with police officers. Boland could only respond that she did not feel the evidence was compelling enough to prosecute the case. He angrily said, "Lady, you better learn what the rules are down in that office you are working in and don't piss off your friends over in the police department." At that point, Boland was losing her patience and told him that if he did not like the decision, he should talk to the district attorney.

The next day she was asked by the district attorney to see him in his office after lunch. She initially thought nothing of his request, but then wondered whether it had anything to do with her dispute with the police lieutenant the previous day. "C'mon in," said District Attorney Witherspoon. "The reason that I am talking to you today is that I got a call from Lieutenant Richmond at the Third District police station today about a case you handled yesterday. I believe the case was against an inebriated individual for disorderly conduct and resisting arrest." "Yes, sir," responded Boland. "Why didn't you process the charge with a criminal complaint? Don't you know that all of these types of cases are prosecuted in this office?" "Sir, the case was lousy and there was not enough evidence to handle it criminally. That's why I referred the case for diversion and alcohol counseling."

District Attorney Witherspoon responded that the office had a good working relationship with the police department and that he wanted to keep it that way. Boland suggested that she did not think it was right for the police department to dictate who gets charged with what and when. Witherspoon said he understood her position, yet she had to learn how to deal with the other criminal justice agencies. He stressed the fact that cooperation with these agencies, especially the police department, was critical to their own survival. He concluded his speech to her by saying, "Don't rock the boat, and keep the conflict at a minimum." Boland walked out depressed and wondered to herself who really made the decisions to charge in her office.

Case Study Questions

1. Discuss possible ways the conflict episode between Prosecutor Boland and the police department could have been avoided.
2. Could the conflict episode between Prosecutor Boland and the police department be viewed as good for both organizations? Why or why not?
3. How could District Attorney Witherspoon reduce potential interorganizational conflict between his department and the police department?

For Discussion

1. Describe a potential conflict situation in a criminal justice setting. Suggest possible ways that this conflict could be resolved. In addition, describe what you believe the role of a criminal justice administrator should be in such a situation and why. Is there a specific conflict behavior that would be useful to deal with this conflict situation and why?

2. Take a conflict situation in one of the components of the criminal justice system and describe its various stages. Discuss in what stage you think the conflict could be managed and the role of the supervisor in the management process. Moreover, are there conflict situations that are

beyond the control of the immediate supervisor? If so mention a few and discuss why they could not be effectively dealt with by management personnel in that component of the criminal justice system.

3. It was mentioned in the chapter that interorganizational conflict is common in the criminal justice system. Suggest methods that could be employed by administrators to decrease this conflict. Is interorganizational conflict in the criminal justice system inevitable?

4. Invite the local police chief to class to discuss the conflicts that arise in the department. Ask the chief to describe the methods employed to decrease conflict. Finally, ask about the position of the department on the role of conflict-management programs in policing. Do you think the programs are useful in reducing conflict?

For Further Reading

Duffee, D. *Correctional Management: Change and Control in Correctional Organizations.* Prospect Heights, Ill.: Waveland, 1986.

Pondy, L. R. "Organizational Conflict: Concepts and Models." *Administrative Science Quarterly,* 1967, *12,* 296–320.

Thomas, K. W. "Conflict and Conflict Management." In *Handbook of Industrial and Organizational Psychology,* edited by M. D. Dunnette, pp. 889–935. Chicago: Rand McNally, 1976.

Tosi, H. L., and Hamner, W. C. (Eds.). *Organizational Behavior and Management.* 4th ed. Cincinnati: Grid, 1985.

PART 4

PROCESSES IN CRIMINAL JUSTICE ORGANIZATIONS

Organizations pursue goals and accomplish tasks. As we will see, these are complicated issues, but they are the issues that differentiate organizations from individuals and groups. Managers must, therefore, be concerned with how their organizations carry out those tasks and how well they perform. These are important concerns in criminal justice, where goals are often unclear and conflicting and where there are few unambiguous measures of accomplishment. In Part Four our focus extends beyond the individual and group to concern with how organizations pursue their goals and accomplish their tasks. We first consider how decisions are made within organizations, and then we examine the difficult process of determining the effectiveness of organizations. In the final chapter we turn our attention to the process of change in criminal justice.

Decision Making

I relish cases where a deal has been worked out. All the pressure is off. No one is on my back. They are really no problem [probation officer discussing sentencing recommendations in plea-bargained cases, quoted in Rosecrance, 1985:542].

A detective was assigned a case in which a man had stabbed his common-law wife in the arm with a kitchen knife. The patrol report on the incident indicated that the woman had been taken to City Hall to sign an arrest warrant, while the man had been arrested on a charge of felony assault and released on his own recognizance. Nominally, the detective was required to collect additional information and evidence relating to the incident and to write a detailed and comprehensive report which would be used in prosecuting the case. However, the detective's interpretation of the incident, based on his understanding of the area in which it occurred and the lifestyles of the persons involved, led him to view any further investigation effort on his part as futile. He remarked: "These drunks, they're always stabbing one another over here. Then you see'em the next day and they're right back together again. She won't show up in court anyhow. Why waste my time and everyone else's on it?" The handling of the case involved only the production of a brief report which concluded: "The victim in this complaint wishes no further investigation by the police department. This complaint is to be classified as closed" [Waegel, 1981:273].

Finally, Dr. Grigson testified that whether Mr. Barefoot was in society at large or in a prison society there was "one hundred percent and absolute" chance that Barefoot would commit future acts of criminal violence that would constitute a continuing threat to society. . . . After an hour of deliberation, the jury answered "yes" to the two statutory questions, and Thomas Barefoot was sentenced to death [*Barefoot* v. *Estelle*, 1983].

We always write in our reports "just what force was necessary." What if you don't take enough force? Well, how in the hell do you know how much force is necessary? I say take all you got in case you need it [corrections officer quoted in Roszell, 1986].

One of the most important concerns for managers in all organizations is decision making. Not only do they engage in it directly, but they also oversee the decisions of their subordinates. We see examples of good and bad decision making all the time. Part of the continued success of Johnson & Johnson has been attributed to the decision to keep Tylenol on the market under its original name despite the publicity about deaths from product tampering with cyanide in the early 1980s. However, the decision to change the formula for Coca-Cola in 1985 met with such resistance that the company had to bring "Classic Coke" back on the market. The space shuttle disaster in 1985 resulted in the death of seven astronauts and set back military and civilian space programs in the United States by three years. That explosion was at least partially attributable to a faulty decision process in which well-known problems with the booster-rocket seals did not lead to redesign efforts, and the fateful launch went forward despite engineers' warnings about the potential effect of the cold weather on the seals' ability to hold.

In criminal justice, decision making is no less important. Severe prison and jail overcrowding has been blamed on decisions that were based on faulty population projections. In 1984 the police decision to drop an incendiary bomb on the roof of a house to evict a cult in Philadelphia ultimately resulted in the burning of some sixty homes and created a costly political firestorm. In the late 1970s the U.S. government's decision to spray the herbicide paraquat on Mexican marijuana led to reduced supplies of the drug but also created concerns about the possible health effects of tainted supplies. This concern ultimately stimulated domestic production of the illegal crop (Brecher, 1986).

Decision making in criminal justice extends well beyond the policy-formulation process with its parallels in the business world. In criminal justice, countless decisions are made about the clients of the system. After the reporting of a crime to the police and through the final discharge of an offender, each step in the criminal process is marked by a decision made by workers in the criminal justice system. Figure 10-1 is a partial list of such decisions. Lipsky (1980) indicates that these decisions, often made by front-line staff, are more important than executive decisions in determining organizational policy. In fact, some scholars have argued that the conglomeration of different criminal justice agencies with different jurisdictions can only be understood as a system by recognizing that the disparate organizations are linked by the decisions made about offenders (Newman, 1986).

In this chapter we examine the process of decision making in criminal justice. We turn first to issues of theory and the growing recognition of the limits of rationality. Next, the focus is on two issues in criminal justice decision making that appear to represent extremes in our assumptions about rationality. First, we investigate discretion in decision making, a topic often criticized by those seeking rational processes. Second, we study prediction, a topic often assumed to be linked to high degrees of rationality. These two issues have engendered more discussion in criminal justice than any other decision-making topics. Finally, we consider the ways in which managers can influence the decision-making process in criminal justice in an effort to increase rationality.

What Is a Decision?

The decisions you made when you opened your closet this morning and the parole board's decision not to parole mass murderer Richard Speck may seem to have little in common. Your choice of garb and Speck's continued incarceration, however, both resulted from processes that share some basic elements. Those elements are shown in figure 10-2.

Figure 10-1   A Partial List of Decisions Made About Criminal Cases

1. Has a crime occurred in the eyes of a victim or bystander?
2. Should a crime be reported to the police?
3. Should police be dispatched to the scene?
4. Should police regard the event as a criminal offense?
5. Should investigators be called in?
6. Should an arrest be made?
7. Should search warrants be issued?
8. Should arrest warrants be issued?
9. Should a police officer fire at a suspect?
10. Should an alleged offender be detained in jail?
11. Should a citation be issued?
12. Should bail be set and at what amount?
13. Should release-on-recognizance be allowed?
14. Should an alleged offender be prosecuted?
15. Should an alleged offender enter a diversion program?
16. With what priority should prosecution be undertaken?
17. Is an alleged offender competent to stand trial?
18. Should motions be granted?
19. Is an alleged offender guilty?
20. Is an alleged offender not guilty due to insanity?
21. Should an offender be incarcerated or allowed to remain in the community?
22. How long should the sentence be?
23. Should there be special conditions to the sentence?
24. What level of security does an offender need?
25. When and how should the levels of security change?
26. Should an incarcerated offender be transferred?
27. Should disciplinary reports be written?
28. Is an offender guilty of disciplinary infractions?
29. What are appropriate sanctions for disciplinary violations?
30. To what program should an offender be assigned?
31. Should an offender be transferred or committed to a mental hospital?
32. Should an incarcerated offender be paroled?
33. Should parole or community release be revoked?
34. Should an offender be discharged?

Figure 10-2 Elements of a Decision

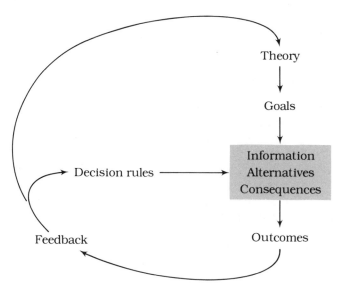

In general, some *theory* or broad framework guides most decisions. As you confront your wardrobe it may simply be your beliefs about what looks good on you, but complex decisions may involve sophisticated theories. In his study of parole-board decision making, for example, Hawkins (1983) found that broad support of classicalism or positivism frames board members' decisions. That is, some members of the parole board place great importance on whether an offender has been punished for a suitable time, while others are concerned with evidence of rehabilitation or change in the offender's outlook. Wilson's (1968) styles of policing may also be seen as broad frameworks within which police officers make decisions to arrest or not arrest. Officers in departments characterized by the "Watchman" style, with its primary focus on order maintenance, may be reluctant to arrest if less drastic means will control a disturbance. Officers in legalistic departments, however, may invoke their power to arrest based solely on whether some statute has been violated.

Goals in the decision-making process are specific to a particular decision. They refer to what a decision maker would like to achieve. In a decision to prosecute a particular case, the goal may be to gain a conviction; and in the decision to dispatch a police car to a burglary scene or to schedule an appointment, a dispatcher's goal may be the efficient use of personnel. Goals may not always be so obvious however. In his study of probation officers' sentencing recommendations, Rosecrance (1985) concluded that "ball-park recommendations" serve the goal of maintaining credibility with the judge and may have little to do with particular cases.

Decision makers also need three kinds of information. First, they must be aware of *alternatives*, or choices. If there are no alternatives, there is no decision to make. Second, they must also be aware of the possible *consequences* of the alternatives. If consequences do not differ or if there are no expectations regarding consequences, an alternative can be selected only at random. Third, some information is needed about the *subject* of the decision in order to guide the selection among the alternatives. A judge's sentencing decision can illustrate the importance of information. Evidence of a convicted offender's crime and criminal history provides a basis for selection among the sentencing alternatives as provided by statute. All of this information is considered in light of the expected consequences of each possible sentence. Among these consequences may be included danger to the public if an offender remains in the community, the possible brutalizing effects of a prison term on a youthful offender, and public dissatisfaction if a substantial penalty is not imposed.

The availability of the information, however, does not necessarily produce a decision. That information must be processed. Processing occurs through the *decision rules*, which govern how the elements of the decision are combined. In criminal justice, many decisions rely on essentially clinical decision rules, which are based on education, training, and experience. Arrest decisions, sentencing decisions, and classification decisions usually rely on the clinical judgments of individuals. At the other extreme are decision rules involving the assignment of numerical weights to pieces of information. Those weights are added to produce a sum, which dictates the decision. Scales based on these principles have been developed for use in prosecution, bail, sentencing, and parole decisions.

The processing of information according to the decision rules produces *outcomes*. People are arrested, sentenced, transferred between prisons, or paroled. Policies are implemented, changed, or dismantled. The outcome is the result of the decision.

In many (but not all) cases the decision process is not completed with the outcome. Many types of decisions are repeated again and again. Police officers soon face new decisions whether to arrest, and judges continue to sentence convicted offenders. In a cybernetic, or self-correcting, decision model the outcome of prior decisions provides *feedback* to influence future decisions. Cybernetic decision processes are based on mechanical models similar to the thermostat in a house. When the heat is turned on, the temperature rises until the preset temperature high is reached, and then the thermostat turns off the heat until the preset low temperature is reached, at which point the heat once again comes on. Criminal justice feedback is not nearly so simple, but the principles apply. Police officers' arrest practices are influenced by prosecutors' decisions to pursue prosecution or dismiss charges. Parole-board decisions are influenced by information regarding the failure of some parolees.

Feedback may affect future decisions through its influence on theory, decision rules, or information, or all three. For example, corrections decision making has been greatly affected by feedback from research in the mid-1970s that suggested that treatment programs had little effect (see Cullen and Gilbert, 1982). Theoretical frameworks supportive of treatment were replaced by just desserts, and decision goals focused on equity in sentencing and time served. In parole, for example, information regarding participation in prison programs became less important than it had been, and some parole boards all but abandoned clinical decision rules and adopted numerical scales to assist in decision making.

Feedback about police intervention in spouse-abuse cases has also influenced arrest decisions. Increasingly, police departments are encouraging or requiring arrest in domestic disputes, especially if there is some sign of physical violence (Morash, 1986). In the past, police and prosecutorial decisions were greatly influenced by feedback showing that many women did not pursue prosecution of husbands or boyfriends in domestic-violence cases. Police officers were encouraged to negotiate settlements at the scene and counsel the participants or make referrals to social service agencies. Feedback with a different content was generated by several well-publicized cases of continued abuse and even homicide and by research studies showing that arrest is most likely to prevent further violence (Sherman and Berk, 1984). That feedback has altered the decision-making process in favor of arrest over mediation.

Decision-Making Theory: From Rationality to the Garbage Can

At first glance, the model of decisions portrayed in figure 10-2 appears to be a model of perfect rationality. The goals of a specific decision are identified and needed information is processed according to agreed-upon decision rules and is considered within some theoretical framework. The model also suggests directions for improving the decision-making process. Increasing consistency in theory, increasing agreement on goals and decision rules, and improving the quality of information will produce increasingly rational decisions. In criminal justice, as in other fields, rationality in decision making may be assumed to be a requirement for effectiveness and efficiency. As Gottfredson (1975) points out, however, although we may strive for rational decisions, achieving rationality is unlikely and probably impossible.

At one time scholars of decision making believed the process could best be understood as a rational one that could produce optimal results or "correct" answers for given situations (Murray, 1986). In this view, there was assumed to be an obviously correct answer to the question of whether a particular suspect should be arrested or paroled. It was assumed that a particular policy regarding the deployment of patrol cars or the choice of a site on which to build a prison could be objectively regarded as the best solution to the problem.

In an influential book, March and Simon (1958) first questioned the rationality of the decision-making process. They pointed out that decisions were made on the basis of "bounded rationality," partly because decision makers are incapable of collecting and handling the kinds of information needed for completely rational decisions. Perrow (1981:2) outlines the thesis of bounded rationality:

> We cannot process large amounts of information but only limited bits, and those slowly. We tend to distort the information as we process it. We cannot gather information very well even if we could process it: we do not always know what is relevant information, inasmuch as we do not understand how things work. Above all, we cannot even be sure of what we want the information for because we cannot be sure what our preferences are. We have trouble discovering what we want. We also have contradictory preferences, or contradictory goals, and are unable to fulfill all of them at once. As a consequence, we do not look for the optimal solutions: we have to settle for "satisficing," taking the first acceptable solution that comes along.

The notion of bounded rationality seems to be especially appropriate for criminal justice decisions. Many decisions, especially those regarding offenders, are characterized by volumes of information about their history and background. It is important to recognize that the information is selectively collected and interpreted and that decision processes are influenced by the organizations of the criminal justice system.

Satisficing, or the attainment of acceptable results rather than optimal results, is also a useful concept in criminal justice. For example, in New York City, detectives will not investigate burglaries in which less than $10,000 in property is taken. This policy is clearly not optimal but is regarded as a minimally acceptable compromise between investigation goals and the need to use manpower efficiently. In the courtroom, the extent to which home detention is used as a response to jail crowding may reflect satisficing between concerns for punishment and concerns about overcrowding.

An extension of the concept of bounded rationality also merits our attention. Cohen, March, and Olsen (1972) use the analogy of the "garbage can" to describe one particular model of decision making. Decision makers handle problems of ambiguity by developing sets of "performance programs," or standardized methods of responding to problems. Organizations thus possess a repertoire of responses, or a "garbage can" full of readymade answers in search of problems. The link to bounded rationality, however, is the idea that the garbage can must also contain the problems. That is, a decision maker will not regard a situation as requiring action until that situation is defined in terms of the solutions that are available (see Pinfield, 1986). When necessary, organization members modify their perceptions of problems to justify actions (Staw and Ross, 1978). Hall (1982) suggests that individuals also possess garbage cans of solutions and problems. Television's comic crime fighter Sledge Hammer, for example, has a standard response to "scum-sucking leeches" in his garbage can. Only after a citizen is defined in those terms does Sledge resort to his limited repertoire of violence. Westley (1970), in fact, found a similar preprogrammed response in his classic study of the police. He reported that a major justification for the use of violence was that a suspect was considered "guilty."

Although the garbage-can analogy may not help us understand all decisions in criminal justice (Mohr, 1976), some research suggests the usefulness of the model. Sudnow's (1965) examination of the public defender's office describes a process by which public defenders' decisions about defense strategies are the results of defining clients by using existing categories rather than individually considering the merits of each case. Public defenders have set practices of encouraging defendants to plead guilty as soon as possible if their cases have the hallmarks of a typical offense, or, as Sudnow calls it, a "normal crime." A young male arrested for burglary and with a prior record for burglary, for example, is encouraged to plead guilty even if he insists on his innocence. Atypical defendants get the benefit of a close examination of the strengths and weaknesses of their case. But typical defendants who resist pressures to plead guilty early may find themselves defined as recalcitrant. As the garbage-can model would suggest, the existing solution for such cases involves proceeding to trial with a public defender who assumes the defendant is guilty. The trial then takes on the characteristics of a ritual-ized conspiracy against the defendant.

In a study of police investigations, Waegel (1981) argues that research strategies that focus on the decision-making processes of individual investigators have severe limitations. It is fruitful, rather, to study the existing shared categorizations of cases. In other words, he supports studying the garbage can of solutions to which police investigations (the problems) will be applied. Much of police investigation, then, involves "mapping the features of a particular case onto a more general and commonly recognized type of case" (1981:265). The most basic categories into which investigations are placed are routine versus nonroutine cases. Characteristics of the victim, offense, and suspects figure into the way the case is viewed. These characteristics trigger different levels of in-vestigation. In some cases the distinction between routine and non-routine is obvious, while in others a fit is forced by the detective. In either case, assumptions about the nature of the incident and the parties involved guide case handling. The ability to type cases quickly is impor-tant in investigations. Waegel points out that the necessity to report on the status of cases influences whether a case is regarded as routine. Cases can be open, closed, or, if leads have been unproductive, suspended. The other side of this process of applying problems to existing solutions is seen in case skimming. A steady stream of arrests is produced by working on only those cases that appear potentially solvable from information in the original patrol officer's report and summarily suspending the remainder of one's cases.

The garbage-can analogy has its appeal as a means of understanding some decision making in criminal justice. We need to be careful, however, not to let the cuteness of the imagery muck up our analysis. It must be remembered that the solutions and problems in the can are not collected in some random fashion. The approach to problems and the problems themselves represent the interests and history of the organization and its members. Thus little in the way of entirely new material is likely to enter into the decision-making process (Hall, 1982:181).

Thus, stability and even routinization of decision making are products of bounded rationality. In this organizational perspective, the boundaries determine the context of decision making, and those boundaries are the product of organizational processes such as limiting the kinds of information available or viewed as relevant, establishing procedures, and requiring reports, as well as less obtrusive controls (see Perrow, 1986:128).

Another important contribution of the concept of bounded rationality is recognition of the cognitive limitations of individual decision makers. Not only must decision makers deal with multiple goals and possibly conflicting theories, and not only are they controlled by organizational practices, but they can effectively handle only small quantities of information. Research has demonstrated, for example, that people can recall only seven or eight bits of information without developing some process or shorthand method for recalling the data (Burnham, 1975). This finding suggests that studying the ways people process information is important to understanding their decisions. In the following sections we first examine characteristics of the decision makers, and then we focus on the characteristics of the information used in decisions.

Characteristics of Decision Makers

Although organizational factors are important in understanding the notion of bounded rationality, some research in criminal justice has focused on the decision makers themselves. In studying parole decision making, Wilkins (1975b) uncovered fundamental differences in the way people process information. He first asked decision makers to make interim decisions after reviewing only limited items of information. Some of the decision makers, however, found it impossible to make decisions based on the limited information even when they were told that they could indicate a low level of confidence in the decision. These decision makers would not consider making a decision without information that they regarded as "sufficient." From this line of research, Wilkins described four types of decision makers. This typology is relevant to a large number of criminal justice decisions, which are characterized by uncertainty and a relatively large amount of available information. These decisions may concern intensity of investigation, sentences, or classification or transfer of prisoners.

Decision makers described by Wilkins as *sequentialists* use their experience to determine what items of information are most important. They then consider items in a sequential fashion, one at a time, based on their view of each item's importance. These decision makers are able to make interim decisions, and each additional item of information adds to or lowers their level of confidence in the decision. Wilkins compares this decision-making process with the logic of the statistical procedure known as step-wise regression, in which the most important information is considered first and it is followed by information that contributes less and less to the end result.

A second type is the *ah yes!* decision maker. These individuals do not employ a sequential search strategy. Instead, they collect large amounts of information and search for patterns in that information. Only after they find a pattern they are familiar with can they exclaim, "Ah, yes, this is the typical. . . ." Then they make a decision. If the data do not fit precisely into existing patterns, these individuals reinterpret the data to fit those patterns.

Although the most pronounced distinctions are between people who process information sequentially and those who do not, Wilkins also identifies two additional types of decision makers. The *simplifyer* reduces complex problems to their simplest form. On a parole board, the simplifyer asks questions like "Anything negative known about this man?" or "What are the problems with this case?" Finally, Wilkins describes the *ratifiers*. Their information-search strategy is to wait for comments by someone else and to associate themselves with that person's viewpoint. These decision makers may review the case file to agree with comments from a caseworker, probation officer, or warden or may look to another member of the parole board for direction.

In his observation study of parole-board decision making, Hawkins (1983) also considered the boundaries of rationality. Rather than focusing on types of decision makers, however, he discusses processes by which "a structure is imposed on the knowledge available in any case." Hawkins indicates that decision makers often use a few master categories in deciding what is relevant. For example, a parole-board member may regard the facts of an offense and the criminal record as central. All board members may not agree however; some, for example, may find a person's record while incarcerated most important. Decision makers in criminal justice also often make certain assumptions about the people involved. When a convict's story varies from the official record, for example, the conflicts are often resolved in favor of the record. This decision is made not by clarifying the fact but by viewing the convict with suspicion because of his or her status. Finally, Hawkins indicates that decision makers often structure their data by resorting to precedent. They categorize cases in ways that allow them to be "handled in the usual way." It is important to recognize that for both Wilkins and Hawkins the categories used and the structure given to information are imposed by the decision maker and are not evident in the content of the information.

Characteristics of Information

Although decision makers must find some way to structure information in order to use it in decisions, some characteristics of the information itself contribute to that process. Clearly the most important characteristic is accuracy. Inaccurate information may be given inappropriate weight or value by a decision maker. The point that improved decisions can be made with accurate information may seem simple, but accuracy of information is a major problem in criminal justice for several reasons. First, case files and other collections of information used by decision makers are compiled from numerous agencies and officials along the way. They often contain incomplete or incorrect information that may be repeated as an offender moves from the police through the courts and to corrections. The information will also resurface if a person is rearrested.

Second, much of the information needed in criminal justice decisions is collected from people who have an interest in the outcomes or the process. Victims want arrests to be made, and convicts want to be paroled. McCleary (1977) has shown that parole officers' records are compiled for purposes that may include threatening a parolee or justifying revocation. Probation officers also write presentence investigations to court the favor of judges (Rosecrance, 1985). This interest in decision outcomes does not necessarily mean that reports are fabrications or that information is intentionally skewed, but it may mean that the data subtly reflect the range of the collector's purposes.

Third, another problem of accuracy in criminal justice information lies in the need for decision makers to use summary information about people. Because criminal histories, personality assessments, and records of adjustment are often presented in summary fashion, distortions are difficult to avoid. Remington, Newman, Kimball, Melli, and Goldstein (1969:697) found these examples in presentence investigations:

> He is a nice looking, clean cut, all-American appearing young man. Beneath this, however, he is as cold as ice. He is an expert manipulator, playing one

person against another, with an amazing ability to say just what he thinks you want to hear.

He is a loser plain and simple. He is sexually inadequate, vocationally inadequate and mentally inadequate. He has failed in everything—schools, jobs, military service, with his family, and with his wife. He has even failed as a crook. There is absolutely no reason to think that he can make it on probation and probably prison won't help him much. The only thing I can recommend is incarceration for as long as possible and then hope for the best.

Because legislation and case law now allow disclosure of presentence investigation reports to most defendants, such generalizations would be rare today. Most probation officers are trained to write less opinionated and more factual reports.

But factual reports do not necessarily eliminate the problem of using summary information. The quest for accuracy is partly responsible for the proliferation of standardized information-collection devices that assign numerical weights to factual data. The addition of the weights creates a score that summarizes the information. Such devices are frequently used in bail, sentencing, and parole decisions. The devices appear to report information with high degrees of accuracy. Assigning a score of zero if a person is employed or a one if unemployed certainly has the appearance of being more accurate than describing an offender as "vocationally inadequate." But the devices can also distort the information. For example, if the offender is a seasonal worker is she to be classified as employed or unemployed? Should criminal histories be based on charges made at the time of arrest or at conviction, when plea bargains may have been struck? Often lengthy and complex instructions are needed to address these and similar problems. In addition, a basic question of accuracy is raised by the fact that the information presented in narrative sentences or numerical scores is often gathered from the offender himself.

Another characteristic of information is the order in which it is presented. Research indicates that because many decision makers use sequential methods to search for and analyze information, the first pieces of information are likely to be more influential than later pieces. This order effect (Burnham, 1975) is important in criminal justice because often the first information used by decision makers is the facts of a crime or an offender's prior record. This order contributes to cautious decision making.

Because of the order effect, new information—that is, information introduced after a tentative decision has been reached—does not have the same influence as if it were introduced earlier. Decision makers using sequential strategies become invested in their decisions and tend to devalue new information. Wilkins (1975b) found that decision makers often continue to ask for items of information long after a tentative decision has been made. In his experience, however, additional items never changed the decision.

Information about the availability of alternatives can also influence decisions. In criminal justice, many decisions are perceived as resulting in one of only two possible solutions. These dichotomous outcome choices include such things as to arrest or not arrest, to prosecute or not prosecute, to parole or not parole. Dichotomies like these often support *minimax strategies* by decision makers. These strategies are designed to minimize the maximum loss that could result from a given decision outcome. They thus produce very conservative or low-risk decisions. A police officer, for example, may arrest a juvenile vandal if the only alternative is doing nothing, and a parole board may deny parole if outright release is the only other option. However, the introduction of alternatives such as diversion programs or prerelease options or even shortening a convict's parole-review date, may alter decision outcomes in a less conservative direction.

It is important to appreciate the boundaries of rationality in decision making. We have examined the origins of those boundaries and have discussed them with reference to organizational processes, the cognitive limitations of decision makers, and the nature of information itself. In the next sections we examine two important topics in criminal justice decision making—discretion and prediction—and focus on the limits of rationality in these areas.

Discretion

In a significant collection of works on the subject, Atkins and Pogrebin (1982) define *discretion* as referring to "a situation in which an official has latitude to make authoritative choices not necessarily specified within the source of authority which governs his decision making." Lipsky (1980) points out that latitude in decision making by front-line staff is one of the defining characteristics of human service organizations. In criminal justice, staff in all organizations have broad discretionary powers to invoke the criminal process or to send a suspect or offender on to the next stage. For police the power is to arrest or not to arrest. Prosecutors exercise broad discretion in the charging decision, and judges have wide latitude in managing the judicial process and in sentencing. In corrections, probation officers, prison staff, and parole officials exercise discretion with regard to program placement, penalties for rule infractions, and release.

Critics of discretionary decision making argue that it often amounts to a total lack of control, "decision making unfettered by constraints of law or policy" (Gottfredson and Gottfredson, 1980:350). The classic statement of that position is provided by Goldstein (1960), who studied police discretion. Goldstein argues that police have a legal mandate to pursue full enforcement of the law. To his regret, however, circumstances such as limitations of time and money as well as ambiguities in the definitions of laws make full enforcement unrealistic. In being forced to adopt selective enforcement practices, the police make decisions that determine the level of law enforcement throughout the criminal process, but no clear guidelines constrain those decisions. Goldstein points out that the decision not to arrest is one that often escapes public scrutiny but one that controls the gate to the entire criminal justice system. Low-visibility decisions, such as police bargains not to seek charges in exchange for information or not to arrest if an assault victim will not sign a complaint, therefore, undermine "a major criminal law objective of imposing upon all persons officially recognized minimum standards of human behavior" (1960:38).

In corrections, the American Friends Service Committee (1971) takes an extreme position on discretion in their classic critique of the rehabilitation model. They argue that the discretion inherent in indeterminate sentences and requirements for program participation often serve illegitimate custodial rather than legitimate treatment aims. They feel that discretion permits prison administrators to use release or denial of parole as a carrot-and-stick control mechanism. Discretion even supports such practices as using offender attitudes or characteristics such as hair length or race as a basis for criminal justice intervention from arrest through parole.

Critics of discretion in criminal justice, then, have argued that the latitude given front-line staff has led to uncontrolled decision making, which results in illegitimate and even corrupt practices. They see a solution to these problems in imposing increased control on decision makers. Thus, the American Friends Service Committee strongly supports determinate sentencing, and Goldstein (1984:40) states that the "ultimate answer is that the police should not be delegated discretion not to invoke the criminal process." His first recommendation is that legislatures should write statutes to reduce or eliminate ambiguity and to make police decisions visible and thus subject to review. These reforms, it would seem, are designed to increase the rationality of decision making by severely restricting or eliminating discretion. Under this view, then, wide discretion is inconsistent with a rational model of organizational decision making.

A somewhat different perspective on discretion is also present in the literature. In their seminal work, March and Simon (1958) suggested there is room for discretion in their theory of bounded rationality. They pointed out that when a general goal in decision making is specified but means remain unspecified, the decision maker is left with supplying the means–ends connection. The choice of means–ends connection, however, is not completely unconstrained. Discretion then can involve, for example, following guidelines that can be triggered only after additional information is obtained, as when a police officer must decide whether violence has occurred in a domestic dispute before deciding whether an arrest is to be made. Discretion may also involve deciding on a course of action based on expectations about others' decisions, as when police officers decide not to arrest in minor cases because they believe the cases will not be prosecuted. Or discretion may involve drawing on memory or experience, as when a police officer does not make an arrest because similar arrests in the past have not led to prosecutions.

This view of discretion, then, is based on the idea that the goals of decisions are often general and complex and that discretionary decisions are not completely unregulated. Three significant implications follow from this perspective. First, discretion can be viewed as necessary and useful. Second, the boundaries or regulations of discretionary decisions can be studied and understood. And, third, because they can be understood, they can be influenced without eliminating discretion.

The view of discretion as necessary is now common in criminal justice. An accepted argument is put forth by Lipsky (1980), who suggests that discretion in the human services is needed because of the complexity of the task. In policing, for example, whether an assault and battery has occurred can be a complex question requiring police discretion. As in all decisions, some order must be imposed on the information available. Questions about the amount of force needed, the level of injury, and the relationship between the parties are complex. This complexity means that discretion is useful. Newman (1981), for example, argues that the discretionary process of plea bargaining can promote fairness by addressing the variability and complexity of offenses. Gottfredson, Hoffman, Sigler, and Wilkins (1975) argue that parole-board discretion fulfills the same purposes.

A bounded-rationality model of discretion also provides direction for the study and reform of decision making. Implicit in the work on sentencing and parole guidelines by Wilkins, Gottfredson, and Kress (Kress, 1980) is the view that such decisions are not completely uncontrolled or lacking in rationality. These authors studied sentence disparity in courts and found that the vast majority of these discretionary decisions could be explained by a small set of information items. An example of these items and the scale used to summarize them is presented in figure 10-3. Items providing information about a defendant, such as prior criminal record, and items about the crime, such as degree of violence or injury to the victim, accounted for 85 percent of sentencing decisions. The remaining 15 percent of sentences could not be explained by the small list of items and would need to be studied as individual cases.

Figure 10-3 Sample Sentencing Guidelines Worksheet. (*From:* Kress, J. *Prescriptions for Justice: The Theory and Practice of Sentencing Guidelines.* Cambridge, Mass.: Ballinger, 1980, p. 311.)

Offender _____ Docket number _____

Judge _____ Date _____

Offense(s) convicted of: _____

_____

_____

Crime score

  A. Injury
    0 = No injury
    1 = Injury
    2 = Death   _____ +

  B. Weapon
    0 = No weapon
    1 = Weapon possessed
    2 = Weapon present and used   _____ +

  C. Drugs
    0 = No sale of drugs
    1 = Sale of drugs   _____ =

                                                  Crime score

Offender score

  A. Current legal status
    0 = Not on probation/parole, escape
    1 = On probation/parole, escape   _____ +

  B. Prior adult misdemeanor convictions
    0 = No convictions
    1 = One conviction
    2 = Two or more convictions   _____ +

  C. Prior adult felony convictions
    0 = No convictions
    2 = One conviction
    4 = Two or more convictions   _____ +

  D. Prior adult probation/parole revocations
    0 = None
    1 = One or more revocations   _____ +

  E. Prior adult incarcerations (over 60 days)
    0 = None
    1 = One incarceration
    2 = Two or more incarcerations   _____ =

                                                  Offender score

Guideline sentence _____

Actual sentence _____

Reasons (if actual sentence does not fall within guideline range):

The recognition that discretionary decisions can be highly predictable also suggests methods of affecting those decisions. Wilkins and Gottfredson and Kress all describe a method of structuring judicial discretion without greatly restricting or eliminating it. Sentence averages or narrow intervals based on sentences that have already been handed down by judges can be constructed for all the combinations of offense and offender scores. The resulting guidelines reflect sentencing policy in the court because they are based on sentences actually given out. Sample guidelines are presented in figure 10-4. Judges are given the guidelines and are told that they can issue sentences outside the guidelines (while remaining inside statutory limitations) but must provide explicit written reasons for the deviation. The guidelines are then updated at regular intervals so that they continue to reflect current court policy.

By structuring rather than eliminating discretion, this process recognizes that sentencing is a complex process in which judicial discretion is useful and beneficial. Instead of viewing discretionary decisions as unconstrained by law or policy, this approach is based on identifying and building on implicit constraints. The patterns of previous decisions reveal those constraints, and studying those patterns provides a productive method for influencing discretion while still noting its importance. The bounded-rationality perspective can thus provide a useful method for addressing problems of discretion.

Prediction

Although some authors have considered discretionary decision making as nearly devoid of rationality from an organizational perspective, the opposite assumptions seem common in discussions of prediction. Although recent advances have involved mathematical models, whether

Figure 10-4   Sample Felony-Sentencing Grid. (*From:* Kress, J. *Prescriptions for Justice: The Theory and Practice of Sentencing Guidelines.* Cambridge, Mass.: Ballinger, 1980, p. 313.)

Crime score				
4-5	4-6 years	5-7 years	6-8 years	8-10 years
3	3-5 years	4-6 years	6-8 years	6-8 years
2	2-4 years	3-5 years	3-5 years	4-6 years
1	Probation	Probation	2-4 years	3-5 years
0	Probation	Probation	Probation	2-4 years
	0-1	2-4	5-7	8-10

Offender score

decisions are made by highly trained experts employing clinical methods or by statisticians applying complex formulas, the prediction of human behavior is generally thought of as a highly rational scientific process. Even when nonexperts make predictive decisions, the lack of expertise is generally not viewed as detracting from the rationality of the process. In this section, we examine the extent to which such assumptions of rationality are justified.

In criminal justice many decisions involve the prediction of future behavior. After reviewing studies of decision making in the field, Gottfredson and Gottfredson (1980:334) describe prediction as "omnipresent" in the criminal justice system. Bail decisions, sentencing decisions, and parole decisions obviously involve predictions, but so do many other decisions made by workers in the criminal justice process. Classification into risk categories for probation involves prediction. Prediction figures into sentencing recommendations by probation officers, into corrections caseworkers' reviews of inmates for transfer, and into assistant prosecutors' determinations of charges and priorities for prosecution. Even police officers' decisions to arrest or issue a citation or use a diversion program involve predictions.

In considering the usefulness of a pure rationality theory of these decisions, let us first consider the methods used in prediction. Two broad categories exist: clinical methods and statistical methods. *Clinical methods* involve assessments that focus on such factors as personality variables, situational variables, and the interaction of these variables. They may or may not involve the use of standardized tests, such as personality assessments, and they may or may not involve personal interviews. In death-penalty cases in Texas, for example, psychiatrists make predictions about the likelihood of future violence by relying on hypothetical descriptions of the criminal record and character of convicted murderers. The heart of clinical methods, then, is the use of expertise in selecting and interpreting data from a variety of sources.

By contrast, *statistical methods* of prediction specify precisely what information is to be used and how it is to be interpreted. These methods use mathematical formulas that incorporate information about individuals to produce probability estimates of behavior. In order to make these estimates, information on the individual whose behavior is being predicted is compared with information on a large sample of individuals whose behavior in similar situations is known. For example, these are the information items that were originally found to be the best predictors of whether a convicted offender would continue to offend at a high rate and therefore should receive a long prison sentence (Greenwood, 1982:50): was convicted before for the same type of offense; was incarcerated more than 50 percent of the preceding two years; was convicted before age sixteen; served time in a state juvenile facility; used drugs in the preceding two years; used drugs as a juvenile; was employed less than 50 percent of the preceding two years. The scale produced with these items was used in support of a policy of selective incapacitation.

In criminal justice, statistical prediction methods were first used in 1928, when Burgess produced expected rates of failures on parole by developing a scale that assigned a point for each characteristic of an individual that was correlated with parole failure in a large sample of previously released offenders. The higher the total score, the more likely a person was to fail on parole, and, therefore, the stronger the argument for denying parole. Since then, sophisticated methods have been developed that use multivariate models to account for the differences in the importance of some predictor items and the interaction effects of the items. The prediction instruments used with this method resemble the instrument in figure 10-3, but all the variables are selected for their strength in predicting some specific behavior such as parole failure or failure on pretrial release.

Currently much of the literature in criminal justice reveals a preference for statistical methods of prediction. An authoritative volume on the subject of prediction and classification in criminal justice does not even mention clinical prediction methods (Gottfredson and Tonry, 1987). Clinical approaches to classification are mentioned only as a stage in the development of more sophisticated models in Brennan (1987). Much of the pessimism surrounding clinical prediction may be related to questions of accuracy (which we will take up later in this section) and to the negative publicity surrounding some cases. A national newsmagazine, for example, dubbed Dr. James Grigson "Doctor Death" after his pronouncement, in the death-penalty hearing of Thomas Barefoot, that he was 100 percent certain in his prediction of future dangerousness. In an amicus curiae brief to the Supreme Court in the Barefoot case, the American Psychiatric Association (1982) maintained that such predictions cannot be made with accuracy and that psychiatrists should not be permitted to testify in death-penalty proceedings regarding predictions of future dangerousness. The court, however, viewed prediction as integral to criminal justice and ultimately rejected the Association's position.

The case in support of statistical methods as well as the criticisms of clinical methods can be overstated however. The American Psychiatric Association rejected only long-term clinical predictions and even questioned statistical predictions in these cases. There is support for short-term clinical predictions, especially when informed by statistical data and by attention to unique conditions in an individual's environment (Monahan, 1981). The point should also be made, however, that incompetent clinical assessments have their parallels in sloppy statistical procedures, which may involve improper sampling or unreliable measurement.

The most important point, however, may be that clinical predictions are unavoidable. For many decisions made in criminal justice, adequate data bases for statistical methods do not exist. There may be little data on the characteristics of those who succeed in a diversion program or on those who fail to adjust in one particular medium security prison. Even where statistical data exist, clinical processes remain relevant. A juvenile vandal's motives will continue to be relevant to a prosecutor deciding on charges, and racist attitudes and the tensions they produce will be relevant to prison placement. On this subject, Monahan (1981) presents a sensible argument that statistical data may be most useful within a context of clinical decision making.

It follows, then, that it can be productive to examine the assumptions about rationality that underlie both clinical and statistical predictions. Toward that end we examine several factors important to all predictions of behavior. First, all decisions based on prediction involve a *criterion*— for example, dangerousness, repeat offending, failure on parole, failure on pretrial release. Defining the criterion variable can be difficult however. Monahan (1981) discusses the difficulties in defining dangerousness. What specific behaviors entail dangerousness? Must they be overt acts? Must they cause injury? At first these questions may seem relevant only to clinical predictions, in which no objective measurement of the criterion is made. With statistical methods, however, equally difficult problems arise. Should predictions about future criminality be made based on official arrest records or on self-report studies of offenders? These two criteria may produce different results (Farrington, 1987). Likewise, success on parole may involve anything from upstanding citizenship to drug-addicted fringe lifestyles in which arrest is avoided. Failures may range from a repetition of major violations to revocation for technical violations (Glaser, 1969). Clearly, viewing prediction as a purely rational process requires an unambiguous criterion variable. In clinical prediction, the failure to define the criterion in unambiguous terms is a problem, while with statistical methods the need for precise measurements may mask the ambiguities.

Predictor variables are the variables used to predict the criterion. In clinical prediction, they may differ from case to case but can include, for example, assessments of stability and subjective views of adjustment. With statistical methods, the predictors are the same for all cases and may include variables like age at first arrest and number of juvenile convictions. With either method, appreciating the limits of rationality remains relevant. It is impossible to know all the variables that may be pertinent, and information may arguably be different for different cases. Another difficulty is that often only the variables available in an official record make it into statistical processes.

Perhaps the most difficult problem in prediction relates to the base rate of the criterion variable. The *base rate* is the proportion of individuals in a population who exhibit the criterion. For example, the base rate for parole failure is the percentage of all paroled inmates who fail. For predictions to be useful then, they must improve on the base rate. If, for example, 20 percent of all parolees fail on parole, then parolees released based on predictions must fail at a rate below 20 percent for the predictions to be useful. If prediction produced failures of more than 20 percent, the parole board would be better off simply releasing everyone because that would produce a failure rate of only 20 percent. Of course, no parole board would abdicate responsibility in this way, but the point illustrates the importance of understanding the base rate.

Base rates are problematical in criminal justice predictions for two reasons. First, the base rate is frequently unknown by decision makers. This is particularly true in clinical predictions where studies to determine base rates may not have been undertaken. Not knowing the base rate may lead to dramatic overpredictions of such things as parole or pretrial-release failures. Base rates also present problems in statistical predictions however. For example, because the base rates for parole failure have generally been based only on the behavior of people released by parole boards, the rate for all potential releases is not known. The rates as well as the predictors have not been calculated on a representative sample of parole-eligible inmates.

Second, base rates are often low—that is, much of the behavior we seek to predict is rare. For example, in Goldkamp's (1985) development of statistical predictions in bail decision making, he found that only 12 percent of pretrial releasees failed to appear in court. For the predictions to be useful then, they must improve on a 12 percent failure rate. The rub is that, for statistical reasons, as base rates get further and further from a proportional distribution of 50/50 in a population, it becomes increasingly difficult to predict. Behavior that is statistically rare, such as violent crime or dangerousness or parole failure, is very difficult to predict.

An additional issue is relevant to our discussion of the rationality of prediction: the consequences of predictions and our view of their accuracy. A parole board would certainly be well regarded if only 10 percent of parolees were rearrested. Although at first glance the board's predictions seem highly accurate, a closer examination is required. Figure 10-5 reveals that there are, in fact, four possible consequences to the parole decision as well as other predictions. Those predicted to succeed will be released and will either succeed or fail. Those predicted to fail, however, will continue to be incarcerated and could succeed or fail but are not given the chance.

In our example, the 10 percent of parolees who fail are known as *false negatives.* The prediction that they would not fail was incorrect. By considering only these however, it is clear that a parole board that releases few inmates will always be regarded as more accurate than a parole board willing to take more risks. To complete the assessment of accuracy then, we must also consider the *false positives,* or the percentage of inmates whom the board predicts would fail and who would, in fact, actually not fail if they were released. In the example in figure 10-5, we see

Figure 10-5 Hypothetical Outcomes from Parole Predictions

Predicted outcome

		Success	Failure
Actual behavior	Success	Accurate 90% Paroled True negative	Inaccurate 60% Parole denied False positive
	Failure	Inaccurate 10% Paroled False negative	Accurate 40% Parole denied True positive
Column total		100%	100%

that 60 percent of those predicted to fail would actually succeed. Of course, there is trouble with this rate. If the board predicts inmates will fail, the board won't let them out. So in reality the false positive rate is rarely known.

Only if our parole board is willing to release the inmates whom they expect to fail can we completely evaluate the success of the predictions. Although such release rightly does not occur, in some instances courts have required the release of offenders who had been predicted to be violent based on clinical prediction methods. Subsequent studies of these offenders have found that approximately 60 percent of them did not engage in violence (see Monahan, 1981). Overall, these studies have prompted the conclusion that clinical predictions of violence are incorrect in approximately two out of three cases. Studies of statistical predictions use statistical procedures to estimate false positive rates. These studies have revealed only slightly better results than the other studies, generally with false positive rates of around 40 percent to 50 percent.

The issue of false positives raises two questions relevant to the rationality of prediction. First, as we already mentioned, the false positive rate is rarely known with regard to actual predictions. Decision makers, then, often do not have information that is critical to the prediction process. Second, the tolerance of different rates of false positives is a policy determination that has nothing to do with scientific methods. Even with some idea of its rate of false positives, a parole board must decide how many offenders it is willing to keep in prison in order to prevent criminal offenses. The lower the acceptable percentage of false positives (i.e., those denied parole who would not fail), the higher will be the percentage of false negatives (i.e., released offenders who commit crimes); and the more we are concerned with reducing the number of false negatives, the higher will be the rate of false positives. It may be appropriate, for example, for the board to release only extremely low-risk candidates, while still knowing that 60 percent (but not knowing which 60 percent) of those they reject for parole would not commit offenses. Whether decision makers should accept false positive rates of 60 percent or higher is a policy question that is distinct from the prediction process itself.

All of this analysis suggests that even under the best circumstances claims about the rationality of prediction can be overstated. In considering the highly technical aspects of prediction, one should not overlook the conceptual problems connected with specifying the criterion, identifying appropriate predictors, appreciating the base rate, and determining the tolerable ratios of false positives and false negatives. Understanding these aspects of prediction can be productive in guiding decision studies and improving prediction. In the final section of this chapter we consider the ways in which managers can influence and improve the decision-making process in criminal justice.

Improving Criminal Justice Decisions

Early in this chapter we noted that improvement in criminal justice decision making meant making rational decisions. Although completely rational decision making may be an unattainable goal, the process can be moved in the direction of being more rational than it now is from an organizational perspective. The question remains, however, What is rational from an organizational perspective? From a theoretical viewpoint this is a complex question, but the matter may be simplified by identifying recurrent themes in the literature on criminal justice decision making. These themes can guide the improvement of decision making.

One theme in criminal justice decision making involves *equity*. Equity with regard to criminal justice processing means that similar offenders in similar circumstances are treated in similar ways. It does not mean that all offenders are treated alike but does mean that differences in treatment should be based on some meaningful distinctions among the offenders. Legal and ethical arguments support the goal of equity in decision making.

A second theme relates to *accuracy*. It is obvious that we should strive to see that persons not guilty of crimes are not arrested and that those released on parole do not commit additional crimes. It is equally important to strive to see that guilty persons are subject to arrest and that those denied parole based on prediction would, in fact, fail.

Equity and accuracy, however, provide only limited direction for decision makers. Sentencing guidelines, for example, may iron out inequities across judges, but the guidelines themselves say little about the purpose of sentencing an offender to prison. A third theme, then, involves *consistency with theory.* Many theories exist regarding such things as the purpose of police intervention or prosecution or the punishment and treatment of offenders. Decision makers should strive to articulate the theories that underlie their decisions and to make future decisions consistent with those theories. We must appreciate, however, that the theories may be inconsistent with concerns for equity and accuracy. Deterrence theory, for example, may require the arrest and prosecution as well as long sentences for only a few people accused of crimes such as tax evasion or failure to register for the draft (see Morris, 1982).

A fourth theme of decision making in criminal justice involves *consistency with resources.* While we strive for consistency with theory, we must also consider pragmatic interests. The decision to arrest or issue a citation should be influenced by the availability of jail space (see Hall, Henry, Perlstein, and Smith, 1985). Prosecutors need to be sensitive to court backlog, and even if there is a disproportionately high number of maximum security prison cells, classification officers must find ways to distinguish between those who will and will not fill those spaces. Although long-term planning can change available resources, decision makers must also confront short-term necessities.

Finally, a fifth theme is evident in the literature of criminal justice. Decisions should *contribute to future decisions.* Both the process and the outcome should help to improve decision making in the future. This theme implies a cybernetic approach to improving decisions. Decision making should be guided by continuing assessments of equity, accuracy, and consistency with theory and resources. Improving decision making is then an ongoing, evolutionary process (Gottfredson and Gottfredson, 1980).

The five general themes we have just discussed also provide specific ideas for influencing the decision-making process. Those ideas involve the development of decision-making policies, concern with the people making decisions, and concern with the information used in decision making.

When similar decisions are made time and time again, as are many criminal justice decisions, organizations need to formulate explicit policies regarding them. Those policies must address the theories underlying the decisions and the goals of particular decisions as well as the types of information to be used and the decision rules for processing information. Without such policies, no guides exist for examining the consequences of decision making and no basis exists for systematically studying and increasing the effectiveness of decisions. Policymakers, however, should appreciate the complexity of criminal justice decisions and the potential uniqueness of individual cases. Decision policies should provide for flexibility. The use of sentencing guidelines illustrates one approach to flexibility. The guidelines allow judges to go outside the expected sentence range but require a written explanation of the reasons for the deviation.

In improving decision making, attention must also be paid to the decision makers themselves. Decision processes should be structured to deemphasize personality variables and subjective confidence levels. When possible, group rather than individual decisions should be encouraged. Groups tend to be more willing to take risks than individuals. Group decisions, then, lessen the conservative influences of minimax criteria. Group discussion about what information is considered relevant and how information is processed also encourages consistency in both the process and outcome of decisions.

Decision makers should also be encouraged to frame their decisions as probability estimates (Burnham, 1975) for two reasons. First, the accuracy of those estimates can then be checked against actual behavior; and, second, policy can dictate the outcome of decisions when probability estimates are made explicit. For example, parole-board policy should dictate whether an offender should be released when that individual is regarded as having a 60 percent chance of succeeding. In addition, decision makers should be trained and retrained by examining both the process and results of previous decisions.

Along with policymakers and decision makers, attention should also be paid to the information used in decision making. Efforts should be made to ensure that the information used is reliable and valid. For example, information such as the seriousness of the offense or the length of criminal history or adjustment to incarceration should be recorded and measured in ways that are consistent across decision makers. And decision makers should be encouraged to use information that research has demonstrated is relevant to the results of the decision. Along with reliability and validity, format is important. When information is presented to decision makers, it should be presented in sequential as well as summary form to accommodate the variety of search processes among decision makers. Efforts should also be made to avoid the influences of order effects and to assure adequate consideration of new information.

Information on alternatives must also be adequate for decision making. When possible, dichotomous outcomes should be avoided because they increase the likelihood that minimax strategies will be invoked. Intermediate steps, such as citation as an alternative to arrest or release and revised parole or classification dates as an alternative to denial, should be encouraged.

Finally, for the improvement of decision making to be an evolutionary process, decision makers should have feedback about decisions they have made in the past. This information is most useful when presented in the form of correct-answer feedback (Burnham, 1975). *Correct-answer feedback* not only tells decision makers whether past decisions were correct but also provides information about why some decisions were correct while others were not. For example, correct-answer feedback to a parole board would report the percentage of parolees who failed and also provide information about the characteristics of offenders who are most likely to fail. This feedback, then, can influence the information decision makers regard as relevant, how the information is combined, and even the theories underlying the decision process. With modern computing and statistical capabilities, even decision makers in small organizations and agencies should have access to correct-answer feedback.

Summary

The decisions made in criminal justice create a system out of disparate agencies and define the organizational policies of those agencies. Decision making pervades the roles of managers and front-line staff members in criminal justice. In few fields are the study and improvement of decision making as important as in this one. In this chapter we considered the theory and process of decision making and examined ways to improve the decisions made in criminal justice.

Improvement in decision making means rational decisions. But that goal must be considered within the context of the limits of rationality in the decision-making process. Organizations, individual decision makers, and information itself constrain decision making and assure that a purely rational model of decisions is not possible under the conditions of ambiguity that exist in criminal justice. Decision makers impose order where goals may conflict and large amounts of information are available. An extension of the theoretical perspective suggests that some decision making can best be understood as a process of defining problems in terms of the solutions that already exist.

Recognition of the limits of rationality can help us understand and improve the decision-making process. Although discretion has sometimes been characterized as unguided by organizational policy, viewing discretionary decisions from the perspective of bounded rationality provides direction for change while still preserving the desirable qualities of discretion. The bounded-rationality perspective also suggests that neither clinical nor statistical prediction should be regarded as an entirely rational process.

The limits of rationality are not inflexible however. Those limits can be pushed back by managers seeking increasingly rational decisions. In the literature of criminal justice, several themes are consistent with the pursuit of increased rationality. The goal of rational decisions suggests attention to equity, accuracy, consistency with theory and resources, and the development of self-correcting processes.

In the next chapter we continue to focus on the question of rationality in criminal justice organizations by examining the complex question of organizational effectiveness in a field where goals are complex and often conflicting.

CASE STUDY

The Parole Board's Dilemma

Caseworker: "Well, that is the case summary and you have had a chance to talk to the man. I've also prepared the parole-prediction form, and the result is that another ten months is recommended for this type of offender and offense."

Member #1: "There doesn't seem to be anything unusual about this case. There is nothing negative in the folder. It is a run-of-the-mill burglary by a run-of-the-mill burglar."

Member #2: "From what I've heard so far, you may be right, and I would feel pretty comfortable denying parole at this time. But I would like to hear some details on what actually happened on his previous offense."

Caseworker: "The previous offense was also a burglary, much like this one. A residence was broken into in broad daylight, and a TV and some jewelry were taken. Jimmy here was fingered by his partner, who was busted trying to pawn the TV."

Member #2: "That's consistent with what I'm thinking."

Member #3: "You people are jumping to conclusions. We need to get a better picture of this man. What was his juvenile record like? How has he spent his time in prison? What does he have going for him on the street? Let me see that folder."

Member #2: "If you want to go through all of that we can, but I don't see that it's going to have any effect on my decision."

Member #4: "Leo's right; we need more details."

Member #1: "See, it's the same old story. This is the same kind of case. We must have seen ten of these last week alone. There is nothing different here. We voted to deny release on all of those guys, and for the sake of consistency we should do the same here."

Member #3: "It's not so simple. If you look at the whole picture, you can see that this guy has turned it around during this bit. During his last sentence, he got a lot of disciplinary infractions and didn't do anything to improve himself. This bit is a complete reversal—no tickets and good program participation. When I look at everything, this guy is typical of the kinds of cases we have been giving a break to."

Member #1: "Yes, he has got some things going for him now. But this is his second time renting a room from the state. The real issue is whether he has served enough time, and I don't think he has."

Member #3: "Served enough time! We are overcrowded here. If the only question was has he served enough time, we wouldn't need a parole board; the judges could determine the exact out date."

Member #2: "We can only let the crowding issue push us so far. What we have here is a burglar who has never used violence but is a two-time loser. Those are the key issues, and they suggest he should spend more time, just like the chart says."

Member #4: "I think we should go with the form and deny for at least another ten months."

Member #2: "OK, let's consider a vote. We need to bear the crowding issue in mind, but that can't influence the decision too much. We need to consider the individual case but also decide whether he has spent enough time in prison. The guidelines are just that, and they give us some leeway. I recommend we deny parole at this time but schedule another hearing in six months instead of ten. All in favor. . . ."

Case Study Questions

1. What theoretical views and goals of the decision makers appear to have influenced the decision of this parole board?
2. How would you describe the decision-making styles of each board member? Can you identify a sequentialist, an ah yes! decision maker, a simplifier, or a ratifier?
3. How did the information itself appear to influence the process and outcome of this decision?

For Discussion

1. Consider a probation officer contemplating a decision to seek revocation of a client's probation. What theories might underlie such a decision? What are the goals? What kinds of information should the officer seek? What kinds of feedback might the probation officer want in order to influence later decisions?

2. A police officer witnesses two people arguing and shoving each other on the street and must decide what to do about it. What do you think is the range of things that the officer can do? How well does a rational model of decision making explain the choices an officer has? How well do other models, including the garbage-can model, explain the officer's position?

3. Of the types of decision makers described in this chapter, which best describes your own approach? If you were a judge making a sentencing decision, what items of information would you want? How many items would you collect? If you could collect only four items, what would they be? Could you make a sentencing decision based on those items? How confident would you be of the decision?

4. Design a process for determining, on a case-by-case basis, which juveniles should be diverted from court processing. Is this a predictive

decision? What is being predicted? How should the decision process be structured? Who should make the decisions? What kinds of information should be used? How should it be presented? How would you evaluate the decisions?

For Further Reading

Atkins, B., and Pogrebin, M. *The Invisible Justice System: Discretion and the Law.* Cincinnati: Anderson, 1981.

Gottfredson, D. M., and Tonry, M. (Eds.). *Prediction and Classification: Criminal Justice Decision Making.* Chicago: University of Chicago Press, 1987.

Gottfredson, M. R., and Gottfredson, D. M. *Decisionmaking in Criminal Justice: Toward a Rational Exercise of Discretion.* Cambridge, Mass.: Ballinger, 1980.

Murray, M. *Decisions: A Comparative Critique.* Marshfield, Mass.: Pitman, 1986.

Organizational Effectiveness

If the original report doesn't call it a [Uniform Crime Reports burglary], the insurance company won't pay off, but a lot of victims don't know that. When they find out, they want to change the report. That's not possible, of course. Once the report's filed, it's all over. So what they do is call the crime in again. We'll dispatch an officer, and in most cases a new complaint report comes in here [city police clerk quoted in McCleary, Nienstedt, and Erven, 1982:364].

There is no future in making collars! I used to be active, but it got me nothing. So now I work off the books [without paying taxes]. That way I keep the money, not the government. I leave the collars to the hotshots that still believe they will get promoted [police officer quoted in Walsh, 1986:282].

The reason the county gets so many child-abuse cases is because the district attorney has encouraged reporting by doctors and other professionals.

Who says we recommended those dispositions? It is the judge who has the responsibility of imposing the sentence.

The reason child molesters avoid jail in this county is judges refuse to send these people to jail [prosecutors explaining their prosecution and sentence records, "Offenders Escape Through Cracks," 1987:2].

I do believe, we all do—from the director to the warden to the boss in the cellblock—that prisons can be run well. Prisons don't have to be unsafe, unclean, uneducational. Good programs and good safety go together with good management [Texas prison major quoted in DiIulio, 1987:146].

For many people, the very concept of organization implies purpose, and the question of how well purposes are met is central to understanding organizations. Organizational effectiveness is thus a central theme in both the pragmatically oriented literature on management and the theoretically oriented literature of organizational behavior. For many managers, determining effectiveness involves identifying the criteria with which to assess effectiveness, measuring these criteria, and weighing the various outcomes. Implicit in these steps, however, are important theoretical questions such as: Effectiveness for whom? How are outcomes to be measured? What is a good outcome? Such inescapable questions illustrate the complexity of the concept of organizational effectiveness.

That complexity is evident in many discussions of organizations (see Peters and Waterman, 1982). For example, Tayloristic managers might cringe at a policy that Minnesota Mining & Manufacturing Co. (3M) finds central to its effectiveness. At 3M some employees are expected to steal company time and material for their own creative enterprises in the hopes that this theft will produce marketable innovations. Those sticky Post-It notes illustrate the potential for success in this approach. Managers at Ford also grappled with definitions of organizational effectiveness when, in the late 1970s, they allegedly used a cost–benefit analysis to decide not to recall Pintos, even though they knew the faulty gas-tank design was linked to fires and the subsequent deaths of some of their customers (Cullen, Mackestad, and Cavender, 1987).

In criminal justice the question of effectiveness is equally complicated. For example, what criteria for effectiveness should drive prison policies regarding overcrowding? In the mid-1980s the Illinois Department of Corrections granted massive numbers of good-time deductions, thus permitting the early release of thousands of prisoners, before the courts intervened to stop the policy. Although the Department argued that the policy was necessary for the effective management of the prison population, prosecutors argued that it violated correction's fundamental purpose of protecting the public from convicted criminals (Austin, 1986).

The complexity of the effectiveness issue is also seen in federal prosecutor Rudolph Giuliani's support of a three-year prison sentence in the largest case of insider stock trading. In late 1987, after an investigation lasting nearly two years, Ivan Boesky was convicted of illegally making hundreds of millions of dollars by trading stocks based on insider information not available to the public. Giuliani defended the sentence, which made Boesky eligible for parole after one year, by pointing out that Boesky had cooperated with the investigation and had provided information useful in several other cases. He argued that cooperation is necessary in such complex cases and that a stiffer sentence may have sent the wrong message to other stock traders considering cooperating with the prosecution.

In this chapter we examine the questions posed by these examples. We begin by defining effectiveness and noting the political consequences of this definition. We then focus on theories of organizational effectiveness, paying special attention to the limitations of the models used frequently in organizational assessments. After examining a variety of methods for assessing effectiveness, the chapter ends with a discussion of key issues to consider when determining the effectiveness of criminal justice organizations.

What Is Organizational Effectiveness?

In the literature on organizations the term *effectiveness* has been used in many ways. Most commonly, effectiveness refers to the degree of congruence between organizational goals and some observed outcome. This definition, however, masks many complicated concerns. For example, some have argued that organizational survival is the best indicator of effectiveness (Hannan and Freeman, 1977). Others have focused on adaptability to the environment rather than simply on survival. Most scholars focusing on organizational goals have also argued that effectiveness is a multidimensional concept and have advocated the use of multiple measures to assess it. In the literature on organizations, then, effectiveness remains a largely ambiguous and ill-defined concept. Some scholars have even questioned the value of the concept in the scientific study of organizations (Pfeffer, 1977b). Few scholars, however, would doubt the value of the concept for management.

Cameron (1981) identifies three reasons why the concept of organizational effectiveness remains muddled. First, there are important differences in the way scholars have conceptualized organizations. Some have suggested that organizations are best viewed as rational entities pursuing goals. In this view, a police department may be viewed as attempting to control all crime. An organization, however, might also be viewed as responding to strategic constituencies. In this view, police managers may be most concerned with their impact on property crime in a business district. Or police organizations may be viewed as primarily meeting the needs of their members through pay schedules or shift and holiday assignments. A second but related reason for the confusion surrounding the concept of effectiveness is the complexity of organizations. To the extent that organizations pursue goals, those goals are often complex, multiple, and conflicting. This complexity prohibits the identification of specific indicators of effectiveness that can be applied across organizations. Third, the confusion has been enhanced by the fact that researchers have often used different, nonoverlapping criteria, thus limiting the accumulation of empirical evidence about organizational effectiveness.

Scholarly discussions of effectiveness do make one thing clear. Effectiveness is not one thing. Organizations can be effective or ineffective in a number of different ways, and these ways may be relatively independent of one another. There is, however, little agreement on the specific criteria that should be considered in examining organizational effectiveness. In a review of the research, Campbell (1977) identified thirty different criteria that have been proposed seriously as indices of organizational effectiveness. The list includes productivity, efficiency, employee absenteeism, turnover, goal consensus, conflict, participation in decision making, stability, and communications. In criminal justice it is easy to imagine as long a list of idiosyncratic measures: crime rates, arrest rates, conviction rates, sentences, victim satisfaction, incapacitation, recidivism, humaneness, attention to legal rights, worker satisfaction, increasing budgets. Obviously, such measures may often be independent or even conflicting.

In light of ambiguities about a general definition of organizational effectiveness, perhaps the best approach is to address first the question of why we try to assess the effectiveness of organizations. Scholars give many answers to that question. They may be interested in accounting for the growth or decline of organizations; they may wish to investigate interactions between organizations and their environments; or they may seek to understand the antecedents of effectiveness.

For managers, however, the answer is straightforward. Beliefs about effectiveness influence how organizations are managed. Notions of effectiveness undergird many management decisions, and effectiveness studies can have direct and tangible consequences for organizations and their members.

In criminal justice organizations, those consequences may be felt in a variety of areas including the organization's budget, its personnel, and even its mission. Treatment programs may be dismantled if they do not lower recidivism rates. Civilian staff may replace sworn officers in traffic control and other assignments when cost effectiveness is considered (Harring, 1982). Managers or their subordinates may be fired in the face of indicators of ineffectiveness. Prison wardens may resign following disturbances or escapes; police chiefs may be forced out by dissatisfied officers. Managers may even redefine their goals in response to effectiveness studies. In the mid-1970s treatment came to be regarded as ineffective, and departments of corrections redefined their mission by emphasizing incapacitation and punishment. Prompted by the same research, probation agencies took on responsibilities for victim services, pretrial supervision, and increased surveillance of offenders.

The point is that concern with effectiveness can often lead to the redistribution of resources within and across organizations. In a completely rational model of organizations, changes in budget, personnel, or mission may appear to be logical consequences of efforts to assess and improve effectiveness. As we pointed out in the previous chapter, however, there are limits to rationality within organizations. Conflicting goals, inadequate information, and the need to "satisfyce" rather than optimize limit organizational rationality. Under these circumstances, effectiveness can be viewed as subject to the same bounded rationality as decision making. Effectiveness, therefore, might best be understood as a normative, value-laden concept used to distribute resources between and within organizations.

Effectiveness studies, then, like all evaluation research, take place within a political context. According to Weiss (1972), this context intrudes in three ways. First, the organizations, programs, or offices are the creatures of political decisions. They have been proposed, created, funded, and staffed through political processes. Second, the results of effectiveness studies feed into the political processes that sustain or change the organization. Third, the studies are political themselves because they involve implicit statements about the legitimacy of goals and interests within the organization.

Appreciation of the complexity of organizations and the political context of evaluation highlights one important question that undergirds all discussions of organizational effectiveness: Effectiveness for whom? Regardless of the theory of effectiveness being considered and regardless of how data may be gathered and analyzed, this question remains relevant.

Many studies of effectiveness adopt the perspective of the dominant coalition in an organization by reflecting the interests of those in power. As Hall (1982:286) notes, effectiveness "lies in the eye and mind of the beholder, with the important qualification that some beholders are more powerful than others." Police managers, for example, may argue that arrest rates are the best indicator of effectiveness. Corrections managers may regard low levels of inmate violence and few escapes as indicators of effectiveness. Other constituencies, however, may have alternative views. Internal constituencies led by union stewards may base an assessment of effectiveness on working conditions. This was the case in 1979 in the largest prison guard strike in history. New York corrections officers had to be replaced by the National Guard when they walked off the job to protest a perceived lack of control over inmates and their low status within the organization (Jacobs and Zimmer, 1983).

One of the most significant cases in the history of prisoner litigation also illustrates the importance of the question of effectiveness-for-whom and the importance of power in determining whose view prevails. Prior to the case of *Ruiz* v. *Estelle* (1980), the Texas Department of Corrections (TDC) was widely regarded as highly effective based on its low costs, low incidence of reported violence, and the general cleanliness of its institutions. A combination of internal and external constituents, however, saw the matter differently. Inmates, prison-reform lawyers, and the federal court came to regard the TDC as grossly ineffective. As one lawyer noted, "While corrections in Texas may be cheap in some senses, the system exacts intolerable costs to the human rights of the citizens in its custody and its unlawful practices must be remedied" (quoted in Martin and Ekland-Olson, 1987). These differing views figured prominently in the longest and most expensive prisoners' rights trial to date, a case that, after long and bitter battles, led to the near-total reorganization of the TDC.

The importance of the question of perspective is also demonstrated in a study of the use of telephones to arrange bail for pretrial inmates. Here another powerful external constituency was involved. An experiment in the Tombs, a detention prison in lower Manhattan, proved that many inmates could raise bail money simply by being given access to telephones. The social scientists conducting the study felt that increased availability of telephones not only would benefit inmates but also would increase organizational effectiveness by reducing crowding and saving large sums of money on pretrial detention. Implementation of increased access to telephones was resisted, however, when prosecutors intervened. This external constituency opposed the policy because it was seen as weakening their position in plea bargaining. Because detained arrestees are more likely than released arrestees to plead guilty, the prosecutors attempted to block increased access to telephones (Lenihan, 1977).

These examples illustrate varying perspectives on organizational effectiveness. Dominant coalitions, powerful internal constituencies, and powerful external constituencies may all have different ideas as to what makes for an effective organization. Because those perspectives may lead to different distributions of resources in organizations, it is critical to understand whose perspective underlies any discussion of the effectiveness of an organization.

Theories of Organizational Effectiveness

Hannan and Freeman (1977) point out that some theoretical perspective must underlie any discussion of effectiveness. Even the question of whether an organization is regarded as succeeding or failing will depend on theory. In this section we review the major theoretical perspectives on the assessment of organizational effectiveness.

The Goal Model

The goal model is the most common theoretical perspective on effectiveness, and, as Hall (1982:278) suggests, it is both simple and complex. In its simplest form, the goal model defines effectiveness as the degree to which an organization realizes its goals (Etzioni, 1964:8). The model posits that organizations can be understood as rational entities. When using this perspective, evaluators assume that an organization's goals can be identified, that organizations are motivated to meet those goals, and that progress toward them can be measured. Evaluating companies by their profits is, perhaps, the most obvious example of this approach. In criminal justice, such measures of effectiveness as arrest rates, conviction rates, and recidivism all reflect the goal model.

There are some difficulties with this model. As we noted in the previous chapter, research has revealed limitations of the rational model of organizations. Many commentators have also noted the difficulties involved in defining an organization's goals (Simon, 1964; Etzioni, 1960); most organizations have multiple and, frequently, conflicting goals. Even manufacturing firms must balance quantity with quality goals and concern for short-term profits with long-term considerations. The situation is still more complicated in criminal justice. Police departments are charged with controlling crime but must also ensure due process. They also generate revenue through enforcement practices, reduce fear of crime, maintain order, and satisfy their employees, as well as pursue many other goals. Identification of some primary goal or goals is clearly a difficult task and one that again raises the question of effectiveness-for-whom.

Nevertheless, all public organizations have numerous goals (Hannan and Freeman, 1977:111). In his study of street-level bureaucracies, Lipsky (1980) considered the impact of these goals on effectiveness. He argues that one of the characteristics of public organizations is that their conflicting goals reflect conflicts absorbed by the organization from society at large. For example, the public generally supports services for welfare recipients, but the same public argues for reductions in welfare rolls and cutbacks in services. The public also wants to see offenders rehabilitated but at the same time wants prison to be, at least, uncomfortable. One implication of Lipsky's argument is that public organizations are designed to be ineffective when effectiveness is ascertained by a broad-based goal model.

A second problem with the goal approach also relates to the question of what goals should be considered but poses that question differently. Perrow (1961) distinguishes between official goals and operative goals. *Official goals* are generally for public consumption and can be found in annual reports and broad policy statements. Such goals as "to serve and to protect," however, provide little guidance for what goes on in an organization on a daily basis. *Operative goals* are generally derived from official goals but tell us exactly what the organization is trying to do.

The difference between official and operative goals is illustrated in Sykes's (1971) study of Trenton Prison. He argues that because we know little of the technology needed to "treat" offenders and because punishment must be tempered with humaneness, prison cannot accomplish either official goal. Instead, the regimen of incarceration reveals an operative goal of simply retaining custody through benign means. The Texas prison system confronted the same dilemma that Sykes describes but apparently resolved it in a different fashion. While neither treatment nor punishment was actively pursued, the TDC did follow a strict and sometimes brutal regimen directed at maintaining order (see DiIulio, 1987). The point is that to consider only official goals would invoke unrealistic standards and ignore goals that are actually being pursued. Considering only operative goals, however, would make it impossible to compare effectiveness across organizations.

A third problem with focusing on organizational goals relates to the consequences of measuring goal attainment. On the one hand, this approach means that behavior that is not viewed as relating to goals is not measured and, therefore, is not viewed as contributing to effectiveness. Police officers' compassion toward the victims of crime or a judge's exhortations to an impressionable juvenile go unrecognized if effectiveness is measured by arrest statistics or cases processed. On the other hand, the effectiveness criteria selected may go further and actually alter desirable behavior that is not recognized in the measurement process. While studying an employment agency, Blau (1963) observed that the choice of evaluation criteria had a dramatic effect on behavior within the organization. When the agency was evaluated on its job-placement rate, employment counselors shifted their focus from clients who were difficult to place to place to clients who were the most likely to find work and who may even have been successful without the agency. Measuring goal attainment, then, not only leaves some activity within an organization unrecognized but may narrow activity so that only those goals whose attainment is measured are met.

A final concern about the goal model of effectiveness deals with the relationship between goal attainment and consequences for the organization. In public organizations this relationship is not at all straightforward. Lipsky (1980:35), for example, suggests that the demand for services in street-level bureaucracies will always increase to meet (or exceed) supply. He illustrates the point with the example of a health-care clinic forced to move out of a poor neighborhood in an effort to control the demand for services. The more successful the clinic was at providing services, the greater was the demand. The evidently bottomless demand necessitated either cutbacks in the quality of services or making services difficult to obtain by increasing transportation problems for clients. The attainment of goals thus led to drastic changes for the organization.

Whereas goal attainment may have negative consequences for some organizations, failure may not only *not* have negative consequences, it may, in fact, have some positive consequences. For example, it is difficult to envision cutbacks in the police because crime rates increase! Likewise, when Martinson (1974) and others declared correctional treatment a failure in the mid-1970s, prison populations and resources for prisons began to soar. When some goals are considered, then, prisons may look ineffective, but the consequences may be positive for the organization.

The goal model, then, is a complex framework in which to consider organizational effectiveness. Despite its limitations, however, the assessment of effectiveness continues to be largely a process of identifying goals, measuring them, and comparing the results against some standard. The reader, however, should be aware of the problems and limitations of this perspective.

Some Alternatives to the Goal Model

The goal model is a broad and complex means of examining organizational effectiveness. In response to problems with this goal approach, several other models have been developed that view effectiveness differently. One such model has been referred to as the *internal process model*. This model is consistent with human relations perspectives in organizational analysis (see Likert, 1967). It argues that effective organizations are those in which there is little internal strain, where information flows easily both horizontally and vertically, and where internal functioning is smooth and characterized by trust and benevolence toward individuals (Cameron, 1981). To the extent that this model is concerned with morale within an organization, it may be seen as simply focusing on a limited set of goals. Such a narrow focus, however, is not without its benefits, especially in fields like criminal justice, when agreement on other goals may be difficult to reach.

Another perspective has been described as the counterparadigm to the goal model (see Hall, 1982:286). *Participant-satisfaction models* or *strategic-constituency models* are not concerned with questions of morale as the names may suggest. Instead they view effective organizations as serving the interests of key constituencies (see Hall, 1982; Cameron, 1981), which may include resource providers, suppliers, users of an organization's products, or even clients in social service agencies. Effective organizations are able to maintain the contributions of these constituencies. For example, this model might highlight the importance of good relations between the police and the prosecutor's office or might explain why public defenders often maintain good relationships with their supposed adversaries in the courtroom. The model may also explain why some organizations fail. The Willowbrook School on Staten Island, a school for the retarded, was closed in the late 1970s after failing to satisfy parents' groups and the courts (Rothman and Rothman, 1984). An investigative reporter had sneaked into the school and revealed deplorable conditions on the local television station. Eventually a parents' group was organized, and it successfully fought the institution.

Another view of organizational effectiveness incorporates many of the elements in the approaches already discussed. Steers (1977) describes this *process approach.* Under this model, effectiveness is described as a process rather than an end state, as might be the case under the goal model. The process approach consists of three related components: goal optimization, a systems perspective, and an emphasis on behavior within organizations. Goal optimization refers to the need to balance goals and thus to optimize multiple goals rather than fully achieve a particular one. A systems view incorporates concerns for changes in an organization's environment. And the behavioral emphasis suggests attention to the possible contributions of individual employees to organizational effectiveness. Under this model, then, the effective organization is one in which goals are responsive to the environment, optimization of multiple goals is pursued, and employees all contribute to meeting those goals.

One last important theory of organizational effectiveness is a substantial deviation from the others. Yuchtman and Seashore (1967) developed the *system–resource model* from an empirical investigation of the effectiveness of seventy-five independent insurance agencies. In this view organizations are not assumed to possess goals, nor is goal accomplishment a relevant consideration. Instead, an organization is effective to the extent that it can obtain needed resources from its environment. As Seashore and Yuchtman note, the effectiveness of an organization can be defined as the "ability to exploit its environment in the acquisition of scarce and valued resources to sustain its functioning" (1967:893).

Thus, whereas the goal model emphasizes output, the system–resource model is concerned with inputs.

This difference in orientation can produce useful insights in areas where the goal model may lead to confusion. For example, under the goal model, the failure of probation agencies to rehabilitate clients may be regarded as ineffectiveness. The system–resource model, however, would lead to the conclusion that these same agencies have been highly effective because they were able to change their mission and attract resources for custodially oriented surveillance programs such as intensive supervision or electronic home monitoring. Likewise, if running safe and humane prisons was a goal of the Louisiana Corrections Department, then a 1975 court decision ordering sweeping reforms indicates that the organization was ineffective. However, then Corrections Secretary C. Paul Phelps has said that "the court order was the best thing that ever happened to corrections in [the] state" (cited in Rideau and Sinclair, 1982). Such a proclamation is understandable under a system–resource perspective because the court order gave the Department considerable political power and financial resources to make needed improvements.

Methods of Assessing Effectiveness

Reviewing a variety of theoretical perspectives on effectiveness is useful because it not only points out the limitations of the goal model but also provides alternative ways of considering organizations. In examining studies of effectiveness, however, it is clear that the goal model dominates efforts to assess organizations. Studies based on this model involve the identification and measurement of some goal or goals. Most frequently this type of study has used a method referred to as *variable analysis*. Sophisticated studies of this type try to examine causal links in the attainment of some goal. For example, they may examine the contribution of training or supervision style to job satisfaction. Before discussing some of the pragmatic uses of this design, it is important to note that other types of effectiveness studies are possible.

Perrow (1977) describes two alternatives to variable analysis. In *gross-malfunctioning analysis*, the target of inquiry is failed or failing organizations. The analysis may examine the reasons behind a commercial bankruptcy, the disappearance of a social service program, a police department reorganization, or a major prison riot. Perrow describes gross-malfunctioning analysis as reflecting a "primordial" concern with effectiveness because it deals with basic questions of outcome. He argues that the subtleties of complex goals or goal displacement become irrelevant when organizations fail dramatically. Gross mismanagement, Perrow suggests, is easy to spot, and understanding it is a useful guide to improving organizations.

One example of gross-malfunctioning analysis can be seen in the report of the National Advisory Commission on Civil Disorders (1968), also known as the Kerner Commission. The group was formed to investigate the causes of the urban riots that occurred in 1967 in major cities across the country including Los Angeles, Newark, Detroit, and New York. The Commission found that blacks in each of the cities complained of police misconduct—harassment, brutality, and even the improper use of deadly force. Although many causes of the riots were cited in the report, these practices along with aggressive patrol practices in urban ghettos were seen as major contributing factors to the unrest. Law-and-order candidates for the presidency rejected its conclusions (Cronin, Cronin, and Milakovich, 1981:66), but the Kerner Commission maintained that, at the height of the civil rights movement, police organizations continued to rely on enforcement strategies that were regarded as reflecting policies of racism and neglect.

The history of Texas prisons also illustrates the potential benefits of gross-malfunctioning analysis. Texas prisons, too, failed to adapt to a changing environment. Prisoner litigation cost millions of dollars, was associated with increased violence and instability, and ultimately led to the reorganization of the prison system. Martin and Ekland-Olson's (1987) history of the litigation makes it clear that the policies of harassing inmate litigants and their lawyers and of ignoring or violating court orders exacerbated problems for the prison system.

Perrow's (1977) second alternative to variable analysis is called *revelatory analysis.* While variable analysis seeks to answer the question of how well some goal is being met, revelatory analysis asks who is getting what from an organization. In other words, revelatory analysis directly addresses the question of effectiveness-for-whom by investigating how organizations are used by groups inside and outside organizations. Prisons, then, may be effective by virtue of the employment opportunities they provide in rural areas. This fact explains why many rural communities have actively sought to attract these institutions, which seem relatively ineffective by a simple variable analysis. Likewise, Perrow suggests that organizations can be effective at meeting the individual needs of employees. A police department, for example, may be regarded as effective, by some, because it offers a work schedule of four ten-hour days per week, which allows officers to maintain second jobs or engage in their favorite hobbies. Under a variable analysis, employee morale may be seen as significant because of its assumed effect on goals such as productivity. In a revelatory analysis, however, morale may be regarded as significant in and of itself.

Variable Analysis in Criminal Justice

In the assessment of organizational effectiveness, *variable analysis* refers to research designs in which there is an attempt to measure the degree of attainment of some goal. Measurement of some outcome variable is often accompanied by investigation of the relationship between that outcome and independent variables. These studies, then, not only lead to general statements about effectiveness based on goal attainment but also provide information on what may contribute to effectiveness and thus on how effectiveness may be enhanced. For example, studies using crime rates as measures of police effectiveness may examine the relationship between that dependent variable and independent variables such as police expenditures, numbers of personnel, or intensity of investigation (Wycoff, 1982).

Variable analysis is the most common approach to studying effectiveness in criminal justice. In this section we examine five issues that are critical to these assessments and reveal the complexity of this approach.

What Domain of Activity Is the Target of the Assessment?

This question recognizes that organizations have multiple goals and that an assessment of effectiveness may not deal with all of them. As with all organizations, you could assess the effectiveness of criminal justice organizations at providing a safe and comfortable working environment for workers or managers or you could assess their effectiveness at garnering or spending budgetary resources. There are also many activities unique to criminal justice organizations. For example, Wycoff (1982) focuses on the effects of crime-control activity by the police. Vanagunas (1982), however, argues that only a small amount of police activity deals with crime-related events and that, for the "consumer" of police services, problems unrelated to crime are more frequent and more important than criminal problems. He suggests using a human service model in the evaluation of the police, which would include evaluating conflict-reduction efforts and emergency services.

Such questions about the activity or activities being assessed are central. Assessments of courts may focus on efficiency in the processing of cases or equity in the dispensation of sentences (see Goodstein and Hepburn, 1985; Hardy, 1983). Likewise, corrections programs have often been assessed on their ability to change offender behavior through rehabilitation, but some observers have suggested focusing on fairness (Fogel and Hudson, 1981), and, most recently, attention has turned to deterrence (Phillips, McCleary, and Dinitz, 1983) and incapacitation (Greenwood, 1982). The National Institute of Justice released a cost–benefit study that analyzed the financial savings brought about by crime reductions due to imprisonment (Zedlewski, 1987).

The selection of the domain of activity is a significant step in the evaluation of effectiveness. That selection bears directly on many of the issues we have discussed—most notably, the question of effectiveness-for-whom, the fact that goals often conflict, and the tendency for effectiveness criteria to influence behavior within organizations.

What Do the Variables Mean?

After some domain of activity is selected, the next important consideration is validity, or finding variables that actually provide measures of effectiveness in the selected domain of activity. The problem is not a simple one. For example, recidivism rates have often been used as a measure of the effectiveness of rehabilitation programs. In fact, Martinson's (1974) famous critique of correctional treatment was based on the programs' failure to reduce recidivism rates. As he summarized his findings, "With few and isolated exceptions, the rehabilitative efforts that have been reported so far have had no appreciable effect on recidivism" (1974:49). That summary influenced the move away from a rehabilitation model and toward a just-desserts, or punishment, model. In fact, however, there is every reason to question the use of recidivism as a satisfactory measure of rehabilitation. As Maltz (1984) points out, without paying attention to how programs are expected to affect recidivism, it is impossible to tell just what recidivism rates measure. They may also be measuring the effects of punitiveness and, therefore, special deterrence rather than rehabilitation. In other words, "it may not be possible to disentangle the effects of the carrot (rehabilitation) from those of the stick (special deterrence)" (Maltz, 1984:11).

The situation is equally complex with other measures of criminal justice effectiveness. For example, Chicago police and prosecutors were criticized for failing to successfully prosecute a large number of people arrested for drug offenses. It was later reported that the primary motive for the drug-possession arrests was to get gang members off the streets for brief periods of time. The police were using the charges in much the way they had once used charges of public intoxication. It was argued, therefore, that successful prosecution was not an appropriate criterion for effectiveness because failure to prosecute did not mean what the critics suggested ("The Court Retorts . . . ," 1987). (Whether arrests should be used in this way raises a completely different question about effectiveness criteria.)

Reported crime, arrest rate, and clearance rate are the most frequently employed outcome measures in assessments of the police. Problems with the validity of these measures, however, have been well documented (see Wycoff, 1982). In one series of case studies, McCleary, Nienstedt, and Erven (1982) demonstrated that official crime statistics may sometimes be the result of organizational behavior that has little to do with effectiveness. In one of the cases, the authors explained a major drop in Uniform Crime Reports (UCR) burglary rates in one city by a significant change in investigation and recording procedures. The city changed procedures to require investigation of burglaries before they were recorded by the UCR clerks rather than have investigations follow the official recording. With the change in procedures, many events that would have been recorded as burglaries based on the initial patrol officers' reports were not viewed as meeting UCR definitions by the investigating detectives.

In a second case study, a "crime wave" coincided with the retirement of a police chief of long tenure. The study argues that the chief had "wished" crime rates down by rewarding district commanders who produced low UCR rates. That "wish" was then passed down through the ranks. With the chief's retirement, the hierarchical authority patterns within the department disintegrated and crime rates rose.

Finally, McCleary, Nienstedt, and Erven found another unsuspected source of a crime wave. In one city, the task of directly supervising police dispatchers was removed from shift sergeants. Without the experience and protection of the sergeants, dispatchers began to send police officers to respond to many calls that otherwise would have been handled informally. Department statisticians experienced the increased dispatches of officers as a crime wave.

One final example illustrates the political issues inherent in defining effectiveness criteria. Morash and Greene (1986) report two studies that came to radically different conclusions about the effectiveness of female police officers. The curious thing is that both studies were done by the same consulting firm in the same city (Philadelphia) in the same year. In the first study, criteria for effectiveness were developed by using sophisticated techniques to find consensus among police administrators. In that study, resolving problems without arrests was an indicator of effectiveness, and female officers were found to be as effective as their male counterparts. Later, as a response to court proceedings and the city administration's concern with violent confrontations, a second study was conducted in which the decision to arrest was viewed as an indicator of effectiveness. By this criterion, women were not found to be as effective as male officers. The studies illustrate that not only do organizational factors influence outcomes but the way those outcomes are viewed is the result of value judgments and political decisions.

How Are the Variables Measured?

The problems just discussed relate to how effectiveness criteria are conceptualized and understood. Another aspect of the problem involves the measurement of the variables. The question is not necessarily one of inaccurate measurements. Although computational errors do occur, the significant problem is the choices made between measures that may all be mathematically correct. Some measures may be more suitable than others to the specific effectiveness problem being addressed. For example, when calculating crime rates in an urban area, considering only the number of crimes per 100,000 residents ignores the fact that many potential victims (and offenders) commute into the city every day.

The literature on measuring recidivism provides many illustrations of the importance of knowing how outcome variables are measured. While there are many examples of inappropriate models and formulas used in recidivism research, even mathematically correct equations may produce widely different results. *Recidivism* can be defined as the proportion of some specified group of offenders who fail, according to some criteria, within some specified time. At a minimum then, measuring recidivism for some group of offenders requires identification of a failure criterion and a follow-up period. Failure may involve anything from rearrest to a return to prison with a new sentence, and the follow-up period may be anything from a few months to many years. Recidivism rates can thus vary greatly according to the failure criterion and the length of the follow-up period. The easier it is to fail and the longer the follow-up, the higher will be the recidivism rate. To illustrate the point, Hoffman and Stone-Meierhoefer (1980) computed recidivism rates on a sample of released prison inmates using various failure criteria and follow-up periods. When return to prison was the criterion for failure and a one-year follow-up was used, the recidivism rate was 8.7 percent. When arrest was used as the failure criterion with a six-year follow-up, the same sample produced a recidivism rate of 60.4 percent.

An inquiry into effectiveness by Wilkins (1976) also demonstrates the complexity of using recidivism measures. The Maryland Institute for Defective Delinquents at Patuxent, a well-known treatment facility, reported a recidivism rate of 7 percent using rearrest with a one-year follow-up. This rate was well below the 65 percent reported by similar facilities. When Wilkins examined the data, he found that the Institute had used a unique way of figuring recidivism. The treatment program involved a period of institutionalization followed by three years of out-patient supervision and services. The Institute counted an offender as a recidivist only if the juvenile was not returned to the institution during the three-year outpatient phase and was later arrested. Those who were returned to the Institution during their period of outpatient services were not counted among the recidivists. Wilkins showed that the likelihood of anyone from any program failing after three years was about 7 percent and that Patuxent did no better than other institutions when the three-year outpatient period was included in the analysis. The research underscores two important points about the measurement of variables. Those conducting studies of effectiveness need to be aware of the implications of selecting different ways of measuring outcomes, and the reader of reports on effectiveness must understand precisely how the outcome variables were measured.

Alternatives to Outcome Measures

Up until now our discussion has focused primarily on outcome variables as indicators of effectiveness. Crime rates, arrest rates, convictions, and recidivism are all measures of the outcome of organizational activity in criminal justice. There are, however, many limitations to such variables. They are complicated and expensive to measure. They can often be assessed only long after some activity has taken place. And many things outside the organization may influence them. It is easy to see, for example, that police can have only a limited impact on crime rates and that many factors other than prison may contribute to an ex-offender's return to crime.

In response to the problems of outcome measures, many managers and researchers have turned to measures of process or structure as indicators of effectiveness (Scott, 1977). *Process measures* are measures of the activities assumed to cause effectiveness within organizations. For example, assessments of probation and parole agencies have incorporated variables such as the length of time probation/parole officers spend in supervision of each case or the length of time they spend in face-to-face contact with parolees. Judges might examine the length of time a case takes to go from indictment to final disposition, and police managers often examine numbers of traffic stops made by officers. The advantage of these measures is that they are easy to collect and are likely to be easier than outcome measures to influence directly. A disadvantage lies in the fact the they may not be as highly related to outcome measures as is often assumed.

Structure measures are still further removed from outcomes. These variables measure organizational features or participant characteristics that are presumed to have an impact on effectiveness. Courts have used the ratio of corrections officers to inmates as a measure of inmate safety in prison. Likewise, the level of training among staff has been used in assessing the effectiveness of many criminal justice agencies. One way of viewing these measures is to regard them as measures of organizational inputs that serve as surrogate measures for outputs.

Using Multiple Measures of Effectiveness

There has been considerable criticism of evaluation efforts that use single measures as indicators of effectiveness (see Chen and Rossi, 1980). Whether structure, process, or outcome variables are used, single measures have often been regarded as too simplistic and often uninformative. Single-variable measures assess achievement of only one goal and are, therefore, based on a lack of appreciation of the complexity of multiple goals within organizations. Furthermore, single-measurement analyses inevitably conclude that a goal either has been reached or has not been reached. A program is thus regarded as a success or as a failure. Such a conclusion provides a static, one-shot view of effectiveness and little information on how an organization might change or improve.

Multigoal/multimeasure designs give a more comprehensive view of organizational effectiveness than single measures do. These deisgns utilize a variety of measures to assess achievement of multiple goals. In doing so, they permit examination of the effectiveness of different domains of organizational activity and examination of the relationship between achievement of various goals. These models can also view effectiveness as an ongoing activity and thus provide information about how an organization can improve.

Blomberg (1983) provides an example of the multigoal/multimeasure approach in assessing the effectiveness of juvenile diversion programs. These programs have often been evaluated from a single-goal perspective. They have often been regarded as failing because the goal of diverting nonserious offenders from the criminal justice system has been displaced as the diversion programs became an add-on intervention rather than an alternative. In other words, through net widening, diversion programs have sometimes come to serve clients who would not even have been arrested if the diversion program did not exist. Where evaluations have focused on rearrest data, these single-outcome measures have also not shown these programs to be effective.

Blomberg is critical of the simplicity of such evaluations. As an alternative he suggests a multigoal/multimeasure approach that incorporates at least three broad measurements. First, measures of structure identify the types of youth served by the diversion programs, including such variables as age, ethnicity, social status, and offense history. Second, measures of services provided by the programs can distinguish between various types and intensities of programs. Finally, outcome measures, such as rearrest data, should be included. Taken together these variables recognize that different types of programs may serve different types of youth. The evaluation, therefore, addresses the question of what-works-for-whom and thus provides information for program improvement.

Another model multigoal/multimeasure evaluation is an assessment of the juvenile corrections system in Massachusetts (Coates, Miller, and Ohlin, 1978). Researchers from the Harvard Center for Criminal Justice carried out the evaluation of the community-based system that replaced the juvenile institutions after they were closed by Jerome Miller, the commissioner of youth services in the early 1970s. The study incorporated a variety of structure, process, and outcome variables.

The assessment began with a theoretical model of community-based corrections as running along a continuum from institutionalization to normalization. Variables such as the types of relationships between staff and inmates and the types and extent of links to the community were used to distinguish between facilities that were more like institutions and facilities that were more open and approximated normal life. The researchers found that some of the programs had social climates and links to the community that nearly duplicated those of institutions. Most often, these programs focused on changing offenders' values rather than reintegrating them into the community. This structural dimension was then examined to see how it related to process and outcome variables.

The process variables were decisions made to place youths in the various types of programs. The researchers found that youths with more extensive records were more likely to be placed in the less open programs. Thus many youths did not benefit from the new treatment programs, and those most needing the innovative programs were least likely to get them.

The study also incorporated a variety of outcome measures. Cost and recidivism outcomes were examined, as were a variety of attitudes in the short and long term. Attitudes were examined at release from the program and again at six months after release. The evaluation revealed that the open, or normalized, programs had the most positive effects but that these modest program effects diminished when the youths returned to their homes.

The complex design of the Massachusetts evaluation permitted conclusions that went far beyond commenting on the success or failure of the community-based programs. The study showed that most youth offenders could be handled in the community-based system. Another finding was that "community based" was an inadequate description and masked a wide range of programs. Another finding was that the more open programs were more likely to be successful. The evaluation also produced significant recommendations for program improvement, which ranged from increasing links to the community to strengthening advocacy work and follow-up in the community.

These five issues illustrate the complexity of variable analysis in the assessment of organizational effectiveness. At first glance these issues may appear to deal with narrow technical problems. Careful consideration, however, reveals that they get to the heart of understanding organizational effectiveness under the goal model. Attention to these issues will require that decisions be made about what goals are relevant to effective organizations, how attainment of those goals can be assessed appropriately, and what benefits their assessment can have for members of the organization. Attention to the issues will also suggest that the assessment of effectiveness can be an ongoing activity that provides information for the continuing change and improvement of organizations.

Summary

In this chapter we have considered what effectiveness may mean and how it might be assessed in criminal justice. These are complex questions in any field and are particularly difficult in criminal justice, where goals are many and often conflicting. For managers, however, some answer to these questions is necessary. Beliefs about how effective an organization is and how it may increase its effectiveness, whether these beliefs are the result of complicated empirical studies or are uninformed by data, influence how resources are distributed and what goes on in the organization.

Given the implications of effectiveness evaluations and the complexity of goals in criminal justice, the importance of the question of effectiveness-for-whom must be recognized. Offenders, front-line staff, managers, and those outside criminal justice may have different ideas of what makes for an effective criminal justice organization. The perspective of those in power within organizations often underlies effectiveness studies, but other constituencies, including organized employees and the courts, can also be influential.

Although there are a variety of theoretical perspectives on organizational effectiveness, the goal model is the one most often adopted by managers. Variable analyses based on this model, however, illustrate how complex the model is. Key conceptual questions must be addressed. Decisions must be made about what goals to measure and how to measure them and about the use of process and structure measures as surrogates for outcomes. One approach to the complex conceptual issues of variable analysis is the use of a multigoal/multimeasure approach. This approach recognizes the complexity of programs and organizations and allows managers to look beyond simple measures of success or failure.

With the proper design, the study of organizational effectiveness need not be a static assessment of how well an organization meets a goal or goals. It can be an ongoing process that produces empirically based recommendations for continued improvement. In the following chapter, we deal directly with the improvement of criminal justice through the process of organizational change.

--------------------- **CASE STUDY** ---------------------
A Probation Officer's View of Effectiveness

Only a week on the job and the new chief probation officer calls a meeting of our whole department with an agenda item ominously titled "plans for a comprehensive evaluation." That's where all the trouble began in the first place. A "comprehensive evaluation" is what led to the resignation of the previous chief.

Of course, that evaluation wasn't done in the department. Six months ago the local newspaper ran a special series on the probation department. For three Sundays in a row they raked us over the coals. In Part I, they showed that over 60 percent of our felony probationers were rearrested within a year. Part II claimed that all we officers do is sit around the office and drink coffee. In Part III, the social service agencies in town chimed in by saying we don't provide any rehabilitation services.

That's not what did the chief in, though. No, we did him in. His reaction to the newspaper stories was to jump all over us. We had to do even more paperwork to show how busy we were. He made us work long hours on cases that were no threat to anyone. He made me spend a week tracking down a shoplifter who missed one appointment. It turned out the guy was in the hospital for a hernia operation. My wife almost put me in the hospital when I had to miss my son's birthday party to prove the shoplifter shouldn't be violated yet.

Yeah, things got pretty nasty around here. So, after a few guys quit and caseloads went up, we started talking union. Now we're part of an organization of county workers all across the country. With our first set of grievances, the boss's ulcer acted up, and pretty soon we were facing this new guy from the outside. Just what we all need, another "comprehensive evaluation."

Later, at the meeting. . . .

Allen Jones, chief probation officer: "OK, now to the next agenda item, plans for a comprehensive evaluation."

Gus Murdock, union steward: "Wait a minute. There's no point in doing an evaluation. As long as caseloads are over a hundred, we know what your numbers will show."

Jones: "Gus, I don't want to do an evaluation to show how bad we are or even how good we are. I think that if we can start to collect some information and see how some things relate to each other, we can start working in a direction that we all find beneficial."

Jan Seltzer, probation officer: "Well, right off, I'm leery of using those same recidivism rates again. Felony probationers are always going to have a high failure rate. At the very least, we have to look at what is also happening with our misdemeanants and other less serious offenders and at differences within those groups."

Murdock: "Let's get back to caseloads. Nothing is gonna change if we don't get the numbers down."

Jones: "OK, Gus, but we can't get the numbers down until we fill our three vacancies. And even then I'm not sure we can expect smaller caseloads to reduce recidivism. The size of the caseload doesn't tell us anything about what probation officers are actually doing with their cases."

Murdock: "Well, what are you suggesting?"

Jones: "First, we need to see how much time the officers are spending with clients. I mean, how much can you spend if you're carrying 100 people on a caseload? And how much time is spent on paperwork?"

Murdock: "Maybe that information can give us some baseline data and show how we can increase the time spent with clients without taking it out of the officers' hides."

Seltzer: "Yeah, but there is more to it than how much time you spend with them. We should also keep track of where the time is spent. I mean, it may make a difference if you spend it with them in the office havin' coffee or out in the field."

Murdock: "You're right. But what you do with the time may also be important. For example, some of you are good at hard-nosed surveillance—keeping them honest. Now maybe that works with some clients. But right now I'm working on getting my cases hooked up with some of these social service agencies. Maybe that will work for some of them too."

Jones: "OK, now we're getting somewhere. We need to look at what the officers do, how that relates to the success or failure of all different kinds of clients, and how it can be improved. And we need to do this sort of thing at least once a year so we can build on the results."

Murdock: "And you're gonna do all of this without increasing our work load?"

Jones: "No false promises, but together we can keep any additional work to a minimum. And one last thing. I think we need to include a good survey of job satisfaction. The bottom line is that we need to make this a good place to work. Now on to the next agenda item. How are we going to train the new officers, and how do we evaluate the training?"

It's probably all baloney, but let's give this evaluation a chance. It may get us back to what probation is supposed to be all about. We'll see.

Case Study Questions

1. Whose interests were served in the newspaper's evaluation of this department and whose will be served by the proposed evaluation?
2. What theory or theories of effectiveness are represented in the proposed new evaluation format?
3. What process and outcome measures are included in the evaluation? What domain of activity do these cover? Is the meaning of the variables clear?

For Discussion

1. Local jails are complex organizations with multiple goals. Consider how you might assess the effectiveness of your own local jail. What internal and external constituencies exist? How might their views of effectiveness differ from that of the jail administration?

2. Describe the goals of your local police department. How do official and operative goals compare? What variables would you suggest using to measure achievement of those goals? Is the meaning of the variables clear?

3. Consider the effectiveness of a probation agency using a variety of theoretical perspectives. Would you reach similar conclusions using a goal model, strategic-constituency model, and system–resource model of effectiveness? Under what circumstances might the theories lead to different conclusions about how effective the agency is?

4. Develop a plan for a multigoal/multimeasure evaluation of a victim–witness assistance program administered through the prosecutor's office. What kinds of structure, process, and outcome variables would you be interested in? How would you use the evaluation procedure to provide information for the ongoing assessment and improvement of the program?

For Further Reading

Flemming, R. B. *Punishment Before Trial: An Organizational Perspective of Felony Bail Processes.* New York: Longman, 1982.

Martin, S. J., and Eckland-Olson, S. *Texas Prisons: The Walls Came Tumbling Down.* Austin: Texas Monthly Press, 1987.

Peters, T. J., and Waterman, R. H. *In Search of Excellence: Lessons from America's Best-Run Companies.* New York: Harper & Row, 1982.

Whitaker, G. P., and Phillips, C. D. (Eds.). *Evaluating Performance of Criminal Justice Agencies.* Beverly Hills, Calif.: Sage, 1983.

Change and Innovation

Many of the criminal justice system's difficulties stem from its reluctance to change old ways, or, to put the same proposition in reverse, its reluctance to try new ones. The increasing volume of crime in America establishes conclusively that many of the old ways are not good enough. Innovation and experimentation in all parts of the criminal justice system are clearly imperative. They are imperative with respect both to entire agencies and to specific procedures. Court systems need reorganization and case-docketing methods need improvement; police–community-relations programs are needed and so are ways of relieving detectives from the duty of typing their own reports; community-based correctional programs must be organized, and the pay of prison guards must be raised. Recruitment and training, organization and management, research and development all require reexamination and reform [President's Commission on Law Enforcement and the Administration of Justice, 1967:14].

Change is inevitable, progress is not [unknown].

This chapter focuses on organizational change within the criminal justice system and its agencies. Organizational change and the concepts and theories surrounding change can apply to minor procedural changes within an agency or to sweeping reforms that change the philosophy and operations of an entire system. At one extreme, changes can take place in an agency because of decisions on the part of agency members. At the other extreme, major, systemwide change is typically the result of reform movements that emanate from cohesive groups within society or the polity in its entirety. Historically, such organizational change takes place within the context of general social changes that create, or are created by, different perspectives, ideas, or paradigms. Rothman (1980), for example, argues that the prison reforms that took place at the beginning of the century were the natural consequence of the "progressive era," during which all social institutions were being questioned and changed.

The perceived need for reform and change in the criminal justice system preceded the progressive era however. Attempts to bring reform to the criminal justice system began at least as early as the mid-1800s. Prison reform was pursued in New York and Pennsylvania. In essence, our present parole system, which is being challenged and has been eliminated in some states, was developed in the late 1800s to emulate the "successful" system of penology developed by Sir Walter Croften in Ireland (Barnes and Teeters, 1959). In 1870, penologists from across the United States met in Cincinnati at the National Congress of Penitentiary and Reformatory Discipline. The goal of the dedicated members of the Congress was to reform and reorganize the existing American penal system. In 1931, the National Commission on Law Observance and Enforcement published the fourteen-volume *Wickersham Commission Report*, which provided recommendations to improve our criminal justice systems' ability to manage crime and delinquency.

The report quoted at the beginning of this chapter was followed in 1973 by massive volumes of recommendations to improve police, courts, corrections, and the juvenile justice system written by the National Advisory Commission on Criminal Justice Standards and Goals. The commission was provided with $1.75 million through the Law Enforcement Assistance Administration (LEAA), which was created in the 1960s to respond to increasing crime, civil and racial disturbances, and looting during riots. The unrest, both civil and political, shed doubt on the ability of criminal justice institutions to impose law and order, rehabilitate and control offenders, and in general impose social control in an efficient and just manner. Change and innovation were desperately needed throughout the system. Millions of dollars in grants were provided to state and local criminal justice agencies through LEAA to assist them in making their operations effective and efficient and in the hope that the standards and goals promulgated by the National Advisory Commission would be implemented.

Today, the effectiveness and practices of the criminal justice system are continually being challenged by society or the political and legal system. Massive overcrowding of prisons and jails and the apparent influx of mentally ill offenders into our correctional institutions are stretching the ability of our corrections system to perform basic tasks. Police agencies are being restructured through the implementation of foot-patrol units or team policing. The practice of indeterminate sentencing and parole has been challenged by both liberal and conservative members of the police (Cullen and Gilbert, 1982); and traditional judicial sentencing practices are being challenged. The perceived need for reform within the criminal justice system is ever present, and both substantive and symbolic changes have been made to meet that need. In the long term, change has been a part of the criminal justice system and will continue to take place in the future. Change is inevitable and leads to progress.

The change manifested in simple agency alterations or in major reforms may be purposive or crescive (Warren, 1977). Crescive change is inadvertent or unplanned and is independent of an organization's control. Crescive change may come about in spite of organizational efforts at self-direction. It can result from environmental influences on an organization or from internal organizational conflict (see chapters 2 and 9 on organizational environments and conflict). Purposive change results from conscious, deliberate, and planned efforts by organizational members, typically managers. Purposive change may be a response to environmental pressures, to internal conflict, or to organizational members' perceived needs to change or improve aspects of their system. Crescive and purposive change are obviously not mutually exclusive processes. Purposive change represents an "intervention into a flow of events that will in any case result in change. . . . Consequently, the decision is not whether or not there will be change, but rather what one's part will be in shaping or channeling inexorable change" (Warren, 1977:10). In this chapter, we will be concerned primarily with purposive, or planned, change as it applies to the agencies of the criminal justice system.

Change may be required or can take place at every level of an organization and in every nook and cranny. An organization may change its mission and social function or may continuously change procedures. It is beyond the scope of this chapter to consider every possible change within an organization. Throughout, we discuss organizational change as a general phenomenon rather than attempt to apply the concept of change to every facet of a criminal justice agency or system.

Why Change Occurs

As we have perhaps overstated, change will occur as a result of pressures from an agency's environment or from conflict within the agency. To the extent that organizational members are aware of environmental changes or internal conflict that may affect the agency's operations or outputs, they may enter into deliberate or planned change efforts. Before organizational executives actively make some form of change effort however, they must first perceive a need for change, that "something is broke and needs to be fixed." When an agency is performing improperly or below capacity, it is suffering a performance gap. A performance gap may be recognized by agency executives, personnel, clients, or other constituencies (Downs, 1967). "Whenever an official detects some performance gap between what he is doing and what he believes he ought to be doing, he is motivated to search for alternative actions satisfactory to him" (1967:191). An agency official will not generally search for alternative policies or methods unless a performance gap is made apparent. Therefore, a change effort will be initiated in an agency after officials perceive a performance gap or are convinced that a performance gap exists.

A performance gap may be produced by any of four major events: employee turnover, internal structural or technical changes, external or environmental changes, and repercussions of an agency's performance (Downs, 1967). Any of these events taken separately or collectively can cause disequilibrium in an agency (Chin, 1966).

Turnover of personnel will lead to differences in the collective behaviors of organizational members regardless of official agency goals. New employees may have different goals, values, or work ethics from older employees. They may also view the mission of the agency differently. Newly appointed executives may cast the agency in a new role and ascertain that existing policies do not match that role. For example, younger corrections officers are less concerned with inmate use of marijuana than older officers are (Kalinich, 1984); and the change in prison composition from traditional inmates to street gangs has affected operations (Irwin, 1980). New organizational members with different values and ethics are, therefore, primary forces for internal change (Steers, 1977) as well as conflict.

Advanced communications and recording technology supplied by computer systems have created a rather clear performance gap in the criminal justice system. Although computer technology provides the potential for increased efficiency in communication and record keeping, most criminal justice practitioners must be trained to work with this advanced technology before it can be useful to criminal justice agencies. In addition, computer crimes are on the increase (Parker, 1976), and criminal justice agencies must learn new techniques to prevent this new kind of white-collar crime as well as to solve computer crimes and prosecute the sophisticated computer-fraud criminal.

Chapter 2 is rich in examples of how the environment creates organizational change. Organizational change can be understood as a bridge that links an organization with its environment. The use of bridging strategies "presumes the presence of decision makers who survey the situation, confront alternatives as well as constraints, and select a course of action" (Scott, 1987:200). In other words, organizations modify their internal workings to adapt to external environmental pressures and constraints. Hence, the adaptation process is a form of purposive change in response to a perceived performance gap. Expansion of the use of community mental health services in county jails, for example, is a response to the increase in the number of mentally ill jail inmates (Swank and Winer, 1976) and contemporary standards of care for inmates imposed on corrections systems (Embert, 1986).

Unexpected and unintended consequences following a routine agency performance may create repercussions that make a performance gap evident. Such routine activities often have the potential to upset the agency's dynamic equilibrium (Downs, 1967; Chin, 1966). For example, the discovery of police corruption will upset the balance and stability of a police agency. Also, prisons may be replete with brutality and corruption or managed by inmate gangs, but this corruption or lack of control by the prison staff may not be apparent until it becomes manifest in a riot or inmate disturbance. Prosecutors and judges may be seen as entering into "liberal" plea bargaining or giving convicted offenders "lenient" sentences if the public suddenly becomes concerned with crime (LaFave, 1970).

If agency directors perceive a performance gap in their organization, they must first determine whether the gap is a short-term, or situational, phenomenon or if the gap is a long-term problem relating to some fundamental aspect of the agency (Spiro, 1958; Kalinich, Stojkovic, and Klofas, 1988). If the performance gap is viewed as a short-term phenomenon, agency executives may choose to ignore it. If it cannot be ignored, they may enter into "sales," or persuasive, tactics to convince their critics that no problem exists (Downs, 1967). If such persuasion is not effective, the agency executives may placate critics by making limited changes in the bureau's "window dressing" (Wilensky, 1967) or symbol structure (Kalinich, Lorinskas, and Banas, 1985). Organizations that passively adapt to pressures for change will typically take this as a first step without analyzing the scope of the problems they are facing. They will routinely seek change that is the least diverse and least costly and that will most readily satisfy or not disrupt its members or external constituents (Downs, 1967; Sharkansky, 1972). As discussed in chapter 2, criminal justice agencies are practiced at altering symbols and window dressing to placate pressure groups. If, however, the agency executives themselves perceive the performance gap as a fundamental organizational problem, they may attempt to bring about substantial change.

The Process of Organizational Change

The optimal approach to creating substantial change in an agency is to enter into a deliberate and rational process of planned change. A behavioral view suggests, however, that most organizational change is not purely rational or deliberate. Planned change requires that decision makers make rational decisions. To do so, they must possess all pertinent information and must not be constrained by time or other resource limitations in the planning and decision-making process. However, decision makers at best operate under "bounded rationality" (March and Simon, 1967), where they have limited knowledge and a finite amount of time and resources to dedicate to the decision-making process. An extension of the concept of bounded rationality is the garbage-can theory, which suggests that organizational change is typically less than a deliberate, rational process (see chapter 10 on decision making).

The garbage-can theory posits a model of organizations in which problems become receptacles for people to toss in solutions that interest them. Thus, agency decision makers have favorite solutions stored away that are searching for problems (Perrow, 1986). The "can" becomes an opportunity for agency members or decision makers to put forward their particular solution, which can include their own agendas. The agenda may be a restructuring of agency priorities, a reallocation of resources, an improvement in one's own status within the agency, or implementation of a favorite program. As competition among organizational members and decision makers over which solution to select proceeds, the original problem may get lost or take on new form or a life of its own (Cohen, March, and Olsen, 1972). As a consequence of the competition among agency decision makers, unintended outcomes no one considered at the beginning of the process can be created.

Solutions that lead to unintended outcomes can be "fatal remedies"— which we discuss later in this chapter—when the outcomes are harmful to the agency's mission (Sieber, 1981). For example, diversion programs created to limit the flow of offenders into the criminal justice and juvenile system have broadened rather than reduced the system's net and thus increased the intake of offenders (Decker, 1985; Doleschal, 1982). To avoid serious organizational change that results from garbage-can selection and that can lead organizations into selecting fatal remedies to close their performance gaps, agencies, ideally, should enter into the process of planned change.

"Planned organizational change refers to a set of activities designed to change individuals, groups, and organization structure and process" (Goodman and Kruke, 1982). Planned change requires innovation and accepts problems as opportunities to pursue real improvement in an agency's performance. Conversely, planned change is not a passive adaptation to environmental pressures or a minimal attempt to reduce organizational tensions (Warren, 1977). Examples of passive change in response to tensions abound in criminal justice. The cliché that criminal justice administrators are reactive rather than proactive suggests that a passive, adaptive approach to change may dominate the criminal justice system. Units to improve police–community relations sprang up after the civil disturbances of the late 1960s in a weak attempt to give police agencies the appearance of being sensitive to minority needs (Radelet, 1986). These units were typically funded poorly and were not much more than a token attempt to respond to a fundamental problem (Block and Specht, 1973). Corrections is famous for changing labels. Guards are now referred to as corrections officers, and convicts became prisoners, then inmates, and in some states residents. Such minimal attempts to meet pressures for change with the least costly approach are habitual for organizations in general (Sharkansky, 1972).

Planned change, however, requires an ongoing and substantive commitment for the long-run health of an organization. The process of planned change demands routine and continuous examination of an agency's operations as well as the expectations and demands of the agency's clients and constituents to discover existing and potential problems that will create performance gaps. Further, problems must be comprehensively examined to discover whether they relate to the substantive nature or mission of the organization or are fundamental or policy-related problems, procedural problems, or circumstantial problems. After problems are understood with some clarity, then solutions can be developed and ultimately implemented. In other words, planned change requires an ongoing examination and continuous restructuring of goals, policies, procedures, practices, and behaviors. An occasional discovery of a performance gap or single look at a problem is insufficient. The basis of successful analysis for decision making, and hence for planning, is a "continuous cycle of formulating the problem, selecting objectives, designing alternatives, correcting data, building models, weighing costs against performance, testing for sensitivity, questioning assumptions and data, re-examining the objectives, . . . and so on, until satisfaction is achieved or time or money forces a cut off" (Quade, 1977:157).

From our general discussion of planned change to this point, it becomes clear that deliberate and extensive effort is required in the process. Typically, organizational members expend their energies pursuing established goals, performing internal maintenance activities, adapting to environmental pressures (Selznik, 1949), and protecting agency routines. Planned change requires a break from these routines. To become free of this habitual momentum, organizations often create a permanent core of executives whose role is the implementation of planned change through a formalized planning process.

Planning in Criminal Justice

Planning can be thought of as the systematic application of the concept of planned change. Planning has been defined as "any deliberate effort to increase the proportion of goals attained by increasing awareness and understanding of the factors involved" (Dahl, 1959:340). More simply, planning is a process that precedes decision making, that gives explicit consideration to the future, and that seeks coordination among sets of interrelated decisions or actions (Hudzik and Cordner, 1983). Planning ideally allows the achievement of ends and the making of rational choices among alternative programs (Davidoff and Reiner, 1962).

The planning process is the first step in developing and implementing planned change. It is a process of "lining up the ducks" by identifying the immediate and future needs of an agency and the goals that must be met, then devising a systematic way in which to meet these needs and goals. In short, the tasks of planners are identifying agency goals and problems, forecasting, and generating and testing alternatives (Hudzik and Cordner, 1983). Each of these tasks deserves additional discussion.

Identifying an agency's goals may sound simplistic, even unnecessary. However, in planning and decision making, it is important to consistently review the basic purposes of the agency as rational planning requires a clear understanding of mission or goals as well as the values implicit in the agency's purpose. Often, the agency mission may be ignored in favor of day-to-day routines or lost in agency folklore about its social role. Hence, frequent reviews of an organization's purpose can remind administrators of the basic mission and goals, facilitate the promulgation of policies and procedures that are congruent with the agency's basic purpose, and assist in long-term planning.

Reviewing the basic mission is also important in viewing an agency's goals in the light of changing environmental demands and constraints. The mission of jails, for example, has changed dramatically over the years. Traditionally, the major purpose of jails was security or to prevent inmates from escaping or rioting. The health, safety, and welfare of inmates were a low-level concern. Although security remains an important function of jails, they must place the health, safety, and welfare of inmates on a par with security concerns. Hence, planning for jails that does not consider the health and welfare of inmates will be, at best, inadequate. Also, police agencies often focus on crime fighting as their major or even sole mission and ignore the vast service aspect of policing (Adams, 1971). Planning that is based on crime-fighting folklore and that excludes crime prevention and the vast array of services provided by police agencies will obviously miss the police system's broader mission. Thus, examining agency goals in the planning process may force agencies to adjust their missions and goals in light of contemporary social demands and expectations rather than in conformity with traditional values or agency folklore.

The *identification of problems* is crucial to planning and to avoiding the garbage-can approach to management. Planners and managers who perceive a performance gap need to analyze the root causes of the gap or problem. This process involves looking through a layer of possibilities to extract the probable basic causal factors. For example, we often hear that low morale in a police agency is causing a low level of productivity. However, morale and productivity are not necessarily causally related (Perrow, 1986), although that is often the common-sense conclusion. What is necessary are the discovery and examination of the basic organizational problems that create both low productivity and low morale. It may be discovered, as often happens, that low levels of productivity and morale both relate to lack of certainty about one's role (March and Simon, 1967), which may relate to the agency's failure to identify its goals with clarity. A lack of clarity about the organization's mission and goals will make it difficult for the agency to promulgate policies and procedures and provide training that relates to current constraints on and expectations of its operational personnel. For example, police officers are often publicly criticized for their behaviors, and jail personnel are made responsible for inmate deaths through civil litigation. If, however, they are not being guided by clear policies, procedures, and training in areas in which they are subject to criticism and legal action, they will react with extreme uncertainty toward their work.

Forecasting is obviously an important aspect of planning, especially long-term planning. Assumptions about the future are implicit in any decision. However, it is often assumed that the future will replicate the present. Forecasting requires that planners and decision makers attempt to project into the future to understand prospective problems and to estimate the impact decisions will have on the agency or its constituents. Predicting crime rates is rather common and can be utilized in assessing the future needs of criminal justice agencies. In retrospect, the overcrowding in prisons could have been predicted, and, in fact, some people within the formal political structure did predict overcrowding and attempted to expand the prison system. Again, the impact of de-institutionalizing the mentally ill has led to an increased number of mentally ill individuals in the nation's prisons and jails, where they are not provided with adequate treatment (Petrich, 1976). Systematic and formal forecasting of the impact of deinstitutionalization might have led to a secondary set of decisions and plans to improve the abilities of correctional institutions to treat mentally ill inmates.

Generating and selecting appropriate alternative solutions to problems is another crucial step in planning. Planners must construct a series of possible alternative solutions for the problems that have been identified. These solutions must take into account present and future constraints. Typically, the generation of alternatives begins with past strategies or ideas that seem to fit within the agency's philosophy, structure, knowledge–technology core, or resource limitations. If alternatives generated within these limitations are not deemed satisfactory, more creative or innovative alternatives then need to be found (Hudzik and Cordner, 1983). As overcrowding continues to plague prisons and jails, alternative solutions are being sought. Efforts are being made to control the influx of offenders into institutions by creating sentencing guidelines for judges (Kratcoski and Walker, 1978), using appearance tickets in lieu of arrests for certain offenses, and creating special bail-bond programs for indigent offenders (Harris, 1984). These alternatives all fall well within the present structure and general philosophy of the criminal justice system, and have been promulgated since the 1930s (Barnes and Teeters, 1959).

In spite of these efforts, the problem of overcrowding continues. Hence, alternatives to incarceration are being sought. New forms of community corrections place incarcerated offenders in work-release programs, weekend or day parole, or community centers prior to their eventual release from confinement. Other innovative alternatives have been utilized to address overcrowding, including emergency release (parole consideration for inmates ninety days away from their minimum sentence date), early release of sentenced, nonviolent jail inmates, and court orders that require jails to refuse arrestees in certain crime categories when those jails are overcrowded. Also home confinement in lieu of a jail or prison sentence has been utilized in conjunction with computer-monitored anklets or bracelets (Schmidt, 1989). These alternatives can be considered innovative to the extent they are not traditional processes in the criminal justice system. But such innovative approaches often prove to be politically unpopular. In fact, the governor of Michigan discontinued the use of emergency release in 1986 in reaction to public criticism.

It is important to point out, however, that the application of these alternatives to institutional overcrowding is not necessarily the result of any long-term planning or planned change. Rather these alternatives were created in reaction to a desperate state of affairs and, in many respects, exemplify the garbage-can approach to change. Legitimate planning would have considered the possibility of overcrowding before the fact, and alternatives would have been implemented in time to meet the crisis. Forecasting overcrowding, understanding the reasons overcrowding would occur, and creating alternatives to deal with overcrowding would have been a good example of rational planning. Had the innovative alternatives been implemented, planned change would have occurred.

Planning in general, as we have described it here, is, at best, difficult and bounded by constraints. Purely rational planning may be especially difficult for criminal justice agencies. Rational planning requires that an agency's goals are congruent rather than contradictory, that the goals are clear and known to the agency members or decision makers, and that means–ends relationships are understood (Hudzik and Cordner, 1983). However, goals for criminal justice agencies are often vague and conflicting. Means–ends relationships and methods to achieve agency goals are often unknown or uncertain (see chapters 1 and 2). Rehabilitation of criminal offenders, for example, can take on several meanings and is but one of many goals of corrections. To the extent that rehabilitation requires a degree of freedom for inmates from prison routines, it may come squarely into conflict with security concerns of the custodial staff. Further, reliable means of achieving some form of long-term behavioral change in offenders do not exist. In fact, empirical evidence to date suggests that most rehabilitation programs have not had any long-term effect on offenders' postrelease behavior (Lipton, Martinson, and Wilkes, 1975). At best, therefore, planning for rehabilitation programs is a disjointed, incremental process in which programs may be developed and then tested for acceptability and effectiveness and to see whether they create any unintended consequences (Lindblom, 1959).

The value of planning for criminal justice agencies should not, however, be minimized. The planning process has the potential of clarifying goals or at least prioritizing agency objectives. Further, means–ends relationships can be developed through agency research-and-development efforts. It is theorized, for example, that prison classification programs can identify inmates who are amenable to particular types of rehabilitation programs (Austin, 1983). Hence, rehabilitation goals and means can be offender-specific and can be devised to take into account the constraints and conflicting goals of the prison system.

However, changing an institution's classification system and developing an array of treatment programs that can coexist with security needs will take a great deal of organizational skill and energy beyond the formal planning process. Planning is the initial and perhaps simplest step in organizational change. The creation of desired planned change throughout an agency may require that its members replace old values, habits, relationships, and routines with a new repertoire of behaviors. New ways of thinking about goals or performing tasks, therefore, will typically meet with resistance. Understanding and overcoming resistance and obstacles to change are, perhaps, the most important and difficult aspects of planned change.

Resistance to Change

Planning is the technical aspect of planned change. Implementing change is the human and more difficult aspect of planned change. The human side requires that agency members change their work behaviors and possibly their values, depending on the breadth or depth of the prescribed change. Also, change may require restructuring of routines. Change efforts may also be confounded by lack of public support. Finally, particular characteristics of innovations, such as cost, may create obstacles for their implementation. Hence, a natural resistance to change exists in almost all organizations. Obstacles and sources of resistance to change must be identified and eliminated or controlled if planned change is to be successful. In this section, we discuss the major sources of resistance to change. Table 12-1 provides a summary of individual and organizational sources.

Table 12-1 Personal and Organizational Sources of Resistance to Change

Personal Sources	Organizational Sources
1. Misunderstanding of purpose, mechanics, or consequences of change	1. Reward system
2. Failure to see need for change	2. Interdepartmental rivalry or conflict, leading to an unwillingness to cooperate
3. Fear of unknown	3. Sunk costs in past decisions and actions
4. Fear of loss of status, security, power, etc.,	4. Fear that change will upset current balance of power between groups and departments
5. Lack of identification or involvement with change	5. Prevailing organizational climate
6. Habit	6. Poor choice of method of introducing change
7. Vested interests in status quo	7. Past history of unsuccessful change attempts and their consequences
8. Group norms and role prescriptions	8. Structural rigidity
9. Threat to existing social relationships	
10. Conflicting personal and organizational objectives	

Source: Steers, R. M., *Organizational Effectiveness: A Behavioral View*, p. 167. Copyright 1977 Goodyear Publishing Company, Inc. Reprinted by permission of the author.

Personal Sources

As table 12-1 shows, change may be resisted by agency employees for a number of reasons personal to them. Corrections officers, for example, may resist the use of due process for inmate discipline as it may necessitate a loss of their power and discretion. Corrections officers may also perceive that the loss of power may lead to a dramatic change in their relationships with inmates. From a broad perspective, changing guard–inmate relationships may interfere with the norms of the corrections officers' subculture (Lombardo, 1985). The fear of loss of control over the inmate population has led to an actual loss of control, perhaps as a self-fulfilling prophecy. In the police area, effecting better police–community relations through programming or training officers to interact differently with civilians has been resisted by police officers who see the world as divided into "us and them" and see community relations as an appeasement program that weakens police authority (Skolnick and Bayley, 1986).

Personal resistance is especially apparent in areas where community policing or foot patrol is being implemented. Community police who walk the beat are viewed by other officers as "social workers" who are "not real cops" (Trojanowicz and Carter, 1988). The role of the community police officer is viewed by many traditional police officers and administrators as being in conflict with their traditional role. They also believe that community policing will bring loss of power as it requires police to associate and identify with civilians who traditionally have been viewed as the recipients of coercive control by law enforcement personnel (Skolnick and Bayley, 1986). Police officers given a foot-patrol assignment must also leave the comfort and security provided by the well-armed patrol car with its communication system.

For courts, the establishment of sentencing guidelines also has the potential of taking discretion and power away from judges, prosecutors, and probation officers, all of whom have a vested interest in criminal sentencing. Utilizing court administrators to manage court procedures and case flow has been accepted in principle. However, court administrators deal with judicial personalities and egos that resist administrative control, which is the substance of such programs. Prosecutors may resist the creation of community corrections programs or liberalized bail-bond systems, seeing these programs as contrary to their role of protecting the community from criminal offenders. In good conscience, prosecuting attorneys have often expressed the fear that reducing confinement in favor of community programs would cause an increase in crime and delay case processing as offenders on liberalized bail-bond programs would more often than not fail to appear for their court hearings. This fear of liberalized bond systems has not proven realistic (Vetter and Territo, 1984).

Organizational Sources

An agency's traditional practices, values, structure, or leadership can influence the success or failure of attempts to implement change. Resistance to change due to organizational climate and sunk costs in past decisions and routines is portrayed in a case study of a local jail. A consent decree promulgated by a federal district court ordered a local jail to modify the existing facility and provide contact visitations and other services to inmates (Schafer, 1986). Immediately following the consent decree, a steering committee comprised of local jail and criminal justice officials was formed to plan the change and provide guidance for the implementation of the consent decree. In spite of the decree and the show of good faith through the formation of a steering committee, county governmental officials and the sheriff actively dragged their feet on compliance. Much of the system's energy was focused on attempting to circumvent and renegotiate the consent decree. The leadership in the jail, as well as the local political leadership, created a negative climate within the jail and community that greatly slowed the process of change. It was not until five years after the original court order that the changes began (Schafer, 1986).

An inappropriate reward–punishment system may hamper desirable change. Since the 1970s, attempts have been made to upgrade the quality of corrections officers in local jails. However, in many jurisdictions, corrections officers receive a lower wage than road patrol officers within the same agency, which motivates corrections officers to strive for a transfer to the road patrol. In addition, corrections officers who perform well in that capacity are typically rewarded by being transferred to the road patrol, leaving the less talented or motivated personnel to continue as corrections officers. There are, of course, other advantages to working in a police department rather than in a correctional facility. However, the reward system described here clearly retards the best efforts of jail administrators to upgrade their staff.

Organizations with rigid structures are typically those with well-established traditions, belief systems, routines, and practices, as well as little history of change. Also, large, powerful organizations that are capable of influencing their environments will typically place more effort into resisting change than into conforming to pressures for change (Scott, 1987).

Organizations that readily facilitate change have several characteristics in common. In addition to having a history of change (Burnes and Stalker, 1961), Hage and Aiken (1977) found that change-ready organizations share the following characteristics:

1. High complexity in terms of professional training of organizational members.

2. High decentralization of power.
3. Low formalization.
4. Low stratification in terms of differential distribution of rewards.
5. Low emphasis on volume (as opposed to quality) of production.
6. Low emphasis on efficiency in terms of cost of production or service.
7. High level of job satisfaction on the part of organizational members.

While these characteristics may be antithetical to change resisters, many are also antithetical to criminal justice agencies. Criminal justice agencies tend to be centralized and highly formalized, and job satisfaction, especially among corrections officers, tends to be low (Toch and Klofas, 1982). Police agencies and often courts tend to emphasize volume, with police agencies often resorting to arrest rates as a benchmark for success and courts placing emphasis on efficient case flow (Grau, 1980).

In addition, organizational change requires, in essence, that the organization's routines be altered. Routines develop in all organizations that survive for an extended period of time. Routines provide certainty and purpose to organizational members. Of equal importance, routines are the skills that govern all aspects of organizations from formal record keeping and daily work practices to the ongoing truce between management and subordinates. It is management's job to maintain routines (Nelson and Winter, 1982). To the extent routines are altered, the basic skills of an organization, guideposts for its members' behavior, are being challenged, and management's role in maintaining routines must be set aside. An organization, and its members, will face uncertainty with the elimination of well-established routines and therefore will resist their elimination.

Routines within the criminal justice system and its agencies are abundant, are typically well established, and emanate from a variety of sources, some of which are beyond the control of the administrators and staff of criminal justice organizations. The criminal justice system has a rich tradition of routines (Atkins and Pogrebin, 1982). Uniquely, many of the established routines relate to important values in society in general. A proposed change for the criminal justice system—one, for example, that limits police authority—could be viewed as a threat to law and order, an important belief of the general public and the law enforcement community. Hence, such a change could be readily resisted.

More specifically, many criminal justice routines are imposed by statute and case law, and subroutines are created within the organization to establish conformity—or the appearance of conformity—to prevailing laws. The court system performs extensive rituals that are considered significant to protect the rights of defendants. For example, defendants appear in a formal courtroom for sentencing. At a criminal sentencing hearing, the defense attorney pleads for leniency, and the prosecuting attorney may counter by requesting the court to impose a harsh sentence to "protect the public." This process is honored and acted out even though sentencing decisions are typically decided well in advance of the formal hearing. The formal hearing is symbolic of the court's duty to protect the rights of the offender. The suggestion that the formal sentencing hearing be dispensed with in cases where a clear decision has been made to place an offender on probation—a suggestion that would save the court time and expense—has not been well received (Robin, 1975). The routine has historical ritualistic value and is difficult to set aside.

In addition, large police agencies and correctional systems are organized along bureaucratic lines and are often considered to be paramilitary organizations. They have a clear chain of command and a hierarchy of authority supported with formal rules and regulations. The rigid formality of such agencies requires and creates a set of routines that are often seen as a statement of organizational purpose and that are difficult to eliminate or alter; hence, agencies are resistant to change. The extent to which change will be resisted is thus, in part, a function of the rigidity or flexibility of an organization and its members.

Resistance to change is also a function of the magnitude and depth of the change that is being proposed. Change that focuses on a single aspect of the behavior of a few agency members or on a limited number of procedures that are not frequently used will be met with much less resistance than proposed change in fundamental aspects of an organization. Fundamental change often requires a shift in agency ideologies, a major shift in operations and programming, and a dramatic shift in the role of the line or service-delivery personnel (Duffee, 1986). Fundamental change therefore encounters a great deal more resistance than attempts to create circumstantial or procedural change. It is easier to create special units within a police agency to focus on police–community relations or crime prevention than to change the policies and procedures of the entire agency. The practices, behaviors, and attitudes of the mass of agency members do not have to be altered if special functions are assigned to a few members included in the specialized units. Similarly, it is easier to use short-term measures to alleviate overcrowding, such as emergency release procedures (described previously), than to build new correctional facilities or expand the use of community corrections. A change as fundamental as creating community corrections centers may run into resistance from the public as well as be a difficult change from an organizational perspective.

Organizations whose members are unionized face another potentially powerful constraint on change. Management–labor contracts often call for specific behavior on the part of both management and labor. These agreements reinforce particular routines and make them unalterable for the duration of the contract. Police unions have had a significant impact on policy decisions in many jurisdictions and have eroded the power and discretion of police administrators to make changes (Swanson, Territo, and Taylor, 1988). Corrections officers' unions have also been on the increase across the nation, and they will ultimately have a powerful impact on corrections policies historically reserved for management. When unions and administrators share the same objectives, the union can be a powerful ally in planning and implementing change. If they are not in accord, unions can become a major obstacle to the implementation of planned change. We must consider, however, that ideally unions represent the interests and views of the rank and file. If the critical mass of the rank and file is opposed to change, implementation of planned change is unlikely regardless of the existence of a union within an organization.

Finally, we must briefly touch on forces in the environment that thwart an organization's attempt at innovation. Successful innovation within an organization is dependent, in part, on the positive association between external pressures for change and internally perceived need for change (Griener, 1967). In other words, when an agency's constituents and members both perceive a performance gap, the momentum for change will be strengthened by the congruent pressures. Public support is, therefore, important to effect planned change. Conversely, public opposition to change or support for the status quo will make major change, or change that will be visible to the public, difficult. Attempts to establish corrections centers in communities, for example, have typically been vociferously challenged by community members (Smykla, 1981). Innovation in police agencies often faces criticism from community members who have a preference for traditional police operations (Skolnick and Bayley, 1986).

Characteristics of Innovations

Previously in this chapter we suggested that the nature of innovation itself would effect resistance to change. For example, we stated that fundamental change would require greater effort than altering the procedures of a system because resistance to a fundamental change would be greater than that to a circumstantial change. In this section, we discuss the characteristics of innovations that affect resistance to change (see Zaltman, Duncan, and Holbeck, 1973).

The first set of characteristics relates to the social and economic cost and cost effectiveness of innovation and change. Innovations with a higher price tag will be entered into with greater reluctance. If the innovation will create a high return on the initial investment or will improve an agency's efficiency, the innovation will be more attractive than one that does not. For example, the initial cost of implementing substantive and comprehensive rehabilitation programs throughout a corrections system may be quite high. If, however, recidivism would be cut drastically by such programs, the long-term savings to corrections and the criminal justice system may pay off the initial investment. The establishment of comprehensive rehabilitation programs would also be attractive if they had the potential of making inmate management efficient.

The extent to which organizational change creates risk or uncertainty will also affect the likelihood of innovation. In this regard, innovations that are compatible with the existing organizational structure and are not complex will pose less risk and uncertainty to an agency than those that are incompatible and complex. Also, change that is reversible creates less apprehension and has less potential for causing risk and uncertainty. Moving from well-established, traditional indeterminate sentencing and parole to the so-called justice system will be difficult to reverse (Cullen and Gilbert, 1982). Hence, most states have resisted such a sweeping change.

Plans for innovations that emanate within organizations and are timely have a better opportunity for acceptance than externally imposed or poorly timed innovations because internal innovations have greater credibility. Timeliness suggests that innovative ideas are put forward to meet a need at a moment when consensus about the problem and its source exists among organizational members. Timely ideas have a stronger chance of survival in an organization than ideas that must be sold to or forced on agency members. The concept of house arrest or home confinement coupled with the use of electronic monitoring techniques of offenders is timely. First, overcrowding has created a desperate situation. Second, monitored home confinement may be more acceptable than traditional forms of community corrections from the public's point of view as it is more punitive, restrictive, and secure.

Finally, the larger the mass of people involved in the change process, the more implementation will be impeded. If innovation is likely to affect the general public or external groups, more individuals will be involved in the process of change than if these groups are not affected. Moving from traditional policing and institutional corrections to community policing and community corrections will ultimately involve community members; and they will be part of the decision-making and innovation process.

To this point, we have discussed obstacles to organizational change on the individual and organizational level. We have also examined some of the characteristics of innovations themselves that may show or prevent their implementation. In the next section, we provide an overview of some of the general prescriptions for overcoming resistance to change in organizations.

Overcoming Resistance to Change

Resistance to change seems to be a natural characteristic of most organizations and organizational members. Efforts to create change within an organization require overcoming its natural resistance to assuming a new or modified mission, creating and implementing new goals and procedures, and ultimately altering the arrangement of its activities (Katz and Kahn, 1978). As we have suggested, recognizing the need for change and planning for change are the first steps in the change process. However, a chief of police or director of a corrections system cannot simply decree change by issuing a memo or direct order through the chain of command. A degree of alienation exists between administrators and line staff in criminal justice agencies (McCleary, 1975; Toch, Grant, and Galvin, 1975). It is therefore likely that decrees from administrators to subordinates may increase resistance to change rather than lead to the implementation of innovations. Change ultimately requires unfreezing, changing, and refreezing the behavior of an organization's members (Lewin, 1958). This process requires a set of strategies to overcome resistance to change.

The responsibility for overcoming resistance to change within an agency typically falls on change agents—usually management (Bennis, 1966). The extent to which managers have a commitment to change and are capable of overcoming change-resistant staff is an important determinant of successful implementation of planned change (Bennis, 1966; Zaltman, Duncan, and Holbeck, 1973; Skolnick and Bayley, 1986). Strategies for change can be aimed at the individuals in an agency, the agency's structure and system, or the organizational climate (the interpersonal style of relationships)—or at combinations of these targets (Huse, 1975; Steers, 1977). Table 12-2 provides a crisp summary of techniques that can be applied to change individual members, organizational structures, or the organizational climate.

Individual Change Strategies

The assumption underlying this approach is that individuals or groups of individuals within an agency must modify their attitudes, skills, and behaviors. For example, corrections officers had to relearn certain aspects of their work to implement the due process model of corrections. Officers who were accustomed to almost complete discretion in disciplining inmates had to adapt to a process that allowed inmates their "day in court" (*Wolf v. McDonnell*, 1974). Shifting corrections officers into the new disciplinary process required some resocialization as they no longer had total discretion in disciplining inmates. It also required a new set of skills for officers as they were required to prepare their cases thoroughly, write a complete report, and testify in a formal hearing. Corrections officers ideally should have been provided with a clear explanation of their new role, with training programs to provide new knowledge, and with skills commensurate with the new task, as well as with programs to help them accept the liberal approach to inmate management (Duffee,

Table 12-2 Comparison of Three General Approaches for Initiating Organizational Changes

Approaches for Initiating Change	Typical Intervention Techniques	Intended Immediate Outcomes	Assumptions About the Major Causes of Behavior in Organizations
Individuals	Education, training, socialization, attitude change	Improvements in skill levels, attitudes, and motivation of people	Behavior in organizations is largely determined by the characteristics of the people who compose the organization
Organizational structure and systems	Modification of actual organizational practices, procedures, and policies that affect what people do at work	Creation of conditions to elicit and reward member behaviors that facilitate organizational goal achievement	Behavior in organizations is largely determined by the characteristics of the organizational situation in which people work
Organizational climate and interpersonal style	Experiential techniques aimed at increasing members' awareness of the social determinants of their behavior and helping them learn new ways of reacting to and relating to each other within the organizational context	Creation of a systemwide climate that is characterized by high interpersonal trust and openness; reduction of dysfunctional consequences of excessive social conflict and competitiveness	Behavior in organizations is largely determined by the emotional and social processes that characterize the relations among organization members

Source: Porter, L. W., Lawler, E. E., III, and Hackman, J. R., *Behavior in Organizations*, p. 440. Copyright 1975 by McGraw-Hill Book Co. Reprinted by permission.

1986). The extent to which corrections officers were provided with these things is not clear. If the due process procedures were implemented by decree, which is within traditional practices for paramilitary systems, the hearing procedures predictably met with strong resistance by corrections officers.

Structural and Systems Change Strategies

Realizing improved methods may require a rearrangement of an organization's policies, procedures, and reward–punishment system. In other words, to achieve desired change, major modifications may be required in the basic structure of the organization as opposed to simply altering the work behaviors of the members. Before workers' behaviors can change, basic structural aspects of the system that constrain their behaviors must be changed. For example, a major performance gap exists in jails. Typical jail operations are not geared to provide the range of care and services that jail inmates are presently entitled to (see Kalinich and Klofas, 1986). It is argued that physical structure is a major constraint that limits jail corrections officers from sufficient contact with inmates to provide adequate supervision and management (Nelson, 1986). Therefore, new jail facilities that are being constructed across the nation—referred to as "new-generation jails"—allow corrections officers to readily observe all inmates whom they are responsible for.

In addition, policies and procedures must be introduced in the new facilities, as well as in traditional facilities, that are congruent with the contemporary mission of jails. Corrections officers are required to take an active role, interacting with inmates and identifying problems before they take on crisis proportions, rather than a passive role of intervening in crises with coercive force.

Similarly, moving from traditional to community policing, controlling sentencing disparity with sentencing guidelines, and expanding the methods and availability of community corrections all require restructuring various aspects of the respective systems. In all the examples, old routines must be set aside in favor of new routines. Also the roles of many of the key actors must be changed. Change in routines and roles may often curtail the authority and discretion of the actors and may require a philosophical reorientation on their part. Providing organizational members with training and making structural changes may not therefore be sufficient to bring about desired change. The core of an organization—its culture, behavioral regularities, rituals, norms, dominant values, and climate—may have to be modified to facilitate the adoption of new routines and member role behaviors required to complete the change process (Schein, 1985; Steers, 1977).

Organizational-Climate Change Strategies

As shown in table 12-2, the assumption behind attacking organizational climate to initiate change is that the behaviors in an organization are largely a product of the organization's culture (Schein, 1985). The routines of an organization and the work behaviors of its members are constrained by the collective value structure of the organization and the emotional and social interaction among its members. An organizational climate may further be described as having the following dimensions (Steers, 1977:102):

1. *Task structure.* The degree to which the methods used to accomplish tasks are spelled out by an organization.
2. *Reward–punishment relationship.* The degree to which the granting of additional rewards such as promotions and salary increases is based on performance and merit instead of other considerations like seniority, favoritism, and so forth.
3. *Decision centralization.* The extent to which important decisions are reserved for top management.
4. *Achievement emphasis.* The desire on the part of the people in an organization to do a good job and contribute to the performance objectives of the organization.
5. *Training and development emphasis.* The degree to which an organization tries to support the performance of individuals through appropriate training and development experiences.
6. *Security versus risk.* The degree to which pressures in an organization lead to feelings of insecurity and anxiety on the part of its members.
7. *Openness versus defensiveness.* The degree to which people try to cover their mistakes and look good rather than communicate freely and cooperate.
8. *Status and morale.* The general feeling among individuals that the organization is a good place in which to work.
9. *Recognition and feedback.* The degree to which employees know what their supervisors and management think of their work and the degree to which management supports employees.
10. *General organizational competence and flexibility.* The degree to which an organization knows what its goals are and pursues them in a flexible and innovative manner. Includes the extent to which it anticipates problems, develops new methods, and develops new skills in people before problems become crises.

The task at hand, therefore, is to create a climate within the organization that facilitates change in its culture and simultaneously affects traditional agency practices and habits to allow changes in the values, attitudes, and personal interactions of its members. For example, if organizational members tend to be defensive and insecure, they will be reluctant to venture into new roles, even if they are prescribed by management. Returning to our example of new-generation jails, corrections officers are being asked to interact with inmates rather than simply keeping them locked up. This change poses a new set of risks for corrections officers. If they feel they will be "burned" by the bosses if they make mistakes, they will attempt to delegate many of their responsibilities back up to their supervisors. In effect, they will cling to their old roles and routines.

In addition, if communication is poor or decision making is centralized, it will be difficult to gain the active participation of organizational members in the change process (Duffee, 1986). If corrections officers are not involved in the transition from a traditional jail to a new-generation jail, they are not likely to have complete knowledge of the change process or to identify with the purpose of the new system. Conversely, management will have, at best, a contaminated feedback loop from the line staff and will not be able to accurately assess the efficacy of the transition. With a contaminated feedback loop, even incremental change will be unsuccessful (Lindblom, 1959).

Creating an organizational climate that is conducive to cooperative change can be an overwhelming task, especially if the change is prompted by extreme conflict within an agency. However, any change within an agency that goes beyond the alteration of simple procedures or change that is consensual will probably face impediments from within the environmental and cultural aspects of the system. Therefore, steps for dealing with an agency's climate should be considered in the early phases of planned change. A series of human relations techniques and training programs that improve an agency's climate have been utilized with some frequency. The approaches utilized loosely fall under the rubric of organizational development.

Organizational Development

Organizational development (OD) focuses on the environmental influences of an organization. The process attempts to alter values, routines, and structures of a system simultaneously in an attempt to create an atmosphere in which obstacles to change can be identified and minimized (French, 1969). Traditionally, OD programs have been the responsibility of a *change agent*, an individual whose sole role is to promote change within a system. The change agent may come from within an agency—usually from management—or may be a consultant from outside the agency. These are some of the objectives of OD programs (French, 1969:24):

1. To increase the level of trust and support among organizational members
2. To increase the incidence of confronting problems rather than ignoring them
3. To create an environment where authority is based on expertise as well as being assigned
4. To increase the level of personal satisfaction among organizational members
5. To increase open communication within the organization

The objectives are congruent with the dimensions of organizational climate shown in table 12-2. This makes sense because OD focuses on organizational practices and social–political systems as each affects the systems environment and vice versa. As a field of social and management science, OD relies on a multidisciplinary approach and draws heavily on psychology, sociology, and anthropology as well as on information from motivation, personality, and learning theory, and on research on group dynamics, leadership, power, and organizational behavior (Hellriegel, Slocum, and Woodman, 1986). The techniques used in OD are based, in part, upon Theory Y assumptions that individuals are responsible and can be motivated most readily when they are given responsibility (see chapter 4 on motivation). Hence the techniques are aimed at getting organizational members' active contribution in identifying agency problems and developing solutions rather than leaving that task to a few of the management elite.

OD techniques and programs include survey feedback, which is a pencil-and-paper method of gathering information from agency members, and team building, which allows agency members to form groups that do not conform to traditional social or authority-oriented patterns. Team building therefore creates fresh subsets of interpersonal communications among agency members and overcomes traditional barriers to communication.

Training, such as sensitivity training, that focuses on agency members' values, perceptions of agency problems, and commitments to agency goals is a common OD technique. Training of this nature facilitates information gathering, open communication, and examination of personal objectives within the framework of role objectives and organizational objectives. Such techniques and programs attempt to get organizational members actively involved in the change process while providing them with an opportunity for open dialogue across ranks to improve communication, examine problems and solutions, and identify impediments to change.

We can discuss the application of OD techniques to criminal justice agencies best in a critical manner. In effect, OD requires active participation of organizational members in the process of management and especially change. Criminal justice agencies are typically bureaucratic, paramilitary organizations, in which communications flow predominantly downward. Upward communication, while theoretically possible, is severely limited (see chapter 3 on communication). Lateral communication is contrary to organizational structure and practices. The preponderance of traditional routines precludes the quality and quantity of member participation in organizational decision making that is requisite to the practice of OD. The management style of corrections administrators, for example, is often autocratic and therefore does not allow for corrections officers' participation in change (Duffee, 1986). Thus, utilizing change agents—outside consultants or internal specialists—on an ad hoc basis when change seems to be inevitable will have limited value. The outcome of ad hoc attempts at change within rigid systems that do not routinely facilitate open communication and participation among members will be changes in written policies and procedures that will be resisted passively by the line staff. The whole notion of planned change is based on a series of attitudes and practices of organizational administrators and managers that run contrary to the traditional attitudes and practices of criminal justice administrators. While planned change is the optimal approach to meeting public demands in an effective way, in criminal justice these plans often produce unintended consequences or fatal remedies. This concept is discussed briefly in the next section.

Unintended Consequences of Change

The final outcomes of a change effort may be different from those desired by change agents or planners. At times, change may be harmful either because the outcomes are unintended or the remedies are "fatal." Fatal remedies are due to the natural regressive effects of social engineering (Sieber, 1981). Earlier scholars, including Weber, Marx, and Engels, have written about regressive effects. More recently, sociologists have studied the fatal remedies of governmental programs (Banfield, 1974). However, the prescriptive literature on organizational change does not address this phenomenon.

In brief, Sieber (1981) advises that social interventions fail as policymakers and planners fall into regressive traps for several reasons (we will cover only a few of Sieber's principles here). The multiplicity and priority of goals of target groups may not be understood thoroughly if they are understood at all. It may be of little value, for example, to provide minimum-wage jobs for teenagers who make large sums of money selling drugs. Interventions may also be exploited by groups tangential to the intervention. It was unfortunately common for federal grants provided for improvement of inner cities during the War on Poverty to end up in the pockets of fraudulent contractors. In addition, goals may be displaced by the bureaucratic emphasis on process rather than outcome. For example, when the Drug Enforcement Administration (DEA) sprayed paraquat, a toxic herbicide, on marijuana crops in Mexico in an attempt to eliminate a major supply source, the poisoned crop harmed consumers.

Program evaluation needs may also pervert the desired ends as agencies may evaluate outcomes of the program that are readily measurable or show favorable results rather than the original ends of a program (Hoos, 1983). Providing a program for one group or creating a change may provoke opposing groups into action to thwart interventions and create their own. In California during the early 1970s, for example, liberal groups unhappy with what they considered the unfair, indeterminate sentencing system fought for the establishment of determinate sentences. Liberals viewed this change as a just and human system and a benefit to offenders and inmates. The inmates' union joined the liberal factions. Once the issue was made public, conservative law-and-order groups also joined the reform movement in favor of the determinate sentencing system. This coalition of groups felt the existing system was excessively lenient and did not provide sufficiently long sentences for inmates. The conservative coalition became more influential than the liberals. Determinate sentences were established. However, the sentence structure implemented provided longer sentences for inmates than the indeterminate system it replaced, contrary to the liberals' original intent (Travis, Latessa, and Vito, 1985).

Other fatal criminal justice remedies are prevalent. The evidence suggests that diversion programs actually widen the criminal justice net rather than divert offenders (Decker, 1985; Doleschal, 1982). In addition, decriminalization of victimless crimes seems to increase arrest for related misdemeanors; and community corrections programs that survive become, in effect, small prisons within the community (Doleschal, 1982). Doleschal argues: "The highly disturbing findings of evaluations show that well-intentioned humanitarian reforms designed to lessen criminal justice penalties either do not achieve their objectives or actually produce consequences opposite [to] those intended" (1982:133).

We have just skimmed the surface of the concept of unintended consequences and fatal remedies. They are often inevitable, as the principles of rational planning do not allow us to deal with unknown and unpredictable phenomena. Often, we fall into the trap of promoting regressive intervention strategies because of our myopic orientations. The successful change agent or reformer is either open and quick enough to foresee and deal with the multitude of contingencies, flexible enough to deal with them as they arise, or lucky.

Implications for Criminal Justice Managers

An important aspect of an administrator's duties is to police the organization's boundaries to keep out disruptive influences and to provide the organization with stability. Also, administrators must enter into calculated exchange relationships with the agency's environment and acquire necessary resources and support (see chapter 2). However, administrators must also be responsive to changing demands from their constituencies and be able to make necessary changes within the organization to provide appropriate services to the community. Ideally, changing conditions, constraints, or demands should be anticipated, and changes made within the agency congruent with environmental shifts. If the ideal is not achieved, performance gaps should be recognized and steps taken to close them, which is easier to say than to do. As we have discussed, many of the obstacles to change lie within the traditional folklore, routines, and structure of criminal justice agencies themselves. The rank and file become infected with their agencies' past, perhaps making them less likely to find change desirable than their bosses, who may develop some degree of environmental sensitivity as a function of their position.

Purposive rather than crescive change in an organization requires a commitment to responsiveness and innovation, at least at the administrative level. Proactive responsiveness requires systematic methods of gathering input from constituents, the work environment, and agency members as well as useful methods of evaluating service delivery and programs. Purposive change also requires that organizational members identify with the goals of the agency and be committed to personal as well as organizational success. This, again, requires that agency members have an opportunity to actively participate in decisions at every level and therefore commit themselves to change. To the extent criminal justice agencies are paramilitary bureaucracies or are managed from the top down, agency members will be discouraged from any form of participation in planned change.

In this regard, change typically will not come about through decrees from the top. Updated policy and procedure manuals may do no more than gather dust. Requiring that staff "read and sign" new memoranda will not change their work-related behavior. Ideally, staff must be involved at all levels of the change process. Staff involvement will allow planners to tap staff expertise and improve the likelihood that staff will accept change. Finally, organizational members must have a fairly clear sense of their new role and possess the knowledge, skills, and tools to carry out the new tasks involved.

Skolnick and Bayley (1986) identify four factors crucial to change and innovation in police agencies attempting to become crime-prevention oriented. First, they cite "the chief's abiding, energetic commitment to the values and implications of a crime-prevention-oriented police department" (1986:220). They argue that the chief must be more than an advocate of new programs. He or she must infuse the entire organization with a sense of purpose that supports the logic of new programs or innovations. Second, the chief must promote the values and programs he or she is advocating by motivating and even manipulating departmental personnel into accepting those values. A series of tactics used to motivate or manipulate personnel was observed (Skolnick and Bayley, 1986:222–223):

1. Influencing younger members, then promoting them to positions of influence
2. Urging retirement of older officers and replacing them with new officers who can be successfully indoctrinated
3. Identifying and enlisting older officers who will buy into new ideas
4. Training middle managers through the chief's office to ensure proper indoctrination
5. Sending trained middle managers into the field in leadership positions to indoctrinate other members of the organization
6. Applying the coercive power of the chief's office to punish those fighting change

Third, once a program is established, conscious efforts must be maintained to keep it in place and protect its integrity. The natural tendency for a police agency is to fall back on old routines.

Fourth, "innovation is unlikely to happen without public support" (Skolnick and Bayley, 1986:223; also see chapter 2). Public support is needed at least to obtain resources for new programs. Public support may come in the demand for better services from a criminal justice agency. A critical public can be an opportunity for a change-oriented executive. Creating new programs to deliver services to a critical public can garner public support. However, criminal justice agencies have traditionally been insular and often subjected to criticism over spurious, highly visible incidents. The public may also be suspicious of new programs developed by criminal justice agencies, thus making it difficult to establish public support for innovation. Nonetheless, public support is crucial and can be obtained only when leadership possesses "an abiding, energetic commitment" to change.

In sum, planned change in criminal justice depends on agency administrators being alert to the need for change and innovation, setting aside traditional management styles, and creating a climate within their agencies that fosters communication and criticism from the ranks. Finally, they must be willing to expend the resources required to implement change. In general, criminal justice managers who would themselves be change agents must free themselves and their personnel from firmly rooted organizational values that, in themselves, contain major obstacles to change.

Summary

In this chapter we have examined the origins of change and the process of organizational change. In addition, we have discussed at length the obstacles and sources of resistance to innovation and change along with prescribed approaches to overcoming resistance to change. We have emphasized the value of planned change and planning.

However, the chapter paints a pessimistic picture of the ability of criminal justice agencies to successfully implement or even consciously enter into a process of planned change. The traditions of the criminal justice system coupled with its often vague and always conflicting and multiple goals mitigate against true planning and creative innovation. We have, however, provided sufficient conceptual knowledge and information for students and practitioners who view planned change as a worthy and important venture.

Out of necessity, we have reiterated most of the concepts put forward throughout this book in this chapter. Planned change and innovation of any magnitude in the criminal justice system and its organizations will invariably involve environmental concerns, communication, decision making, job design and enrichment, personnel motivation, and power, as well as all the other topics we have covered. Whether we wish it or not, the criminal justice system is dynamic not static. An agency's ability to manage change is manifest in good management. Good management is based, in part, on a sound cognitive, if not intuitive, grasp of theories of organizational behavior and administrative theory as they apply to criminal justice agencies. To that end, we hope we have provided a service.

CASE STUDY

A New Jail and a New Philosophy of Inmate Supervision

Local officials and jail administrators are attempting to close a traditional jail, build a new-generation jail, and change the existing practices of administrators, middle managers, and line staff to conform to the philosophy required to properly run such a jail. The change began as a result of external pressures. First, the jail was almost always overcrowded. Second, inmates were often brutalized by fellow inmates, and inmate suicides occurred with some frequency. Resulting law suits were a costly indicator of a performance gap within the jail system. Finally, the federal district court issued an order restricting the number of inmates that could be housed and requiring an upgrading of medical and social services for inmates. It was clear to local leaders that drastic steps would have to be taken, and a decision was made to build a new jail.

Different types of construction were considered by a committee of county commissioners, judges, and other criminal justice personnel as well as jail management. After consulting with the National Institute of Corrections, several other outside consultants, and a number of architects, it was decided to build a new-generation jail that would have the capacity for 380 inmates, 100 more than the existing facility. The selling point, made by the architectural firm, was that the new jail could be managed with a reduced staff during the 12:00 A.M. to 8:00 A.M. shift with the aid of a television monitoring system. The reduction of staff presumably would pay the cost of the new jail in thirty years.

Briefly, in a new-generation jail inmates are free to congregate in the day room during the day. Corrections officers are in the day room and actively interact with the inmates. Social service workers also circulate throughout the day rooms rather than interview inmates in their offices. They are subordinate to corrections officers. Middle managers are expected-to act as coaches rather than superiors in the traditional chain of command. In other words, the corrections officer becomes the key actor in the system in almost all respects.

A new sheriff was elected after the plans for the new jail were made. He proposed a participative management approach for the department, appointed a core of managers he felt were "progressive," and fully supported the new-generation jail. His commitment was supported by local officials, who granted his department the substantial training budget he requested. He also authorized his jail administrator to appoint a transition team composed of a cross-section of personnel to plan the transition to the new jail. Members of the transition team were released from their routine duties and worked full time on transition planning.

Outside OD trainers were utilized at retreat seminars attended by management and selected staff to open up communication, discuss problems that would be faced in the new jail, and develop solutions. The transition team created policies and procedures for the new jail and developed sophisticated training programs for all members of the staff. The trainers were selected by application from staff members. Rank and experience were not requirements for application. The selection was based on commitment to the change, communication skills, and basic knowledge. Those selected were trained by professional trainers. Members of the jail command staff as well as other selected veteran corrections officers and social service workers were flown to two functioning new-generation jails in other states to observe the operations. They all came back impressed.

Case Study Questions

1. In this case, the pressures for change came from sources outside the local political system. Why do you think that was necessary to force the building of a new jail?
2. Do you think many of the corrections officers will resist the move to the new inmate-management philosophy? What would you do to motivate them to accept the new system?
3. In what ways do you think the transition team is going to help the change process? What are some of the inherent dangers in appointing a transition team to make many of the key decisions for the transition process?

For Discussion

1. To what extent does an agency's reliance on its folklore to enhance its self-image impede planned change? Police agencies, for example, may see themselves as fighting a war on crime, or corrections administrators may see the primary role of their institutions as rehabilitation.

2. A growing number of line-level criminal justice practitioners have college degrees. Will the advanced education of these practitioners create greater or less resistance to change from within criminal justice organizations?

3. What must a corrections administrator consider in deciding whether to police the agency's boundaries or succumb to pressures for change?

4. Define a criminal justice agency problem that you are familiar with and understand in some depth. Discuss why the problem exists, develop alternative solutions, decide which solution is the most feasible, and finally consider what negative or unintended consequences might result from implementing your selected alternative solution.

5. To what extent does the classic paramilitary structure of police and corrections organizations create a climate that is not conducive to change?

For Further Reading

Duffee, D. *Correctional Management: Change and Control in Correctional Organizations.* Prospect Heights, Ill.: Waveland, 1986.

Hudzik, J., and Cordner, G. *Planning in Criminal Justice Organizations and Systems.* New York: Macmillan, 1983.

Sieber, S. *Fatal Remedies: The Ironies of Social Intervention.* New York: Plenum, 1981.

Skolnick, J. H., and Bayley, D. H. *The New Blue Line: Police Innovation in Six American Cities.* New York: Free Press, 1986.

References

Adams, T. F. *Police Patrol: Tactics and Techniques.* Englewood Cliffs, N.J.: Prentice-Hall, 1971.

Allison, G. T. *Essence of Decision.* Boston: Little, Brown, 1969.

Alpert, G. P., and Dunham, R. G. *Policing Urban America.* Prospect Heights, Ill.: Waveland, 1988.

American Friends Service Committee. *Struggle for Justice.* New York: Hill and Wang, 1971.

American Psychiatric Association. *Brief Amicus Curiae in the Case of* Barefoot *v.* Estelle. Washington, D. C.: American Psychiatric Association, 1982.

Angell, J. E. "Towards an Alternative to Classical Police Organizational Arrangements." *Criminology,* 1971, *19,* 19–29.

Archambeault, W. G., and Archambeault, B. J. *Correctional Supervisory Management: Principles of Organization, Policy and Law.* Englewood Cliffs, N.J.: Prentice-Hall, 1982.

Archambeault, W. G., and Wierman, C. L. "Critically Assessing the Utility of Police Bureaucracies in the 1980's: Implications of Management Theory Z." *Journal of Police Science and Administration,* 1983, *11*(4), 420–429.

Argyris, C. *Interpersonal Competence and Organizational Effectiveness.* Homewood, Ill.: Dorsey Press, 1962.

Atkins, B., and Pogrebin, M. *The Invisible Justice System: Discretion and the Law.* Cincinnati: Anderson, 1981.

Atkins, B., and Pogrebin, M. "Discretionary Decision-Making in the Administration of Justice." In *The Invisible System of Justice,* edited by B. Atkins and M. Pogrebin, pp. 3–15. Cincinnati: Anderson, 1982.

Austin, J. "Assessing the New Generation of Prison Classification Models." *Crime and Delinquency,* 1983, *29,* 523.

Austin, J. "Using Early Release to Relieve Prison Crowding: A Dilemma for Public Policy." *Crime and Delinquency,* 1986, *32,* 404–502.

Auten, J. H. "Police Management in Illinois." *Journal of Police Science and Administration*, 1985, *13*(4), 325–337.

Bacharach, S. B., and Lawler, E. E. *Power and Politics in Organizations*. San Francisco: Jossey-Bass, 1980.

Baker, T. J. "Designing the Job to Motivate." *FBI Law Enforcement Bulletin*, 1976, *45*(11), 3–7.

Banfield, E. *The Unheavenly City*. Boston: Little, Brown, 1974.

Barak-Glantz, I. L. "The Anatomy of Another Prison Riot." In *Prison Violence in America*, edited by M. Braswell, S. Dillingham, and R. Montgomery, Jr., pp. 47–72. Cincinnati: Anderson, 1985.

Barefoot v. *Estelle*, 103 S. Ct. 3383 (1983).

Barnard, C. *The Functions of the Executive*. Cambridge, Mass.: Harvard University Press, 1938.

Barnes, H., and Teeters, N. *New Horizons in Criminology*. Englewood Cliffs, N.J.: Prentice-Hall, 1959.

Bass, B. M. (Ed.). *Stodgill's Handbook of Leadership*. New York: Free Press, 1981.

Baugher, D. *Measuring Effectiveness*. San Francisco: Jossey-Bass, 1951.

Bennett, B. "Motivation Hang-Ups of the Police Mystique." *Police Human Relations*, 1981, *1*, 136–146.

Bennett, R. R. "Becoming Blue: A Longitudinal Study of Police Recruit Occupational Socialization." *Journal of Police Science and Administration*, 1984, *12*, 47–58.

Bennis, W. "Leadership in Administrative Behavior." In *The Planning of Change*, edited by W. Bennis, K. Benne, and R. Chin, pp. 62–79. New York: Holt, Rinehart & Winston, 1966.

Benton, W., and Silberstein, J. "State Prison Expansion: An Explanatory Model." *Journal of Criminal Justice*, 1983, *11*, 121–128.

Bierstedt, R. "An Analysis of Social Power." *American Sociological Review*, 1950, *15*(6), 730–738.

Blake, R. R., and Mouton, J. S. *The Managerial Grid*. Houston: Gulf, 1964.

Blanchard, K. H., and Hersey, P. *Management of Organizational Behavior*. Englewood Cliffs, N.J.: Prentice-Hall, 1977.

Blau, P. *The Dynamics of Bureaucracy*. Boston: Little, Brown, 1955.

Blau, P. *Exchange and Power in Social Life*. New York: Wiley, 1964.

Block, P. B., and Specht, D. *Neighborhood Team Policing*. Washington, D.C.: U.S. Government Printing Office, 1973.

Blomberg, T. "Diversion's Disparate Results and Unresolved Questions: An Integrative Evaluation Perspective." *Journal of Research in Crime and Delinquency*, 1983, *20*, 24–38.

Blumberg, A. "The Practice of Law as a Confidence Game." *Law and Society Review*, 1967, *1*, 15–39.

Book, C., Terrance, A., Atkin, C., Bettinghaus, E., Donohue, W., Farace, R.,

Greenberg, B., Hleper, H., Milkovich, M., Miller, G., Ralph, D., and Smith, T. *Human Communication: Principles, Context, and Skills.* New York: St. Martin's Press, 1980.

Booth, W., and Harwick, C. "Physical Ability Testing for Police Officers in the 80's." *The Police Chief,* January 1984, 39–41.

Bopp, W. J. "Organizational Democracy in Law Enforcement." In *Administration of Justice System: An Introduction,* edited by D. T. Shanahan, pp. 84–102. Boston: Holbrook Press, 1977.

Brecher, E. M. "Drug Laws and Drug Law Enforcement: A Review Based on 111 Years of Experience." *Drugs and Society,* 1986, *1,* 1–28.

Brennan, T. "Classification: An Overview of Selected Methodological Issues." In *Prediction and Classification: Criminal Justice Decision Making,* edited by D. M. Gottfredson and M. Tonry, pp. 201–248. Chicago: University of Chicago Press, 1987.

Brief, A. P., Munro, J., and Aldag, R. J. "Correctional Employees' Reactions to Job Characteristics: A Data Based Argument for Job Enlargement." *Journal of Criminal Justice,* 1976, *4,* 223–230.

Brown, D. C. *Civilian Review of Complaints Against the Police: A Survey of the United States Literature.* Research and Planning Paper 19. London: Home Office, 1983.

Brown, W. J. "Operation Citizen Participation: A Report on Public Perceptions of Police Service Delivery." *Journal of Police Science and Administration,* 1983, *1*(2), 129–135.

Bureau of Justice Statistics. *Prisoners in 1987.* Washington, D.C.: U.S. Department of Justice, 1988.

Burgess, E. W. "Factors Determining Success or Failure on Parole." In *The Workings of the Indeterminate Sentence Law and the Parole System in Illinois,* edited by A. Bruce, E. W. Burgess, and A. J. Harno. Springfield, Ill.: Illinois State Board of Parole, 1928.

Burnes, T., and Stalker, G. *The Management of Innovation.* London: Tavistock, 1961.

Burnham, W. R. "Modern Decision Theory and Corrections." In *Decision-Making in the Criminal Justice System: Review and Essays,* edited by D. M. Gottfredson, pp. 93–103. Rockville, Md.: National Institute of Mental Health, 1975.

Buzawa, E. S. "Determining Patrol Officer Job Satisfaction." *Criminology,* 1984, *22,* 61–81.

Byham, W. C., and Thornton, G. C. *Assessment Centers and Managerial Performance.* New York: Academic Press, 1982.

Cameron, K. "The Enigma of Organizational Effectiveness." In *Measuring Effectiveness,* edited by D. Baugher. San Francisco: Jossey-Bass, 1981.

Campbell, J. "On the Nature of Organizational Effectiveness." In *New Perspectives on Organizational Effectiveness,* edited by P. S. Goodman and J. S. Pennings, pp. 13–55. San Francisco: Jossey-Bass, 1977.

Carlisle, H. M. *Management: Concepts and Situations.* Chicago: SRA, 1976.

Carp, R., and Wheeler, R. "Sink or Swim: The Socialization of a Federal District Judge." *Journal of Public Law,* 1972, *21,* 359–393.

Carroll, L. *Hacks, Blacks and Cons: Race Relations in a Maximum Security Prison.* Lexington, Mass.: Lexington Books, 1974.

Carroll, S. J., and Tosi, H. L. *Management by Objectives: Applications and Research.* New York: Macmillan, 1973.

Carter, R. M., and Wilkins, L. T. "Caseloads: Some Conceptual Models." In *Probation, Parole and Community Corrections,* edited by R. M. Carter and L. T. Wilkins, pp. 211–232. New York: Wiley, 1976.

Center for Assessment of the Juvenile Justice System. *Youthful Gangs and Appropriate Police Response* 1982.

Center for the Study of Mass Communications Research. *Media Crime Prevention Campaign.* University of Denver, 1982.

Chapper, J. "Oral Argument and Expediting Appeals: A Compatible Combination." *Journal of Law Reform* 1983, *16*(3), 517–526.

Charles, M. T. *Policing the Streets.* Springfield, Ill.: Charles C Thomas, 1986.

Cheek, F., and Miller, M. *Prisoners of Life: A Study of Occupational Stress Among State Corrections Officers.* Washington, D.C.: American Federation of State, County, and Municipal Employees, 1982.

Cheek F., and Miller, M. "The Experience of Stress for Corrections Officers." *Journal of Criminal Justice,* 1983, *11,* 105–120.

Chen, H., and Rossi, P. "The Multi-Goal, Theory Driven Approach to Evaluation: A Model Linking Basic and Applied Social Science." *Social Forces,* 1980, *59,* 106–120.

Cherniss, C. *Staff Burnout: Job Stress in the Human Services.* Beverly Hills, Calif.: Sage, 1980.

Chin, R. "The Utility of System Models and Developmental Models for Practitioners." In *The Planning of Change,* edited by W. Bennis, K. Benne, and R. Chin, pp. 297–313. New York: Holt, Rinehart & Winston, 1966.

Clear, T. R., and O'Leary, V. *Controlling the Offender in the Community.* Lexington, Mass.: Lexington Books, 1983.

Clynch, E. J., and Neubauer, D. W. "Trial Courts as Organizations: A Critique and Synthesis." *Law and Policy Quarterly,* 1981, *3,* 69–94.

Coates, R., Miller, A., and Ohlin, L. *Diversity in a Youth Correctional System.* Cambridge, Mass.: Ballinger, 1978.

Cohen, M. D., March, J. G., and Olsen, J. P. "A Garbage Can Model of Organizational Choice." *Administrative Science Quarterly,* 1972, *17,* 1–25.

Cole, G. *The American System of Criminal Justice.* Pacific Grove, Calif.: Brooks/Cole, 1983.

Cole, G. (Ed.). *Criminal Justice: Law and Politics.* 5th ed. Pacific Grove, Calif.: Brooks/Cole, 1988.

Cole, G., Hanson, R., and Silbert, J. "Mediation: Is It an Effective Alternative to

Adjudication in Resolving Prisoner Complaints?" *Judicature,* 1982, 5(10), 481–489.

Conser, J. A. "Motivational Theory Applied to Law Enforcement Agencies." *Journal of Police Science and Administration,* 1979, 7(3), 285–291.

Cordner, G. W. "Review of Work Motivation Theory and Research for the Police Manager." *Journal of Police Science and Administration,* 1978, 6(3), 286–292.

Cordner, G. W., and Hudzik, J. *Planning in Criminal Justice Organizations.* New York: Macmillan, 1983.

"The Court Retorts. . . ." *Chicago Tribune,* August 10, 1987, p. 2.

Craig, M. "Improving Jury Deliberations: A Reconsideration of Lesser Included Offense Instructions." *Journal of Law Reform,* 1983, 16(3), 561–584.

Cronin, T., Cronin, T. Z., and Milakovich, M. *U.S. v. Crime in the Streets.* Bloomington, Ind.: Indiana University Press, 1981.

Crouch, B., and Marquart, J. "On Becoming a Prison Guard." In *The Keepers: Prison Guards and Contemporary Corrections,* edited by B. M. Crouch, pp. 1–22. Springfield, Ill.: Charles C Thomas, 1980.

Crozier, M. *The Bureaucratic Phenomenon.* Chicago: University of Chicago Press, 1964.

Cullen, F. T., and Gilbert, K. *Reaffirming Rehabilitation.* Cincinnati: Anderson, 1982.

Cullen, F. T., Maakestad, W. J., and Cavender, G. *Corporate Crime Under Attack: The Ford Pinto Case and Beyond.* Cincinnati: Anderson, 1987.

Cushman, D., and Whiting, G. "An Approach to Communications Theory: Toward Consensus on Rules." *Journal of Communications,* 1972, 22, 217–238.

Dahl, R. "The Concept of Power." *Behavioral Science,* 1957, 2(3), 201–215.

Dahl, R. "The Politics of Planning." *International Social Science Journal,* 1959, 11, 340–353.

Dalton, M. *Men Who Manage.* New York: Wiley, 1959.

Danzinger, S., and Weinstein, M. "Employment Location and Wage Rates of Poverty-Area Residents." *Journal of Urban Economics,* 1976, 44, 425–448.

Davidoff, P., and Reiner, T. "A Choice Theory of Planning." *Journal of the American Institute of Planners,* 1962, 30, 258–274.

Decker, S., "A Systematic Analysis of Diversion: Net Widening and Beyond." *Journal of Criminal Justice,* 1985, 3(8), 207–216.

Dershowitz, A. *The Best Defense.* New York: Random House, 1983.

Dickinson, G. "Change in Communications Policies." *Corrections Today,* 1984, 46(1), 58–60.

DiIulio, J. *Governing Prisons: A Comparative Study of Correctional Management.* New York: Free Press, 1987.

Doering, C. D. *A Report on the Development of Penological Treatment at Norfolk Prison Colony in Massachusetts*. New York: Bureau of Social Hygiene, 1940.

Doleschal, G. "The Dangers of Criminal Justice Reform." *Criminal Justice Abstracts*, 1982, 133–152.

Downs, A. *Inside Bureaucracy*. Boston: Little, Brown, 1967.

Dubin, R. "Power, Function, and Organization." *Pacific Sociological Review*, 1963, 6(1), 16–24.

DuBrin, A. *Fundamentals of Organizational Behavior*. New York: Pergamon Press, 1978.

Duffee, D. *Correctional Management: Change and Control in Correctional Organizations*. Englewood Cliffs, N.J.: Prentice-Hall, 1980.

Duffee, D. "The Interaction of Organization and Political Constraints on Community Prerelease Programs." In *The Politics of Crime and Justice*, edited by E. Fairchild and V. Webb, pp. 99–119. Beverly Hills, Calif.: Sage, 1985.

Duffee, D. *Correctional Management: Change and Control in Correctional Organizations*. Prospect Heights, Ill.: Waveland, 1986.

Duffee, D., and O'Leary, V. "Formulating Correctional Goals: The Interaction of Environment, Belief, and Organizational Structure." In *Correctional Management*, edited by D. Duffee, Englewood Cliffs, N.J.: Prentice-Hall, 1980.

Duncan, R. B. "The Characteristics of Organizational Environments and Perceived Environmental Uncertainty." *Administrative Science Quarterly*, 1972, *17*, 313–327.

Eisenstein, J. *Politics and the Legal Process*. New York: Harper & Row, 1973.

Eisenstein, J., Flemming, R., and Nardulli, P. *The Contours of Justice: Communities and Their Courts*. Boston: Little, Brown, 1988.

Ellsworth, R. B., and Ellsworth, J. J. "The Psychiatric Aide: Therapeutic Agent or Lost Potential?" *Journal of Psychiatric Nursing and Mental Health Services*, 1970, *8*, 7–13.

Embert, P. "Correctional Law and Jails." In *Sneaking Inmates Down the Alley: Problems and Prospects in Jail Management*, edited by D. Kalinich and J. Klofas, pp. 63–84. Springfield, Ill.: Charles C Thomas, 1986.

Emerson, R. E. "Power-Dependence Relations." *American Sociological Review*, 1962, *27*(1), 31–40.

Emmery, F., and Emmery, M. "Participative Design: Work and Community Life." In *Democracy at Work*, edited by F. Emmery and E. Thorsund, pp. 147–170. Leiden, The Netherlands: Martinus, Nijhoff, 1974.

Emmery, F., and Trist, E. L. "The Causal Texture of Organizational Environments." *Human Relations*, 1965, *18*, 21–32.

Ermer, V. B. "Recruitment of Female Police Officers in New York City." *Journal of Criminal Justice*, 1978, *6*, 233–246.

Etzioni, A. "New Direction in the Study of Organizations and Society." *Social Research*, 1960, *27*, 223–228.

Etzioni, A. *A Comparative Analysis of Complex Organizations.* New York: Free Press, 1961.

Etzioni, A. *Modern Organizations.* Englewood Cliffs, N.J.: Prentice-Hall, 1964.

Fairchild, E. "Interest Groups in the Criminal Justice Process." *Journal of Criminal Justice,* 1981, *9,* 181–194.

Fairchild, E., and Webb, V. (Eds.). *The Politics of Crime and Justice.* Beverly Hills, Calif.: Sage, 1985.

Farace, R., Monge, P., and Russell, H. *Communicating and Organizing.* New York: Random House, 1977.

Farrington, D. P. "Predicting Individual Crime Rates." In *Prediction and Classification: Criminal Justice Decision Making,* edited by D. M. Gottfredson and M. Tonry, pp. 52–102. Chicago: University of Chicago Press, 1987.

Festinger, L. *A Theory of Cognitive Dissonance.* Evanston, Ill.: Row, Peterson, 1957.

Fiedler, F. A. *A Theory of Leadership Effectiveness.* New York: McGraw-Hill, 1967.

Fielding, N. G., and Fielding, J. L. "A Study of Resignation During British Police Training." *Journal of Police Science and Administration,* 1987, *15,* 24–36.

Fischer, F., and Sirianni, C. *Critical Studies in Organization and Bureaucracy.* Philadelphia: Temple University Press, 1984.

Fogel, D., and Hudson, J. *Justice as Fairness.* Cincinnati: Anderson, 1981.

Frankel, M. E. *Criminal Sentences: Law Without Order.* New York: Hill and Wang, 1973.

Frazier, C., and Block, W. "Effects of Court Officers on Sentencing Severity." *Criminology,* 1982, *20,* 257–272.

French, J. R. P., and Raven, B. "The Bases of Social Power." In *Group Dynamics* (3rd ed.), edited by D. Cartwright and A. Zander, pp. 259–269. New York: Harper & Row, 1968.

French, W. L. "Organizational Development: Objectives, Assumptions and Strategies." *California Management Review,* 1969, *12*(2), 23–35.

French, W. L. "The Emergence and Early History of Organizational Development with Reference to Influences upon and Interactions Among Some of the Key Actors." In *Contemporary Organization Development: Current Thinking and Applications,* edited by D. Warrick, pp. 12–27. Glenview, Ill.: Scott, Foresman, 1985.

Frey, W. "Central City White Flight: Racial and Non-Racial Causes." *American Sociological Review,* 1979, *44,* 435–448.

Gaines, L. K., Tubergen, N. V., and Paiva, M. A. "Police Officer Perceptions of Promotion as a Source of Motivation." *Journal of Criminal Justice,* 1984, *12*(3), 265–274.

Galliher, J. "Explanations of Police Behavior: A Critical Review and Analysis." In *The Ambivalent Force,* edited by A. Blumberg and E. Niederhoffer, New York: Holt, Rinehart & Winston, 1985.

Gandz, J., and Murray, V. "The Experience of Workplace Politics." *Academy of Management Journal,* 1980, *23,* 237–251.

Geller, W. A. (Ed.). *Police Leadership in America: Crisis and Opportunity.* Chicago: American Bar Association, 1985.

Ghorpade, J., and Atchison, T. J. "The Concept of Job Analysis: A Review and Some Suggestions." *Public Personnel Management,* 1980, *9,* 134–144.

Glaser, D. *Effectiveness of a Prison and Parole System.* Indianapolis: Bobbs-Merrill, 1969.

Glauser, M., and Tullar, W. "Communicator Style of Police Officers and Citizen Satisfaction with Officer/Citizen Telephone Conversations." *Journal of Police Science and Administration,* 1985, *13*(1), 70–77.

Goffman, E. *Asylums.* Garden City, N.Y.: Doubleday, 1961.

Goldkamp, J. S. *Policy Guidelines for Bail: An Experiment in Court Reform.* Philadelphia: Temple University Press, 1985.

Goldstein, H. "Police Discretion Not to Invoke the Criminal Process." *Yale Law Journal,* 1960, *69,* 33–42.

Goldstein, H. "Police Discretion Not to Invoke the Criminal Process: Low-Visibility Decisions in the Administration of Justice." In *Criminal Justice: Law and Politics* (4th ed.), edited by G. F. Cole, pp. 77–91. Pacific Grove, Calif.: Brooks/Cole, 1984.

Goodman, P. S., and Kurke, L. B. "Studies of Change in Organizations: A Status Report." In *Changes in Organizations: New Perspectives on Theory, Research, and Practice,* pp. 280–315. San Francisco: Jossey-Bass, 1982.

Goodstein, L., and Hepburn, J. *Determinate Sentencing and Imprisonment: A Failure of Reform.* Cincinnati: Anderson, 1985.

Gottfredson, D. M. *Decision-Making in the Criminal Justice System: Review and Essays.* Rockville, Md.: National Institute of Mental Health, 1975.

Gottfredson, D. M., Hoffman, P. B., Sigler, M. H., and Wilkins, L. T. "Making Parole Policy Explicit." *Crime and Delinquency,* 1975, *21,* 7–17.

Gottfredson, D. M., and Tonry, M. (Eds.). *Prediction and Classification: Criminal Justice Decision Making.* Chicago: University of Chicago Press, 1987.

Gottfredson, M. R., and Gottfredson, D. M. *Decisionmaking in Criminal Justice: Toward a Rational Exercise of Discretion.* Cambridge, Mass.: Ballinger, 1980.

Grau, C. W. "Limits of Planned Change in Courts." In *Misdemeanor Courts—Policy Concerns and Research Perspectives,* edited by J. J. Alfini, pp. 271–300. Racine, Wis.: Johnson Foundation, 1980.

Greene, J., Bynum, T., and Cordner, G. "Planning and the Play of Power: Resource Acquisition Among Criminal Justice Agencies." *Journal of Criminal Justice,* 1986, *14,* 529–544.

Greenwood, P. *Selective Incapacitation.* Santa Monica, Calif.: Rand, 1982.

Griener, L. "Antecedents of Planned Change." *Journal of Applied Behavioral Sciences,* 1967, *21,* 51–86.

Griffin, G. R., Dunbar, R. L. M., and McGill, M. E. "Factors Associated with Job

Satisfaction Among Police Personnel." *Journal of Police Science and Administration,* 1978, *6*(1), 77–85.

Grubb, N. "The Flight to the Suburbs of Population Employment." *Journal of Urban Economics,* 1982, *11*, 348–367.

Guy, E., Platt, J., and Zwerling, S. "Mental Health Status of Prisoners in an Urban Jail." *Criminal Justice and Behavior,* 1985, *12*, 29–53.

Guyot, D. "Political Interference Versus Political Accountability in Municipal Policing." In *The Politics of Crime and Justice,* edited by E. Fairchild and V. Webb, pp. 120–143. Beverly Hills, Calif.: Sage, 1985.

Gyllenhammer, P. "Changing Work Organization at Volvo." In *Perspectives on Job Enrichment,* edited by W. Soujaren, pp. 77–99. Atlanta: School of Business Administration, Georgia State University, 1975.

Hackman, J. R., and Oldham, G. R. *Work Redesign.* Reading, Mass.: Addison-Wesley, 1980.

Hagan, J. *Victims Before the Law: The Organizational Domination of Criminal Law.* Toronto: Butterworth, 1983.

Hage, J., and Aiken, M. *Social Change in Complex Organizations.* New York: Random House, 1970.

Hage, J., and Dewar, R. "Elite Values Versus Organizational Structure in Predicting Innovation." *Administrative Science Quarterly,* 1973, *18*(3), 279–290.

Hahn, H. "A Profile of Urban Police." In *The Police Community,* edited by J. Goldsmith and S. Goldsmith. Pacific Palisades, Calif.: Palisades Publishers, 1974.

Hall, A., Henry, D. A., Perlstein, J. J., and Smith, W. F. *Alleviating Jail Crowding: A Systems Perspective.* Washington, D.C.: U.S. Government Printing Office, 1985.

Hall, R. H. *Organizations: Structure and Process.* Englewood Cliffs, N.J.: Prentice-Hall, 1982.

Halperin, M. "Shaping the Flow of Information." In *Bureaucratic Power in National Politics* (3rd ed.), edited by R. Rourke, pp. 102–115. Boston: Little, Brown, 1978.

Hannan, M. T., and Freeman, J. "Obstacles to Comparative Studies." In *New Perspectives on Organizational Effectiveness,* edited by P. S. Goodman and J. M. Pennings, pp. 106–131. San Francisco: Jossey-Bass, 1977.

Hannan, M. T., and Freeman, J. "Structural Inertia and Organizational Change." *American Sociological Review,* 1984, *49*, 929–964.

Hardy, K. "Equity in Court Dispositions." In *Evaluating Performance of Criminal Justice Agencies,* edited by G. P. Whitaker and C. D. Phillips, pp. 151–173. Beverly Hills, Calif.: Sage, 1983.

Harring, S. "Taylorization of Police Work." *Insurgent Sociologist,* 1982, *4*, 25–32.

Harris, P. W., and Hartland, G. R. "Developing and Implementing Alternatives to Incarceration—A Problem of Planned Change in Criminal Justice." *University of Illinois Law Review,* 1984, *2*, 319–364.

Harris, R. N. *The Police Academy: An Inside View.* New York: Wiley, 1973.

Hatry, H. P., and Greiner, J. M. *How Police Departments Better Apply Management-by-Objectives and Quality Circle Programs.* Washington, D.C.: National Institute of Justice, U.S. Department of Justice, 1984.

Hawkins, K. "Assessing Evil." *British Journal of Criminology,* 1983, *23,* 101–127.

Hayslip, D. *Can Correction Officers Be Motivated?* Paper presented at the annual meeting of the Academy of Criminal Justice Sciences, Louisville, Ky., 1982.

Hellriegel, D., and Slocum, J. W. *Organizational Behavior.* St. Paul: West, 1979.

Hellriegel, D., Slocum, J. W., and Woodman, R. W. *Organizational Behavior.* 4th ed. St. Paul: West, 1986.

Henderson, M., and Hollin, C. "A Critical Review of Social Skills Training with Young Offenders." *Criminal Justice and Behavior,* 1983, *10*(3), 316–341.

Henry, N. *Public Administration and Public Affairs.* Englewood Cliffs, N.J.: Prentice-Hall, 1975.

Hepburn, J. R. "The Exercise of Power in Coercive Organizations: A Study of Prison Guards." *Criminology,* 1985, *23*(1), 145–164.

Hernandez, A. P. "Motivation and Municipal Police Departments—Models and an Empirical Analysis." *Journal of Police Science and Administration,* 1982, *10*(3), 284–288.

Herzberg, F. *Work and the Nature of Man.* New York: World, 1966.

Herzberg, F. "Participation Is Not a Motivator." *Industry Week,* 1978, *198,* 39–44.

Herzberg, F., Mausner, B., and Snyderman, B. B. *The Motivation to Work.* New York: Wiley, 1959.

Hicksen, D., Hinings, C., Lee, C., Schenck, R., and Pennings, J. "A Strategic Contingencies Theory of Intraorganizational Power." In *Readings in Organizational Behavior and Human Performance,* edited by W. J. Scott and L. L. Cummings, pp. 63–96. Homewood, Ill.: Richard D. Irwin, Inc. 1973.

Hinings, C. R., Pugh, D. S., Hicksen, D. J., and Turner, C. "An Approach to the Study of Bureaucracy." *Sociology,* 1967, *1*(1), 61–72.

Hoffman, P., and Stone-Meierhoefer, B. "Reporting Recidivism Rates: The Criterion and Follow-Up Issues." *Journal of Criminal Justice,* 1980, *8,* 53–60.

Hoos, I. R. *Systems Analysis in Public Policy.* Los Angeles: University of California Press, 1983.

Houghland, J. G., Shepard, J. M., and Wood, J. R. "Discrepancies in Perceived Organizational Control: Their Decrease and Importance in Local Churches." *The Sociological Quarterly,* 1979, *20*(1), 63–76.

Houghland, J. G., and Wood, J. R. "Control in Organizations and Commitment of Members." *Social Forces,* 1980, *59*(1), 85–105.

House, R. J. *Power in Organizations: A Social Psychological Perspective.* Unpublished manuscript, University of Toronto, 1984.

House, R. J., and Mitchell, T. R. "Path–Goal Theory of Leadership." In *Organizational Behavior and Management* (4th ed.), edited by H. L. Tosi and W. C. Hamner, pp. 491–500. Cincinnati: Grid, 1985.

Hudzik, J., and Cordner, G. *Planning in Criminal Justice Organizations and Systems.* New York: Macmillan, 1983.

Huse, E. *Organizational Development and Change.* Minneapolis: West Publishing, 1975.

Ideus, K. *Staffing and Personnel Management—A Humanistic Look.* Rockville, Md.: National Institute of Justice, 1978.

Inbau, F., Reid, J., and Buckley, J. *Criminal Interrogation and Confession.* Baltimore: Williams & Wilkins, 1986.

Irwin, J. *Prisons in Turmoil.* Boston: Little, Brown, 1980.

Irwin, J. *The Jail: Managing the Underclass in American Society.* Berkeley, Calif.: University of California Press, 1986.

Jacks, I. "Positive Interaction: Everyday Principles of Correctional Rehabilitation." In *Psychological Approaches to Crime and Its Correction: Theory, Research, Practice,* edited by I. Jacks, pp. 424–443. Chicago: Nelson-Hall, 1984.

Jacobs, D. "Dependency and Vulnerability: An Exchange Approach to the Control of Organizations." *Administrative Science Quarterly,* 1974, *19,* 45–59.

Jacobs, J. B. *Stateville: The Penitentiary in Mass Society.* Chicago: University of Chicago Press, 1977.

Jacobs, J. B. *The Unionization of the Guards.* Proceedings of the Thirteenth Interagency Workshop, Sam Houston State University, Huntsville, Tex., 1978.

Jacobs, J. B. (Ed.). *New Perspectives on Prisons and Imprisonment.* Ithaca, N.Y.: Cornell University Press, 1983a.

Jacobs, J. B. "The Prisoners' Rights Movement and Its Impacts." In *New Perspectives on Prisons and Imprisonment,* edited by J. B. Jacobs, pp. 33–60. Ithaca, N.Y.: Cornell University Press, 1983b.

Jacobs, J. B., and Grear, M. P. "Drop Outs and Rejects: An Analysis of the Prison Guard's Revolving Door." *Criminal Justice Review,* 1977, *2,* 57–70.

Jacobs, J. B., and Retsky, H. C. "Prison Guard." *Urban Life,* 1975, *4,* 5–29.

Jacobs, J. B., and Zimmer, L. "Collective Bargaining and Labor Unrest." In *New Perspectives on Prisons and Imprisonment,* edited by J. B. Jacobs, pp. 142–159. Ithaca, N.Y.: Cornell University Press, 1983.

Johnson, R. "Informal Helping Networks in Prison: The Shape of Grass-Roots Correctional Intervention." *Journal of Criminal Justice,* 1977, *7,* 53–70.

Joint Commission on Correctional Manpower and Training. *A Time to Act.* Washington, D.C.: U.S. Government Printing Office, 1969.

Josephson, E., and Josephson, M. *Man Alone: Alienation in Modern Society.* New York: Laurel, 1975.

Julian, J. "Compliance Patterns and Communication Blocks in Complex Organizations." *American Sociological Review,* 1966, *31*(3), 382–389.

Jurik, N. C., and Winn, R. "Describing Correctional–Security Dropouts and

Rejects: An Individual or Organizational Profile?" *Criminal Justice and Behavior,* 1987, *14*(1), 5–25.

Kagehiro, D., and Werner, C. "Divergent Perceptions of Jail Inmates and Correctional Officers: The 'Blame the Other—Expect to Be Blamed' Effect." *Journal of Applied Social Psychology,* 1981, *11*(6), 507–528.

Kalinich, D. *Power, Stability, and Contraband: The Inmate Economy.* Prospect Heights, Ill.: Waveland, 1984.

Kalinich, D. "Criminal Justice Education: Coming in in the Middle of the Movie." In *The Future of Criminal Justice Education,* edited by R. Muraskins. Brookville, N.Y.: Long Island University Criminal Justice Institute, 1987.

Kalinich, D., and Banas, D. "Systems Maintenance and Legitimization: An Historical Illustration of the Impact of National Task Forces and Committees on Corrections." *Journal of Criminal Justice,* 1984, *12,* 61–71.

Kalinich, D., and Klofas, J. (Eds.) *Sneaking Inmates Down the Alley: Problems and Prospects of Jail Management.* Springfield, Ill.: Charles C Thomas, 1986.

Kalinich, D., Lorinskas, L., and Banas, D. "Symbolism and Rhetoric: The Guardians of the Status Quo in the Criminal Justice System." *Criminal Justice Review,* 1985, *10,* 41–46.

Kalinich, D., and Stojkovic, S. "Contraband: The Basis for Legitimate Power in a Prison Social System." *Criminal Justice and Behavior,* 1985, *12,* 435–451.

Kalinich, D., Stojkovic, S., and Klofas, J. "Toward a Political-Community Theory of Prison Organization." *Journal of Criminal Justice,* 1988, *16*(3), 217–230.

Karger, H. "Burnout as Alienation." *Social Service Review,* 1981, *55,* 270–283.

Katz, D., and Kahn, R. L. *The Social Psychology of Organizations.* 2nd ed. New York: Wiley, 1978.

Katzev, R., and Wishart, S. "The Impact of Judicial Commentary Concerning Eyewitness Identifications on Jury Decision Making." *The Journal of Criminal Law and Criminology,* 1985, *76*(3), 733–745.

Kaufman, H. "Organization Theory and Political Theory." *The American Political Science Review,* 1964, *58*(1), 5–14.

Kaufman, H. "Administrative Decentralization and Political Power." *Public Administration Review,* 1969, *29,* 3–15.

Kelling, G. L. *Police and Communities: The Quiet Revolution.* Washington D. C.: National Institute of Justice, 1988.

Kelly, J. E. *Scientific Management, Job Redesign and Work Performance.* New York: Academic Press, 1982.

Klofas, J., Smith, S., and Meister, E. "Harnessing Human Resources in Local Jails: Toward a New Generation of Planners." In *Sneaking Inmates Down the Alley,* edited by D. Kalinich and J. Klofas, pp. 193–208. Springfield, Ill.: Charles C Thomas, 1986.

Klofas, J., and Toch, H. "The Guard Subculture Myth." *Journal of Research in Crime and Delinquency,* 1982, *19,* 169–175.

Knapp Commission. *Report on Police Corruption.* New York: Geo. Braziller, 1972.

Kohfeld, C. W. "Rational Cops, Rational Robbers, and Information." *Journal of Criminal Justice,* 1983, *11*(5), 459–466.

Kolonski, H., and Mendelsohn, R. *The Politics of Local Justice.* Boston: Little, Brown, 1970.

Kratcoski, P. C., and Walker, D. B. *Criminal Justice in America.* Glenview, Ill.: Scott, Foresman, 1978.

Kreman, B. "Search for a Better Way of Work: Lordstown, Ohio." In *Humanizing the Workplace,* edited by R. P. Fairchild, pp. 17–41. Buffalo, N.Y.: Prometheus, 1973.

Kress, J. *Prescriptions for Justice: The Theory and Practice of Sentencing Guidelines.* Cambridge, Mass.: Ballinger, 1980.

Kuykendall, J. "Police Managerial Styles—A Grid Analysis." *American Journal of Police,* 1985, *4*(1), 38–70.

Kuykendall, J., and Unsinger, P. C. "The Leadership Styles of Police Managers." *Journal of Criminal Justice,* 1982, *10*(4), 311–322.

LaFave, W. L. "The Prosecutor's Discretion in the United States." *American Journal of Comparative Law,* 1970, *18,* 532–548.

Lasky, G. L., Gordon, B. C., and Srebalus, D. J. "Occupational Stressors Among Federal Correctional Officers Working in Different Security Levels." *Criminal Justice and Behavior,* 1986, *13,* 317–327.

Lawrence, P. R., and Lorsch, J. W. "Differentiation and Integration in Complex Organizations." *Administrative Science Quarterly,* 1967, *12*(1), 1–47.

Lawrence, R. "Professionals or Civil Servants?: An Examination of the Probation Officer's Role." *Federal Probation,* 1984, *48,* 3–13.

Lee, J. H., and Visano, L. H. "Official Deviance in the Legal System." In *Law and Deviance,* edited by H. L. Ross, pp. 215–250. Beverly Hills, Calif.: Sage, 1981.

Lenihan, K. J. "Telephones and Raising Bail: Some Lessons in Evaluation Research." *Evaluation Quarterly,* 1977, *1,* 569–586.

Levinson R., and Gerard, R. "Functional Units: A Different Correctional Approach." *Federal Probation,* 1973, *37,* 8–16.

Lewin, K. *Readings in Social Psychology.* New York: Holt, Rinehart & Winston, 1958.

Liebentritt, D. *The Making of a Prison Guard.* Unpublished manuscript, Center for Studies in Criminal Justice, University of Chicago Law School, 1974.

Likert, R. *New Patterns of Management.* New York: McGraw-Hill, 1961.

Likert, R. *The Human Organization.* New York: McGraw-Hill, 1967.

Lindblom, C. "The Science of Muddling Through." *Public Administration Review,* 1959, *19,* 79–88.

Lindquist, C. A., and Whitehead, J. T. "Guards Released from Prison: A Natural Experiment in Job Enlargement." *Journal of Criminal Justice,* 1986, *14,* 283–294.

Lipsky, M. *Street-Level Bureaucracy.* New York: Russell Sage Foundation, 1980.

Lipsky, M. "Toward a Theory of Street-Level Bureaucracy." In *Criminal Justice: Law and Politics* (5th ed.), edited by G. F. Cole, pp. 55–73. Pacific Grove, Calif.: Brooks/Cole, 1988.

Lipton, D., Martinson, R., and Wilkes, J. *The Effectiveness of Correctional Treatment: A Survey of Treatment Evaluation Studies.* New York: Praeger, 1975.

Lodahl, J., and Gordon, G. "Funding the Sciences in University Departments." *Educational Record,* 1973, *54,* 74–82.

Lombardo, L. X. *Guards Imprisoned: Correctional Officers at Work.* New York: Elsevier, 1981.

Lombardo, L. X. "Group Dynamics and the Prison Guard Subculture: Is the Subculture an Impediment to Helping Inmates?" *International Journal of Offender Therapy and Comparative Criminology,* 1985, *29,* 79–90.

Long, N. "Power and Administration." *Public Administration Review,* 1949, *9,* 257–264.

Longenecker, C. O., Gioia, D. A., and Sims, H. P., Jr. "Behind the Mask: The Politics of Employee Appraisal." *Executive,* 1987, *1*(3), 183–194.

Lord, R. G. "Functional Leadership Behavior: Measurement and Relation to Social Power and Leadership Perceptions." *Administrative Science Quarterly,* 1977, *22*(1), 114–133.

Lovell, R., and Stojkovic, S. "Myths, Symbols, and Policymaking in Corrections." *Criminal Justice Review,* in press.

Lynch, R. G. *The Police Manager: Police Leadership Skills.* 3rd ed. New York: Random House, 1986.

Maltz, M. *Recidivism.* New York: Academic Press, 1984.

Manning, P. K., and Redlinger, L. J. "Invitational Edges of Corruption: Some Consequences of Narcotics Law Enforcement." In *Drugs and Politics,* edited by P. Rock, pp. 279–310. New Brunswick, N.J.: Transaction Books, 1977.

March, J. G. "The Business Firm as a Political Coalition." *Journal of Politics,* 1962, *24,* 662–678.

March, J. G., and Simon, H. A. *Organizations.* New York: Wiley, 1958.

Marquart, J. W. "Doing Research in Prison: The Strengths and Weaknesses of Full Participation as a Guard." *Justice Quarterly,* 1986a, *3,* 15–32.

Marquart, J. W. "Prison Guards and the Use of Physical Coercion as a Mechanism of Prisoner Control." *Criminology,* 1986b, *24*(2), 347–366.

Marsden, P. V. "Introducing Influence Processes into a System of Collective Decisions." *American Journal of Sociology,* 1981, *86,* 1203–1235.

Martin, S. J., and Ekland-Olson, S. *Texas Prisons: The Walls Came Tumbling Down.* Austin: Texas Monthly Press, 1987.

Martinson, R. "What Works? Questions and Answers About Prison Reform." *Public Interest,* 1974, *35,* 22–54.

Maslach, C. "Burned-Out." *Human Behavior,* 1976, *5,* 16–22.

Maslach, C., and Jackson, S. "Burned-Out Cops and Their Families." *Psychology Today*, 1979, *12*, 59–62.

Maslach, C., and Jackson, S. "The Measurement of Experienced Burnout." *Journal of Occupational Behavior*, 1981, *2*, 99–113.

Maslow, A. H. "A Theory of Motivation." *Psychological Review*, 1943, *50*, 370–396.

Mayo, E. *The Human Problems of Industrial Civilization.* Boston: Harvard Business School, 1946.

McCleary, R. "How Parole Officers Use Records." *Social Problems*, 1977, *24*, 576–589.

McCleary, R. *Dangerous Men.* Beverly Hills, Calif.: Sage, 1978.

McCleary, R. "How Structural Variables Constrain the Parole Officer's Use of Discretionary Power." *Social Problems*, 1985, *32*, 141–152.

McCleary, R., Nienstedt, B. C., and Erven, J. M. "Uniform Crime Reports as Organizational Outcomes: Three Time Series Experiments." *Social Problems*, 1982, *29*, 361–372.

McClelland, D. A. "Toward a New Theory of Motive Acquisition." *American Psychologist*, 1965, *20*, 321–323.

McGregor, D. M. "The Human Side of Enterprise." In *Classics of Organizational Behavior*, edited by W. E. Natemeyer, pp. 12–18. Oak Park, Ill.: Moore, 1978.

Melancon, D. "Quality Circles: The Shape of Things to Come?" *Police Chief*, 1984, *51*(11), 54–55.

Melone, A. "Criminal Code Reform and Interest Group Politics of the American Bar Association." In *The Politics of Crime and Justice*, edited by E. Fairchild and V. Webb, pp. 37–56. Beverly Hills, Calif.: Sage, 1985.

Menke, B. A., Zupan, L. L., and Lovrich, N. P. *A Comparison of Work-Related Attitudes Between New Generation Correction Officers and Other Public Employees.* Paper presented at the annual meeting of the Academy of Criminal Justice Sciences, Orlando, Fla., 1986.

Meyer, J., and Rowan, B. "Institutionalized Organizations: Formal Structures as Myths and Ceremony." *American Journal of Sociology*, 1978, *83*, 340–363.

Michels, R. *Political Parties.* New York: Free Press, 1949.

Missonelie, J., and D'Angelo, J. *Television and Law Enforcement.* Springfield, Ill.: Charles C Thomas, 1984.

Mohr, L. B. "Organizations, Decisions, and Courts." *Law and Society*, 1976, *10*, 621–642.

Monahan, J. *Predicting Violent Behavior: An Assessment of Clinical Techniques.* Beverly Hills, Calif.: Sage, 1981.

Moran, T. K., and Lindner, C. "Probation and the Hi-Technology Revolution: Is a Reconceptualization of the Traditional Probation Officer Role Model Inevitable?" *Criminal Justice Review*, 1985, *10*, 25–32.

Morash, M. "Wife Battering." *Criminal Justice Abstracts*, 1986, *18*, 252–271.

Morash, M., and Greene, J. "Evaluating Women on Patrol." *Evaluation Review*, 1986, *10*, 230–255.

More, H. W., Jr. *Criminal Justice Management: Text and Readings*. St. Paul: West, 1977.

Morgenbesser, L. "Psychological Screening Mandated for New York Correctional Officer Applicants." *Corrections Today*, 1984, *46*, 28–29.

Morris, N. *Madness and the Criminal Law*. Chicago: University of Chicago Press, 1982.

Morse, J. J. "A Contingency Look at Job Design." *California Management Review*, 1973, *16*, 67–75.

Murphy, P. V. "The Prospective Chief's Negotiation of Authority with the Mayor." In *Police Leadership in America: Crisis and Opportunity*, edited by W. A. Geller, pp. 30–41. Chicago: American Bar Association, 1985.

Murray, M. *Decisions: A Comparative Critique*. Marshfield, Mass.: Pitman, 1986.

National Advisory Commission on Civil Disorders. *Report of the National Advisory Commission on Civil Disorders*. New York: Dutton, 1968.

National Advisory Commission on Criminal Justice Standards and Goals. *Corrections*. Washington, D.C.: U.S. Government Printing Office, 1973a.

National Advisory Commission on Criminal Justice Standards and Goals. *Police*. Washington, D.C.: U.S. Government Printing Office, 1973b.

National Jail Coalition *Covering the Jail*. Washington, D.C.: 1984.

Nelson, R. "Changing Concepts in Jail Design." In *Sneaking Inmates Down the Alley: Problems and Prospects in Jail Management*, edited by D. Kalinich and J. Klofas, pp. 167–180. Springfield, Ill.: Charles C Thomas, 1986.

Nelson, R., and Winter, S. *An Evolutionary Theory of Economic Change*. Boston: Belknap Press, 1982.

Newman, D. "Plea Bargaining." In *Order Under Law*, edited by R. Culbertson and M. Tezak, pp. 166–179. Prospect Heights, Ill.: Waveland, 1981.

Newman, D. *Introduction to Criminal Justice*. New York: Random House, 1986.

Niederhoffer, A. *Behind the Shield: The Police in Urban Society*. New York: Doubleday, 1969.

Nokes, P. "Purpose and Efficiency in Human Social Institutions." *Human Relations*, 1960, *13*, 141–155.

Nuchia, S. M. "First Amendment Freedom of Speech and the Police Officer's Criticism of Departmental Policy and His Superiors." *Journal of Police Science and Administration*, 1983, *11*(4), 395–401.

"Offenders Escape Through Cracks." *Boston Globe*, November 10, 1987, pp. 1–3.

O'Keefe, G., and Mendelsohn, H. *Taking a Bite Out of Crime: The Impact of a Mass Media Crime Prevention Campaign*. Washington, D.C.: U.S. Government Printing Office, 1984.

Olsen, M. *The Logic of Collective Action: Public Goods and the Theory of Groups*. Cambridge, Mass.: Harvard University Press, 1973.

O'Reilly, C. A., and Pondy, L. R. "Organizational Communications." In *Organizational Behavior*, edited by S. Kerr, pp. 138–162. Cincinnati: Grid, 1979.

O'Reilly, C. A., and Roberts, K. H., "Information Filtering and Organizations: Three Experiments." *Organizational Behavior and Human Performance*, 1974, *11*(2), 253–265.

Osborn, R., and Hunt, J. "Environmental and Organizational Effectiveness." *Administrative Science Quarterly*, 1974, *19*, 231–246.

Ouchi, W. *Theory Z: How American Business Can Meet the Japanese Challenge*. Reading, Mass.: Addison-Wesley, 1981.

Pandarus, P. "One's Own Primer of Academic Politics." *American Scholar*, 1973, *42*, 569–592.

Parker, D. *Crime by Computer*. New York: Scribner's, 1976.

Perrow, C. "The Analysis of Goals in Complex Organizations." *American Sociological Review*, 1961, *26*, 194–208.

Perrow, C. "Departmental Power and Perspective in Industrial Firms." In *Power in Organizations*, edited by M. Zald, pp. 59–89. Nashville: Vanderbilt University Press, 1970.

Perrow, C. "Three Types of Effectiveness Studies." In *New Perspectives on Organizational Effectiveness*, edited by P. S. Goodman and J. M. Pennings, pp. 96–105. San Francisco: Jossey-Bass, 1977.

Perrow, C. "Disintegrating Social Sciences." *New York University Educational Quarterly*, Winter 1981, 2–9.

Perrow, C. *Complex Organizations: A Critical Essay*. 3rd ed. New York: Random House, 1986.

Peters, T. J., and Waterman, R. H. *In Search of Excellence: Lessons from America's Best-Run Companies*. New York: Harper & Row, 1982.

Petrich, J. "Psychiatric Treatment in Jail: An Experiment in Health-Care Delivery." *Hospital and Community Psychiatry*, 1976, 413–415.

Pettigrew, A. M. *The Politics of Organizational Decision-Making*. London: Tavistock, 1973.

Pfeffer, J. "Power and Resource Allocation in Organizations." In *New Directions in Organizational Behavior*, edited by B. Staw and G. R. Salancik, pp. 235–265. Chicago: St. Clair Press, 1977a.

Pfeffer, J. "Usefulness of the Concept." In *New Perspectives on Organizational Effectiveness*, edited by P. S. Goodman and J. M. Pennings, pp. 132–145. San Francisco: Jossey-Bass, 1977b.

Pfeffer, J. "The Micropolitics of Organizations." In *Environments and Organizations*, edited by M. W. Meyer, pp. 29–50. San Francisco: Jossey-Bass, 1978.

Pfeffer, J. *Power in Organizations*. Marshfield, Mass.: Pitman, 1981.

Pfeffer, J., and Salancik, G. R. "Organizational Decision-Making as a Political Process: The Case of a University Budget." *Administrative Science Quarterly*, 1974, *19*(2), 135–151.

Philliber, S. "Thy Brother's Keeper: A Review of the Literature on Correctional Officers." *Justice Quarterly*, 1987, 4(1), 9–38.

Phillips, C. D., McCleary, B. W., and Dinitz, S. "The Special Deterrent Effect of Incarceration." In *Evaluating Performance of Criminal Justice Agencies*, edited by G. P. Whitaker and C. D. Phillips, pp. 237–264. Beverly Hills, Calif.: Sage, 1983.

Pindur, W., and Lipiec, S. "Creating Positive Police–Prosecutor Relations." *Journal of Police Science and Administration*, 1982, 10(1), 28–33.

Pinfield, L. T. "A Field Evaluation of Perspectives on Organizational Decision Making." *Administrative Science Quarterly*, 1986, 31, 365–388.

Podsakoff, P. M., and Schriesheim, C. A. "Field Studies of French and Raven's Bases of Power: Reanalysis, Critique, and Suggestions for Future Research." *Psychological Bulletin*, 1985, 97(3), 387–411.

Pondy, L. R. "Organizational Conflict: Concepts and Models." In *Organizational Behavior and Management* (4th ed.), edited by H. L. Tosi and W. C. Hamner, pp. 381–391. Cincinnati: Grid, 1985.

Poole E. D., and Regoli, R. M. "Role Stress, Custody Orientation and Disciplinary Actions: A Study of Prison Guards." *Criminology*, 1980, 18, 215–226.

Porter, L. W. *Organizations as Political Animals.* Presidential address to the Division of Industrial Organizational Psychology, 84th annual meeting of the American Psychological Association, Washington, D.C., 1976.

Porter, L. W., Allen, R. W., and Angle, H. L. "The Politics of Upward Influence in Organizations." *Research in Organizational Behavior*, 1981, 3, 109–149.

Porter, L. W., Lawler, E. E., III, and Hackman, J. H. *Behavior in Organizations.* New York: McGraw-Hill, 1975.

Powers, R. *Secrecy and Power: The Life of J. Edgar Hoover.* New York: Free Press, 1987.

President's Commission on Law Enforcement and the Administration of Justice. *Task Force Report: Corrections.* Washington, D.C.: U.S. Government Printing Office, 1967.

Price, B. "A Study of Leadership Strength of Female Police Executives." *Journal of Police Science and Administration*, 1974, 2, 219–226.

Pritchard, R., and Karasick, B. "The Effects of Organizational Climate on Managerial Job Performance." *Organizational Behavior and Human Performance*, 1973, 9, 128–147.

Quade, E. "Systems Analysis Techniques for Public Policy Problems." In *Perspectives on Public Bureaucracy*, edited by F. Kramer, pp. 151–174. Cambridge, Mass.: Winthrop, 1977.

Quinney, R. *Critique of the Legal Order.* Boston: Little, Brown, 1974.

Radelet, L. *The Police and the Community.* 4th ed. New York: Macmillan, 1986.

Reddin, T. "Are You Oriented to Hold Them?" *Police Chief*, 1966, 33, 12–20.

Reid, S. *Crime and Criminology.* New York: Holt, Rinehart & Winston, 1982.

Reiss, A. J. "Career Orientations, Job Satisfaction and the Assessment of Law Enforcement Problems by Police Officers." In *Studies in Crime and Law Enforcement*, by the President's Commission on Law Enforcement and the Administration of Justice. Washington, D.C.: U.S. Government Printing Office, 1967.

Reiss, A. J. *The Police and the Public*. New Haven, Conn.: Yale University Press, 1971.

Remington, F., Newman, D., Kimball, E., Melli, M., and Goldstein, H. *Criminal Justice Administration*. Indianapolis: Bobbs-Merrill, 1969.

Rideau, W., and Sinclair, B. *Inside Angola*. New Orleans: Louisiana Department of Corrections, 1982.

Roberg, R. R. *Police Management and Organizational Behavior: A Contingency Approach*. St. Paul: West, 1979.

Robin, G. D. "Judicial Resistance to Sentencing Allowability." *Crime and Delinquency*, 1975, *21*, 201–212.

Roethlisberger, F. J., and Dickson, W. J. *Management and the Worker*. Cambridge, Mass.: Harvard University Press, 1939.

Rokeach, M., Miller, G., and Snyder, J. A. "The Value Gap Between the Police and the Policed." *Journal of Social Issues*, 1971, *27*, 155–171.

Rosch, J. "Crime as an Issue in American Politics." In *The Politics of Crime and Justice*, edited by E. Fairchild and V. Webb, pp. 19–34. Beverly Hills, Calif.: Sage, 1985.

Rosecrance, J. "The Probation Officer's Search for Credibility: Ball Park Recommendations." *Crime and Delinquency*, 1985, *31*, 539–554.

Roszell, S. *Other Prisoners*. Chicago: John Howard Association, 1987.

Rothman, D. J. *Conscience and Convenience*. Boston: Little, Brown, 1980.

Rothman, D. J., and Rothman, S. M. *The Willowbrook Wars*. New York: Harper & Row, 1984.

Rottman, D. B., and Kimberly, J. R. "The Social Context of Jails." *Sociology and Social Research*, 1975, *59*, 344–361.

Rourke, F. *Bureaucracy, Politics, and Public Policy*. Boston: Little, Brown, 1976.

Rourke, F. *Bureaucratic Power in National Politics*. 4th ed. Boston: Little, Brown, 1986.

Ruiz v. Estelle, 503 F. Supp. 1265 (1980).

Ryan, E. *A Multidimensional Analysis of Conflict in the Criminal Justice System*. Jonesboro, Tenn.: Pilgrimage, 1981.

Saari, D. J. *American Court Management: Theories and Practices*. Westport, Conn.: Quorum Books, 1982.

Salancik, G. R., and Pfeffer, J. "Who Gets Power—and How They Hold on to It: A Strategic Contingency Model of Power." *Organizational Dynamics* (American Management Association), Winter 1977, *5*, 3–21.

Sarrata, B., and Jeppensen, J. C. "Job Design and Staff Satisfaction in Human Service Settings." *Journal of Community Psychology*, 1977, *5*, 229–236.

Schafer, N. "Jails and Judicial Review: Special Problems for Local Facilities." In *Sneaking Inmates Down the Alley: Problems and Prospects in Jail Management*, edited by D. Kalinich and J. Klofas, pp. 127–146. Springfield, Ill.: Charles C Thomas, 1986.

Schein, E. H. *The Psychological Contract: Organizational Psychology*. 2nd ed. Englewood Cliffs, N.J.: Prentice-Hall, 1970.

Schein, E. H. "The Individual, the Organization and the Career: A Conceptual Scheme." *Journal of Applied Behavioral Science*, 1971, *7*, 401–426.

Schein, E. H. *Organizational Culture and Leadership*. San Francisco: Jossey-Bass, 1985.

Schlesinger, A. M., Jr. "Roosevelt as Chief Administrator," *The Coming of the New Deal*. Boston: Houghton Mifflin, 1958.

Schmidt, A. K. "Electronic Monitoring of Offenders Increases." *National Institute of Justice Reports*, 1989, *212*, 2–5.

Scott, E. *Police Referral in Metropolitan Areas: A Summary Report*. Washington, D.C.: U.S. National Institute of Justice, 1981.

Scott, R. *Organizations: Rational, Natural, and Open Systems*. Englewood Cliffs, N.J.: Prentice-Hall, 1987.

Scott, W. R. "Effectiveness of Organizational Effectiveness Studies." In *New Perspectives on Organizational Effectiveness*, edited by P. S. Goodman and J. M. Pennings, pp. 63–95. San Francisco: Jossey-Bass, 1977.

SEARCH Group, Inc. "State Law and the Confidentiality of Juvenile Records." *Security and Privacy*, 1982, *5*(2), 1–12.

Selke, W., and Bartoszek, M. "Police and Media Relations: The Seed of Conflict." *Criminal Justice Review*, 1984, *9*(2), 25–30.

Sellin, T. "Historical Glimpses of Training for Prison Service." *Journal of the American Institute of Criminal Law and Criminology*, 1934, *25*.

Selznick, P. *TVA and the Grass Roots*. Berkeley: University of California Press, 1949.

Selznick, P. *Leadership in Administration*. New York: Harper & Row, 1957.

Sharkansky, I. *Public Administration: Policy Making in Governmental Agencies*. Chicago: Markham, 1972.

Sharp, E. B. "Street-Level Discretion in Policing: Attitudes and Behaviors in the Deprofessionalization Syndrome." *Law and Policy Quarterly*, 1982, *4*, 167–189.

Sheppard, H. L., and Herrick, N. Q. *Where Have All the Robots Gone?* New York: Free Press, 1972.

Sherman, L. W. "Becoming Bent: Moral Career Concepts of Corrupt Policemen." In *Police Corruption: A Sociological Perspective*, edited by L. Sherman, pp. 191–208. New York: Doubleday, 1974.

Sherman, L. W. "Middle Management and Police Democratization: A Reply to John E. Angell." *Criminology,* 1975, *12*(4), 363–377.

Sherman, L. W., and Berk, R. "The Specific Deterrent Effects of Arrest in Domestic Assault." *American Sociological Review,* 1984, *49,* 261–272.

Sherman, L. W., Milton, C. H., and Kelly, T. V. *Team Policing: Seven Case Studies.* Washington, D.C.: Police Foundation, 1973.

Sieber, S. *Fatal Remedies: The Irony of Social Intervention.* New York: Plenum Press, 1981.

Siedman, H. *Politics, Position, and Power.* New York: Oxford University Press, 1970.

Simon, H. "On the Concept of Organizational Goal." *Administrative Science Quarterly,* 1964, *9,* 1–22.

Simpson, R. L., and Simpson, I. H. "The Psychiatric Attendant: Development of an Occupational Self-Image in a Low Status Occupation." *American Sociological Review,* 1959, *24,* 389–392.

Skolnick, J. H. *Justice Without Trial: Law Enforcement in a Democratic Society.* New York: Wiley, 1966.

Skolnick, J. H., and Bayley, D. H. *The New Blue Line: Police Innovation in Six American Cities.* New York: Free Press, 1986.

Skolnick, J. H., and McCoy, C. "Police Accountability and the Media." *American Bar Foundation Research Journal,* 1984, *3,* 521–557.

Smykla, J. D., *Community Based Corrections: Principles and Practices.* New York: Macmillan, 1981.

Snyder, R., and Morris, J. "Organizational Communications and Performance." *Journal of Applied Psychology,* 1984, *69*(3), 461–465.

Sparrow, M. K. *Implementing Community Policing.* Washington D. C.: National Institute of Justice, 1988.

Spiro, H. "Comparative Politics: A Comprehensive Approach." *American Political Science Review,* 1958, *56*(3), 577–595.

Stastny, C., and Tyrnauer, G. *Who Rules the Joint: The Changing Political Culture of Maximum-Security Prisons in America.* Lexington, Mass.: Heath, 1982.

Staw, B. M., and Ross, J. "Commitment to a Policy Decision: A Multi-Theoretical Perspective." *Administrative Science Quarterly,* 1978, *23,* 40–64.

Steadman, H., Monahan, J., Duffee, B., Hartstone, E., and Robbins, P. "The Impact of the State Mental Hospital Deinstitutionalization on United States Prison Populations, 1968–1978." *The Journal of Criminal Law and Criminology,* 1984, *75,* 474–490.

Steers, R. M. *Organizational Effectiveness: A Behavioral View.* Santa Monica, Calif.: Goodyear, 1977.

Stoddard, E. R. "Blue Coat Crime." In *Thinking About Police: Contemporary Readings,* edited by C. B. Klockars New York: McGraw-Hill, 1983.

Stojkovic, S. "Social Bases of Power and Control Mechanisms Among Prisoners in a Prison Organization." *Justice Quarterly*, 1984, *1*(4), 511–528.

Stojkovic, S. "Social Bases of Power and Control Mechanisms Among Correctional Administrators in a Prison Organization." *Journal of Criminal Justice*, 1986, *14*, 157–166.

Stojkovic, S. *An Examination of Compliance Structures in a Prison Organization: A Study of the Types of Correctional Officer Power.* Unpublished manuscript, University of Wisconsin, Milwaukee, 1987.

Stoller, H. E. *Need for Achievement in Work Output Among Policemen.* Unpublished doctoral dissertation, Illinois Institute of Technology, 1977.

Stolz, B. "Congress and Criminal Justice Policy Making: The Impact of Interest Groups and Symbolic Politics." *Journal of Criminal Justice*, 1985, *13*, 307–320.

Stone, C., and Stoker, R. *Deprofessionalization and Dissatisfaction in Urban Service Agencies.* Paper presented at the 37th annual meeting of the Midwest Political Science Association, Chicago, 1979.

Studt, E. *Surveillance and Service in Parole.* Washington, D.C.: U.S. Department of Justice, 1978.

Styskal, R. A. "Power and Commitment in Organizations: A Test of the Participation Thesis." *Social Forces*, 1980, *57*(4), 925–943.

Sudnow, D. "Normal Crimes: Sociological Features of the Penal Code in a Public Defender Office." *Social Problems*, 1965, *12*, 255–276.

Sutherland, E., and Cressey, R. *Criminology.* Philadelphia: Lippincott, 1978.

Swank, G. E., and Winer, D. "Occurrence of Psychiatric Disorders in County Jail Populations." *American Journal of Psychiatry*, 1976, *133*(11) 1331–1337.

Swanson, C. R., and Territo, L. "Police Leadership and Interpersonal Communication Styles." In *Managing Police Work: Issues and Analysis*, edited by J. R. Greene, pp. 123–139. Beverly Hills, Calif.: Sage, 1982.

Swanson, C. R., Territo, L., and Taylor, R. W. *Police Administration: Structures, Processes, and Behavior.* 2nd ed. New York: Macmillan, 1988.

Sykes, G. *The Society of Captives.* Princeton, N.J.: Princeton University Press, 1958.

Sykes, G., and Messinger, S. L. "The Inmate Social System." In *Theoretical Studies in Social Organization of the Prison*, edited by R. A. Cloward, D. R. Cressey, G. H. Grosser, R. McCleary, L. E. Ohlin, G. Sykes, and S. Messinger. New York: Social Science Research Council, 1960.

Tannenbaum, A. S. "Control in Organizations: Individual Adjustment and Organizational Performance." *Administrative Science Quarterly*, 1962, *7*(2), 236–257.

Taylor, F. W. *Two Papers on Scientific Management.* London: Routledge & Kegan Paul, 1919.

Taylor, F. W. *Scientific Management.* New York: Harper & Row, 1947.

Terkel, S. *Working.* New York: Random House, 1974.

Territo, L., Swanson, J. R., and Chamelin, N. "The Police Selection Process." In *Policing Society,* edited by W. C. Terry, pp. 187–196. New York: Wiley, 1985.

Terry, W. C. "Police Stress as an Administrative Problem: Some Conceptual and Theoretical Difficulties." *Journal of Police Science and Administration,* 1983, *11,* 156–164.

Thomas, K. W. "Organizational Conflict." In *Organizational Behavior and Management* (4th ed.), edited by H. L. Tosi and W. C. Hamner, pp. 392–416. Cincinnati: Grid, 1985.

Thompson, J. *Organizations in Action.* New York: McGraw-Hill, 1967.

Thompson, J., Svirdoff, M., and McElroy, J. *Unemployment and Crime: A Review of Theories and Research.* Washington, D.C.: U.S. Department of Justice, 1981.

Tifft, L. L. "Control Systems, Social Bases of Power and Power Exercise in Police Organizations." In *Policing: A View from the Street,* edited by P. K. Manning and J. Van Maanen, pp. 90–104. Santa Monica, Calif.: Goodyear, 1978.

Toch, H. "Is a 'Correction Officer' Always a 'Screw'?" *Criminal Justice Review,* 1978, *3,* 19–35.

Toch, H., and Grant, J. D. *Reforming Human Services: Change Through Participation.* Beverly Hills, Calif.: Sage, 1982.

Toch, H., Grant, J. D., and Galvin, R. *Agents of Change: A Study of Police Reform.* Cambridge, Mass.: Schenkman, 1975.

Toch, H., and Klofas, J. "Alienation and Desire for Job Enrichment Among Correction Officers." *Federal Probation,* 1982, *46,* 322–327.

Tosi, H. L., Rizzo, J. R., and Carroll, S. J. *Managing Organizational Behavior.* Marshfield, Mass.: Pitman, 1986.

Travis, L., Latessa, E., and Vito, G. "Adding a Building in Criminal Justice: The Case of Determinant Sentencing." *American Journal of Criminal Justice,* 1985, *X*(1), 1–21.

Trojanowicz, R. *An Evaluation of the Neighborhood Foot Patrol Program in Flint, Michigan.* East Lansing, Mich.: National Neighborhood Foot Patrol Center, 1983.

Trojanowicz, R., and Banas, D. *Perceptions of Safety: A Comparison of Foot Patrol Versus Motor Patrol Officers.* East Lansing, Mich.: National Neighborhood Foot Patrol Center, 1985.

Trojanowicz, R., and Carter, D. *The Philosophy and Role of Community Policing.* East Lansing, Mich.: National Neighborhood Foot Patrol Center, 1988.

Trojanowicz, R., Steele, M., and Trojanowicz, S. *Community Policing: A Taxpayer's Perspective.* East Lansing, Mich.: National Neighborhood Foot Patrol Center, 1986.

Tullar, W. L., and Glauser, M. J. "Communicator Style of Police Officer and Citizen Satisfaction with Officer/Citizen Telephone Conversations." *Journal of Police Science and Administration,* 1985, *13*(1), 70–72.

Tully, H., Winter, J., Wilson, T., and Scanlon, T. "Correctional Institution Impact and Host Community Resistance." *Canadian Journal of Criminology,* 1982, *24*(2), 133–139.

Vanagunas, S. "Planning for the Delivery of Urban Police Services." In *Managing Police Work: Issues and Analysis,* edited by J. Greene, pp. 203–216. Beverly Hills, Calif.: Sage, 1982.

Van Maanen, J. "Observations on the Making of a Policeman." *Human Organization,* 1973, *4,* 407–418.

Van Maanen, J. "Police Socialization: A Longitudinal Examination of Job Attitudes in an Urban Police Department." *Administrative Science Quarterly,* 1975, *20,* 266–278.

Van Maanen, J. "People Processing: Strategies of Organizational Socialization." In *Managing Organizations,* edited by D. A. Nadler, M. L. Tushman, and N. G. Hatvany, pp. 144–157. Boston: Little, Brown, 1982.

Van Maanen, J. "Learning the Ropes." In *Policing Society,* edited by W. C. Terry. New York: Wiley, 1985.

Vetter, H., and Territo, L. *Crime and Justice in America: A Human Perspective.* St. Paul: West, 1984.

Waegel, W. B. "Case Routinization in Investigative Police Work." *Social Problems,* 1981, *28,* 263–275.

Wahler, C., and Gendreau, P. "Assessing Correctional Officers." *Federal Probation,* 1985, *49,* 70–74.

Waldron, R. J. *The Criminal Justice System.* Boston: Houghton Mifflin, 1984.

Walker, S. *Sense and Nonsense About Crime: A Policy Guide.* Pacific Grove, Calif.: Brooks/Cole, 1985.

Walmsley, G., and Zald, M. *The Political Economy of Public Organizations.* Lexington, Mass.: Heath, 1973.

Walsh, W. F. "Patrol Officer Arrest Rates: A Study of the Social Organization of Police Work." *Justice Quarterly,* 1986, *3,* 271–290.

Waltman, J. "Nonverbal Communications in Interrogation: Some Applications." *Journal of Police Science and Administration,* 1983, *11*(2), 166–169.

Warren, D. I. "Power, Visibility, and Conformity in Formal Organizations." *American Sociological Review,* 1968, *33*(6), 951–970.

Warren, E. "The Economic Approach to Crime." In *Criminal Justice Studies,* edited by G. Misner, pp. 172–180. St. Louis: C. V. Mosby, 1981.

Warren, R. *Social Change and Human Purpose: Toward Understanding and Action.* Chicago: Rand McNally, 1977.

Weber, M. *The Theory of Social and Economic Organization.* New York: Free Press, 1947.

Weimann, G. "Sex Differences in Dealing with Bureaucracy." *Sex Roles,* 1985, *12,* 777–790.

Weiner, J., and Johnson, R. "Organization and Environment: The Case of Correctional Personnel Training Programs." *Journal of Criminal Justice*, 1981, *9*, 441–450.

Weiss, C. H. "Evaluation Research in the Political Context." In *Handbook of Evaluation Research*, edited by E. L. Struening and M. Guttentag, pp. 13–26. Beverly Hills, Calif.: Sage, 1972.

Westley, W. *Violence and the Police: A Sociological Study of Law, Custom and Morality.* Cambridge, Mass.: MIT Press, 1970.

Whitehead, J. T. "Job Burnout in Probation and Parole: Its Extent and Intervention Implications." *Criminal Justice and Behavior*, 1985, *12*, 91–110.

Whitehead, J. T., and Lindquist, C. A. "Correctional Officer Job Burnout: A Path Model." *Journal of Research in Crime and Delinquency*, 1986, *23*, 23–42.

Wildavsky, A. *The Politics of the Budgetary Process.* Boston: Little, Brown, 1974.

Wilensky, H. *Organizational Intelligence.* New York: Basic Books, 1967.

Wilkins, L. T. "Information Overload: Peace or War with the Computer." In *Parole: Legal Issues/Decision-Making/Research*, edited by W. E. Amos and C. L. Newman, pp. 141–157. New York: Federal Legal Publications, 1975a.

Wilkins, L. T. "A Typology of Decision-Makers?" In *Parole: Legal Issues/Decision-Making/Research*, edited by W. E. Amos and C. L. Newman, pp. 159–168. New York: Federal Legal Publications, 1975b.

Wilkins, L. T. "Treatment of Offenders at Patuxent." *Rutgers Law Review*, 1976, *29*, 45–60.

Willett, T. C. "The 'Fish Screw' in the Canadian Penitentiary Service." *Queen's Law Journal*, 1977, *3*, 424–449.

Williamson, O. E. "The Economics of Organizations: The Transactions–Cost Approach." *American Journal of Sociology*, 1981, *87*, 548–577.

Wilson, J. Q. *Varieties of Police Behavior.* Cambridge, Mass.: Harvard University Press, 1968.

Witham, D. C. "Management Control Through Motivation." *FBI Law Enforcement Bulletin*, 1980, *49*(2), 6–11.

Wolff v. McDonnell, 94 S. Ct. 2963 (1974).

Wright, K. "The Desirability of Goal Conflict Within the Criminal Justice System." *Journal of Criminal Justice*, 1981, *9*, 209–218.

Wycoff, M. A. "Evaluating the Crime-Effectiveness of Municipal Police." In *Managing Police Work: Issues and Analysis*, edited by J. Greene, pp. 15–36. Beverly Hills, Calif.: Sage, 1982.

Yeager, M. "Unemployment and Imprisonment." *Journal of Criminal Law and Criminology*, 1979, *75*, 586–593.

Yuchtman, E., and Seashore, S. "A System–Resource Approach to Organizational Effectiveness." *American Sociological Review*, 1967, *32*, 891–903.

Yukl, G. A. *Leadership in Organizations.* Englewood Cliffs, N.J.: Prentice-Hall, 1981.

Zaltman, G., Duncan, R., and Holbeck, J. *Innovations and Organizations.* New York: Wiley, 1973.

Zander, A. "Resistance to Change: Its Analysis and Prevention." *Advanced Management,* 1950, *15–16,* 9–11.

Zedlewski, E. W. "Making Confinement Decisions." Washington, D.C.: National Institute of Justice, 1987.

Author Index

Subject Index